HEALTHY
COOKING
ANNUAL RECIPES

Taste of Home

RDA ENTHUSIAST BRANDS, LLC • MILWAUKEE, WI

HEALTHY COOKING
ANNUAL RECIPES

22

237

© **2018 RDA ENTHUSIAST BRANDS, LLC**
1610 N. 2ND ST., SUITE 102
MILWAUKEE, WI 53212-3906

**INTERNATIONAL STANDARD
BOOK NUMBER:** 978-1-61765-777-1

**INTERNATIONAL STANDARD
SERIAL NUMBER:** 1944-7736

COMPONENT NUMBER: 117900047H

COVER PHOTOGRAPHY:
TASTE OF HOME PHOTO STUDIO

PICTURED ON FRONT COVER:
Sesame Chicken Slaw Salad, p. 146

PICTURED ON BACK COVER:
Spaghetti Squash Meatball Casserole,
p. 129; Black Bean Turkey Chili, p. 34;
Spinach Dip Burgers, p. 125; Chocolate-
Topped Strawberry Cheesecake, p. 252;
Blackberry-Sauced Pork Chops, p. 192.

PICTURED ON TITLE PAGE:
Mediterranean Pork & Orzo, p. 190.

PRINTED IN USA
1 3 5 7 9 10 8 6 4 2

Contents

Eat great and feel great the whole year through with 410+ amazing heart-smart dishes. Discover comforting entrees, slow cooker classics and fiery grilled specialties, all just pages away. You'll also find golden breads, eye-opening breakfasts and showstopping sweets to make this your best year yet!

186

Eating Right Is a Cornerstone for Lifelong Health

Help your family eat right with *Healthy Cooking Annual Recipes.*

As a registered dietitian nutritionist, I thought it would be easy to get my kids to eat healthy meals and snacks. After all, most of my education and career have been spent learning about healthy foods and making them taste great. But it wasn't that simple. Now that my kids are 7 and 5, I can look back at the habits I tried to teach them and sort out the ones that have really made a difference.

Try a bite of everything. It could take up to 10 tries for a child to know if they really like a new food or not, so I have them try a bite of everything. I also continue to make foods that they've said they don't like because I know their tastes are constantly changing.

All foods can fit. It's true! Whether it's cheesecake on a holiday, nachos at the game or just a cookie or two after dinner, they can all be part of a healthy diet–in moderation.

Eat a variety of foods. For every meal, I try to include lots of options for them to choose from. Not only does this encourage them to eat a variety for better health, but then I also know there's something on their plate that they will like.

Eat vegetables because they taste good. Encouraging kids to eat veggies because "they're good for you" sets them up to think healthy foods will taste bad. Instead, I give veggies a positive description like, "You'll love those sugar snap peas. They're sweet and crunchy."

If you're in a rut with your kids, try something new. Maybe it's time to get them involved with meal prep or in the family garden. And, of course, experiment with new recipes from *Healthy Cooking Annual Recipes.* They're family favorites from readers just like you and they're test-kitchen approved. If you need a place to start, my family loves **MEXI-MAC SKILLET (P. 123).** It's nutritious and done in 30 minutes, and it leaves me with only one dish to wash, which is a win-win-win in my book.

Happy Cooking,

Peggy

Peggy Woodward, RDN

About Our Nutrition Facts

The *Healthy Cooking Annual Recipes* cookbook provides a variety of recipes that fit into a healthy lifestyle.

- Whenever a choice of ingredients is given (such as ½ cup sour cream or plain yogurt), the first ingredient is used in our calculations.

- When a range is given for an ingredient, we calculate using the first amount.

- Only the amount of a marinade absorbed is calculated.

- Optional ingredients are not included in our calculations.

We have also added total sugars to our Nutrition Facts: 294 cal., 12g fat (2g sat. fat), 64mg chol., 218mg sodium, 20g carb. (13g sugars, 3g fiber), 24g pro.
Note: This represents added sugars plus naturally occurring sugars.

SPECIAL INDICATORS
To help those on restricted diets easily find dishes to suit their needs, we clearly mark recipes that are especially low in fat, sodium or carbohydrates, as well as those that contain no meat. You will find these icons, plus quick-to-fix recipes and healthy insights throughout the book:

HEALTH TIP Peggy shares her best secrets to help you make healthy mealtime choices.

F One serving contains 3 grams fat or less.

S One serving contains 140 milligrams sodium or less.

C One serving contains 15 grams carbohydrates or less.

M Recipe contains no gelatin, Worcestershire or other meat products.

FAST FIX Dish is table-ready in 30 minutes or less.

uild Healthy Habits with Foods You'll Love

Healthy habit: All foods can fit.

ating healthy doesn't have to mean hat desserts are off-limits. Missouri ook **Carleta Foltz** lightens up her **UMMY ZUCCHINI CHOCOLATE AKE** with canola oil and applesauce, ut it still tastes oh-so-good. **P. 234**

Healthy habit: Eat vegetables because they taste good.

Holly Sander of Florida won the grand prize in our 5-ingredient contest with her tasty **PARMESAN ROASTED BROCCOLI** recipe. This easy side was up against appetizers, main dishes and even desserts! Goes to show: Veggies can be delicious, too. **P. 69**

Healthy habit: Eat a variety of foods.

Skip Taco Tuesday and try **SOUTHWEST VEGETARIAN BAKE** from ***Trish Gale.*** The Illinois cook's simple dinner not only offers a unique twist on Tex-Mex, but it's loaded with brown rice, beans, corn and tomatoes, which provide a variety of nutrients. **P. 226**

The Salty Six

nother key to healthy eating is limiting sodium intake. These common foods contribute the most sodium to diets, ccording to the American Heart Association. Here's how to choose smart.

1 BREADS AND ROLLS
Bread isn't super salty, but it's not uncommon for Americans to eat toast for reakfast and a sandwich at lunch, nd include a roll with dinner, which eally makes the sodium add up over day. Look for thinly sliced bread and ompare sodium between brands to nd the best options.

2 PIZZA
Pizza is usually loaded with higher-sodium foods: bread, cheese, cured meats, olives and pizza sauce. Reduce the cheese and meat and increase fresh veggies. Instead of pizza sauce, try no-salt-added tomato sauce doctored up with herbs and spices.

3 CHICKEN
Chicken isn't inherently high in sodium, but it's how we prepare it that makes a difference. A sodium solution is often added to plump up raw chicken. Read the food label to find brands that have less than 100mg sodium per serving. Chicken nuggets, strips and patties are all much higher in sodium than plain chicken, too.

4 COLD CUTS AND CURED MEATS
Since salt is used to preserve deli meats, most re loaded with sodium. However, educed-sodium versions do exist. ook for them at the deli counter and onsider using leftover cooked meat nstead of processed meats in recipes nd sandwiches.

5 SOUP
Canned soups are typically high in sodium and the homemade versions can be, too. Look for heart-smart canned soups that are lower in sodium. If you're making soup at home, reach for no-salt or reduced-sodium stock, beans and tomato products.

6 SANDWICHES
Like pizza, sandwiches are typically made up of foods that are higher in sodium: bread, cold cuts, cheese and condiments. Use less meat and cheese and more veggies, or eat a half sandwich and round out your meal with fresh fruit or veggies.

STARTERS & SNACKS

"My love for Greece inspired this fast-to-fix Mediterranean dip. It's great for parties and is a delicious way to include garden-fresh veggies on your menu."
—Cheryl Snavely, Hagerstown, MD

Hot Cider Punch (p. 18) Spicy Peanut Chicken Kabobs (p. 11) Green & Gold Salsa (p. 8)
Goat Cheese Mushrooms (p. 16) Layered Hummus Dip (p. 18) Garlic-Dill Deviled Eggs (p. 19)

LIME-MARINATED
SHRIMP SALAD

LIME-MARINATED
SHRIMP SALAD F S C

*Ceviche is a seafood dish of raw fish
marinated in citrus juice, which cooks
the fish without heat. This version starts
with cooked shrimp and adds tomatoes,
cucumbers and serrano peppers.*
—Adan Franco, Milwaukee, WI

Prep: 25 min. + chilling
Makes: 10 cups

- 1 large onion, quartered
- 2 to 4 serrano peppers, seeded and
  coarsely chopped
- 2 medium cucumbers, peeled,
  quartered and seeds removed
- 2 large tomatoes, cut into chunks
- 6 green onions, coarsely chopped
  (about ¾ cup)
- 2 pounds peeled and deveined cooked
  shrimp (26-30 per pound)
- ¾ cup lime juice
- ½ teaspoon salt
- ¼ teaspoon pepper
  Tortilla chips or tostada shells

1. Place onion and peppers in a food
processor; pulse until very finely chopped.
Transfer to a large bowl. Place cucumbers,
tomatoes and green onions in a food
processor; pulse until finely chopped.
Add to bowl.
2. Place shrimp in food processor; pulse
until chopped. Add shrimp, lime juice, salt
and pepper to vegetable mixture; toss to
coat. Refrigerate until cold. Serve with
tortilla chips or tostada shells.
Note: Wear disposable gloves when
cutting hot peppers; the oils can burn
skin. Avoid touching your face.
Per ½ cup: 61 cal., 1g fat (0 sat. fat),
69mg chol., 128mg sod., 4g carb. (1g
sugars, 1g fiber), 10g pro.
Diabetic exchanges: 1 lean meat.

GREEN & GOLD SALSA
F S C M FAST FIX
(PICTURED ON P. 7)

*Looking for a healthy alternative to
calorie-laden creamy dips to serve at your
next football party? With its green and gold
colors, this unique salsa will please Green
Bay Packers supporters. But other teams'
fans will love it, too!*
—Maggie Lovat, Green Bay, WI

Start to Finish: 10 min.
Makes: 3 cups

- 1 cup frozen shelled edamame, thawed
- 1 cup (about 5 ounces) frozen corn,
  thawed
- 1 cup cubed avocado
- 1 cup pico de gallo
  Sliced cucumber and tortilla chips

Combine edamame, corn, avocado and
pico de gallo until well blended. Serve with
cucumbers and chips for dipping.
Per ¼ cup: 48 cal., 3g fat (0 sat. fat),
0 chol., 4mg sod., 5g carb. (1g sugars,
2g fiber), 2g pro.

GRILLED CHIPOTLE SHRIMP F S C

I created this for a Cinco de Mayo party one year, and it was a hit! It's so easy to make, yet has a serious wow factor. The creamy dipping sauce mellows out the shrimp's heat perfectly.
—Mandy Rivers, Lexington, SC

Prep: 25 min. + marinating • **Grill:** 10 min.
Makes: about 5 dozen (1¼ cups sauce)

- ¼ cup packed brown sugar
- 2 chipotle peppers in adobo sauce, chopped, plus ¼ cup adobo sauce
- 6 garlic cloves, minced
- 2 tablespoons water
- 2 tablespoons lime juice
- 1 tablespoon olive oil
- ¼ teaspoon salt
- 2 pounds uncooked large shrimp, peeled and deveined

CILANTRO CREAM SAUCE
- 1 cup sour cream
- ⅓ cup minced fresh cilantro
- 2 garlic cloves, minced
- 1½ teaspoons grated lime peel
- ¼ teaspoon salt
- ¼ teaspoon minced fresh mint

1. In a small saucepan, bring the brown sugar, chipotles, adobo sauce, garlic, water, lime juice, oil and salt to a boil. Reduce heat; cook and stir 2 minutes longer. Remove from the heat; cool completely.
2. Transfer mixture to a large resealable plastic bag. Add the shrimp; seal bag and turn to coat. Refrigerate for up to 2 hours.
3. Meanwhile, combine the sauce ingredients; chill until serving.
4. Drain and discard marinade. Thread shrimp onto metal or soaked wooden skewers.
5. Grill shrimp on an oiled rack, covered, over medium heat or broil 4 in. from the heat for 6-8 minutes or until shrimp are pink, turning once. Serve with sauce.

Per shrimp with 1 teaspoon sauce: 27 cal., 1g fat (1g sat. fat), 21mg chol., 47mg sod., 1g carb. (1g sugars, 0 fiber), 3g pro.

TORTELLINI APPETIZERS C

These cute, light kabobs will lend a little Italian flavor to any get-together. Cheese tortellini is marinated in salad dressing, then skewered onto toothpicks along with stuffed olives, salami and cheese.
—Patricia Schmidt, Sterling Heights, MI

Prep: 25 min. + marinating
Makes: 1½ dozen

- 18 refrigerated cheese tortellini
- ¼ cup fat-free Italian salad dressing
- 6 thin slices (4 ounces) reduced-fat provolone cheese
- 6 thin slices (2 ounces) Genoa salami
- 18 large pimiento-stuffed olives

1. Cook tortellini according to package directions; drain and rinse in cold water. In a resealable plastic bag, combine the tortellini and salad dressing. Seal bag and refrigerate for 4 hours.
2. Place a slice of cheese on each slice of salami; roll up tightly. Cut into thirds. Drain tortellini and discard dressing. For each appetizer, thread a tortellini, salami roll-up and olive on a toothpick.

Per appetizer: 63 cal., 4g fat (1g sat. fat), 10mg chol., 267mg sod., 4g carb. (0 sugars, 0 fiber), 4g pro.

GRILLED CHIPOTLE SHRIMP

CAPRESE SCALLOP STACKS

Scallops and zucchini put a creative and tasty twist on the traditional caprese recipe. The red and green colors make these stacks perfect for the Christmas season.
—Roxanne Chan, Albany, CA

Start to Finish: 30 min.
Makes: 1 dozen

- 1 medium zucchini
- 12 sea scallops (about 1½ pounds)
- 4 tablespoons olive oil, divided
- ¼ cup chopped roasted sweet red peppers
- 1 tablespoon pine nuts, toasted
- 1 tablespoon lemon juice
- 1 garlic clove, minced
- 1 teaspoon dried currants
- 1 teaspoon capers, drained
- ½ teaspoon Dijon mustard
- ¼ teaspoon grated lemon peel
  Watercress, optional

1. Cut zucchini into ⅓-in.-thick slices; place in a steamer basket over 1 in. of water. Bring to a boil; cover and steam for 1-2 minutes or until crisp-tender.
2. Meanwhile, cut the scallops in half horizontally. In a large skillet, saute scallops in 1 tablespoon oil until firm and opaque. Remove and keep warm.
3. To serve, place zucchini slices on a serving plate. Layer each with a scallop half, some chopped roasted pepper and a scallop half. In a small bowl, combine pine nuts, lemon juice, garlic, currants, capers, mustard, lemon peel and the remaining oil; spoon over stacks. Garnish with watercress if desired.
Per appetizer: 98 cal., 5g fat (1g sat. fat), 18mg chol., 120mg sod., 3g carb. (1g sugars, 0 fiber), 10g pro.
Diabetic exchanges: 1 lean meat, 1 fat.

MANGO GUACAMOLE

I needed a change from the standard guacamole recipe, so I added mango for more sweetness. It tempers the heat from the chili pepper and adds nice color, too.
—Adam Landau, Englewood Cliffs, NJ

Start to Finish: 20 min.
Makes: 3 cups

- 2 medium ripe avocados, peeled and quartered
- 1 medium mango, peeled and chopped
- ½ cup finely chopped red onion
- ¼ cup minced fresh cilantro
- 1 jalapeno pepper, seeded and finely chopped
- 2 tablespoons lime juice
- 1½ teaspoons grated lime peel
- ½ teaspoon salt
- ⅛ teaspoon coarsely ground pepper
  Tortilla or pita chips

In a small bowl, mash avocados. Stir in the mango, onion, cilantro, jalapeno, lime juice, lime peel, salt and pepper. Serve the guacamole with chips.
Note: Wear disposable gloves when cutting hot peppers; the oils can burn skin. Avoid touching your face.
Per ¼ cup: 63 cal., 5g fat (1g sat. fat), 0 chol., 101mg sod., 6g carb. (3g sugars, 2g fiber), 1g pro.
Diabetic exchanges: ½ starch, ½ fat.

CAPRESE
SCALLOP STACKS

SPICY PEANUT
CHICKEN KABOBS

WATERMELON-STRAWBERRY COOLER F S M

We love watermelon so this frosty cooler gets gulped down fast, especially on hot Texas days. The strawberries give it an extra pop of sweetness.
—Joan Hallford, North Richland Hills, TX

Prep: 10 min. + chilling
Makes: 10 servings (1 cup each)

- 2 cups water
- ½ cup lemon juice
- 12 cups cubed watermelon (about 3½ pounds)
- 2 cups fresh strawberries or raspberries
- ⅔ cup sugar
- 1½ teaspoons minced fresh mint
  Small watermelon wedges and fresh mint leaves

1. Place 1 cup water, ¼ cup lemon juice, 6 cups watermelon, 1 cup berries, ⅓ cup sugar and ¾ teaspoon minced mint in a blender; cover and process until smooth. Transfer to a large pitcher. Repeat with remaining water, lemon juice, fruit, sugar and minced mint.
2. Refrigerate 1 hour or until cold. If desired, press through a fine-mesh strainer. Serve with watermelon wedges and mint leaves.
Per cup: 119 cal., 0 fat (0 sat. fat), 0 chol., 2mg sod., 30g carb. (26g sugars, 1g fiber), 1g pro.

SPICY PEANUT
CHICKEN KABOBS F C

A little sweet, a little sour, and a whole lot of flavor—that's what makes these kabobs so great! They're a fun accompaniment for any party or get-together.
—Nancy Zimmerman
Cape May Court House, NJ

Prep: 20 min. + marinating • **Grill:** 10 min.
Makes: 8 appetizers

- ¼ cup reduced-fat creamy peanut butter
- 3 tablespoons reduced-sodium soy sauce
- 4½ teaspoons lemon juice
- 1 tablespoon brown sugar
- 1½ teaspoons ground coriander
- 1 teaspoon ground cumin
- ¾ teaspoon salt
- ¼ teaspoon pepper
- ¼ to ½ teaspoon cayenne pepper
- 1 garlic clove, minced
- 1 large onion, finely chopped
- 1 pound boneless skinless chicken breasts, cut into 1-inch cubes

1. In a small bowl, combine the first 10 ingredients. Set aside 3 tablespoons marinade for sauce. Pour remaining marinade into a large resealable plastic bag; add onion and chicken. Seal bag and turn to coat; refrigerate overnight. Cover and refrigerate sauce.
2. Drain and discard marinade. Thread chicken onto eight metal or soaked wooden skewers.
3. Grill chicken, covered, on an oiled rack over medium heat or broil 4 in. from the heat for 4-5 minutes on each side or until no longer pink. Brush with reserved sauce before serving.
Per kabob: 94 cal., 3g fat (1g sat. fat), 31mg chol., 275mg sod., 4g carb. (2g sugars, 1g fiber), 13g pro.
Diabetic exchanges: 2 lean meat, ½ fat.

SKINNY QUINOA VEGGIE DIP

SKINNY QUINOA VEGGIE DIP
F S C M

Don't let the name fool you. This good-for-you recipe will appeal to the health-conscious, but it has plenty of flavor to satisfy everyone. We use crunchy cucumber slices for dippers.
—Jennifer Gizzi, Green Bay, WI

Prep: 20 min. • **Cook:** 15 min.
Makes: 32 servings

- 2 cans (15 ounces) black beans, rinsed and drained
- 1½ teaspoons ground cumin
- 1½ teaspoons paprika
- ½ teaspoon cayenne pepper
- 1⅔ cups water, divided
  Salt and pepper to taste
- ⅔ cup quinoa, rinsed
- 5 tablespoons lime juice, divided
- 2 medium ripe avocados, peeled and coarsely chopped
- 2 tablespoons plus ¾ cup sour cream, divided
- ¼ cup minced fresh cilantro
- 3 plum tomatoes, chopped
- ¾ cup peeled, seeded and finely chopped cucumber
- ¾ cup finely chopped zucchini
- ¼ cup finely chopped red onion
  Cucumber slices

1. Pulse beans, cumin, paprika, cayenne and ⅓ cup water in food processor until smooth. Add salt and pepper to taste.
2. In a small saucepan, cook quinoa with remaining 1⅓ cups water according to package directions. Fluff with fork; sprinkle with 2 tablespoons lime juice. Set aside. Meanwhile, mash together avocados, 2 tablespoons sour cream, cilantro and remaining lime juice.
3. In a 2½-qt. dish, layer bean mixture, quinoa, avocado mixture, remaining sour cream, tomatoes, chopped cucumber, zucchini and onion. Serve immediately with cucumber slices for dipping, or refrigerate until serving.
Note: Look for quinoa in the cereal, rice or organic food aisle.
Per ¼ cup: 65 cal., 3g fat (1g sat. fat), 4mg chol., 54mg sod., 8g carb. (1g sugars, 2g fiber), 2g pro.
Diabetic exchanges: ½ starch, ½ fat.

PROSCIUTTO-WRAPPED ASPARAGUS WITH RASPBERRY SAUCE **F C** **FAST FIX**

Grilling the prosciutto with the asparagus gives this appetizer a salty crunch that's perfect for dipping into a sweet glaze. When a delicious appetizer is this easy to prepare, you owe it to yourself to try it!
—Noelle Myers, Grand Forks, ND

Start to Finish: 30 min.
Makes: 16 appetizers

- ⅓ pound thinly sliced prosciutto or deli ham
- 16 fresh asparagus spears, trimmed
- ½ cup seedless raspberry jam
- 2 tablespoons balsamic vinegar

1. Cut prosciutto slices in half. Wrap a prosciutto piece around each asparagus spear; secure ends with toothpicks. .
2. Grill asparagus, covered, on an oiled rack over medium heat for 6-8 minutes or until prosciutto is crisp, turning once. Discard toothpicks.
3. In a small microwave-safe bowl, microwave jam and vinegar on high for 15-20 seconds or until jam is melted. Serve with asparagus.
Per asparagus spear with 1½ teaspoons sauce: 50 cal., 1g fat (0 sat. fat), 8mg chol., 184mg sod., 7g carb. (7g sugars, 0 fiber), 3g pro.
Diabetic exchanges: ½ starch.

PROSCIUTTO-WRAPPED ASPARAGUS WITH RASPBERRY SAUCE

SESAME OMELET SPINACH SPIRALS

ICED HONEYDEW MINT TEA
F S M FAST FIX

I grow mint in the garden on my balcony, so I get excited when I find tasty recipes where I can use it. In this one, I blend two of my favorite beverages—Moroccan mint tea and honeydew agua fresca.
—Sarah Batt, Throne El Cerrito, CA

Start to Finish: 20 min.
Makes: 10 servings

- 4 cups water
- 24 fresh mint leaves
- 8 individual green tea bags
- ⅔ cup sugar
- 5 cups diced honeydew melon, divided
- 3 cups ice cubes, divided
  Additional ice cubes

1. In a large saucepan, bring water to a boil; remove from heat. Add mint leaves and tea bags; steep, covered, 3-5 minutes according to taste, stirring occasionally. Discard mint and tea bags. Stir in sugar.
2. Place 2½ cups honeydew, 2 cups tea and 1½ cups ice in a blender; cover and process until blended. Serve over ice. Repeat with remaining ingredients.

Per cup: 83 cal., 0 fat (0 sat. fat), 0 chol., 15mg sod., 21g carb. (20g sugars, 1g fiber), 0 pro.
Diabetic exchanges: 1 starch, ½ fruit.

SESAME OMELET SPINACH SPIRALS F S C M

These pretty appetizer spirals remind me of sushi and are perfect for a buffet of international hors d'oeuvres. The dipping sauce is an exotic accompaniment.
—Roxanne Chan, Albany, CA

Prep: 25 min. • **Cook:** 10 min.
Makes: about 2½ dozen (⅓ cup sauce)

- 4 tablespoons tahini
- 4 spinach tortillas (8 inches), warmed
- 6 eggs
- 2 tablespoons each finely chopped green onion, sweet red pepper and canned water chestnuts
- 2 tablespoons shredded carrot
- 1 teaspoon minced fresh gingerroot
- ¼ teaspoon crushed red pepper flakes
- 2 teaspoons sesame oil, divided

DIPPING SAUCE
- ¼ cup reduced-sodium soy sauce
- 1 tablespoon minced fresh cilantro
- 1 garlic clove, minced
- 1 teaspoon sesame seeds, toasted
- 1 teaspoon rice vinegar
- 1 teaspoon sesame oil
- ¼ teaspoon grated orange peel

1. Spread tahini over tortillas; set aside. In a small bowl, whisk the eggs, onion, red pepper, water chestnuts, carrot, ginger and pepper flakes.
2. Heat a large nonstick skillet over medium heat; lightly brush with some of the oil. Pour ⅓ cup egg mixture into the pan; cook for 1 minute or until set. Flip egg mixture and cook 30 seconds to 1 minute longer or until lightly browned. Place omelet on a tortilla; roll up. Repeat three times, brushing skillet as needed with remaining oil. Cut wraps into 1-in. slices.
3. Combine the sauce ingredients; serve with spirals.

Per spiral: 51 cal., 3g fat (1g sat. fat), 40mg chol., 121mg sod., 4g carb. (0 sugars, 0 fiber), 2g pro.

APPLE-NUT BLUE CHEESE TARTLETS C M

These tasty appetizers look and taste gourmet, but they're easy to make and have loads of blue cheese flavor. The phyllo shells and filling can be made in advance—just fill the cups and warm them in the oven before serving.
—Trisha Kruse, Eagle, ID

Prep: 25 min. • **Bake:** 10 min.
Makes: 15 appetizers

- 1 large apple, peeled and finely chopped
- 1 medium onion, finely chopped
- 2 teaspoons butter
- 1 cup (4 ounces) crumbled blue cheese
- 4 tablespoons finely chopped walnuts, toasted, divided
- ½ teaspoon salt
- 1 package (1.9 ounces) frozen miniature phyllo tart shells

1. In a small nonstick skillet, saute apple and onion in butter until tender. Remove from the heat; stir in the blue cheese, 3 tablespoons walnuts and salt. Spoon a rounded tablespoonful into each tart shell.

2. Place on an ungreased baking sheet. Bake at 350° for 5 minutes. Sprinkle with remaining walnuts; bake 2-3 minutes longer or until lightly browned.

Freeze option: Freeze cooled pastries in a freezer container, separating layers with waxed paper. To use, reheat pastries on a baking sheet in a preheated 350° oven until crisp and heated through.

Per tartlet: 76 cal., 5g fat (2g sat. fat), 7mg chol., 200mg sod., 5g carb. (2g sugars, 0 fiber), 3g pro.

Diabetic exchanges: 1 fat, ½ starch.

APPLE-NUT BLUE CHEESE TARTLETS

ROSY APPLESAUCE F S M

I end up with a surplus of fresh rhubarb each summer. Because it's a tad bitter, many recipes call for a lot of sugar. This one relies mostly on fruit to sweeten. I refrigerate the sauce overnight to help the flavors blend.
—Amy Nelson, Weston, WI

Prep: 25 min. • **Cook:** 25 min.
Makes: 6 cups

- 5 large Red Delicious apples, peeled and finely chopped
- 4 cups finely chopped fresh or thawed frozen rhubarb (about 8 stalks)
- 4 cups fresh strawberries, hulled and halved
- ½ cup sugar
- ¼ cup water
- 1 teaspoon vanilla extract

1. In a Dutch oven, combine apples, rhubarb, strawberries, sugar and water; bring to a boil. Reduce heat; simmer, covered, 18-22 minutes or until fruit is tender, stirring occasionally.

2. Remove from heat; stir in vanilla. If a smoother consistency is desired, cool slightly and, in batches, process in a blender. Serve warm or cold.

Freeze option Freeze cooled applesauce in freezer containers. To use, thaw in the refrigerator overnight. Serve applesauce cold or heat through in a saucepan, stirring occasionally.

Per ½ cup: 93 cal., 0 fat (0 sat. fat), 0 chol., 2mg sod., 23g carb. (19g sugars, 3g fiber), 1g pro.

Diabetic exchanges: 1 fruit, ½ starch.

HOT CRAB PINWHEELS F S C

I got the recipe for these crabmeat bites from a friend. What amazed me most is that my husband, who hates seafood, couldn't stop eating them.
—Kitti Boesel, Woodbridge, VA

Prep: 15 min. + chilling • **Bake:** 10 min.
Makes: 3 dozen

- 1 package (8 ounces) reduced-fat cream cheese
- 1 can (6 ounces) crabmeat, drained, flaked and cartilage removed
- ¾ cup diced sweet red pepper
- ½ cup shredded reduced-fat cheddar cheese
- 2 green onions, thinly sliced
- 3 tablespoons minced fresh parsley
- ¼ to ½ teaspoon cayenne pepper
- 6 flour tortillas (6 inches)

1. Beat cream cheese until smooth; stir in crab, red pepper, cheese, green onions, parsley and cayenne. Spread ⅓ cup filling over each tortilla; roll up tightly. Wrap in plastic, twisting ends to seal; refrigerate at least 2 hours.

2. To serve, preheat oven to 350°. Unwrap rolls; trim ends and cut each into six slices. Place on baking sheets coated with cooking spray. Bake until bubbly, about 10 minutes. Serve warm.
Per pinwheel: 44 cal., 2g fat (1g sat. fat), 10mg chol., 98mg sod., 3g carb. (0 sugars, 0 fiber), 2g pro.

CATHERINE'S GUACAMOLE

CATHERINE'S GUACAMOLE S C M

Get the scoop on making a standout guacamole. A handful of chopped celery adds some fun crunch in this avocado dip—everyone's favorite fiesta starter.
—Catherine Cassidy, Milwaukee, WI

Prep: 15 min. + chilling
Makes: 2½ cups

- 3 medium ripe avocados, peeled and pitted
- ⅓ cup chopped sweet onion
- 1 small tomato, seeded and chopped
- 1 celery rib, finely chopped
- 2 garlic cloves, minced
- 2 tablespoons lemon or lime juice
- 2 teaspoons Worcestershire sauce
- ½ teaspoon salt
- ¼ teaspoon pepper
- ¼ to ⅓ cup chopped fresh cilantro, optional
  Tortilla chips

In a small bowl, mash avocados. Stir in onion, tomato, celery, garlic, lemon juice, Worcestershire, salt, pepper and, if desired, cilantro. Chill 1 hour before serving. Serve with chips.
Per ¼ cup: 75 cal., 6g fat (1g sat. fat), 0 chol., 136mg sod., 5g carb. (1g sugars, 3g fiber), 1g pro.
Diabetic exchanges: 1 fat.

GOAT CHEESE MUSHROOMS
F S C M FAST FIX
(PICTURED ON P. 6)

Stuffed mushrooms are superstars in the hot appetizer category. I load baby portobellos with creamy goat cheese and sweet red peppers.
—Mike Bass, Alvin, TX

Start to Finish: 30 min.
Makes: 2 dozen

- 24 baby portobello mushrooms (about 1 pound), stems removed
- ½ cup crumbled goat cheese
- ½ cup chopped drained roasted sweet red peppers
  Pepper to taste
- 4 teaspoons olive oil
  Chopped fresh parsley

1. Preheat oven to 375°. Place the mushroom caps in a greased 15x10x1-in. baking pan. Fill each with 1 teaspoon cheese; top each with 1 teaspoon red pepper. Sprinkle with pepper; drizzle with oil.

2. Bake 15-18 minutes or until mushrooms are tender. Sprinkle with parsley.
Per stuffed mushroom: 19 cal., 1g fat (0 sat. fat), 3mg chol., 31mg sod., 1g carb. (1g sugars, 0 fiber), 1g pro.

SAUCY ASIAN MEATBALLS F S C

This meatball recipe originally called for beef and pork and a different blend of seasonings. I used ground turkey and altered the seasonings to create a healthy, fresh-flavored variation.
—Lisa Varner, El Paso, TX

Prep: 20 min. • **Bake:** 20 min.
Makes: about 3 dozen

- 1 pound lean ground turkey
- 2 garlic cloves, minced
- 1 teaspoon plus ¼ cup reduced-sodium soy sauce, divided
- ½ teaspoon ground ginger
- ¼ cup rice vinegar
- ¼ cup tomato paste
- 2 tablespoons molasses
- 1 teaspoon hot pepper sauce

1. Preheat oven to 350°. Place turkey in a large bowl. Sprinkle with garlic, 1 teaspoon soy sauce and ginger; mix lightly but thoroughly. Shape into 1-in. balls; place in a 15x10x1-in. baking pan. Bake until cooked through, 20-25 minutes.
2. In a large saucepan, combine vinegar, tomato paste, molasses, pepper sauce and remaining soy sauce; cook and stir over medium heat 3-5 minutes. Add meatballs; heat through, stirring gently to coat.
Per meatball: 26 cal., 1g fat (0 sat. fat), 10mg chol., 87mg sod., 2g carb. (1g sugars, 0 fiber), 2g pro.

SAUCY ASIAN MEATBALLS

LEMONY HUMMUS
C M FAST FIX ▶

I love the nutty flavor tahini adds to hummus, but it's high in fat. I modified a traditional recipe, slashing the fat.
—Josephine Piro, Easton, PA

Start to Finish: 15 min.
Makes: 1½ cups

- 2 garlic cloves, peeled
- 1 can (15 ounces) chickpeas or garbanzo beans, rinsed and drained
- ¼ cup lemon juice
- 3 tablespoons water
- 2 tablespoons tahini
- 1 teaspoon ground cumin
- ¼ teaspoon salt
- ¼ teaspoon pepper
  Pita breads, warmed and cut into wedges
  Carrot and celery sticks

Process garlic in a food processor until minced. Add the chickpeas, lemon juice, water, tahini, cumin, salt and pepper; cover and process until smooth. Transfer to a small bowl. Serve with pita wedges and vegetables.
Per ¼ cup: 106 cal., 5g fat (1g sat. fat), 0 chol., 192mg sod., 13g carb. (2g sugars, 3g fiber), 4g pro.
Diabetic exchanges: 1 starch, 1 fat.

BUTTERNUT SQUASH BUTTER

STARTERS & SNACKS

BUTTERNUT SQUASH BUTTER F S C M

Looking for a tasty way to use up those pumpkins and have a wonderful gift to share during the holidays? My homemade squash butter is delicious on biscuits or bread, and also makes a tempting filling for miniature tart shells.
—Wanda Richardson, Somers, MT

Prep: 20 min. • **Cook:** 1 hour
Makes: 6 cups

- 6 cups mashed cooked butternut squash or pumpkin
- 2 cups apple cider or juice
- 1¼ cups packed brown sugar
- 1 teaspoon ground cinnamon
- ½ teaspoon ground ginger
- ½ teaspoon ground nutmeg
- ⅛ teaspoon ground cloves

Place all ingredients in a Dutch oven. Bring to a boil. Reduce heat; simmer, uncovered, until mixture reaches a thick, spreadable consistency, 1-1½ hours. Cool to room temperature. Store in an airtight container in the refrigerator up to 3 weeks.
Per 2 tablespoons: 39 cal., 0 fat (0 sat. fat), 0 chol., 4mg sod., 10g carb. (7g sugars, 1g fiber), 0 pro.
Diabetic exchanges: ½ starch.

LAYERED HUMMUS DIP
C FAST FIX ▶
(PICTURED ON P. 7)

My love for Greece inspired this fast-to-fix Mediterranean dip. It's great for parties and is a delicious way to include garden-fresh veggies on your menu.
—Cheryl Snavely, Hagerstown, MD

Start to Finish: 15 min.
Makes: 12 servings

- 1 carton (10 ounces) hummus
- ¼ cup finely chopped red onion
- ½ cup Greek olives, chopped
- 2 medium tomatoes, seeded and chopped
- 1 large English cucumber, chopped
- 1 cup crumbled feta cheese
  Baked pita chips

Spread hummus into a shallow 10-in. round dish. Layer with onion, olives, tomatoes, cucumber and cheese. Refrigerate until serving. Serve with chips.
Per serving: 88 cal., 5g fat (2g sat. fat), 5mg chol., 275mg sod., 6g carb. (1g sugars, 2g fiber), 4g pro.
Diabetic exchanges: 1 fat, ½ starch.

HOT CIDER PUNCH F S M
(PICTURED ON P. 6)

This hot fruit punch has been a family fave since 1993. It's so refreshing and soothing it's no wonder we've loved it for 25 years! The clove-studded orange wedges make it look especially pretty on a spread.
—Anita Bell, Hermitage, TN

Prep: 5 min. • **Cook:** 30 min.
Makes: 12 servings

- 3½ cups apple cider or juice
- 2 tablespoons sugar
- 1 cinnamon stick (3 inches)
- ½ teaspoon ground nutmeg
- 3 cups orange juice
- 3 cups unsweetened pineapple juice
- 1 teaspoon whole cloves
- 1 medium orange, cut into wedges

1. Place cider, sugar, cinnamon stick and nutmeg in a large saucepan; bring to a boil. Reduce heat; simmer, covered, 20 minutes.
2. Stir in orange and pineapple juices. Insert cloves into orange wedges; add to cider mixture and heat through. Discard cinnamon stick. Serve warm.
Per ¾ cup: 107 cal., 0 fat (0 sat. fat), 0 chol., 15mg sod., 26g carb. (21g sugars, 0 fiber), 0 pro.

HOMEMADE PEANUT BUTTER
S **C** **FAST FIX**

We eat a lot of peanut butter, so I decided to compare the cost of store-bought peanut butter here in Alaska with the cost of peanuts, salt and honey. I discovered making my own at home is much cheaper. I also have the added value of knowing what goes into it.
—Marge Austin, North Pole, AK

Start to Finish: 15 min.
Makes: about 1 cup

- 2 cups unsalted dry roasted peanuts
- ½ teaspoon salt
- 1 tablespoon honey

Process the peanuts and salt in a food processor until desired consistency, about 5 minutes, scraping down sides as needed. Add honey; process just until blended. Store peanut butter in an airtight container in refrigerator.

Per tablespoon: 111 cal., 9g fat (1g sat. fat), 0 chol., 75mg sod., 5g carb. (2g sugars, 2g fiber), 4g pro.
Diabetic exchanges: 2 fat.

SPICY EDAMAME **F** **C** **FAST FIX**

Edamame (pronounced ay-duh-MAH-may) are young soybeans in their pods. In our Test Kitchen, we boiled and seasoned them with salt, ginger, garlic powder and red pepper flakes.
—*Taste of Home* Test Kitchen

Start to Finish: 20 min.
Makes: 6 servings

- 1 package (16 ounces) frozen edamame pods
- 2 teaspoons kosher salt
- ¾ teaspoon ground ginger
- ½ teaspoon garlic powder
- ¼ teaspoon crushed red pepper flakes

Place edamame in a large saucepan and cover with water. Bring to a boil. Cover and cook for 4-5 minutes or until tender; drain. Transfer to a large bowl. Add the seasonings; toss to coat.

Per serving: 52 cal., 2g fat (0 sat. fat), 0 chol., 642mg sod., 5g carb. (1g sugars, 2g fiber), 4g pro.

GARLIC-DILL DEVILED EGGS **S** **C**

Easter isn't complete without deviled eggs. I like to experiment with my recipes, and was pleasantly pleased with how the fresh dill perked up the flavor of these irresistible appetizers.
—Kami Horch, Calais, ME

Prep: 20 min. + chilling
Makes: 2 dozen

- 12 hard-boiled large eggs
- ⅔ cup mayonnaise
- 4 teaspoons dill pickle relish
- 2 teaspoons snipped fresh dill
- 2 teaspoons Dijon mustard
- 1 teaspoon coarsely ground pepper
- ¼ teaspoon garlic powder
- ⅛ teaspoon paprika or cayenne pepper

1. Cut eggs lengthwise in half. Remove yolks, reserving whites. In a bowl, mash yolks. Stir in all remaining ingredients except paprika. Spoon or pipe into egg whites.
2. Refrigerate, covered, for at least 30 minutes before serving. Sprinkle with paprika.

Per stuffed egg half: 81 cal., 7g fat (1g sat. fat), 94mg chol., 81mg sod., 1g carb. (0 sugars, 0 fiber), 3g pro.

HOMEMADE PEANUT BUTTER

SOUPS

"Tender cubes of chicken, fresh vegetables and wild rice make this soup hearty enough for a meal. You can't beat the down-home comfort of a warm bowlful. I like to serve it with whole-wheat rolls."
—J. Beatrice Hintz, Neenah, WI

**MAKEOVER CHEESY
HAM & POTATO SOUP**

SOUPS

WATERMELON GAZPACHO
F **M** **FAST FIX** ▶

*My refreshing gazpacho is a delightfully
simple, elegant dish. Serve it as a side
or with pita and hummus for a meal.*
—Nicole Deelah, Nashville, TN

Start to Finish: 25 min.
Makes: 4 servings

- 4 cups cubed watermelon, seeded,
  divided
- 2 tablespoons lime juice
- 1 tablespoon grated lime peel
- 1 teaspoon minced fresh gingerroot
- 1 teaspoon salt
- 1 cup chopped tomato
- ½ cup chopped cucumber
- ½ cup chopped green pepper
- ¼ cup minced fresh cilantro
- 2 tablespoons chopped green onion
- 1 tablespoon finely chopped seeded
  jalapeno pepper

1. Puree 3 cups watermelon in a blender.
Cut remaining watermelon into ½-inch
pieces; set aside.
2. In a large bowl, combine watermelon
puree, lime juice, lime peel, ginger and salt.
Stir in tomato, cucumber, green pepper,
cilantro, onion, jalapeno and cubed
watermelon. Chill until serving.
Note: Wear disposable gloves when
cutting hot peppers; the oils can burn
skin. Avoid touching your face.
Per cup: 58 cal., 0 fat (0 sat. fat), 0 chol.,
599mg sod., 18g carb. (15g sugars,
2g fiber), 1g pro.
Diabetic exchanges: 1 fruit.

MAKEOVER CHEESY HAM
& POTATO SOUP **FAST FIX** ▶

*This better-for-you version of an all-time
classic uses lean ham, canola oil, fat-free
milk and reduced-fat cheddar cheese.
Potatoes and dry milk powder help keep
the soup's thick creamy texture.*
—*Taste of Home* Test Kitchen

Start to Finish: 30 min.
Makes: 7 servings

- 2¼ cups cubed potatoes
- 1½ cups water
- 1½ cups cubed fully cooked lean ham
- 1 large onion, chopped
- 2 teaspoons canola oil
- ¼ cup nonfat dry milk powder
- 3 tablespoons all-purpose flour
- ¼ teaspoon pepper
- 3 cups fat-free milk
- 1½ cups finely shredded reduced-fat
  cheddar cheese
- 1 cup frozen broccoli florets, thawed
  and chopped

1. In a saucepan, bring potatoes and
water to a boil. Cover and cook for 10-15
minutes or until tender. Drain, reserving
1 cup cooking liquid. In a blender or food
processor, process reserved liquid and
¼ cup cooked potatoes until smooth;
set aside. Set remaining potatoes aside.
2. In a large saucepan, saute ham and
onion in oil until onion is tender. In a bowl,
combine milk powder, flour, pepper, milk
and processed potato mixture until
smooth. Stir into ham and onion. Bring
to a boil; cook and stir for 2 minutes or
until thickened.
3. Reduce heat to low. Add the cheese,
broccoli and reserved potatoes; cook and
stir over low heat until cheese is melted
and heated through. Serve immediately.
Per cup: 238 cal., 8g fat (4g sat. fat),
31mg chol., 604mg sod., 23g carb.
(8g sugars, 2g fiber), 19g pro.
Diabetic exchanges: 1 starch, 2 lean
meat, ½ fat-free milk.

SWEET POTATO SOUP

Ginger and peanut butter make this dazzling orange soup unique. It has a mild, not spicy, taste with a lovely Asian flair.

—Hilda Fallas, Kirkland, WA

Prep: 25 min. • **Cook:** 20 min.
Makes: 8 servings (2 quarts)

- 1 large onion, chopped
- 1 medium sweet red pepper, chopped
- 2 medium carrots, chopped
- 2 teaspoons canola oil
- 1 teaspoon minced fresh gingerroot
- 1 garlic clove, minced
- ½ teaspoon cayenne pepper
- ½ teaspoon coarsely ground pepper
- 1 carton (32 ounces) plus 1 can (14½ ounces) reduced-sodium chicken broth
- 1 can (14½ ounces) diced tomatoes, undrained
- 1 large sweet potato, peeled and cubed
- ⅔ cup creamy peanut butter
- 2 teaspoons honey
- 4 green onions, chopped

1. In a large saucepan, saute the onion, red pepper and carrots in canola oil for 3 minutes. Stir in ginger, garlic, cayenne and pepper; cook 2 minutes longer. Add the broth, tomatoes and sweet potato. Bring to a boil. Reduce heat; cover and simmer for 15-20 minutes or until the potatoes are tender.

2. Cool slightly. In a blender, cover and process soup in batches until smooth. Return all to pan and heat through. Stir in peanut butter and honey. Cook and stir until peanut butter is melted. Garnish servings with green onions.

Per cup: 213 cal., 12g fat (2g sat. fat), 0 chol., 655mg sod., 20g carb. (11g sugars, 4g fiber), 9g pro.

CHILLED SUMMER BERRY BISQUE F S M

A blend of yogurt and spices thickens this cold blueberry soup and tempers the sweetness. It makes an attractive and healthy first course for a summer menu.

—Arlene Knick, Newport News, VA

Prep: 20 min. + chilling
Makes: 8 servings

- 4½ cups fresh or frozen blueberries, thawed, divided
- 1 cup unsweetened apple juice
- 1 cup orange juice
- ¼ cup honey
- 2 teaspoons minced fresh gingerroot
- 1 teaspoon grated orange peel
- ¼ teaspoon ground cinnamon
- ⅛ teaspoon ground nutmeg
- 2 cups (16 ounces) plain yogurt
  Fresh mint leaves

1. In a large saucepan, combine 4 cups blueberries, apple juice, orange juice, honey, ginger, orange peel, cinnamon and nutmeg. Bring to a boil, stirring occasionally. Cool slightly.

2. In a blender, process the blueberry mixture and yogurt in batches until smooth. Refrigerate until chilled. Just before serving, garnish with mint and remaining blueberries.

Per ¾ cup: 145 cal., 2g fat (1g sat. fat), 8mg chol., 30mg sod., 30g carb. (26g sugars, 2g fiber), 3g pro.
Diabetic exchanges: 1 starch, 1 fruit.

SWEET POTATO SOUP

CREAM OF WILD RICE SOUP
FAST FIX ▶

Tender cubes of chicken, fresh vegetables and wild rice make this soup hearty enough for a meal. You can't beat the down-home comfort of a warm bowlful. I like to serve it with whole-wheat rolls.
—J. Beatrice Hintz, Neenah, WI

Start to Finish: 30 min.
Makes: 10 servings (2½ quarts)

- 1 large onion, chopped
- 1 large carrot, shredded
- 1 celery rib, chopped
- ¼ cup butter
- ½ cup all-purpose flour
- 8 cups reduced-sodium chicken broth
- 3 cups cooked wild rice
- 1 cup cubed cooked chicken breast
- ¼ teaspoon salt
- ¼ teaspoon pepper
- 1 cup fat-free evaporated milk
- ¼ cup minced chives

In a large saucepan, saute onion, carrot and celery in butter until tender. Stir in flour until blended. Gradually add broth. Stir in rice, chicken, salt and pepper. Bring to a boil over medium heat; cook and stir 2 minutes or until thickened. Add milk; cook 3-5 minutes longer. Garnish with chives.
Per cup: 176 cal., 5g fat (3g sat. fat), 24mg chol., 600mg sod., 21g carb. (5g sugars, 2g fiber), 11g pro.
Diabetic exchanges: 1½ starch, 1 lean meat, 1 fat.

BLOODY MARY SOUP WITH BEANS

BLOODY MARY SOUP WITH BEANS **F**

A good Bloody Mary inspired this soup. It packs a spicy punch to warm you right up on a chilly day. For a meat-free meal, substitute vegetarian Worcestershire and veggie broth.
—Amber Massey, Argyle, TX

Prep: 20 min. • **Cook:** 55 min.
Makes: 16 servings (4 quarts)

- 1 tablespoon olive oil
- 1 large onion, chopped
- 2 celery ribs, chopped
- 1 large carrot, finely chopped
- 1 poblano pepper, seeded and chopped
- 3 garlic cloves, minced
- 1 carton (32 ounces) reduced-sodium chicken broth
- 1 can (28 ounces) crushed tomatoes
- 1 can (14½ ounces) fire-roasted diced tomatoes, undrained
- ¼ cup tomato paste
- 2 cans (15 ounces each) white kidney or cannellini beans, rinsed and drained
- ¼ cup vodka
- 2 tablespoons Worcestershire sauce
- ½ teaspoon sugar
- 2 tablespoons lemon juice
- 1 tablespoon prepared horseradish
- ½ teaspoon pepper
  Minced fresh parsley, celery ribs, lemon wedges and hot pepper sauce, optional

1. In a Dutch oven, heat oil over medium-high heat. Add onion, celery, carrot and poblano pepper; cook and stir 4-5 minutes or until crisp-tender. Add the garlic; cook 1 minute longer.
2. Stir in broth, tomatoes and tomato paste. Bring to a boil. Reduce the heat; simmer, covered, 15 minutes. Add beans, vodka, Worcestershire sauce and sugar; return to a boil. Reduce heat; simmer, uncovered, 25-30 minutes or until vegetables are tender, stirring occasionally.
3. Stir in lemon juice, horseradish and pepper. If desired, sprinkle servings with parsley and serve with celery ribs, lemon wedges and pepper sauce.
Note: Wear disposable gloves when cutting hot peppers; the oils can burn skin. Avoid touching your face.
Per cup without toppings: 99 cal., 1g fat (0 sat. fat), 0 chol., 405mg sod., 16g carb. (5g sugars, 4g fiber), 4g pro.

APPLE SQUASH SOUP

I add a little ginger and sage to apples and squash to make this creamy soup. My family loves it when autumn rolls around.
—Crystal Ralph-Haughn, Bartlesville, OK

Prep: 10 min. • **Cook:** 35 min.
Makes: 5 servings

- 2 tablespoons butter
- 1 large onion, chopped
- ½ teaspoon rubbed sage
- 1 can (14½ ounces) chicken or vegetable broth
- 2 medium tart apples, peeled and finely chopped
- ¾ cup water
- 1 package (12 ounces) frozen cooked winter squash, thawed
- 1 teaspoon ground ginger
- ½ teaspoon salt
- ½ cup fat-free milk

1. In a large saucepan, heat butter over medium-high heat. Add onion and sage; cook and stir 2-4 minutes or until tender. Add the broth, apples and water; bring to a boil. Reduce heat; simmer, covered, 12 minutes.
2. Add squash, ginger and salt; return to a boil. Reduce heat; simmer, uncovered, 10 minutes to allow the flavors to blend. Remove from heat; cool slightly.
3. Process in batches in a blender until smooth; return to pan. Add milk; heat through, stirring occasionally (do not allow to boil).

Freeze option: Freeze cooled soup in freezer containers. To use, partially thaw in refrigerator overnight. Heat through in a saucepan, stirring occasionally and adding a little broth if necessary.

Per cup: 119 cal., 5g fat (3g sat. fat), 15mg chol., 641mg sod., 18g carb. (8g sugars, 3g fiber), 3g pro.
Diabetic exchanges: 1 starch, ½ fruit, 1 fat.

APPLE SQUASH SOUP

TOMATO GREEN BEAN SOUP
F **C**

This colorful soup is delicious at any time of year. When I can't use home-grown tomatoes and green beans, I've found that frozen beans and canned tomatoes (or even stewed tomatoes) work just fine.
—Bernice Nolan, Granite City, IL

Prep: 10 min. • **Cook:** 35 min.
Makes: 9 servings

- 1 cup chopped onion
- 1 cup chopped carrots
- 2 teaspoons butter
- 6 cups reduced-sodium chicken or vegetable broth
- 1 pound fresh green beans, cut into 1-inch pieces
- 1 garlic clove, minced
- 3 cups diced fresh tomatoes
- ¼ cup minced fresh basil or 1 tablespoon dried basil
- ½ teaspoon salt
- ¼ teaspoon pepper

1. In a large saucepan, saute onion and carrots in butter for 5 minutes. Stir in the broth, beans and garlic; bring to a boil. Reduce heat; cover and simmer for 20 minutes or until vegetables are tender.
2. Stir in the tomatoes, basil, salt and pepper. Cover and simmer for another 5 minutes.

Per cup: 58 cal., 1g fat (1g sat. fat), 2mg chol., 535mg sod., 10g carb. (5g sugars, 3g fiber), 4g pro.
Diabetic exchanges: 2 vegetable.

QUICK MUSHROOM
BARLEY SOUP

QUICK MUSHROOM BARLEY SOUP Ⓜ FAST FIX ▸

I surprised my mother with a visit some years ago, and she was preparing this soup when I walked in. It was so wonderful that I asked for the recipe, and I've been fixing it ever since.
—Edie Irwin, Cornwall, NY

Start to Finish: 30 min.
Makes: 6 servings

- 1 tablespoon olive oil
- 1 cup sliced fresh mushrooms
- ½ cup chopped carrot
- ⅓ cup chopped onion
- 2 cups water
- ¾ cup quick-cooking barley
- 2 tablespoons all-purpose flour
- 3 cups whole milk
- 1½ teaspoons salt
- ½ teaspoon pepper

1. In a large saucepan, heat the oil over medium heat. Add mushrooms, carrot and onion; cook and stir 5-6 minutes or until tender. Add water and barley. Bring to a boil. Reduce heat; simmer, uncovered, 12-15 minutes or until barley is tender.
2. In a small bowl, mix flour, milk, salt and pepper until smooth; stir into soup. Return to a boil, stirring constantly; cook and stir 1-2 minutes or until thickened.
Per cup: 196 cal., 7g fat (3g sat. fat), 12mg chol., 654mg sod., 27g carb. (7g sugars, 5g fiber), 8g pro.
Diabetic exchanges: 1½ starch, ½ whole milk, ½ fat.

★ ★ ★ ★ ★ **READER REVIEW**

"I really like this soup! Very easy, satisfying and delicious. A treat I'm looking forward to is enjoying the leftovers!"
PVHDEERFIELD TASTEOFHOME.COM

HEARTY BEEF VEGETABLE SOUP

My stew-like soup is loaded with nutritious ingredients, yet it is so easy to prepare. I make homemade bread or breadsticks to serve with it.
—Sherman Snowball, Salt Lake City, UT

Prep: 20 min. • **Cook:** 2 hours
Makes: 8 servings (about 2½ quarts)

- 3 tablespoons all-purpose flour
- ½ teaspoon salt
- ¼ teaspoon pepper
- 1 pound beef stew meat, cut into ½-inch cubes
- 2 tablespoons olive oil
- 1 can (14½ ounces) Italian diced tomatoes
- 1 can (8 ounces) tomato sauce
- 2 tablespoons red wine vinegar
- 2 tablespoons Worcestershire sauce
- 3 garlic cloves, minced
- 1 teaspoon dried oregano
- 3 cups water
- 4 medium potatoes, peeled and cubed
- 6 medium carrots, sliced
- 2 medium turnips, peeled and cubed
- 1 medium zucchini, halved lengthwise and sliced
- 1 medium green pepper, julienned
- 1 cup sliced fresh mushrooms
- 1 medium onion, chopped
- 1 can (4 ounces) chopped green chilies
- 2 tablespoons sugar

1. In a large resealable plastic bag, combine the flour, salt and pepper. Add beef, a few pieces at a time, and shake to coat.
2. In a Dutch oven, brown beef in oil. Stir in the tomatoes, tomato sauce, vinegar, Worcestershire sauce, garlic and oregano. Bring to a boil. Reduce heat; cover and simmer for 1 hour.
3. Stir in the remaining ingredients. Bring to a boil. Reduce heat; cover and simmer for 1 hour or until meat and vegetables are tender.
Per 1½ cups: 276 cal., 8g fat (2g sat. fat), 35mg chol., 638mg sod., 38g carb. (14g sugars, 5g fiber), 15g pro.
Diabetic exchanges: 2½ starch, 2 lean meat.

HEARTY BEEF VEGETABLE SOUP

SEAFOOD SOUP

SHORTCUT SAUSAGE MINESTRONE FAST FIX ▶

I call this surprisingly good dish my magic soup for its soothing powers. My daughter-in-law always asks for it when she needs a healing touch.
—Marta Smith, Claremont, PA

Start to Finish: 25 min.
Makes: 6 servings (2 quarts)

- ¾ pound Italian turkey sausage links, casings removed
- 1 small green pepper, chopped
- 1 small onion, chopped
- 2 cups cut fresh green beans or frozen cut green beans
- 2 cups water
- 1 can (16 ounces) kidney beans, rinsed and drained
- 1 can (14½ ounces) diced tomatoes with basil, oregano and garlic, undrained
- 1 can (14½ ounces) reduced-sodium chicken broth
- ¾ cup uncooked ditalini or other small pasta

1. In a 6-qt. stockpot, cook the sausage, pepper and onion over medium heat 5-7 minutes or until sausage is no longer pink, breaking up sausage into crumbles; drain.
2. Add green beans, water, kidney beans, tomatoes and broth; bring to a boil. Stir in ditalini; cook, uncovered, 10-11 minutes or until pasta is tender, stirring occasionally.
Per 1⅓ cups: 232 cal., 4g fat (1g sat. fat), 21mg chol., 773mg sod., 34g carb. (6g sugars, 7g fiber), 16g pro.

SEAFOOD SOUP C

Salmon, shrimp and loads of veggies make this a flavorful, hearty meal in a bowl. What a tasty change of pace.
—Valerie Bradley, Beaverton, OR

Prep: 20 min. • **Cook:** 50 min.
Makes: 6 servings

- 1 tablespoon olive oil
- 1 small onion, chopped
- 1 small green pepper, chopped
- 2 medium carrots, chopped
- 1 garlic clove, minced
- 1 can (15 ounces) tomato sauce
- 1 can (14½ ounces) diced tomatoes, undrained
- ¾ cup white wine or chicken broth
- 1 bay leaf
- ½ teaspoon dried oregano
- ¼ teaspoon dried basil
- ¼ teaspoon pepper
- ¾ pound salmon fillets, skinned and cut into ¾-inch cubes
- ½ pound uncooked medium shrimp, peeled and deveined
- 3 tablespoons minced fresh parsley

1. In a large saucepan, heat the oil over medium heat. Add the onion and green pepper; cook and stir until tender. Add carrots and garlic; cook 3 minutes longer. Stir in tomato sauce, tomatoes, wine and seasonings. Bring to a boil. Reduce heat; simmer, covered, 30 minutes.
2. Stir in salmon, shrimp and parsley. Cook, covered, 7-10 minutes longer or until the fish flakes easily with a fork and shrimp turn pink. Discard bay leaf.
Per cup: 213 cal., 9g fat (1g sat. fat), 74mg chol., 525mg sod., 12g carb. (5g sugars, 3g fiber), 18g pro.
Diabetic exchanges: 2 lean meat, 2 vegetable, ½ fat.

CREAMY ASPARAGUS CHOWDER

While this soup is best when made with fresh asparagus, you can also use frozen or canned. I like to blanch and freeze asparagus in portions just right for the recipe. This way, I can make our favorite chowder all year.
—Shirley Beachum, Shelby, MI

....

Prep: 10 min. • **Cook:** 30 min.
Makes: about 2½ quarts

- 2 medium onions, chopped
- 2 cups chopped celery
- ¼ cup butter
- 1 garlic clove, minced
- ½ cup all-purpose flour
- 1 large potato, peeled and cut into ½-inch cubes
- 4 cups whole milk
- 4 cups chicken broth
- ½ teaspoon dried thyme
- ½ teaspoon dried marjoram
- 4 cups chopped fresh asparagus, cooked and drained
  Salt and pepper to taste
  Sliced almonds
  Shredded cheddar cheese
  Chopped fresh tomato

1. In a Dutch oven, saute onions and celery in butter until tender. Add garlic; cook 1 minute longer. Stir in flour. Add the potato, milk, broth and herbs; cook over low heat, stirring occasionally until the potato is tender and soup is thickened, about 20-30 minutes.
2. Add the asparagus, salt and pepper; heat through. To serve, sprinkle with almonds, cheese and chopped tomato.
Per cup: 187 cal., 8g fat (5g sat. fat), 26mg chol., 491mg sod., 23g carb. (9g sugars, 3g fiber), 7g pro.
Diabetic exchanges: 1½ starch, 1½ fat.

TURKEY SOUP F C

I like making this soup around the holidays after a big turkey dinner. It's especially good on cold winter nights when it is snowing—which happens a lot where I live!
—Carol Brethauer, Denver, CO

....

Prep: 30 min. • **Cook:** 4 hours
Makes: 12 servings (5 quarts)

- 1 leftover turkey carcass (from a 14-pound turkey)
- 3 quarts water
- 2 cans (14½ ounces each) reduced-sodium chicken broth
- ½ cup uncooked long-grain rice
- 1 medium onion, finely chopped
- 4 celery ribs, finely chopped
- 2 medium carrots, grated
- 1 bay leaf
  Dash poultry seasoning
  Salt, optional
  Pepper
  Onion powder
  Garlic powder

1. In a stock pot, place turkey carcass, water and broth. Bring to a boil. Reduce heat; cover and simmer for 4-5 hours.
2. Remove carcass from stock. Remove any meat and dice. Return to stock along with rice, onion, celery, carrots, bay leaf and poultry seasoning. Add remaining seasonings to taste. Cover and simmer over medium-low heat until the rice is cooked. Discard bay leaf.
Per 1⅔ cups: 147 cal., 2g fat (0 sat. fat), 28mg chol., 412mg sod., 15g carb. (3g sugars, 1g fiber), 12g pro.
Diabetic exchanges: 1 starch, 1 lean meat.

CREAMY ASPARAGUS CHOWDER

BARBARA'S ITALIAN WEDDING SOUP `FAST FIX`

We had an amazing soup with orzo at an Italian restaurant. I tweaked it to make it healthier, but kept the comforting flavor.
—Barbara Spitzer, Lodi, CA

Start to Finish: 30 min.
MAKES: 6 servings

- 1 package (19½ ounces) Italian turkey sausage links, casings removed
- 2 shallots, finely chopped
- 3 garlic cloves, minced
- 1 carton (32 ounces) reduced-sodium chicken broth
- ¾ cup uncooked whole wheat orzo pasta
- ¼ teaspoon pepper
- 10 cups coarsely chopped escarole or spinach
- ½ cup coarsely chopped fresh Italian parsley

1. In a 6-qt. stockpot, cook the sausage, shallots and garlic over medium heat 6-8 minutes or until sausage is no longer pink, breaking up sausage into crumbles. Drain.
2. Add broth to sausage mixture; bring to a boil. Stir in orzo, pepper and escarole; return to a boil. Reduce the heat; simmer, uncovered, 10-12 minutes or until orzo is tender. Stir in parsley before serving.
Per cup: 197 cal., 6g fat (1g sat. fat), 34mg chol., 780mg sod., 20g carb. (1g sugars, 6g fiber), 16g pro.

CHICKEN & BLACK BEAN SOUP

CHICKEN & BLACK BEAN SOUP `F` `FAST FIX`

This spicy soup is one of my husband's favorites. It's quick to make but tastes like it simmered all day, and what a great way to use up the last tortilla chips in a bag. It's even delicious reheated!
—Linda Lashley, Redgranite, WI

Start to Finish: 30 min.
Makes: 6 servings (2 quarts)

- ½ pound boneless skinless chicken breasts, cut into 1-inch cubes
- 2 cans (14½ ounces each) reduced-sodium chicken broth, divided
- 2 cups frozen corn
- 1 can (15 ounces) black beans, rinsed and drained
- 1 can (10 ounces) diced tomatoes and green chilies, undrained
- 1 jalapeno pepper, seeded and chopped
- 2 tablespoons minced fresh cilantro
- 3 teaspoons chili powder
- ½ teaspoon ground cumin
- 1 tablespoon cornstarch
- 18 tortilla chips
  Shredded reduced-fat Mexican cheese blend, optional

1. Place a large nonstick saucepan coated with cooking spray over medium heat. Add the chicken; cook and stir it 4-6 minutes or until no longer pink. Reserve 2 tablespoons broth; add remaining broth to pan. Stir in corn, beans, tomatoes, jalapeno, cilantro, chili powder and cumin. Bring to a boil. Reduce the heat; simmer it, uncovered, for 15 minutes.
2. Mix the cornstarch and reserved broth until smooth; gradually stir into the soup. Bring to a boil; cook and stir 2 minutes or until thickened. Top servings with crushed chips and, if desired, cheese.
Note: Wear disposable gloves when cutting hot peppers; the oils can burn skin. Avoid touching your face.
Per 1⅓ cups without cheese: 194 cal., 2g fat (0 sat. fat), 24mg chol., 752mg sod., 29g carb. (2g sugars, 5g fiber), 17g pro.
Diabetic exchanges: 2 starch, 2 lean meat.

MEATBALL ALPHABET SOUP

Bite-size meatballs made from ground turkey perk up this fun alphabet soup. A variety of vegetables mix into a rich tomato broth seasoned with herbs.
—*Taste of Home* Test Kitchen

Prep: 20 min. • **Cook:** 35 min.
Makes: 9 servings

- 1 large egg, lightly beaten
- 2 tablespoons quick-cooking oats
- 2 tablespoons grated Parmesan cheese
- ¼ teaspoon garlic powder
- ¼ teaspoon Italian seasoning
- ½ pound lean ground turkey
- 1 cup chopped onion
- 1 cup chopped celery
- 1 cup chopped carrots
- 1 cup diced peeled potatoes
- 1 tablespoon olive oil
- 2 garlic cloves, minced
- 4 cans (14½ ounces each) reduced-sodium chicken broth
- 1 can (28 ounces) diced tomatoes, undrained
- 1 can (6 ounces) tomato paste
- ¼ cup minced fresh parsley
- 1 teaspoon dried basil
- 1 teaspoon dried thyme
- ¾ cup uncooked alphabet pasta

1. In a bowl, combine the first five ingredients. Crumble turkey over mixture and mix well. Shape into ½-in. balls. In a nonstick skillet, brown meatballs in small batches over medium heat until no longer pink. Remove from the heat; set aside.
2. In a large saucepan or Dutch oven, saute onion, celery, carrots and potatoes in oil for 5 minutes or until crisp-tender. Add garlic; saute for 1 minute longer.
3. Stir in the broth, tomatoes, tomato paste, parsley, basil and thyme; bring to a boil. Add pasta; cook for 5-6 minutes. Reduce heat; add meatballs. Simmer, uncovered, for 15-20 minutes or until vegetables are tender.
Per 1½ cups: 192 cal., 5g fat (1g sat. fat), 39mg chol., 742mg sod., 26g carb. (8g sugars, 4g fiber), 13g pro.

BROWN RICE TURKEY SOUP
FAST FIX

I don't recall where I got this recipe, but it's my all-time favorite turkey soup. Everyone who has tried it agrees. The sweet red pepper is what gives the soup its distinctive flavor.
—Bobby Langley, Rocky Mount, NC

Start to Finish: 30 min.
Makes: 5 servings

- 1 cup diced sweet red pepper
- ½ cup chopped onion
- ½ cup sliced celery
- 2 garlic cloves, minced
- 2 tablespoons butter
- 3 cans (14½ ounces each) reduced-sodium chicken broth
- ¾ cup white wine or additional reduced-sodium chicken broth
- 1 teaspoon dried thyme
- ¼ teaspoon pepper
- 2 cups cubed cooked turkey breast
- 1 cup instant brown rice
- ¼ cup sliced green onions

1. In a Dutch oven, saute the red pepper, onion, celery and garlic in butter for 5-7 minutes or until vegetables are tender. Add the broth, wine or additional broth, thyme and pepper. Bring to a boil.
2. Reduce the heat; cover and simmer for 5 minutes. Stir in the turkey and rice. Bring to a boil; simmer it, uncovered, for 5 minutes or until rice is tender. Garnish with green onions.
Per 1½ cups: 264 cal., 7g fat (3g sat. fat), 57mg chol., 815mg sod., 22g carb. (4g sugars, 2g fiber), 23g pro.
Diabetic exchanges: 3 lean meat, 1½ starch, 1 fat.

MEATBALL ALPHABET SOUP

SOUTHWESTERN CHICKEN TORTILLA SOUP F

The spices really liven up the flavor in this filling soup. This recipe is easily doubled and freezes well.
—Anne Smithson, Cary, NC

Prep: 10 min. • **Cook:** 1¼ hours
Makes: 8 servings

- 1 carton (32 ounces) plus 1 can (14½ ounces) reduced-sodium chicken broth
- 1 can (14½ ounces) crushed tomatoes, undrained
- 1 can (14½ ounces) diced tomatoes, undrained
- 1 pound boneless skinless chicken breast, cut into ½-inch cubes
- 1 large onion, chopped
- ⅓ cup minced fresh cilantro
- 1 can (4 ounces) chopped green chilies
- 1 garlic clove, minced
- 1 teaspoon chili powder
- 1 teaspoon ground cumin
- ½ teaspoon dried oregano
- ¼ teaspoon cayenne pepper
- 3 cups frozen corn, thawed
  Crushed tortilla chips and reduced-fat Mexican cheese blend

In a large saucepan, combine the first 12 ingredients. Bring to a boil. Reduce heat; cover and simmer for 1 hour. Add corn; cook 10 minutes longer. Top with tortilla chips and cheese.
Per 1½ cups without chips and cheese: 158 cal., 2g fat (0 sat. fat), 31mg chol., 748mg sod., 20g carb. (7g sugars, 4g fiber), 17g pro.

TURKEY TOMATO SOUP F
(PICTURED ON P. 21)

Turkey and tomatoes are high on my list of favorite foods. My husband grows the best tomatoes ever, and I made up this recipe to highlight both ingredients. It's wonderful any time of year, but I prefer to make it when the tomatoes, green peppers, basil and garlic are all fresh from our garden.
—Carol Brunelle, Ascutney, VT

Prep: 10 min. • **Cook:** 2½ hours
Makes: 12 servings (3 quarts)

- 4 pounds tomatoes, seeded and chopped (about 8 large tomatoes)
- 3 medium green peppers, chopped
- 2 cans (14½ ounces each) reduced-sodium chicken broth
- 1 can (14½ ounces) vegetable broth
- 1½ cups water
- 1½ teaspoons beef bouillon granules
- 2 garlic cloves, minced
- 1 teaspoon dried oregano
- 1 teaspoon dried basil
- ½ teaspoon pepper
- 3 cups cubed cooked turkey breast
- 3 cups cooked elbow macaroni
  Minced fresh basil, optional

In a Dutch oven, combine the first 10 ingredients. Bring to a boil. Reduce heat; cover and simmer for 2 hours. Stir in turkey and macaroni; heat through. Garnish with fresh basil if desired.
Per cup: 139 cal., 1g fat (0 sat. fat), 28mg chol., 443mg sod., 17g carb. (5g sugars, 3g fiber), 15g pro.
Diabetic exchanges: 1 starch, 1 lean meat, 1 vegetable.

HEARTY LIMA BEAN SOUP

This colorful soup has a golden broth dotted with tender vegetables and lima beans. It makes an excellent lunch or first course.

—Betty Korcek, Bridgman, MI

Prep: 20 min. + standing
Cook: 2 hours 50 min.
Makes: 14 servings (3½ quarts)

1 pound dried lima beans
1 large meaty ham bone or 2 ham hocks
2½ quarts water
5 celery ribs, cut into chunks
5 medium carrots, cut into chunks
1 garlic clove, minced
2 tablespoons butter
2 tablespoons all-purpose flour
2 teaspoons salt
½ teaspoon pepper
  Pinch paprika
1 cup cold water
1 can (14½ ounces) stewed tomatoes

1. Place beans in a Dutch oven; add water to cover by 2 in. Bring to a boil; boil for 2 minutes. Remove from the heat; cover and let stand for 1 hour. Drain and discard liquid; return beans to pan.
2. Add ham bone and 2½ qt. water; bring to a boil. Reduce heat; cover and simmer for 1½ hours.
3. Debone ham and cut meat into chunks; return to pan. Add celery and carrots. Cover and simmer for 1 hour or until beans are tender.
4. In a small skillet, saute garlic in butter for 1 minute. Stir in the flour, salt, pepper and paprika. Add cold water; bring to a boil. Reduce heat; cook and stir for 2 minutes or until thickened.
5. Stir in the tomatoes; simmer for 10 minutes or until heated through.

Per cup: 172 cal., 4g fat (2g sat. fat), 12mg chol., 437mg sod., 26g carb. (6g sugars, 8g fiber), 9g pro.

MEXICAN CABBAGE ROLL SOUP C FAST FIX
(PICTURED ON P. 20)

I love sharing our humble and hearty soup made with beef, cabbage and green chilies. A blast of cilantro gives it a full-flavored finish.

—Michelle Beal, Powell, TN

Start to Finish: 30 min.
Makes: 6 servings (2 quarts)

1 pound lean ground beef (90% lean)
½ teaspoon salt
¾ teaspoon garlic powder
¼ teaspoon pepper
1 tablespoon olive oil
1 medium onion, chopped
6 cups chopped cabbage (about 1 small head)
3 cans (4 ounces each) chopped green chilies
2 cups water
1 can (14½ ounces) reduced-sodium beef broth
2 tablespoons minced fresh cilantro
  Pico de gallo and reduced-fat sour cream, optional

1. In a large saucepan, cook and crumble beef with seasonings over medium-high heat until no longer pink, 5-7 minutes. Remove from pan.
2. In same pan, heat oil over medium-high heat; saute the onion and cabbage until they are crisp-tender, 4-6 minutes. Stir in beef, chilies, water and broth; bring to a boil. Reduce the heat; simmer, covered, to allow the flavors to blend, about 10 minutes. Stir in cilantro. If desired, top with pico de gallo and sour cream.
Freeze option: Freeze cooled soup in freezer containers. To use, partially thaw in refrigerator overnight. Heat through in a saucepan, stirring occasionally.
Per 1⅓ cups: 186 cal., 9g fat (3g sat. fat), 49mg chol., 604mg sod., 10g carb. (4g sugars, 4g fiber), 17g pro.
Diabetic exchanges: 2 lean meat, 2 vegetable, ½ fat.

HEARTY LIMA BEAN SOUP

HEARTY VEGETABLE SOUP ▣
(PICTURED ON P. 21)

A friend gave me the idea to use V8 juice in soup because it provides more flavor. This recipe is great to make on a crisp autumn afternoon or cold winter night.
—Janice Steinmetz, Somers, CT

Prep: 25 min. • **Cook:** 1 hour 20 min.
Makes: 16 servings (4 quarts)

- 1 tablespoon olive oil
- 8 medium carrots, sliced
- 2 large onions, chopped
- 4 celery ribs, chopped
- 1 large green pepper, seeded and chopped
- 1 garlic clove, minced
- 2 cups chopped cabbage
- 2 cups frozen cut green beans (about 8 ounces)
- 2 cups frozen peas (about 8 ounces)
- 1 cup frozen corn (about 5 ounces)
- 1 can (15 ounces) garbanzo beans or chickpeas, rinsed and drained
- 1 bay leaf
- 2 teaspoons chicken bouillon granules
- 1½ teaspoons dried parsley flakes
- 1 teaspoon salt
- 1 teaspoon dried marjoram
- 1 teaspoon dried thyme
- ½ teaspoon dried basil
- ¼ teaspoon pepper
- 4 cups water
- 1 can (28 ounces) diced tomatoes, undrained
- 2 cups V8 juice

1. In a stockpot, heat oil over medium-high heat; saute carrots, onions, celery and green pepper until crisp-tender. Add garlic; cook and stir 1 minute. Stir in remaining ingredients; bring to a boil.
2. Reduce heat; simmer, covered, until vegetables are tender, 1 to 1½ hours. Remove bay leaf.

Per cup: 105 cal., 2g fat (0 sat. fat), 0 chol., 488mg sod., 20g carb. (9g sugars, 5g fiber), 4g pro.
Diabetic exchanges: 1 starch.

BLACK BEAN TURKEY CHILI
FAST FIX ▸

This busy-day chili is packed with flavor. Very often, I'll make it ahead and freeze it for nights when time is extra tight.
—Marisela Segovia, Miami, FL

Start to Finish: 30 min.
Makes: 6 servings

- 1 pound lean ground turkey
- 1 large green pepper, chopped
- 1 medium onion, chopped
- 2 tablespoons chili powder
- ½ teaspoon salt
- ¼ teaspoon pepper
- ⅛ to ¼ teaspoon cayenne pepper
- 1 can (15 ounces) no-salt-added tomato sauce
- 1 can (15 ounces) black beans, rinsed and drained
- 1½ cups frozen corn (about 8 ounces), thawed
- 1 large tomato, chopped
- ½ cup water
  Shredded cheddar cheese, optional

1. In a 6-qt stockpot, cook and crumble turkey with green pepper and onion over medium-high heat until no longer pink, 5-7 minutes. Stir in seasonings; cook 1 minute.
2. Stir in tomato sauce, beans, corn, tomato and water; bring to a boil. Reduce heat; simmer, uncovered, to allow flavors to blend, about 10 minutes, stirring occasionally. If desired, serve with cheese.

Freeze option: Freeze cooled chili in freezer containers. To use, partially thaw in refrigerator overnight. Heat through in a saucepan, stirring occasionally and adding a little water if necessary.

Per cup: 247 cal., 7g fat (2g sat. fat), 52mg chol., 468mg sod., 27g carb. (7g sugars, 7g fiber), 21g pro.
Diabetic exchanges: 3 lean meat, 1½ starch, 1 vegetable.

MISO SOUP WITH TOFU & ENOKI C M FAST FIX

Here is a great way to mix up your menus! The traditional Japanese soup is soothing and mild, and made with easy-to-find ingredients. Sliced green onions give it a nice table presentation.
—Bridget Klusman, Otsego, MI

Start to Finish: 30 min.
Makes: 5 servings

- 2 packages (3½ ounces each) fresh enoki mushrooms or ½ pound sliced fresh mushrooms
- 1 medium onion, chopped
- 2 garlic cloves, minced
- 1 teaspoon minced fresh gingerroot
- 1 tablespoon canola oil
- 4 cups water
- ¼ cup miso paste
- 1 package (16 ounces) firm tofu, drained and cut into ¾-inch cubes
  Thinly sliced green onions

In a Dutch oven, saute the mushrooms, onion, garlic and ginger in oil until tender. Add the water and miso paste. Bring to a boil. Reduce heat; simmer, uncovered, for 15 minutes. Add tofu; heat through. Ladle into bowls; garnish with green onions.
Note: Look for miso paste in natural food or Asian markets.
Per cup: 147 cal., 8g fat (1g sat. fat), 0 chol., 601mg sod., 10g carb. (4g sugars, 2g fiber), 10g pro.
Diabetic exchanges: 1½ fat, 1 lean meat, ½ starch.

HEARTY NAVY BEAN SOUP F

Bean soup is a family favorite that I make often. Use thrifty dried beans and a ham hock to create this comfort-food classic, and follow the directions for a thicker soup if that's what your family likes best.
—Mildred Lewis, Temple, TX

Prep: 30 min. + soaking • **Cook:** 1¾ hours
Makes: 10 servings (2½ quarts)

- 3 cups (1½ pounds) dried navy beans
- 1 can (14½ ounces) diced tomatoes, undrained
- 1 large onion, chopped
- 1 meaty ham hock or 1 cup diced cooked ham
- 2 cups chicken broth
- 2½ cups water
  Salt and pepper to taste
  Minced fresh parsley

1. Rinse and sort beans; soak according to package directions.
2. Drain and rinse beans, discarding liquid. Place in a Dutch oven. Add the tomatoes with juice, onion, ham hock, broth, water, salt and pepper. Bring to a boil. Reduce heat; cover and simmer until beans are tender, about 1½ hours.
3. Add more water if necessary. Remove ham hock and let stand until cool enough to handle. Remove the meat from bone; discard bone. Cut the meat into bite-size pieces; set aside. (For a thicker soup, cool slightly, then puree the beans with a food processor or blender and return to pan.) Return ham to soup and heat through. Garnish with parsley.
Per cup: 245 cal., 2g fat (0 sat. fat), 8mg chol., 352mg sod., 42g carb. (5g sugars, 16g fiber), 18g pro.
Diabetic exchanges: 3 starch, 2 lean meat.

SIDE
SALADS

"*For a fruit salad that's extra fast and hits the spot on a hot summer day, I combine a variety of berries and citrus with a honey-lime dressing.*"
—Carrie Howell, Lehi, UT

Colorful Quinoa Salad (p. 47) Sweet Potato & Chickpea Salad (p. 49) Green Beans & Radish Salad with Tarragon Pesto (p. 42)
Wheat Berry Salad (p. 50) Tangy Poppy Seed Fruit Salad (p. 39) Cranberry-Avocado Tossed Salad (p. 46)

GARDEN TOMATO SALAD C M FAST FIX

For as long as I can remember, my mom made a salad of tomatoes and cucumbers. Now I make it whenever tomatoes are in season.

—Shannon Copley, Upper Arlington, OH

Start to Finish: 15 min.
Makes: 8 servings

- 3 large tomatoes, cut into wedges
- 1 large sweet onion, cut into thin wedges
- 1 large cucumber, sliced

DRESSING
- ¼ cup olive oil
- 2 tablespoons cider vinegar
- 1 garlic clove, minced
- 1 teaspoon minced fresh basil
- 1 teaspoon minced chives
- ½ teaspoon salt

In a large bowl, combine tomatoes, onion and cucumber. In a small bowl, whisk dressing ingredients until blended. Drizzle over salad; gently toss to coat. Serve immediately.
Per cup: 92 cal., 7g fat (1g sat. fat), 0 chol., 155mg sod., 7g carb. (5g sugars, 1g fiber), 1g pro.
Diabetic exchanges: 1½ fat, 1 vegetable.

CRANBERRY ALMOND SPINACH SALAD

CRANBERRY ALMOND SPINACH SALAD C M FAST FIX

If you want something new to try for your Christmas menu, toss this salad together. Fresh spinach leaves are mixed with toasted almonds and dried cranberries and drizzled with poppy seed dressing. It's likely to become a holiday tradition at your house, too.

—Michelle Krzmarzick, Torrance, CA

Start to Finish: 15 min.
Makes: 12 servings

- ¼ cup sugar
- 2 tablespoons cider vinegar
- 2 tablespoons white wine vinegar
- 1 teaspoon dried minced onion
- ¾ teaspoon poppy seeds
- ⅛ teaspoon paprika
- ¼ cup canola oil

- 10 ounces fresh baby spinach (about 12 cups)
- ¾ cup dried cranberries
- 2 green onions, sliced
- ¾ cup sliced almonds, toasted

Whisk together the first six ingredients; gradually whisk in oil. In a large bowl, toss spinach, cranberries and green onions with dressing; sprinkle with almonds. Serve immediately.
Note: To toast nuts, bake in a shallow pan in a 350° oven for 5-10 minutes or cook in a skillet over low heat until lightly browned, stirring occasionally.
Per cup: 121 cal., 8g fat (1g sat. fat), 0 chol., 19mg sod., 13g carb. (10g sugars, 2g fiber), 2g pro.
Diabetic exchanges: 1½ fat, 1 vegetable, ½ starch.

MIXED GREENS WITH LEMON CHAMPAGNE VINAIGRETTE

S **C** **M** **FAST FIX**

Here, you've got crunch from walnuts and sweetness from pomegranate seeds. This is a great way to enjoy spinach and arugula, too! Best of all, it's so simple.
—Ray Uyeda, Mountain View, CA

Start to Finish: 15 min.
Makes: 10 servings

- 2 tablespoons champagne vinegar
- 2 teaspoons lemon juice
- 1 teaspoon Dijon mustard
- 1 shallot, finely chopped
- ½ cup olive oil
- 4 cups torn leaf lettuce
- 4 cups fresh spinach
- 2 cups fresh arugula
- ¾ cup chopped walnuts, toasted
- ½ cup pomegranate seeds

1. In a small bowl, whisk vinegar, lemon juice, mustard and shallot. Gradually whisk in the oil.

2. In a large bowl, combine lettuce, spinach and arugula. Pour vinaigrette over salad; toss to coat. Top with walnuts and pomegranate seeds. Serve immediately.
Note: To toast nuts, bake in a shallow pan in a 350° oven for 5-10 minutes or cook in a skillet over low heat until lightly browned, stirring occasionally.
Per cup: 169 cal., 17g fat (2g sat. fat), 0 chol., 27mg sod., 5g carb. (2g sugars, 1g fiber), 2g pro.
Diabetic exchanges: 3 fat, 1 vegetable.

TANGY POPPY SEED FRUIT SALAD **F** **S** **M** **FAST FIX**

(PICTURED ON P. 37)

For a fruit salad that's extra fast and hits the spot on a hot summer day, I combine a variety of berries and citrus with a honey-lime dressing.
—Carrie Howell, Lehi, UT

Start to Finish: 20 min.
Makes: 10 servings

- 1 can (20 ounces) unsweetened pineapple chunks, drained
- 1 pound fresh strawberries, quartered
- 2 cups fresh blueberries
- 2 cups fresh raspberries
- 2 medium navel oranges, peeled and sectioned
- 2 medium kiwifruit, peeled, halved and sliced

DRESSING
- 2 to 4 tablespoons honey
- ½ teaspoon grated lime peel
- 2 tablespoons lime juice
- 2 teaspoons poppy seeds

Place all fruit in a large bowl. In a small bowl, whisk dressing ingredients. Drizzle over fruit; toss gently to combine.
Per ⅔ cup: 117 cal., 1g fat (0 sat. fat), 0 chol., 3mg sod., 29g carb. (21g sugars, 5g fiber), 2g pro.
Diabetic exchanges: 2 fruit.

MIXED GREENS WITH LEMON CHAMPAGNE VINAIGRETTE

LEMONY ZUCCHINI RIBBONS

C **M** **FAST FIX**

Fresh zucchini gets a shave and a drizzle of lemony goodness in this change-of-pace salad. Sprinkle on the goat cheese or feta and dive right in.
—Ellie Martin Cliffe, Milwaukee, WI

Start to Finish: 15 min.
Makes: 4 servings

- 1 tablespoon olive oil
- ½ teaspoon grated lemon zest
- 1 tablespoon lemon juice
- ½ teaspoon salt
- ¼ teaspoon pepper
- 3 medium zucchini
- ⅓ cup crumbled goat or feta cheese

1. For dressing, in a small bowl, mix the first five ingredients. Using a vegetable peeler, shave the zucchini lengthwise into very thin slices; arrange on a serving plate.
2. To serve, drizzle with dressing and toss lightly to coat. Top with cheese.
Per ¾ cup: 83 cal., 6g fat (2g sat. fat), 12mg chol., 352mg sod., 5g carb. (3g sugars, 2g fiber), 3g pro.
Diabetic exchanges: 1 vegetable, 1 fat.
HEALTH TIP Making this colorful salad with zucchini instead of spaghetti saves 130 calories.

STRAWBERRY, CUCUMBER & HONEYDEW SALAD

STRAWBERRY, CUCUMBER & HONEYDEW SALAD

F **S** **C** **M** **FAST FIX**

Strawberries and cucumbers together— I just love this combination! We used to eat a lot of cucumbers growing up in upstate New York. We'd get them, along with strawberries and melons, from fruit and veggie stands to make this sweet and tangy salad.
—Melissa McCabe, Victor, NY

Start to Finish: 20 min.
Makes: 8 servings

- 1 container (16 ounces) fresh strawberries, halved
- 1 English cucumber, halved lengthwise and cut into ¼-inch slices
- 1 cup cubed honeydew melon (½-inch pieces)
- 3 tablespoons honey
- 2 tablespoons lime juice
- 1 teaspoon grated lime peel

1. In a large bowl, combine strawberries, cucumber and honeydew. Chill until it's time to serve.
2. In a small bowl, whisk the remaining ingredients. Just before serving, drizzle over the strawberry mixture; toss gently to coat.
Per ¾ cup: 56 cal., 0 fat (0 sat. fat), 0 chol., 6mg sod., 15g carb. (12g sugars, 2g fiber), 1g pro.
Diabetic exchanges: 1 fruit.

NECTARINE ARUGULA SALAD

HONEY KALE CURRANT & ALMOND SALAD C M FAST FIX

This honey-flavored kale salad makes our taste buds tingle. It has subtle sweetness from currants and a nutty almond crunch. Add grated Asiago and you've got a stellar side dish for any entree.
—Ally Phillips, Murrells Inlet, SC

Start to Finish: 10 min.
Makes: 4 servings

- 4 **cups thinly sliced fresh kale**
- ¼ **cup slivered almonds**
- ¼ **cup dried currants**
- 2 **tablespoons grated Asiago cheese**
- 1 **tablespoon balsamic vinegar**
- 1 **tablespoon olive oil**
- 1 **tablespoon honey mustard**
- 1½ **teaspoons honey**
- ¾ **teaspoon coarsely ground pepper**
- ½ **teaspoon sea salt**

Place kale, almonds and currants in a large bowl. In a small bowl, whisk remaining ingredients until blended. Drizzle over salad; toss to coat.
Per cup: 135 cal., 8g fat (1g sat. fat), 3mg chol., 287mg sod., 15g carb. (11g sugars, 2g fiber), 3g pro.
Diabetic exchanges: 1½ fat, 1 vegetable, ½ starch.

NECTARINE ARUGULA SALAD S C M FAST FIX

Here's a summer salad that brightens any supper. The homemade dressing with a hint of berries is perfect with arugula, nectarines and blue cheese.
—Christine Laba, Arlington, VA

Start to Finish: 20 min.
Makes: 8 servings

- 4 **cups fresh arugula or baby spinach**
- 4 **cups torn Bibb or Boston lettuce**
- 3 **medium nectarines, sliced**
- 2 **tablespoons pine nuts, toasted**
- 2 **tablespoons crumbled blue cheese**
  DRESSING
- 2 **tablespoons raspberry vinegar**
- 2 **teaspoons sugar**
- 1 **teaspoon Dijon mustard**
- ⅛ **teaspoon salt**
  Dash pepper
- 3 **tablespoons olive oil**

In a large bowl, combine the first five ingredients. In a small bowl, whisk vinegar, sugar, mustard, salt and pepper. Gradually whisk in oil until blended. Drizzle over salad; toss to coat.
Note: To toast nuts, bake in a shallow pan in a 350° oven for 5-10 minutes or cook in a skillet over low heat until lightly browned, stirring occasionally.
Per 1 cup: 101 cal., 7g fat (1g sat. fat), 2mg chol., 86mg sod., 9g carb. (7g sugars, 1g fiber), 2g pro.
Diabetic exchanges: 1½ fat, ½ starch.

APPLE MAPLE
PECAN SALAD

APPLE MAPLE PECAN SALAD S C M

A well-made salad has good flavor and pleasing crunch. With cabbage, apples and pecans, this one gets high marks for both, with extra points for ease.
—Emily Tyra, Milwaukee, WI

Prep: 15 min. + standing
Makes: 12 servings

- ¼ cup lemon juice
- ¼ cup canola oil
- ¼ cup maple syrup
- 1½ teaspoons Dijon mustard
- ½ teaspoon coarsely ground pepper
- 4 cups shredded cabbage
- 3 large Granny Smith apples, julienned
- ½ cup crumbled Gorgonzola cheese
- 1 cup chopped pecans, toasted

Whisk first five ingredients until well blended. Combine cabbage, apples and Gorgonzola; toss with dressing to coat. Let stand 30 minutes before serving. Sprinkle with pecans.

Note: To toast nuts, bake in a shallow pan in a 350° oven for 5-10 minutes or cook in a skillet over low heat until lightly browned, stirring occasionally.
Per ¾ cup: 169 cal., 13g fat (2g sat. fat), 4mg chol., 84mg sod., 14g carb. (9g sugars, 3g fiber), 2g pro.
Diabetic exchanges: 2½ fat, 1 starch.

GREEN BEANS & RADISH SALAD WITH TARRAGON PESTO S C M FAST FIX
(PICTURED ON P. 37)

Whichever way my garden grows, I usually build my salad with green beans, radishes and a pesto made with tarragon. That adds a hint of licorice.
—Lily Julow, Lawrenceville, GA

Start to Finish: 25 min.
Makes: 10 servings

- 1½ pounds fresh green beans, trimmed
- 2 cups thinly sliced radishes
- ½ cup pecan or walnut pieces, toasted
- ¼ cup tarragon leaves
- 3 tablespoons grated Parmesan cheese
- ½ garlic clove
- ¼ teaspoon coarse sea salt or kosher salt
- ⅛ teaspoon crushed red pepper flakes
- 1½ teaspoons white wine vinegar
- ¼ cup olive oil

1. In a 6-qt. stockpot, bring 8 cups water to a boil. Add the beans in batches; cook, uncovered, 2-3 minutes or just until they are crisp-tender. Remove the beans and immediately drop into ice water. Drain and pat dry. Toss together beans and radishes.
2. Place pecans, tarragon, cheese, garlic, salt and pepper flakes in a small food processor; pulse until chopped. Add vinegar; process until blended. Continue processing while gradually adding oil in a steady stream. Toss with bean mixture.
Per 1 cup: 115 cal., 10g fat (1g sat. fat), 1mg chol., 89mg sod., 7g carb. (2g sugars, 3g fiber), 2g pro.
Diabetic exchanges: 2 fat, 1 vegetable.

BACKYARD RED POTATO SALAD M

Here's a potato salad that has no mayo. I think it's perfect for outdoor picnics, plus it looks just as good as it tastes.

—Holly Bauer, West Bend, WI

Prep: 25 min. • **Grill:** 10 min.
Makes: 9 servings

2½ pounds small red potatoes
1 medium onion, cut into ½-inch slices
½ cup olive oil, divided
1 teaspoon salt, divided
½ teaspoon pepper, divided
3 tablespoons balsamic vinegar
2 tablespoons lemon juice
1 tablespoon Dijon mustard
2 teaspoons sugar
2 garlic cloves, minced
¼ cup minced fresh tarragon

1. Place potatoes in a large saucepan and cover with water. Bring to a boil. Reduce heat; cover and cook for 10 minutes. Drain; cool slightly. Cut each in half.
2. In a large bowl, combine the potatoes, onion, ¼ cup oil, ½ teaspoon salt and ¼ teaspoon pepper; toss to coat. Arrange vegetables, cut side down, on a grilling grid; place on a grill rack. Grill, covered, over medium heat for 8-10 minutes or until vegetables are tender and lightly browned, turning occasionally. Chop onion. Place onion and potatoes in bowl.
3. In a small bowl, whisk the vinegar, lemon juice, mustard, sugar, garlic and remaining oil, salt and pepper. Add to potato mixture; toss to coat. Sprinkle with tarragon. Serve warm or at room temperature. Refrigerate leftovers.

Note: If you do not have a grilling grid, use a disposable foil pan. Poke holes in the bottom of the pan with a meat fork to allow any liquid to drain.

Per ¾ cup: 215 cal., 12g fat (2g sat. fat), 0 chol., 312mg sod., 24g carb. (4g sugars, 3g fiber), 3g pro.
Diabetic exchanges: 2 fat, 1½ starch.

★ ★ ★ ★ ★ **READER REVIEW**

"These were so flavorful and such a great new twist on basic red potatoes. The addition of the Dijon just makes this dish what it is!"

HKAROW9713 TASTEOFHOME.COM

POMEGRANATE-CRANBERRY SALAD S

Juicy pomegranate seeds give this cranberry gelatin a refreshing twist. For the crowning touch, top the salad with low-fat whipped topping and a sprinkling of pecans.

—Lorie Mckinney, Marion, NC

Prep: 15 min. + chilling
Makes: 8 servings

1 package (.3 ounce) sugar-free cranberry gelatin
1 cup boiling water
½ cup cold water
1⅔ cups pomegranate seeds
1 can (14 ounces) whole-berry cranberry sauce
1 can (8 ounces) unsweetened crushed pineapple, drained
¾ cup chopped pecans
Frozen whipped topping, thawed, optional
Additional chopped pecans, optional

In a large bowl, dissolve gelatin in boiling water. Add cold water; stir. Add the pomegranate seeds, cranberry sauce, pineapple and pecans. Pour into a 1½-qt. serving bowl. Refrigerate for 4-5 hours or until firm. If desired, top with whipped topping and additional pecans.

Per ¾ cup without toppings: 190 cal., 8g fat (1g sat. fat), 0 chol., 41mg sod., 30g carb. (21g sugars, 2g fiber), 2g pro.
Diabetic exchanges: 1½ fat, 1 starch, 1 fruit.

BACKYARD RED POTATO SALAD

PASTA & SUN-DRIED
TOMATO SALAD

KIWI-STRAWBERRY SPINACH SALAD S C FAST FIX ▶

This pretty salad is always a hit when I serve it! The recipe came from a cookbook, but I personalized it. Sometimes just a small change in ingredients can make a big difference.
—Laura Pounds, Andover, KS

Start to Finish: 20 min.
Makes: 12 servings (1 cup each)

- ¼ cup canola oil
- ¼ cup raspberry vinegar
- ¼ teaspoon Worcestershire sauce
- ⅓ cup sugar
- ¼ teaspoon paprika
- 2 green onions, chopped
- 2 tablespoons sesame seeds, toasted
- 1 tablespoon poppy seeds
- 12 cups torn fresh spinach (about 9 ounces)
- 2 pints fresh strawberries, halved
- 4 kiwifruit, peeled and sliced

1. Place the first five ingredients in a blender; cover and process 30 seconds or until blended. Transfer to a bowl; stir in the green onions, sesame seeds and poppy seeds.
2. In a large bowl, combine spinach, strawberries and kiwi. Drizzle with dressing; toss to coat.

Per 1 cup: 113 cal., 6g fat (1g sat. fat), 0 chol., 76mg sod., 15g carb. (10g sugars, 3g fiber), 2g pro.
Diabetic exchanges: 1 vegetable, 1 fat, ½ starch, ½ fruit.

PASTA & SUN-DRIED TOMATO SALAD F M

The best thing about this dish is that it can be prepared ahead of time, making it ideal for casual picnics and cookouts.
—Dawn Williams, Scottsboro, AL

Prep: 20 min. • **Cook:** 15 min.
Makes: 8 servings

- 1 can (49 ounces) reduced-sodium chicken broth
- 1 package (16 ounces) orzo pasta
- ¼ cup chopped oil-packed sun-dried tomatoes plus 2 teaspoons oil from the jar
- 1 garlic clove, minced
- ¾ teaspoon salt
- ¼ teaspoon pepper
- ⅓ cup shredded Parmesan cheese
- 4 fresh basil leaves, thinly sliced
  Optional toppings: crumbled feta cheese and chickpeas

1. In a large saucepan, bring the broth to a boil. Stir in the orzo; return to a boil. Cook for 8-10 minutes or until tender, stirring occasionally.
2. Drain orzo; transfer to a large bowl. (Discard the broth or save for another use.) Stir in the tomatoes, oil from sun-dried tomatoes, garlic, salt and pepper; cool completely.
3. Add Parmesan cheese and basil; toss to combine. Cover and refrigerate until serving. Serve with toppings if desired.

Per ¾ cup without optional toppings: 255 cal., 3g fat (1g sat. fat), 2mg chol., 570mg sod., 44g carb. (3g sugars, 2g fiber), 11g pro.

WINTER BEET SALAD S M

To save a little time, we recommend using packaged salad greens for this pretty dish. The perfect addition to cold-weather menus, it's a lovely change of pace.
—*Taste of Home* Test Kitchen

Prep: 20 min. • **Bake:** 1 hour + cooling
Makes: 4 servings

- 2 medium fresh beets
- 1 package (5 ounces) mixed salad greens
- 2 medium navel oranges, peeled and sliced
- 1 small fennel bulb, halved and thinly sliced
- ¼ cup chopped hazelnuts, toasted

DRESSING
- 3 tablespoons olive oil
- 2 tablespoons orange juice
- 1 tablespoon balsamic vinegar
- 2 teaspoons grated orange peel
- ¼ teaspoon onion powder

Preheat oven to 425°. Cut slits in beets; place on a baking sheet. Bake until tender, about 1 hour. When cool enough to handle, peel beets and cut into wedges. Divide the greens among salad plates; top with beets, oranges, fennel and hazelnuts. Combine the dressing ingredients in a jar with a tight-fitting lid; shake well. Drizzle over salads.

Note: To toast nuts, bake in a shallow pan in a 350° oven for 5-10 minutes or cook in a skillet over low heat until lightly browned, stirring occasionally.

Per serving: 213 cal., 15g fat (2g sat. fat), 0 chol., 80mg sod., 21g carb. (12g sugars, 6g fiber), 4g pro.
Diabetic exchanges: 3 fat, 2 vegetable, ½ starch.

GREEN SALAD WITH BERRIES
S C M FAST FIX

For snappy salad that draws a crowd, I do a wonderful combo of spinach, berries and oniony things. Raise your fork for this one, and add it to your list of favorites.
—*Aysha Schurman, Ammon, ID*

Start to Finish: 15 min.
Makes: 4 servings

- 1 cup torn romaine
- 1 cup fresh baby spinach
- 1 cup sliced fresh strawberries
- ½ cup thinly sliced celery
- ½ small red onion, thinly sliced
- ½ cup coarsely chopped walnuts
- 2 green onions, chopped
- ¼ cup raspberry vinaigrette
- 1 cup fresh raspberries

In a large bowl, combine the first seven ingredients. To serve, drizzle it with vinaigrette and toss to combine. Top with raspberries.

Per Serving: 157 cal., 10g fat (1g sat. fat), 0 chol., 50mg sod., 15g carb. (8g sugars, 5g fiber), 4g pro.
Diabetic exchanges: 2 fat, 1 vegetable, ½ fruit.

HEALTH TIP The berries in this salad provide more than half the daily value of vitamin C.

RICE VEGETABLE SALAD
M FAST FIX

Packed with vegetables, this dish has a touch of Indian flair. I first had it at a party and loved the bright look and taste.
—*Sandy Heley, Grand Junction, CO*

Start to Finish: 25 min.
Makes: 5 servings

- ½ cup uncooked basmati rice
- 1 can (15 ounces) black beans, rinsed and drained
- 2 medium carrots, finely chopped
- ¾ cup fresh or frozen corn, thawed
- ¾ cup chopped tomatoes
- ¼ cup minced fresh cilantro
- ¼ cup minced fresh parsley
- 2 tablespoons finely chopped red onion
- ¼ cup lime juice
- ¼ cup olive oil
- 1 teaspoon ground cumin
- ⅛ teaspoon salt
- ⅛ teaspoon pepper

1. Cook rice according to the package directions. Meanwhile, in a large bowl, combine the beans, carrots, corn, tomatoes, cilantro, parsley and onion.
2. In a small bowl, whisk the lime juice, oil, cumin, salt and pepper. Stir rice into bean mixture. Drizzle with the dressing; toss to coat.

Per ¾ cup: 279 cal., 12g fat (2g sat. fat), 0 chol., 245mg sod., 38g carb. (4g sugars, 6g fiber), 7g pro.

GREEN SALAD WITH BERRIES

CRANBERRY-AVOCADO TOSSED SALAD S M FAST FIX
(PICTURED ON P. 37)

The red and green colors in this salad make it a natural for a yuletide dinner, but we like it all year. The dressing and ingredients give it a sweet-tangy flavor.
—Marsha Postar, Lubbock, TX

Start to Finish: 30 min.
Makes: 10 servings (about 1 cup vinaigrette)

- ¼ cup sugar
- ¼ cup white wine vinegar
- ¼ cup thawed cranberry juice concentrate
- 4 teaspoons ground mustard
- ½ teaspoon salt
- ½ teaspoon pepper
- ½ cup canola oil

SALAD

- 1 medium ripe avocado, peeled and cubed
- 1 tablespoon lemon juice
- 4 cups torn romaine
- 4 cups fresh baby spinach
- 1 package (5 ounces) dried cranberries
- 1 small red onion, chopped
- ⅓ cup slivered almonds, toasted if desired
- ⅓ cup sunflower kernels

1. In a small bowl, whisk the first six ingredients until blended. Gradually whisk in the oil.
2. Gently toss avocado with lemon juice. In a large bowl, combine romaine, spinach, cranberries, onion and avocado; drizzle with ½ cup vinaigrette. Sprinkle with almonds and sunflower kernels; serve it immediately. Drizzle with some additional vinaigrette or save for another use.
Note: To toast nuts, bake in a shallow pan in a 350° oven for 5-10 minutes or cook in a skillet over low heat until lightly browned, stirring occasionally.
Per ¾ cup: 212 cal., 13g fat (1g sat. fat), 0 chol., 91mg sod., 25g carb. (16g sugars, 4g fiber), 3g pro.
Diabetic exchanges: 2 fat, 1 starch, 1 vegetable.

FIESTA COLESLAW

FIESTA COLESLAW
C M FAST FIX

Coleslaw with a touch of heat makes a zesty side for barbecue chicken or pork. I also pile it on fish tacos and po'boys.
—Fay Moreland, Wichita Falls, TX

Start to Finish: 20 min.
Makes: 10 servings

- 1 package (14 ounces) coleslaw mix
- 1 cup chopped peeled jicama
- 6 radishes, halved and sliced
- 4 jalapeno peppers, seeded and finely chopped
- 1 medium onion, chopped
- ⅓ cup minced fresh cilantro
- ½ cup mayonnaise
- ¼ cup cider vinegar
- 2 tablespoons sugar
- ½ teaspoon salt
- ½ teaspoon celery salt
- ¼ teaspoon coarsely ground pepper
  Lime wedges, optional

1. Using a large bowl, combine the first six ingredients. In a small bowl, whisk together the mayonnaise, vinegar, sugar and seasonings. Pour over the coleslaw mixture; toss to coat.
2. Refrigerate, covered, until serving. If desired, serve with lime wedges.
Note: Wear disposable gloves when cutting hot peppers; the oils can burn skin. Avoid touching your face.
Per ¾ cup: 114 cal., 9g fat (1g sat. fat), 4mg chol., 242mg sod., 8g carb. (5g sugars, 2g fiber), 1g pro.
Diabetic exchanges: 2 fat, 1 vegetable.

SIDE SALADS

ROASTED APPLE SALAD WITH SPICY MAPLE-CIDER VINAIGRETTE M

We bought loads of apples and needed to use them. To help the flavors come alive, I roasted the apples and tossed them with a sweet dressing.
—Janice Elder, Charlotte, NC

Prep: 15 min. • **Bake:** 20 min. + cooling
Makes: 8 servings

- 4 medium Fuji, Gala or other firm apples, quartered
- 2 tablespoons olive oil

DRESSING
- 2 tablespoons cider vinegar
- 2 tablespoons olive oil
- 1 tablespoon maple syrup
- 1 teaspoon Sriracha Asian hot chili sauce
- ½ teaspoon salt
- ¼ teaspoon pepper

SALAD
- 1 package (5 ounces) spring mix salad greens
- 4 pitted dates, quartered
- 1 log (4 ounces) fresh goat cheese, crumbled
- ½ cup chopped pecans, toasted

1. Preheat oven to 375°. Place apples in a foil-lined 15x10x1-in. baking pan; drizzle with oil and toss to coat. Roast for 20-30 minutes or until apples are tender, stirring occasionally. Cool completely.
2. In a small bowl, whisk the dressing ingredients until blended. In a large bowl, combine salad greens and dates. Drizzle dressing over salad and toss to coat.
3. Divide mixture among eight plates. Top with the goat cheese and roasted apples; sprinkle with pecans. Serve immediately.
Note: To toast nuts, bake in a shallow pan in a 350° oven for 5-10 minutes or cook in a skillet over low heat until lightly browned, stirring occasionally.
Per cup: 191 cal., 13g fat (3g sat. fat), 9mg chol., 240mg sod., 17g carb. (12g sugars, 3g fiber), 3g pro.
Diabetic exchanges: 2 fat, 1 vegetable, ½ fruit.

COLORFUL QUINOA SALAD S M
(PICTURED ON P. 36)

My youngest daughter recently learned she has to avoid gluten, dairy and eggs, which gave me a new challenge in the kitchen. I put this dish together as a side we could all share, and it was a hit. We even love the leftovers.
—Catherine Turnbull, Burlington, ON

Prep: 30 min. + cooling
Makes: 8 servings

- 2 cups water
- 1 cup quinoa, rinsed
- 2 cups fresh baby spinach, thinly sliced
- 1 cup grape tomatoes, halved
- 1 medium cucumber, seeded and chopped
- 1 medium sweet orange pepper, chopped
- 1 medium sweet yellow pepper, chopped
- 2 green onions, chopped

DRESSING
- 3 tablespoons lime juice
- 2 tablespoons olive oil
- 4 teaspoons honey
- 1 tablespoon grated lime peel
- 2 teaspoons minced fresh gingerroot
- ¼ teaspoon salt

1. In a large saucepan, bring the water to a boil. Add the quinoa. Reduce heat; simmer, covered, 12-15 minutes or until the liquid is absorbed. Remove from the heat; fluff with a fork. Transfer to a large bowl; cool completely.
2. Stir the spinach, tomatoes, cucumber, peppers and green onions into quinoa. In a small bowl, whisk dressing ingredients until blended. Drizzle over quinoa mixture; toss to coat. Refrigerate until serving.
Per ¾ cup: 143 cal., 5g fat (1g sat. fat), 0 chol., 88mg sod., 23g carb. (6g sugars, 3g fiber), 4g pro.
Diabetic exchanges: 1 starch, 1 vegetable, 1 fat.

ROASTED APPLE SALAD WITH SPICY MAPLE-CIDER VINAIGRETTE

GRILLED MANGO & AVOCADO SALAD M FAST FIX

A big hit with my family, this light salad is so easy to make! The healthy combo of mango and avocado is simply the best combination you could serve. Who knew you could grill mango?
—Amy Liesemeyer, Tucson, AZ

Start to Finish: 25 min.
Makes: 8 servings

- 4 medium-firm mangoes, peeled
- 1 tablespoon canola oil
- ¼ cup lime juice
- ¼ cup olive oil
- 1 tablespoon black sesame seeds
- ½ teaspoon salt
- 2 tablespoons minced fresh cilantro, optional
- 1 tablespoon minced fresh mint, optional
- 2 medium cucumbers, peeled, seeded and coarsely chopped
- 2 medium-ripe avocados, peeled and coarsely chopped

1. Cut a thin slice off the bottom of each mango. Standing mango upright, slice off a large section of flesh, cutting close to the pit. Rotate and repeat until all flesh is removed.
2. Brush mangoes with canola oil; place on greased grill rack. Cook, covered, over medium heat or broil 4 in. from heat 6-8 minutes or until lightly browned, turning once. Cool slightly. Cut into ¾-inch cubes.
3. In a large bowl, whisk lime juice, olive oil, sesame seeds, salt and, if desired, cilantro and mint. Add the mangoes, cucumbers and avocados; toss to coat.
Per ¾ cup: 249 cal., 15g fat (2g sat. fat), 0 chol., 152mg sod., 31g carb. (24g sugars, 6g fiber), 3g pro.
Diabetic exchanges: 3 fat, 2 starch.

GRAPEFRUIT & FENNEL SALAD WITH MINT VINAIGRETTE

GRAPEFRUIT & FENNEL SALAD WITH MINT VINAIGRETTE S C M FAST FIX

My father has a red grapefruit tree and he shares his crop with me. I toss the grapefruit with onion, fennel and mint for a fresh, fabulous salad.
—Catherine Wilkinson, Dewey, AZ

Start to Finish: 15 min.
Makes: 4 servings

- 1 medium red grapefruit
- 1 medium fennel bulb, halved and thinly sliced
- ¼ cup thinly sliced red onion

VINAIGRETTE
- 3 tablespoons fresh mint leaves
- 2 tablespoons sherry vinegar
- 1½ teaspoons honey
- ⅛ teaspoon salt
- ⅛ teaspoon coarsely ground pepper
- 2 tablespoons olive oil

1. Cut a thin slice from the top and the bottom of the grapefruit; stand grapefruit upright on a cutting board. With a knife, cut off peel and outer membrane from grapefruit. Cut along the membrane of each segment to remove fruit. Arrange the fennel, grapefruit and onion on a serving platter.
2. Place mint, vinegar, honey, salt and pepper in a small food processor; cover and process until mint is finely chopped. While processing, gradually add oil in a steady stream. Drizzle over salad.
Per serving: 114 cal., 7g fat (1g sat. fat), 0 chol., 107mg sod., 13g carb. (9g sugars, 3g fiber), 1g pro.
Diabetic exchanges: 1½ fat, 1 vegetable, ½ fruit.

HONEYDEW SALAD WITH LIME DRESSING
F **S** **M** **FAST FIX**

Green is my favorite color, and this refreshing salad with grapes, cucumber and kiwi is green to the max. If you want more, add green apples and pears.
—Melissa McCabe, Victor, NY

Start to Finish: 20 min.
Makes: 8 servings

- ¼ cup lime juice
- ¼ cup honey
- 1 tablespoon minced fresh mint leaves
- 4 cups cubed honeydew melon (about 1 small)
- 2 cups green grapes
- 4 medium kiwifruit, peeled, halved lengthwise and sliced
- 1 medium cucumber, halved lengthwise and sliced

For dressing, in a small bowl, whisk lime juice, honey and mint until blended. Place fruit and cucumber in a large bowl; add dressing and toss to coat. Refrigerate until serving.

Per cup: 120 cal., 0 fat (0 sat. fat), 0 chol., 22mg sod., 31g carb. (26g sugars, 3g fiber), 1g pro.
Diabetic exchanges: 1 starch, 1 fruit.
HEALTH TIP Swap the honeydew for cantaloupe and get a boost of vitamin A. One cup of cantaloupe has a whopping 120 percent of the daily value, whereas the honeydew only provides 2 percent. Most other nutrient amounts are similar between the melons.

SWEET POTATO & CHICKPEA SALAD **M**
(PICTURED ON P. 36)

Take this colorful dish to the buffet at a family gathering, or enjoy it as a satisfying meal all by itself.
—Brenda Gleason, Hartland, WI

Prep: 15 min. • **Bake:** 20 min.
Makes: 8 servings

- 2 medium sweet potatoes (about 1 pound), peeled and cubed
- 1 tablespoon olive oil
- ½ teaspoon salt
- ¼ teaspoon pepper
- 1 can (15 ounces) garbanzo beans or chickpeas, rinsed and drained

DRESSING
- 2 tablespoons seasoned rice vinegar
- 4 teaspoons olive oil
- 1 tablespoon minced fresh gingerroot
- 1 garlic clove, minced
- ¼ teaspoon salt
- ¼ teaspoon pepper

SALAD
- 4 cups spring mix salad greens
- ¼ cup crumbled feta cheese

1. In a large bowl, combine the sweet potatoes, oil, salt and pepper; toss to coat. Transfer to a 15x10x1-in. baking pan coated with cooking spray. Roast at 425° for 20-25 minutes or until tender, stirring once.
2. In a large bowl, combine garbanzo beans and sweet potatoes. In a small bowl, whisk the dressing ingredients. Add to sweet potato mixture; toss to coat. Serve over salad greens; top with cheese.

Per ½ cup sweet potato mixture with ½ cup greens and 1½ teaspoons cheese: 134 cal., 6g fat (1g sat. fat), 2mg chol., 466mg sod., 18g carb. (6g sugars, 4g fiber), 4g pro.
Diabetic exchanges: 1 starch, 1 fat.

HONEYDEW SALAD WITH LIME DRESSING

![SHAVED BRUSSELS SPROUT SALAD]

SHAVED BRUSSELS SPROUT SALAD

SHAVED BRUSSELS SPROUT SALAD S M

The first time my friends tasted this side dish, they said it was phenomenal. I hope you feel the same. The longer you let it chill in the fridge, the more tender the sprouts will end up.
—Nick Iverson, Denver, CO

Prep: 20 min. + chilling
Makes: 6 servings

- 1 tablespoon cider vinegar
- 1 tablespoon Dijon mustard
- 2 teaspoons honey
- 1 small garlic clove, minced
- 2 tablespoons olive oil
- 1 pound Brussels sprouts, halved and thinly sliced
- 1 small red onion, halved and thinly sliced
- ⅓ cup dried cherries, chopped
- ⅓ cup chopped pecans, toasted

1. Whisk together first four ingredients; gradually whisk in oil until blended.

2. Place the Brussels sprouts, onion and cherries in a large bowl; toss with dressing. Refrigerate, covered, at least 1 hour. Stir in pecans just before serving.

Note: To toast nuts, bake in a shallow pan in a 350° oven for 5-10 minutes or cook in a skillet over low heat until lightly browned, stirring occasionally.

Per ¾ cup: 156 cal., 9g fat (1g sat. fat), 0 chol., 79mg sod., 18g carb. (10g sugars, 4g fiber), 3g pro.
Diabetic Exchanges: 2 fat, 1 vegetable, ½ starch.

WHEAT BERRY SALAD S M

(PICTURED ON P. 36)

I'm a former junk-food fan who discovered the beauty of wheat berries. They're tender yet chewy in this lemony salad that's tossed with cherries and walnuts.
—Nancy Lange, Phoenix, AZ

Prep: 20 min. • **Cook:** 1 hour + cooling
Makes: 6 servings

- 1½ cups wheat berries
- 2 celery ribs, finely chopped
- ½ cup dried cherries, chopped
- ½ cup chopped walnuts, toasted
- ¼ cup minced fresh parsley
- 1 green onion, chopped
- 3 tablespoons olive oil
- 2 tablespoons lemon juice
- ¼ teaspoon salt
- ¼ teaspoon pepper
  Mixed salad greens, optional

1. Place the wheat berries in a large saucepan; add water to cover by 2 in. Bring to a boil. Reduce heat; simmer, covered, about 1 hour or until tender. Drain; transfer to a large bowl. Cool berries completely.

2. Add celery, cherries, walnuts, parsley and green onion to wheat berries. In a small bowl, whisk oil, lemon juice, salt and pepper until blended; add to salad and toss to coat. If desired, serve over greens.

Note: To toast nuts, bake in a shallow pan in a 350° oven for 5-10 minutes or cook in a skillet over low heat until lightly browned, stirring occasionally.

Per ¾ cup without salad greens: 323 cal., 14g fat (2g sat. fat), 0 chol., 112mg sod., 45g carb. (7g sugars, 7g fiber), 8g pro.

GRILLED ROMAINE TOSS M

I often double this fantastic salad, and it's always history by the end of the night. During inclement weather, simply prepare it under the broiler.
—Trisha Kruse, Eagle, ID

Prep: 25 min. • **Grill:** 10 min.
Makes: 10 servings

- ¼ cup olive oil
- 3 tablespoons sugar
- 1 teaspoon dried rosemary, crushed
- 1 teaspoon dried thyme
- ¼ teaspoon salt
- ¼ teaspoon pepper
- 8 plum tomatoes, quartered
- 2 large sweet onions, thinly sliced

GRILLED ROMAINE

- 4 romaine hearts
- 2 tablespoons olive oil
- ¼ teaspoon salt
- ¼ teaspoon pepper

DRESSING

- ¼ cup olive oil
- ¼ cup balsamic vinegar
- 3 garlic cloves, peeled and halved
- 2 tablespoons brown sugar
- ¼ cup grated Parmesan cheese

1. In a large bowl, combine the first six ingredients. Add tomatoes and onions; toss to coat. Transfer to a grill wok or basket. Grill, covered, over medium heat for 8-12 minutes or until tender, stirring frequently. Set aside.
2. For grilled romaine, cut romaine hearts in half lengthwise, leaving ends intact. Brush with oil; sprinkle with salt and pepper. Place romaine halves cut sides down on grill. Grill, covered, over medium heat for 3-4 minutes on each side or until slightly charred and wilted.
3. For dressing, place oil, vinegar, garlic and brown sugar in a food processor; cover and process until smooth.
4. Coarsely chop the romaine; divide among 10 salad plates. Top with tomato mixture; drizzle with dressing. Sprinkle with cheese.

Note: If you do not have a grill wok or basket, use a disposable foil pan. Poke holes in the bottom of the pan with a meat fork to allow liquid to drain.

Per cup: 198 cal., 14g fat (2g sat. fat), 2mg chol., 164mg sod., 16g carb. (12g sugars, 2g fiber), 3g pro.

COLOR IT RUBY SALAD C M FAST FIX

Just looking at this bright red salad cheers me up—and then I get to taste it! For a garnish, sprinkle on fresh chives and mild white cheese.
—Lorraine Caland, Shuniah, ON

Start to Finish: 20 min.
Makes: 12 servings

- 2 tablespoons red wine vinegar
- 1 tablespoon Dijon mustard
- ½ teaspoon kosher salt
- ¼ teaspoon pepper
- ⅓ cup extra virgin olive oil
- 1 pound small tomatoes, quartered
- ¾ pound cherry tomatoes, halved
- ¾ pound fresh strawberries, hulled and sliced
- 2 cans (15 ounces each) beets, drained and chopped

Mix vinegar, mustard, salt and pepper; gradually whisk in oil until blended. Toss with tomatoes, strawberries and beets. Serve immediately.

Per cup: 98 cal., 6g fat (1g sat. fat), 0 chol., 251mg sod., 10g carb. (7g sugars, 3g fiber), 1g pro.
Diabetic exchanges: 1 fat, ½ starch.

GRILLED ROMAINE TOSS

GREEN BEAN & WALNUT SALAD S C M

Cranberries make this side dish extra colorful. Everyone will love the crunchy walnuts as well.

—Deborah Giusti, Hot Springs, AR

Prep: 15 min. • **Cook:** 5 min. + chilling
Makes: 12 servings

- 3 pounds fresh green beans, trimmed
- ¾ cup chopped walnuts
- ⅓ cup dried cranberries

VINAIGRETTE

- 6 tablespoons olive oil
- 6 tablespoons red wine vinegar
- 3 garlic cloves, minced
- ½ teaspoon salt
- ½ teaspoon pepper

1. Place the beans in a Dutch oven and cover with water. Bring to a boil. Cover and cook for 4-7 minutes or until they are crisp-tender; drain.

2. In a large bowl, combine the beans, walnuts and cranberries. In a small bowl, whisk the vinaigrette ingredients. Pour over the bean mixture; toss to coat. Cover and refrigerate until chilled. Toss before serving.

Per 1 serving: 152 cal., 12g fat (1g sat. fat), 0 chol., 105mg sod., 12g carb. (5g sugars, 4g fiber), 3g pro.
Diabetic exchanges: 2 vegetable, 2 fat.

SOUR CREAM CUCUMBERS

SOUR CREAM CUCUMBERS F S C M

This is especially good during the summer with fresh-picked cucumbers from the garden. It's been a tradition at our house to serve it along with the other Hungarian specialties my mom learned to make from the women at church..

—Pamela Eaton, Monclova, OH

Prep: 15 min. + chilling
Makes: 8 servings

- ½ cup sour cream
- 3 tablespoons white vinegar
- 1 tablespoon sugar
  Pepper to taste
- 4 medium cucumbers, peeled if desired and thinly sliced
- 1 small sweet onion, thinly sliced and separated into rings

In a large bowl, whisk sour cream, vinegar, sugar and pepper until blended. Add the cucumbers and onion, then toss to coat. Refrigerate it, covered, at least 4 hours. Serve with a slotted spoon.

Cucumbers with Dill: Omit the first four ingredients. Mix ¾ cup white vinegar, ⅓ cup snipped fresh dill, ⅓ cup sugar and ¾ teaspoon pepper. Stir in cucumbers.

Per ¾ cup: 62 cal., 3g fat (2g sat. fat), 10mg chol., 5mg sod., 7g carb. (5g sugars, 2g fiber), 2g pro.
Diabetic exchanges: 1 vegetable, ½ fat.

✳

TEST KITCHEN TIP
When storing sweet onions, keep them cool, dry and separate. Place in a single layer, wrapped separately in foil or paper towels, in the vegetable bin of the refrigerator.

POMEGRANATE PERSIMMON SALAD M FAST FIX

To bring some sunshine to the table, I toss up this bright salad featuring persimmons and pomegranate seeds, dressed with a puckery vinaigrette.
—Linda Tambunan, Dublin, CA

Start to Finish: 15 min
Makes: 12 servings

- ½ cup olive oil
- ½ cup maple syrup
- ¼ cup rice vinegar
- 2 tablespoons Dijon mustard
- ¼ teaspoon salt
- ¼ teaspoon pepper

SALAD

- 3 ripe Fuyu persimmons or 3 plums, sliced
- 2 packages (10 ounces each) baby kale salad blend
- 1 cup pomegranate seeds

1. Place first six ingredients in a jar with a lid; shake well. Refrigerate until serving.
2. To serve, shake vinaigrette and toss ½ cup with persimmons. Toss remaining vinaigrette with salad blend. Top with persimmons and pomegranate seeds.
Per 1½ cups: 175 cal., 9g fat (2g sat. fat), 0 chol., 220mg sod., 23g carb. (17g sugars, 3g fiber), 2g pro.
Diabetic exchanges: 2 vegetable, 2 fat, ½ starch, ½ fruit.

BARLEY CORN SALAD M

A great alternative to pasta salads, this fresh, fast and easy dish adds summery flavor to barley and sweet corn. Take it to your next get-together and see how fast it will disappear!
—Mary Ann Kieffer, Lawrence, KS

Prep: 15 min. + chilling
Makes: 6 servings

- 2 cups cooked medium pearl barley
- 2 cups frozen corn, thawed
- ½ cup chopped sweet red pepper
- ½ cup chopped green pepper
- 3 green onions, chopped
- 1 tablespoon minced fresh cilantro
- 2 tablespoons lemon juice
- 2 tablespoons canola oil
- ½ teaspoon salt
- ½ teaspoon dried thyme
- ⅛ teaspoon pepper

In a large bowl, combine the first six ingredients. In a jar with a tight-fitting lid, combine the lemon juice, oil, salt, thyme and pepper; shake well. Drizzle over salad and toss to coat. Cover and refrigerate for at least 2 hours before serving.
Freeze option: Prepare salad without onions and cilantro. Transfer to freezer containers; freeze. To use, thaw completely in refrigerator. Gently stir in onions, cilantro and a little oil if necessary.
Per ⅔ cup: 156 cal., 5g fat (0 sat. fat), 0 chol., 202mg sod., 26g carb. (2g sugars, 4g fiber), 3g pro.
Diabetic exchanges: 1½ starch, 1 fat.

POMEGRANATE PERSIMMON SALAD

SIDE
DISHES

"On cold winter days, I pull out the bacon, tomatoes and lima beans for a veggie-packed meal that nourishes the family."
—Karen Kumpulainen, Forest City, NC

Rosemary Cauliflower (p. 63) **Holiday Brussels Sprouts** (p. 66) **Lemon Mushroom Orzo** (p. 68)
Roasted Tater Rounds with Green Onions & Tarragon (p. 69) **Beans, Bacon & Tomato Bake** (p. 71) **Cilantro Ginger Carrots** (p. 65)

THYME-ROASTED
CARROTS

GARDEN-FRESH
RAINBOW CHARD C FAST FIX ▶

Chard is a member of the beet family, prized for its green leaves and colorful stalks. Stir up these good-for-you greens with garlic and red onion.
—*Taste of Home* Test Kitchen

Start to Finish: 20 min.
Makes: 4 servings

- 2 tablespoons olive oil
- 1 medium red onion, halved and sliced
- 3 garlic cloves, sliced
- ¼ cup chicken broth
- 2 bunches rainbow Swiss chard, coarsely chopped (about 16 cups)
- 2 tablespoons lemon juice
- ¼ teaspoon salt
- ¼ teaspoon pepper

1. In a 6-qt. stockpot, heat the oil over medium-high heat. Add onion; cook and stir 2-3 minutes or until tender. Add garlic; cook 1 minute longer.

2. Add broth and chard; cook and stir for 5-6 minutes or until the chard is tender. Remove from heat; stir in lemon juice, salt and pepper.

Per ½ cup: 115 cal., 7g fat (1g sat. fat), 0 chol., 631mg sod., 11g carb. (4g sugars, 4g fiber), 4g pro.
Diabetic exchanges: 2 vegetable, 1½ fat.

THYME-ROASTED CARROTS
F C M FAST FIX ▶

Cutting the carrots lengthwise makes this dish look extra pretty. For a little more elegance and color, garnish with fresh thyme or parsley sprigs.
—Deirdre Cox, Kansas City, MO

Start to Finish: 30 min.
Makes: about 12 servings (2 carrot halves each)

- 3 pounds medium carrots, halved lengthwise
- 2 tablespoons minced fresh thyme or 2 teaspoons dried thyme
- 2 tablespoons canola oil
- 1 tablespoon honey
- 1 teaspoon salt

Preheat oven to 400°. Divide the carrots between two greased 15x10x1-in. baking pans. In a small bowl, mix thyme, oil, honey and salt; brush over carrots. Roast for 20-25 minutes or until tender.

Per 2 carrot halves: 73 cal., 3g fat (0 sat. fat), 0 chol., 275mg sod., 12g carb. (7g sugars, 3g fiber), 1g pro.
Diabetic exchanges: 1 vegetable, ½ starch, ½ fat.

LEMON ALMOND ASPARAGUS
S C M FAST FIX ▶

Here's my time-saving way to dress up fresh asparagus: Just drizzle butter and lemon juice over the cooked spears, then top them with almonds and lemon peel. Simply delicious.
—Linda Barry, Yakima, WA

Start to Finish: 20 min.
Makes: 8 servings

- 3 tablespoons butter
- 5 teaspoons lemon juice
- 2 pounds fresh asparagus, trimmed
- ⅓ cup sliced almonds, toasted
    Lemon peel strips, optional

Melt butter; stir in lemon juice. In a large saucepan, bring 4 cups water to a boil. Add asparagus in batches; cook 2-4 minutes or until crisp-tender. Drain and place on a serving plate. Drizzle with the butter mixture; top with almonds and, if desired, lemon peel.

Note: To toast nuts, bake in a shallow pan in a 350° oven for 5-10 minutes or cook them in a skillet over low heat until lightly browned, stirring occasionally.

Per serving: 78 cal., 7g fat (3g sat. fat), 11mg chol., 36mg sod., 4g carb. (1g sugars, 1g fiber), 2g pro.
Diabetic exchanges: 1 vegetable, 1 fat.

LEMON ROASTED FINGERLINGS & BRUSSLELS SPROUTS

GARLIC MASHED CAULIFLOWER C M FAST FIX

I order cauliflower mash every time we're at our favorite restaurant. One night, I figured out how to make it at home—it was so easy!
—Barry Keiser, West Chester, PA

Start to Finish: 25 min.
Makes: 4 servings

- 5 cups fresh cauliflowerets
- 1 garlic clove, thinly sliced
- 3 tablespoons fat-free milk
- 3 tablespoons reduced-fat mayonnaise
- ½ teaspoon salt
- ⅛ teaspoon white pepper
  Cracked black pepper and minced fresh chives, optional

1. Place 1 in. of water in a large saucepan; add the cauliflower and garlic. Bring to a boil. Reduce heat; simmer, covered, until tender, 10-15 minutes, stirring cauliflower and garlic occasionally. Drain; return to the pan.
2. Mash cauliflower mixture to desired consistency. Stir in milk, mayonnaise, salt and white pepper. If desired, sprinkle with cracked pepper and chives.
Per ½ cup: 74 cal., 4g fat (1g sat. fat), 4mg chol., 428mg sod., 8g carb. (4g sugars, 3g fiber), 3g pro.
Diabetic exchanges: 1 vegetable, 1 fat.

✱
TEST KITCHEN TIP
You can tightly wrap an unwashed head of cauliflower and refrigerate for up to 5 days. Before using, wash and remove the leaves at the base and trim the stem.

LEMON ROASTED FINGERLINGS & BRUSSELS SPROUTS M

My trick to roasting veggies is to pair ones that cook in the same amount of time. Here Brussels sprouts and potatoes combine for a vibrant and flavorful dinner accompaniment.
—Courtney Gaylord, Columbus, IN

Prep: 15 min. • **Bake:** 20 min.
Makes: 8 servings

- 1 pound fingerling potatoes, halved
- 1 pound Brussels sprouts, trimmed and halved
- 6 tablespoons olive oil, divided
- ¾ teaspoon salt, divided
- ¼ teaspoon pepper
- 3 tablespoons lemon juice
- 1 garlic clove, minced
- 1 teaspoon Dijon mustard
- 1 teaspoon honey

1. Preheat oven to 425°. Place potatoes and Brussels sprouts in a greased 15x10x1-in. baking pan. Drizzle with 2 tablespoons oil; sprinkle with ½ teaspoon salt and the pepper. Toss to coat. Roast 20-25 minutes or until tender, stirring once.
2. In a small bowl, whisk lemon juice, garlic, mustard, honey and remaining oil and salt until blended. Transfer vegetables to a large bowl; drizzle with lemon mixture and toss to coat. Serve warm.
Per ¾ cup: 167 cal., 10g fat (1g sat. fat), 0 chol., 256mg sod., 17g carb. (3g sugars, 3g fiber), 3g pro.
Diabetic exchanges: 2 fat, 1 starch, 1 vegetable.

SAUTEED SQUASH WITH TOMATOES & ONIONS
C **M** **FAST FIX** ▶

My favorite dishes showcase my love for family and food, like this one— ratatouille, Mexican style.
—Adan Franco, Milwaukee, WI

Start to Finish: 20 min.
Makes: 8 servings

- 2 tablespoons olive oil
- 1 medium onion, finely chopped
- 4 medium zucchini, chopped
- 2 large tomatoes, finely chopped
- 1 teaspoon salt
- ¼ teaspoon pepper

1. In a large skillet, heat oil over medium-high heat. Add onion; cook and stir 2-4 minutes or until tender. Add zucchini; cook and stir 3 minutes.

2. Stir in tomatoes, salt and pepper; cook and stir 4-6 minutes longer or until squash is tender. Serve with a slotted spoon.
Per ¾ cup: 60 cal., 4g fat (1g sat. fat), 0 chol., 306mg sod., 6g carb. (4g sugars, 2g fiber), 2g pro.
Diabetic exchanges: 1 vegetable, ½ fat.

BRUSSELS SPROUTS WITH GARLIC **C** **FAST FIX** ▶

These Brussels sprouts are special enough for Thanksgiving dinner and any company occasions. If you can't find fresh sprouts, try using frozen.
—Myra Innes, Auburn, KS

Start to Finish: 30 min.
Makes: 6 servings

- 1½ pounds fresh Brussels sprouts
- 2 teaspoons olive oil
- 3 teaspoons butter, divided
- 4 garlic cloves, chopped
- ½ cup reduced-sodium chicken broth
- ¼ teaspoon salt
- ⅛ teaspoon pepper

1. Trim Brussels sprout stems. Using a paring knife, cut an X in the bottom of each one.

2. In a large saucepan, heat the oil and 1 teaspoon butter over medium heat. Add garlic; cook and stir 1-2 minutes or until garlic begins to color. Immediately add the Brussels sprouts, stirring to coat.

3. Stir in the broth, salt and pepper; bring to a boil. Reduce heat; simmer, covered, 8-10 minutes or until Brussels sprouts are tender. Drain. Add remaining butter; toss to coat.
Per ⅔ cup: 78 cal., 4g fat (1g sat. fat), 5mg chol., 187mg sod., 10g carb. (2g sugars, 4g fiber), 4g pro.
Diabetic exchanges: 1 vegetable, ½ fat.

SMOKY QUINOA WITH MUSHROOMS Ⓜ

Add quinoa cooked with smoked paprika to your list of top sides. If desired, saute the spinach leaves to serve them warm.
—Ellen Kanner, Miami, FL

Prep: 15 min. • **Cook:** 35 min.
Makes: 4 servings

- 4 teaspoons olive oil
- 1 pound sliced fresh mushrooms
- 3 garlic cloves, minced
- 3 tablespoons tomato paste
- 2 tablespoons smoked paprika
- 2 tablespoons lemon juice
- 1 teaspoon ground cumin
- ½ teaspoon salt
- 1 cup water or vegetable broth
- ¾ cup quinoa, rinsed
- 4 cups fresh baby spinach
  Minced fresh cilantro and lemon wedges

1. In a large saucepan, heat the oil over medium-high heat. Add mushrooms; cook and stir 6-8 minutes or until mushrooms are tender. Add the garlic; cook 1 minute longer. Reduce heat to medium-low; cook, covered, 10 minutes.
2. Stir in tomato paste, paprika, lemon juice, cumin and salt until blended. Add water; bring to a boil. Add quinoa. Reduce heat; simmer, covered, 15-18 minutes or until liquid is absorbed. Remove from heat; fluff with a fork.
3. Arrange spinach on a serving plate; spoon quinoa over spinach. Sprinkle with cilantro; serve with lemon wedges.
Per ⅔ cup quinoa mixture with 1 cup spinach: 217 cal., 8g fat (1g sat. fat), 0 chol., 337mg sod., 31g carb. (4g sugars, 6g fiber), 10g pro.
Diabetic exchanges: 2 vegetable, 1½ starch, 1 fat.

HERBED POTATO PACKS Ⓜ `FAST FIX` ▸

Fingerlings are small, firm and waxy potatoes, so they cook faster than chunkier varieties and leap from grill to table in one convenient pouch.
—*Taste of Home* Test Kitchen

Start to Finish: 25 min.
Makes: 4 servings

- 2 pounds fingerling potatoes
- 2 tablespoons olive oil
- 2 garlic cloves, minced
- 1 teaspoon salt
- 2 teaspoons minced fresh thyme
- ½ teaspoon coarsely ground pepper

1. Pierce potatoes with a fork. Place in a large microwave-safe dish; cover and microwave for 4-7 minutes or until crisp-tender, stirring halfway. Add the remaining ingredients; toss to coat.
2. Place one-fourth of the potatoes on a double thickness of heavy-duty foil (about 14 x12 in.); fold foil around potatoes and seal tightly. Repeat three times with remaining potatoes.
3. Grill, covered, over medium-high heat for 6-9 minutes on each side or until potatoes are tender. Open foil carefully to allow steam to escape.
Per packet: 178 cal., 4g fat (0 sat. fat), 0 chol., 597mg sod., 30g carb. (1g sugars, 4g fiber), 5g pro.
Diabetic exchanges: 2 starch, ½ fat.

★ ★ ★ ★ ★ **READER REVIEW**

"Although we grill all 12 months a year, I have not done a lot of veggie grilling. But this is a keeper! Easy, fast and so good. There are so many ways you could make this—add mushrooms, kernel corn, spice it up. Loved it!"

KATKOS TASTEOFHOME.COM

SMOKY QUINOA WITH MUSHROOMS

RAINBOW HASH M FAST FIX

I incorporate lots of color in my cooking to entice my family to eat outside their comfort zone. This happy hash combines a rainbow of veggies and flavors.
—Courtney Stultz, Weir, KS

Start to Finish: 30 min.
Makes: 2 servings

- 2 tablespoons olive or coconut oil
- 1 medium sweet potato, peeled and cubed
- 1 medium purple potato, peeled and cubed
- 1 large carrot, peeled and cubed
- ½ teaspoon dried oregano
- ½ teaspoon dried basil
- ½ teaspoon sea salt
- ½ teaspoon pepper
- 2 cups fresh kale or spinach, coarsely chopped
- 1 small garlic clove, minced

In a large skillet, heat oil over medium heat. Cook and stir potatoes, carrot and seasonings until vegetables are tender, 10-12 minutes. Add kale and garlic; continue cooking until vegetables are lightly browned and the kale is tender, 2-4 minutes.
Per cup: 304 cal., 14g fat (2g sat. fat), 0 chol., 523mg sod., 43g carb. (12g sugars, 5g fiber), 4g pro.

COLCANNON IRISH POTATOES

COLCANNON IRISH POTATOES M FAST FIX

My mother came from Ireland as a teen and brought this traditional recipe with her. What a great way to get my family to eat cooked cabbage...hidden in Grandma's mashed potatoes!
—Marie Pagel, Lena, WI

Start to Finish: 30 min.
Makes: 10 servings

- 2½ pounds potatoes (about 6 medium), peeled and cut into 1-inch pieces
- 2 cups chopped cabbage
- 1 large onion, chopped
- 1 teaspoon salt
- ¼ teaspoon pepper
- ¼ cup butter, softened
- 1 cup 2% milk

1. Place potatoes in a 6-qt. stockpot; add water to cover. Bring to a boil. Reduce heat to medium; cook, covered, until potatoes are almost tender, 8-10 minutes.
2. Add cabbage and onion; cook, covered, until cabbage is tender, 5-7 minutes. Drain; return to pot. Add salt and pepper; mash to desired consistency, gradually adding butter and milk.
Per ¾ cup: 129 cal., 5g fat (3g sat. fat), 14mg chol., 290mg sod., 19g carb. (4g sugars, 2g fiber), 3g pro.
Diabetic exchanges: 1 starch, 1 fat.

GARLICKY KALE F M

This zippy side dish features fresh kale and sweet raisins. It's wonderful hot or cold.
—Clara Coulson Minney, Washington Court House, OH

Prep: 20 min. • **Cook:** 15 min.
Makes: 6 servings

- 3 cups water
- 2 bunches kale, trimmed and coarsely chopped
- 4 garlic cloves, minced
- 1 teaspoon olive oil
- ½ cup golden raisins
- ¼ cup pitted ripe olives, sliced
- ¼ teaspoon salt
- ¼ teaspoon crushed red pepper flakes

1. In a large saucepan, bring water to a boil. Stir in kale. Cover and cook for 6-8 minutes or until almost tender; drain and set aside.
2. In a large nonstick skillet coated with cooking spray, cook the garlic in oil for 1 minute. Stir in the raisins, olives, salt and pepper flakes; cook 1 minute longer. Stir in kale; cook for 3-4 minutes or until tender.
Per ⅔ cup: 88 cal., 2g fat (0 sat. fat), 0 chol., 187mg sod., 17g carb. (8g sugars, 2g fiber), 3g pro.
Diabetic exchanges: 2 vegetable, ½ fruit.

ZUCCHINI RICE PILAF FAST FIX

I created this colorful rice and veggie side dish one night with ingredients I had on hand. We've been making it ever since.
—Lori Blevins, Douglasville, GA

Start to Finish: 25 min.
Makes: 4 servings

- ½ teaspoon dried basil
- 2 tablespoons butter
- 2¼ cups hot water
- 1¼ teaspoons chicken bouillon granules
- 1 cup uncooked long grain rice
- ½ cup shredded carrot
- 1 small zucchini, halved and thinly sliced

1. In a large skillet, saute the basil in butter for 2 minutes. Add water and bouillon; bring to a boil. Stir in rice and carrot. Reduce heat; cover and simmer for 10 minutes.

2. Add zucchini; cover and simmer 5 minutes longer or until rice is tender.

Per cup: 231 cal., 6g fat (4g sat. fat), 15mg chol., 318mg sod., 40g carb. (1g sugars, 1g fiber), 4g pro.

Diabetic exchanges: 2 starch, 2 vegetable, ½ fat.

SWISS CHARD WITH ONIONS & GARLIC M FAST FIX

I dress up Swiss chard with flavorful garlic, onions and crunchy walnuts. It's a perfect side, but for a main dish we serve it with pasta. My boys love this recipe any way it appears on the table and ask for it often.
—Rebekah Chappel, Portales, NM

Start to Finish: 25 min.
Makes: 6 servings

- 2 tablespoons olive oil
- 2 medium onions, chopped
- 6 garlic cloves, sliced
- ½ cup white balsamic vinegar
- 2 bunches Swiss chard, coarsely chopped (about 16 cups)
- ½ cup walnut halves, toasted
- ¼ teaspoon salt
- ¼ teaspoon pepper

1. In a 6-qt. stockpot, heat the oil over medium-high heat. Add onions; cook and stir until tender. Add garlic; cook 1 minute longer.

2. Add vinegar, stirring to loosen any browned bits from pot. Add remaining ingredients; cook 4-6 minutes or until chard is tender, stirring occasionally.

Note: To toast nuts, bake in a shallow pan in a 350° oven for 5-10 minutes or cook in a skillet over low heat until lightly browned, stirring occasionally.

Per ⅔ cup: 159 cal., 10g fat (1g sat. fat), 0 chol., 381mg sod., 16g carb. (9g sugars, 3g fiber), 4g pro.

Diabetic exchanges: 2 fat, 1 starch.

ZUCCHINI RICE PILAF

HARVEST VEGETABLES S C M

This is my favorite vegetable side dish to serve whenever we have company. It pairs well with any kind of roasted meat.
—Amy Logan, Mill Creek, PA

Prep: 20 min. • **Bake:** 30 min.
Makes: 9 servings

- 8 small red potatoes, quartered
- 2 small onions, quartered
- 1 medium zucchini, halved and sliced
- 1 medium yellow summer squash, halved and sliced
- ½ pound fresh baby carrots
- 1 cup fresh cauliflowerets
- 1 cup fresh broccoli florets
- ¼ cup olive oil
- 1 tablespoon garlic powder
- 1½ teaspoons dried rosemary, crushed
- ½ teaspoon dried thyme
- ¼ teaspoon salt
- ¼ teaspoon pepper

1. Place vegetables in a large bowl. Combine the remaining ingredients; drizzle over vegetables and toss to coat.
2. Transfer to two greased 15x10x1-in. baking pans. Bake vegetables at 400° for 30-35 minutes or until tender, stirring mixture occasionally.
Per ¾ cup: 114 cal., 6g fat (1g sat. fat), 0 chol., 97mg sod., 13g carb. (4g sugars, 3g fiber), 2g pro.
Diabetic exchanges: 1 vegetable, 1 fat, ½ starch.

★ ★ ★ ★ ★ **READER REVIEW**

"I would absolutely make this again and again! So easy to toss together with very little cleanup. It's wonderful as a side dish for just about anything...grilled chicken, burgers, steak, tuna, even hard-boiled eggs!

BANSLUG000 TASTEOFHOME.COM

ROASTED
CARROTS & FENNEL

ROASTED CARROTS & FENNEL M

This addictive combo is a fresh take on one of my mother's standard wintertime dishes. I usually add more carrots—as many as the pans will hold.
—Lily Julow, Lawrenceville, GA

Prep: 15 min. • **Bake:** 40 min.
Makes: 8 servings

- 2½ pounds medium carrots, peeled and cut in half lengthwise
- 1 large fennel bulb, cut into ½-inch wedges
- 1 large red onion, cut into ½-inch wedges
- 1 medium lemon, thinly sliced
- ¼ cup olive oil
- 2 teaspoons ground coriander
- 1 teaspoon ground cumin
- ½ teaspoon salt
- ¼ teaspoon pepper
  Thinly sliced fresh basil leaves

1. Preheat oven to 375°. In a large bowl, combine carrots, fennel, onion and lemon. Mix oil, coriander, cumin, salt and pepper; drizzle over carrot mixture and toss to coat. Transfer to two foil-lined 15x10x1-in. baking pans.
2. Roast 40-50 minutes or until vegetables are tender, stirring occasionally. Sprinkle with basil.
Per serving: 139 cal., 7g fat (1g sat. fat), 0 chol., 262mg sod., 18g carb. (9g sugars, 6g fiber), 2g pro.
Diabetic exchanges: 2 vegetable, 1½ fat.

LEMON PEPPER
ROASTED BROCCOLI

ROSEMARY CAULIFLOWER
F C M FAST FIX

(PICTURED ON P. 54)

Roasting cauliflower in the oven gives it an amazingly rich and nutty flavor. Sprinkle on Parmesan to take it over the top!
—Joann Fritzler, Belen, NM

Start to Finish: 30 min.
Makes: 6 servings

- 1 medium head cauliflower (about 2½ pounds), broken into florets
- 2 tablespoons olive oil
- 2 teaspoons minced fresh rosemary or ¾ teaspoon dried rosemary, crushed
- ½ teaspoon salt

Preheat oven to 450°. Toss all ingredients; spread in a greased 15x10x1-in. pan. Roast until tender and lightly browned, 20-25 minutes, stirring occasionally.

Per ¾ cup: 65 cal., 5g fat (1g sat. fat), 0 chol., 226mg sod., 5g carb. (2g sugars, 2g fiber), 2g pro.
Diabetic exchanges: 1 vegetable, 1 fat.

LEMON PEPPER ROASTED BROCCOLI **S C M FAST FIX**

Fresh green broccoli florets turn tangy and tasty when roasted with lemon juice and pepper. A sprinkle of almonds adds a pleasant crunch.
—Liz Bellville, Jacksonville, NC

Start to Finish: 25 min.
Makes: 8 servings

- 1½ pounds fresh broccoli florets (about 12 cups)
- 2 tablespoons olive oil
- ½ teaspoon lemon juice
- ¼ teaspoon salt

- ¼ teaspoon coarsely ground pepper, divided
- ¼ cup chopped almonds
- 2 teaspoons grated lemon peel

1. Preheat oven to 450°. Place broccoli in a large bowl. Whisk oil, lemon juice, salt and ⅛ teaspoon pepper until blended; drizzle over broccoli and toss to coat. Transfer to a 15x10x1-in. baking pan.
2. Roast 10-15 minutes or until tender. Transfer to a serving dish. Sprinkle with almonds, lemon peel and the remaining pepper; toss to combine.
Per cup: 84 cal., 6g fat (1g sat. fat), 0 chol., 103mg sod., 7g carb. (0 sugars, 4g fiber), 4g pro.
Diabetic exchanges: 1 vegetable, 1 fat.

WHITE BEANS & SPINACH

WHITE BEANS & SPINACH

F **M** **FAST FIX**

This skillet side is a variation of a recipe I received from my Italian mother. I've prepared spinach like this for years—because my kids will eat it this way!
—Lucia Johnson, Massena, NY

Start to Finish: 10 min.
Makes: 2 servings

- 2 tablespoons water
- 2 garlic cloves, minced
- 8 cups fresh spinach (about 6 ounces)
- ¾ cup canned cannellini or white kidney beans, rinsed and drained
- ⅛ teaspoon salt
  Dash cayenne pepper
  Dash ground nutmeg

Place water, garlic and spinach in a large skillet. Cook, covered, over medium heat just until tender, 2-3 minutes, stirring occasionally. Stir in remaining ingredients; heat through.

Per ½ cup: 116 cal., 1g fat (0 sat. fat), 0 chol., 561mg sod., 21g carb. (1g sugars, 7g fiber), 7g pro.
Diabetic exchanges: 1½ starch.

CILANTRO GINGER CARROTS

F **C** **M** **FAST FIX**

(PICTURED ON P. 55)

Peppery-sweet ginger and cooling cilantro have starring roles in this colorful side of crisp-tender carrots. They go from pan to plate in an instant.
—Taste of Home Test Kitchen

Start to Finish: 15 min.
Makes: 4 servings

- 1 tablespoon butter
- 1 pound fresh carrots, sliced diagonally
- 1½ teaspoons minced fresh gingerroot
- 2 tablespoons chopped fresh cilantro
- ½ teaspoon salt
- ¼ teaspoon pepper

In a large skillet, heat butter over medium-high heat. Add carrots; cook and stir 4-6 minutes or until crisp-tender. Add ginger; cook 1 minute longer. Stir in cilantro, salt and pepper.

Per ½ cup: 73 cal., 3g fat (2g sat. fat), 8mg chol., 396mg sod., 11g carb. (5g sugars, 3g fiber), 1g pro.
Diabetic exchanges: 1 vegetable, ½ fat.

CRANBERRY-WALNUT SWEET POTATOES

CRANBERRY-WALNUT SWEET POTATOES **S** **M**

My favorite dish at Thanksgiving is the sweet potatoes. You can make the sauce for these up to a day ahead; just leave out the walnuts until you're ready to serve.
—Mary Wilhelm, Sparta, WI

Prep: 25 min. • **Bake:** 1 hour
Makes: 8 servings

- 4 large sweet potatoes
- 1 tablespoon butter
- ¼ cup finely chopped onion
- 1 cup fresh or frozen cranberries
- ⅓ cup maple syrup
- ¼ cup cranberry juice
- ¼ teaspoon salt, divided
- ½ cup chopped walnuts, toasted
- 1 teaspoon Dijon mustard
- ¼ teaspoon pepper
- 2 tablespoons minced fresh chives

1. Preheat oven to 400°. Scrub sweet potatoes; pierce several times with a fork. Bake 1 hour or until tender.
2. Meanwhile, in a small saucepan, heat butter over medium-high heat. Add onion; cook and stir until tender. Stir in the cranberries, syrup, cranberry juice and ⅛ teaspoon salt. Bring to a boil. Reduce heat; simmer, covered, 10-15 minutes or until berries pop, stirring occasionally. Stir in walnuts and mustard; heat through.
3. When cool enough to handle, cut each potato lengthwise in half; sprinkle with pepper and remaining salt. Top with cranberry mixture; sprinkle with chives.

Note: To toast nuts, bake in a shallow pan in a 350° oven for 5-10 minutes or cook in a skillet over low heat until lightly browned, stirring occasionally.

Per sweet potato half: 284 cal., 6g fat (1 sat. fat), 4mg chol., 120mg sod., 55g carb. (27g sugars, 9g fiber), 4g pro.

GERMAN RED CABBAGE

GERMAN RED CABBAGE
F S M

Sunday afternoons were a time for family gatherings when I was a kid. While my uncles played cards, my aunts had fun in the kitchen making traditional German recipes such as this red cabbage.
—Jeannette Heim, Dunlap, TN

Prep: 10 min. • **Cook:** 65 min.
Makes: 10 servings

- 1 **medium onion, halved and sliced**
- 1 **medium apple, sliced**
- 1 **medium head red cabbage, shredded (about 8 cups)**
- ⅓ **cup sugar**
- ⅓ **cup white vinegar**
- ¾ **teaspoon salt, optional**
- ¼ **teaspoon pepper**

In a large Dutch oven coated with cooking spray, cook and stir onion and apple over medium heat until onion is tender, about 5 minutes. Stir in remaining ingredients; cook, covered, until cabbage is tender, about 1 hour, stirring occasionally. Serve warm or cold.
Per cup: 64 cal., 0 fat (0 sat. fat), 0 chol., 23mg sod., 16g carb. (12g sugars, 2g fiber), 1g pro.
Diabetic exchanges: 1 vegetable, ½ starch.

HOLIDAY BRUSSELS SPROUTS
C FAST FIX

(PICTURED ON P. 54)

Make Brussels sprouts extra special for the holidays or any time of year with peas, celery and bacon. This recipe easily doubles if you're serving a crowd.
—Jodie Beckman, Council Bluffs, IA

Start to Finish: 25 min.
Makes: 6 servings

- 1 **package (16 ounces) frozen Brussels sprouts**
- 1 **package (10 ounces) frozen peas**
- 2 **tablespoons butter**
- 2 **celery ribs, chopped**
- 2 **bacon strips, cooked and crumbled**
- 2 **tablespoons minced fresh chives**

1. Cook Brussels sprouts and peas according to package directions; drain.
2. In a large skillet, heat butter over medium-high heat. Add celery; cook and stir until crisp-tender. Add the Brussels sprouts, peas, bacon and chives; toss to combine.
Per ⅔ cup: 115 cal., 5g fat (3g sat. fat), 12mg chol., 147mg sod., 13g carb. (3g sugars, 5g fiber), 6g pro.
Diabetic exchanges: 2 vegetable, 1 fat.

SICILIAN STEAMED LEEKS
F S M FAST FIX▶

I love the challenge of developing new recipes for my garden leeks, a delicious but underrated vegetable. This family favorite has full, Mediterranean flavor.
—Roxanne Chan, Albany, CA

Start to Finish: 20 min.
Makes: 6 servings

- 6 medium leeks (white portion only), halved lengthwise, cleaned
- 1 large tomato, chopped
- 1 small navel orange, peeled, sectioned and chopped
- 2 tablespoons minced fresh parsley
- 2 tablespoons sliced Greek olives
- 1 teaspoon capers, drained
- 1 teaspoon red wine vinegar
- 1 teaspoon olive oil
- ½ teaspoon grated orange peel
- ½ teaspoon pepper
  Crumbled feta cheese

In a Dutch oven, place steamer basket over 1 in. of water. Place leeks in basket. Bring water to a boil. Reduce heat to maintain a low boil; steam, covered, until tender, for 8-10 minutes. Meanwhile, combine next nine ingredients. Transfer leeks to a serving platter. Spoon tomato mixture over top; sprinkle with cheese.

Per serving: 83 cal., 2g fat (0 sat. fat), 0 chol., 77mg sod., 16g carb. (6g sugars, 3g fiber), 2g pro.
Diabetic exchanges: 1 starch, ½ fat.

CUMIN-ROASTED CARROTS
C M

Carrots make a super side—they're big on flavor and a breeze to cook. Plus, I can actually get my husband to eat these fragrant, deeply spiced veggies.
—Taylor Kiser, Brandon, FL

Prep: 20 min. • **Cook:** 35 min.
Makes: 12 servings

- 2 tablespoons coriander seeds
- 2 tablespoons cumin seeds
- 3 pounds carrots, peeled and cut into 4x½-inch sticks
- 3 tablespoons coconut oil or butter, melted
- 8 garlic cloves, minced
- 1 teaspoon salt
- ½ teaspoon pepper
  Minced fresh cilantro, optional

1. Preheat oven to 400°. In a dry small skillet, toast coriander and cumin seeds over medium heat 45-60 seconds or until aromatic, stirring frequently. Cool slightly. Grind in a spice grinder, or with a mortar and pestle, until finely crushed.
2. Place carrots in a large bowl. Add melted coconut oil, garlic, salt, pepper and crushed spices, and toss to coat. Divide carrots between two 15x10x1-in. baking pans coated with cooking spray, spreading pieces evenly.
3. Roast 35-40 minutes or until crisp-tender and lightly browned, stirring and rotating pans halfway. Before serving, sprinkle with cilantro if desired.
Note: Two tablespoons each ground coriander and ground cumin may be substituted for whole spices. Before using, toast ground spices in a dry skillet until aromatic, stirring frequently.
Per serving: 86 cal., 4g fat (3g sat. fat), 0 chol., 277mg sod., 13g carb. (5g sugars, 4g fiber), 1g pro.
Diabetic exchanges: 1 vegetable, 1 fat.
HEALTH TIP The fat in coconut oil will give these carrots a subtle coconut flavor. While this oil includes medium-chain triglycerides, their health benefits are still unproven, and coconut oil probably won't help you shed pounds.

SICILIAN STEAMED LEEKS

ROASTED SQUASH,
CARROTS & WALNUTS

ROASTED SQUASH, CARROTS & WALNUTS Ⓜ

After the main dish is done cooking, I dial up the oven temperature and roast carrots and squash for this yummy side. It's great for Thanksgiving or any time you want a special accompaniment.
—Lily Julow, Lawrenceville, GA

Prep: 15 min. • **Bake:** 35 min.
Makes: 8 servings

- 2 **pounds carrots (about 12 medium), peeled**
- 1 **medium butternut squash (3 pounds), peeled and cubed**
- ¼ **cup packed brown sugar**
- ¼ **cup olive oil**
- 2 **teaspoons kosher salt**
- ½ **teaspoon ground cinnamon**
- ¼ **teaspoon ground nutmeg**
- 1 **cup chopped walnuts**

1. Preheat oven to 400°. Cut carrots in half lengthwise, then in half crosswise.
2. In a large bowl, toss squash and carrots with brown sugar, oil, salt, cinnamon and nutmeg. Transfer the vegetables to two greased foil-lined 15x10x1-in. baking pans. Roast 30 minutes, stirring occasionally.
3. Sprinkle walnuts over vegetables. Roast 5-10 minutes longer or until the vegetables are tender.

Per serving: 305 cal., 17g fat (2g sat. fat), 0 chol., 567mg sod., 40g carb. (17g sugars, 10g fiber), 5g pro.

LEMON MUSHROOM ORZO
Ⓜ **FAST FIX** ▶

(PICTURED ON P. 55)

Sometimes I'll serve this side dish chilled; other times I'll serve it hot. It has a lovely appearance and also goes well with almost any entree.
—Shelly Nelson, Akeley, MN

Start to Finish: 25 min.
Makes: 12 servings

- 1 **package (16 ounces) orzo pasta**
- 3 **tablespoons olive oil, divided**
- ¾ **pound sliced fresh mushrooms**
- ¾ **cup chopped pecans, toasted**
- ½ **cup minced fresh parsley**
- 1 **teaspoon grated lemon peel**
- 3 **tablespoons lemon juice**
- 1 **teaspoon salt**
- ½ **teaspoon pepper**

1. Cook orzo according to package directions. Meanwhile, in a large skillet, heat 2 tablespoons oil over medium-high heat. Add mushrooms; cook and stir until tender and lightly browned. Drain orzo.
2. In a large bowl, place orzo, mushroom mixture, pecans, parsley, lemon peel, lemon juice, salt, pepper and remaining oil; toss to combine.

Per ¾ cup: 225 cal., 9g fat (1g sat. fat), 0 chol., 202mg sod., 31g carb. (2g sugars, 2g fiber), 6g pro.

Diabetic exchanges: 2 starch, 1½ fat.

PARMESAN ROASTED BROCCOLI C M FAST FIX

Sure, it's simple and healthy, but this roasted broccoli is delish! Cutting the stalks into tall trees turns ordinary veggies into a standout side dish.

—Holly Sander, Lake Mary, FL

Start to Finish: 30 min.
Makes: 4 servings

- 2 small broccoli crowns (about 8 ounces each)
- 3 tablespoons olive oil
- ½ teaspoon salt
- ½ teaspoon pepper
- ¼ teaspoon crushed red pepper flakes
- 4 garlic cloves, thinly sliced
- 2 tablespoons grated Parmesan cheese
- 1 teaspoon grated lemon zest

1. Preheat oven to 425°. Cut broccoli crowns into quarters from top to bottom. Drizzle with oil; sprinkle with seasonings. Place broccoli in a parchment paper-lined 15x10x1-in. pan.
2. Roast broccoli until crisp-tender, 10-12 minutes. Sprinkle with garlic; roast about 5 minutes. Sprinkle with cheese; roast until cheese is melted and stalks of broccoli are tender, 2-4 minutes longer. Sprinkle with lemon zest.

Per 2 broccoli pieces: 144 cal., 11g fat (2g sat. fat), 2mg chol., 378mg sod., 9g carb. (2g sugars, 3g fiber), 4g pro.
Diabetic exchanges: 2 fat, 1 vegtable.

PARMESAN ROASTED BROCCOLI

ROASTED TATER ROUNDS WITH GREEN ONIONS & TARRAGON F M
(PICTURED ON P. 54)

I'm crazy for roasted potatoes. Toss them with fresh herbs and green onions for a bold finish.

—Ally Phillips, Murrells Inlet, SC

Prep: 25 min. • **Broil:** 10 min.
Makes: 8 servings

- 4 pounds potatoes (about 8 medium), sliced ¼ inch thick
  Cooking spray
- 2 teaspoons sea salt
- 1 teaspoon coarsely ground pepper
- 6 green onions, thinly sliced (about ¾ cup)
- 3 tablespoons minced fresh parsley
- 2 tablespoons minced fresh tarragon
  Olive oil, optional

1. Preheat broiler. Place potatoes in a large microwave-safe bowl; spritz with cooking spray and toss to coat. Microwave, covered, on high 10-12 minutes or until almost tender, stirring halfway through cooking.
2. Spread the potatoes into greased 15x10x1-in. baking pans. Spritz slices with additional cooking spray; sprinkle with salt and pepper.
3. Broil 4-6 in. from heat 10-12 minutes or until golden brown, stirring halfway through cooking. In a small bowl, mix green onions, parsley and tarragon. Sprinkle over potatoes; toss to coat. If desired, drizzle with olive oil.

Per ¾ cup: 185 cal., 1g fat (0 sat. fat), 0 chol., 497mg sod., 41g carb. (2g sugars, 5g fiber), 5g pro.

★ ★ ★ ★ ★ **READER REVIEW**
"Absolutely love these potatoes. They have a fresh taste from the green onions and tarragon. I'll be adding these to my recipe box to make again."

CATBIRD513 TASTEOFHOME.COM

ROASTED HERB & LEMON CAULIFLOWER C M

A standout cauliflower dish, this side is easy to prepare with just a few herbs and seasonings. Crushed red pepper flakes add a nice touch of heat.
—Susan Hein, Burlington, WI

Prep: 15 min. • **Bake:** 20 min.
Makes: 4 servings

1 medium head cauliflower, cut into florets (about 6 cups)
4 tablespoons olive oil, divided
¼ cup minced fresh parsley
1 tablespoon minced fresh rosemary
1 tablespoon minced fresh thyme
1 teaspoon grated lemon peel
2 tablespoons lemon juice
½ teaspoon salt
¼ teaspoon crushed red pepper flakes

1. Preheat oven to 425°. Place cauliflower in an ungreased 15x10x1-in. baking pan. Drizzle with 2 tablespoons oil and toss to coat. Roast 20-25 minutes or until golden brown and tender, stirring occasionally.
2. In a small bowl, combine remaining ingredients; stir in remaining oil. Transfer cauliflower to a large bowl; drizzle with herb mixture and toss to combine.
Per ¾ cup: 161 cal., 14g fat (2g sat. fat), 0 chol., 342mg sod., 8g carb. (3g sugars, 3g fiber), 3g pro.
Diabetic exchanges: 3 fat, 1 vegetable.

ZUCCHINI MUSHROOM BAKE

ZUCCHINI MUSHROOM BAKE C M

Just a 10-minute prep to dress up my garden-fresh zucchini with mushrooms, onion, cheddar and a sprinkle of basil.
—Jacquelyn Smith, Carmel, ME

Prep: 10 min. • **Bake:** 30 min.
Makes: 4 servings

3 cups sliced zucchini
2 cups sliced fresh mushrooms
⅓ cup sliced onion
½ teaspoon dried basil
¼ teaspoon salt
½ cup shredded cheddar cheese

1. Preheat oven to 350°. Toss together first five ingredients; place in a greased 2-qt. shallow baking dish.
2. Bake, covered, 30 minutes. Sprinkle with cheese; bake, uncovered, until vegetables are tender, about 10 minutes.
Per ⅔ cup: 83 cal., 5g fat (3g sat. fat), 14mg chol., 249mg sod., 5g carb. (3g sugars, 1g fiber), 5g pro.
Diabetic exchanges: 1 medium-fat meat, 1 vegetable.

GRILLED STREET CORN M

My grandmother loves Mexican food. I wanted a perfect side for her legendary tacos, and this chile-lime grilled corn turned out to be just right.
—Ashley Crainshaw, Shawnee, KS

Prep: 15 min. • **Grill:** 20 min.
Makes: 6 servings

- 6 medium ears sweet corn
- ½ cup sour cream
- ¼ cup grated Parmesan cheese
- 1 tablespoon lime juice
- ½ teaspoon chili powder
- ¼ teaspoon salt
- ⅛ teaspoon pepper

1. Carefully peel back corn husks to within 1 in. of bottoms; remove silk. Rewrap corn in husks; secure with kitchen string. Rinse corn under water, moistening husks. Grill corn, covered, over medium heat 20-25 minutes or until tender, turning often.

2. In a small bowl, mix the remaining ingredients until blended. Cut string from corn and peel back husks. Spread corn with sour cream mixture.

Per ear of corn with about 1 tablespoon sour cream mixture: 143 cal., 6g fat (3g sat. fat), 16mg chol., 180mg sod., 20g carb. (7g sugars, 2g fiber), 5g pro.
Diabetic exchanges: 1 starch, 1 fat.

BEANS, BACON & TOMATO BAKE

(PICTURED ON P. 55)

On cold winter days, I pull out the bacon, tomatoes and lima beans for a veggie-packed meal that nourishes the family.
—Karen Kumpulainen, Forest City, NC

Prep: 10 min. • **Bake:** 35 min.
Makes: 12 servings (⅔ cup each)

- 8 bacon strips, cut into 1-inch pieces
- 1 cup finely chopped onion
- ⅔ cup finely chopped celery
- ½ cup finely chopped green pepper
- 2 garlic cloves, minced
- 2 teaspoons all-purpose flour
- 2 teaspoons sugar
- 2 teaspoons salt
- ¼ teaspoon pepper
- 2 cans (14½ ounces each) diced tomatoes, undrained
- 8 cups frozen lima beans (about 42 ounces), thawed

1. Preheat oven to 325°. In a 6-qt. stockpot, cook bacon, onion, celery and green pepper over medium heat until bacon is crisp and vegetables are tender. Add garlic; cook 1 minute longer. Stir in flour, sugar, salt and pepper. Add the tomatoes. Bring mixture to a boil, stirring constantly; cook and stir 1-2 minutes or until thickened. Stir in beans.

2. Transfer to a greased 3-qt. baking dish or 13x9-in. baking pan. Bake, covered, 35-40 minutes or until beans are tender.

Per ⅔ cup: 230 cal., 8g fat (3g sat. fat), 12mg chol., 666mg sod., 30g carb. (6g sugars, 9g fiber), 11g pro.
Diabetic exchanges: 2 starch, 1½ fat.

GRILLED STREET CORN

EGGPLANT FRIES C M FAST FIX

My kids love this snack—and I like that it's healthy. Coated with Italian seasoning, Parmesan and garlic salt, these veggie sticks are broiled, not fried, so there's no guilt when you crunch into them.
—Mary Murphy, Atwater, CA

Start to Finish: 20 min.
Makes: 6 servings

- 2 large eggs
- ½ cup grated Parmesan cheese
- ½ cup toasted wheat germ
- 1 teaspoon Italian seasoning
- ¾ teaspoon garlic salt
- 1 medium eggplant (about 1¼ pounds)
  Cooking spray
- 1 cup meatless pasta sauce, warmed

1. Preheat broiler. In a shallow bowl, whisk together eggs. In another shallow bowl, mix cheese, wheat germ and seasonings.
2. Trim ends of eggplant; cut eggplant lengthwise into ½-in.-thick slices. Cut slices lengthwise into ½-in. strips. Dip eggplant in eggs, then coat with cheese mixture. Place the strips on a baking sheet coated with cooking spray.
3. Spritz eggplant with additional cooking spray. Broil 4 in. from heat 3 minutes. Turn eggplant; spritz with additional cooking spray. Broil until golden brown, for 1-2 minutes. Serve eggplant immediately with pasta sauce.
Per serving: 135 cal., 5g fat (2g sat. fat), 68mg chol., 577mg sod., 15g carb. (6g sugars, 4g fiber), 9g pro.
Diabetic exchanges: 1 medium-fat meat, 1 vegetable, ½ starch.

ASIAN RICE PILAF

ASIAN RICE PILAF FAST FIX

We love this rice pilaf. It's loaded with veggies and has a fresh hint of ginger. It pairs nicely with so many main dishes, and even the picky eaters in our family love it!
—Teri Lindquist, Gurnee, IL

Start to Finish: 30 min.
Makes: 6 servings

- 3 tablespoons butter
- ½ cup sliced carrot
- ½ cup sliced celery
- ½ cup chopped onion
- 1 cup uncooked long grain rice
- 2 cups hot water
- 2 tablespoons soy sauce
- 2 teaspoons sugar
- 2 teaspoons dried parsley flakes
- 2 teaspoons chicken bouillon granules
- ½ teaspoon ground ginger
- 2½ cups frozen peas (about 10 ounces), thawed

1. In a large saucepan, heat butter over medium-high heat; saute carrot, celery and onion until tender, 3-5 minutes. Stir in rice until coated.
2. Stir in water, soy sauce, sugar and seasonings; bring to a boil. Reduce heat; simmer, covered, until liquid is absorbed and rice is tender, about 15 minutes.
3. Gently stir in peas. Cover and heat through.
Per ¾ cup: 233 cal., 6g fat (4g sat. fat), 15mg chol., 699mg sod., 38g carb. (5g sugars, 3g fiber), 6g pro.

MARINATED MUSHROOMS & ARTICHOKES F C M

I marinate mushrooms and artichokes with fresh tarragon and thyme, and they turn out totally irresistible.
—Marcia Doyle, Pompano, FL

Prep: 15 min. + marinating
Makes: 16 servings (½ cup each)

- 2 pounds medium fresh mushrooms, halved
- 2 cans (14 ounces each) water-packed quartered artichoke hearts, drained
- 1½ cups water
- 1 cup cider vinegar
- ½ cup olive oil
- 1 bay leaf
- 1½ teaspoons salt
- 1½ teaspoons minced fresh tarragon or ½ teaspoon dried tarragon
- 1½ teaspoons minced fresh thyme or ½ teaspoon dried thyme
- 1 garlic clove, minced
- ½ teaspoon pepper
- 1 tablespoon minced fresh parsley
  Additional parsley

In a nonreactive bowl, combine first twelve ingredients. Refrigerate, covered, to allow flavors to blend, 3-4 hours. Serve with additional parsley.

Per ½ cup: 43 cal., 1g fat (0 sat. fat), 0 chol., 162mg sod., 5g carb. (0 sugars, 0 fiber), 3g pro.
Diabetic exchanges: 1 vegetable.

MARINATED MUSHROOMS & ARTICHOKES

SAUTEED SPRING VEGETABLES S C M

Fresh summer squash, asparagus and sweet red onion help usher in the flavors of the warmer months. For an Asian flavor twist, substitute soy sauce for the balsamic vinegar and reduce the added salt. Crushed red pepper flakes bring a little heat; skip if you prefer it milder.
—Billy Hensley, Mount Carmel, TN

Prep: 20 min. + marinating
Cook: 10 min.
Makes: 9 servings

- 2 medium yellow summer squash, sliced
- 1 pound fresh asparagus, trimmed and cut into 1½-inch pieces
- 1 medium zucchini, sliced
- 1 small red onion, cut into thin wedges
- 1 cup green pepper strips
- ½ cup sweet red pepper strips

MARINADE
- ¼ cup olive oil
- 2 tablespoons balsamic vinegar
- 1 tablespoon lemon juice
- 2 garlic cloves, minced
- ½ teaspoon salt
- ½ teaspoon pepper
- ⅛ to ½ teaspoon crushed red pepper flakes

1. Place the vegetables in a large bowl. In a small bowl, whisk the marinade ingredients. Pour over vegetables; toss to coat. Cover and refrigerate for up to 1 hour.

2. In a large skillet, saute the vegetable mixture in batches for 3-6 minutes or until crisp-tender.

Per ¾ cup: 82 cal., 6g fat (1g sat. fat), 0 chol., 139mg sod., 6g carb. (3g sugars, 2g fiber), 2g pro.
Diabetic exchanges: 1 vegetable, 1 fat.

PORTOBELLO & GREEN BEAN SAUTE S C FAST FIX

The key to delectable veggies is simplicity: everyday ingredients combined to be fantastic. If you like to add salt to taste, be sure to not add too much, as the bouillon granules do the job. If baby portobello mushrooms are not available, white button mushrooms work well.
—Elaine Shoemake, Sedgewickville, MO

Start to Finish: 20 min.
Makes: 10 servings

- 1   pound fresh green beans, trimmed and halved
- 1   pound baby portobello mushrooms, quartered
- 1   medium onion, finely chopped
- ¼   cup butter, cubed
- 2   garlic cloves, minced
- 1   teaspoon chicken bouillon granules
- 4   plum tomatoes, peeled and chopped
- 1   teaspoon dried marjoram
- ¼   teaspoon pepper
- ¼   cup minced fresh parsley

1. Place beans in a large saucepan and cover with water; bring to a boil. Cover and cook for 3-5 minutes or until beans are crisp-tender.
2. Meanwhile, in a large skillet, saute mushrooms and onion in butter until tender. Add garlic and bouillon; cook 1 minute longer. Drain green beans; add to skillet and toss to coat. Remove from the heat. Stir in the tomatoes, marjoram and pepper. Sprinkle with parsley.

Per ¾ cup: 77 cal., 5g fat (3g sat. fat), 12mg chol., 123mg sod., 8g carb. (3g sugars, 3g fiber), 3g pro.
Diabetic exchanges: 1 vegetable, 1 fat.

LIME & SESAME GRILLED EGGPLANT F C M FAST FIX

I fell in love with eggplant when I lived in Greece. My recipe's seasonings have an Asian flair, but to me this dish is still reminiscent of Greek food.
—Allyson Meyler, Greensboro, NC

Start to Finish: 20 min.
Makes: 6 servings

- 3   tablespoons lime juice
- 1   tablespoon sesame oil

LIME & SESAME GRILLED EGGPLANT

- 1½   teaspoons reduced-sodium soy sauce
- 1   garlic clove, minced
- ½   teaspoon grated fresh gingerroot or ¼ teaspoon ground ginger
- ½   teaspoon salt
- ⅛   teaspoon pepper
- 1   medium eggplant (1¼ pounds), cut lengthwise into ½-inch slices
- 2   teaspoons honey
- ⅛   teaspoon crushed red pepper flakes
       Thinly sliced green onion and sesame seeds

1. In a small bowl, whisk the first seven ingredients until blended; brush about 2 tablespoons juice mixture over both sides of eggplant slices. Grill, covered, over medium heat 4-6 minutes on each side or until tender.
2. Transfer eggplant to a serving plate. Stir honey and pepper flakes into the remaining juice mixture; drizzle over eggplant. Sprinkle with green onion and sesame seeds.

Per serving: 50 cal., 2g fat (0 sat. fat), 0 chol., 246mg sod., 7g carb. (4g sugars, 2g fiber), 1g pro.
Diabetic exchanges: 1 vegetable, ½ fat.

ROASTED BALSAMIC RED POTATOES M

When I found a potato recipe that called for vinegar, I was intrigued. I didn't have all the ingredients on hand, so I had to improvise with Italian seasoning and balsamic vinegar. It turned out great!
—Lisa Varner, El Paso, TX

Prep: 10 min. • **Bake:** 30 min.
Makes: 6 servings

- 2   pounds small red potatoes, cut into wedges
- 2   tablespoons olive oil
- ¾   teaspoon garlic pepper blend
- ½   teaspoon Italian seasoning
- ¼   teaspoon salt
- ¼   cup balsamic vinegar

1. Preheat oven to 425°. Toss potatoes with the oil and seasonings; spread in a 15x10x1-in. pan.
2. Roast 25 minutes, stirring halfway. Drizzle with vinegar; roast until potatoes are tender, 5-10 minutes.

Per ¾ cup: 159 cal., 5g fat (1g sat. fat), 0 chol., 143mg sod., 27g carb. (4g sugars, 3g fiber), 3g pro.
Diabetic exchanges: 2 starch, 1 fat.

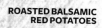

GOOD
MORNINGS

"I work at a farmers market, and honey blueberry jam is my top seller. You've gotta taste it with fresh goat cheese and toasted candied pecans."
—Krystal Wertman, Humble, TX

Asparagus Frittata (p. 85) **Fruit-Filled French Toast Wraps** (p. 87) **Blueberry Cornmeal Muffins** (p. 80)
Chunky Cherry & Peach Preserves (p. 79) **Honey Blueberry Cobbler Jam** (p. 84) **Brunch Enchiladas** (p. 78)

LEMON CHIA SEED
PARFAITS

LEMON CHIA SEED PARFAITS
S M FAST FIX

*These bright and tangy
parfaits start the day on a
healthy note, but they'll
double as a light and
refreshing dessert.*
—Crystal Schlueter, Babbitt, MN

Start to Finish: 15 min.
Makes: 4 servings

- 2 **cups reduced-fat plain Greek yogurt**
- ¼ **cup agave nectar or honey**
- 2 **tablespoons lemon juice**
- 2 **teaspoons grated lemon peel**
- 2 **tablespoons chia seeds or ground flaxseed**
- 1 **teaspoon vanilla extract**
- 1 **cup fresh raspberries**
- 1 **cup fresh blueberries**

Combine the first six ingredients. Layer
half of the yogurt mixture into four small
parfait glasses or custard cups. Top with
half of the berries. Repeat layers.
Per parfait: 214 cal., 4g fat (2g sat. fat),
7mg chol., 48mg sod., 33g carb. (26g
sugars, 5g fiber), 13g pro.
Diabetic exchanges: 1½ starch, ½ fruit,
½ reduced-fat milk.

BRUNCH ENCHILADAS
M FAST FIX

(PICTURED ON P. 77)

*If you want something a little different
for brunch, try this one—folks love it!*
—Linda Braun, Park Ridge, IL

Start to Finish: 30 min.
Makes: 8 servings

- 8 **hard-boiled large eggs, chopped**
- 1 **can (8¼ ounces) cream-style corn**
- ⅔ **cup shredded cheddar cheese**
- 1 **can (4 ounces) chopped green chilies**
- 2 **teaspoons taco seasoning**
- ¼ **teaspoon salt**
- 8 **corn tortillas, warmed**
- 1 **bottle (8 ounces) mild taco sauce**
  Sour cream, optional

1. Preheat oven to 350°. Combine the
first six ingredients; spoon ½ cup down
the center of each tortilla. Roll up tightly.
Place, seam side down, in a greased
13x9-in. baking dish. Top with taco sauce.
2. Bake, uncovered, for 15 minutes or
until heated through. Serve with sour
cream if desired.
Per enchilada: 208 cal., 9g fat (4g sat.
fat), 222mg chol., 600mg sod., 22g carb.
(3g sugars, 2g fiber), 11g pro.
Diabetic exchanges: 1½ starch,
1 medium-fat meat.

CINNAMON APPLE PANCAKES
M FAST FIX ▶

My family loves these fluffy and spicy apple pancakes. And best of all, they're sweet enough to enjoy even without any syrup.
—Kim McConnell, Tulsa, OK

Start to Finish: 25 min.
Makes: 6 servings

- 2 **cups whole wheat flour**
- 4 **teaspoons baking powder**
- 1 **teaspoon ground cinnamon**
- ½ **teaspoon salt**
- 2 **large eggs**
- 2 **cups fat-free milk**
- 2 **tablespoons honey**
- 1 **tablespoon canola oil**
- 1 **medium apple, chopped**

1. In a bowl, whisk together first four ingredients. In another bowl, whisk together eggs, milk, honey and oil; add to dry ingredients, stirring just until moistened. Stir in apple.

2. Preheat a lightly greased griddle over medium heat. Pour batter by ⅓ cupfuls onto griddle; cook until bubbles on the top begin to pop and the bottoms are golden brown.

Per 2 pancakes: 241 cal., 5g fat (1g sat. fat), 64mg chol., 576mg sod., 42g carb. (12g sugars, 5g fiber), 10g pro.
Diabetic exchanges: 3 starch, 1 lean meat, ½ fat.

HEALTH TIP According to a study from the Harvard School of Public Health, people who ate the most whole grains, compared to those who ate little or no whole grains, lived longer and had a lower risk of cancer and heart disease.

CINNAMON APPLE PANCAKES

CHUNKY CHERRY & PEACH PRESERVES **F S C M**
(PICTURED ON P. 76)

Out of all the jams I make, this is my grandmother's favorite. She eagerly waits for late June to come because she knows I'll put up as many batches as I can while peaches and cherries are at their peak.
—Amy Seiger, McLoud, OK

Prep: 40 min. • **Process:** 10 min.
Makes: 7 half-pints

- 4 **cups chopped peeled fresh peaches (about 7 medium)**
- 4 **cups chopped pitted fresh tart cherries (about 2 pounds)**
- 2 **tablespoons lemon juice**
- 1 **package (1¾ ounces) pectin for lower sugar recipes**
- 3 **cups sugar**
- ¼ **teaspoon almond extract**

1. In a Dutch oven, combine peaches, cherries and lemon juice; stir in pectin. Bring to a full rolling boil over high heat, stirring constantly. Stir in sugar; return to a full rolling boil. Boil and stir 1 minute. Stir in extract.

2. Remove from heat; skim off foam. Ladle hot mixture into seven hot half-pint jars, leaving ¼-in. headspace. Remove air bubbles and adjust headspace, if necessary, by adding hot mixture. Wipe rims. Center lids on jars; screw on bands until fingertip tight.

3. Place jars into canner with simmering water, ensuring they are completely covered with water. Bring to a boil; process for 10 minutes. Remove jars and cool.

Note: The processing time listed is for altitudes of 1,000 feet or less. Add 1 minute to the processing time for each 1,000 feet of additional altitude.

Per 2 tablespoons: 53 cal., 0 fat (0 sat. fat), 0 chol., 10mg sod., 13g carb. (13g sugars, 0 fiber), 0 pro.
Diabetic exchanges: 1 starch.

BLUEBERRY CORNMEAL MUFFINS Ⓜ
(PICTURED ON P. 77)

When I bring treats to work, I try to keep them on the healthful side—which this moist muffin is. The cornmeal adds an interesting texture.
—Elizabeth Bergeron, Denver, CO

Prep: 20 min. • **Bake:** 20 min.
Makes: 1 dozen

- 1 cup yellow cornmeal
- ½ cup all-purpose flour
- ½ cup whole wheat flour
- ½ cup plus 1½ teaspoons sugar, divided
- 4 teaspoons baking powder
- ½ teaspoon salt
- 2 large eggs
- ¾ cup fat-free milk
- ¼ cup canola oil
- 1 teaspoon vanilla extract
- 2 cups fresh or frozen blueberries

1. Preheat oven to 350°. In a small bowl, combine cornmeal, the flours, ½ cup sugar, baking powder and salt. In another bowl, combine the eggs, milk, oil and vanilla. Stir into dry ingredients just until moistened. Fold in blueberries.
2. Fill greased muffin cups three-fourths full; sprinkle with the remaining sugar. Bake for 18-22 minutes or until a toothpick inserted in muffin comes out clean. Cool for 5 minutes before removing from pan to a wire rack. Serve warm.
Note: If using frozen blueberries, use without thawing to avoid discoloring the batter.
Per muffin: 185 cal., 6g fat (1g sat. fat), 36mg chol., 251mg sod., 30g carb. (12g sugars, 2g fiber), 4g pro.
Diabetic exchanges: 2 starch, 1 fat.

GRUYERE & PROSCIUTTO STRATA

GRUYERE & PROSCIUTTO STRATA

Prosciutto, sweet onions and Gruyere combine for a perfect make-ahead brunch dish, and there are never any leftovers.
—Patti Lavell, Islamorada, FL

Prep: 15 min. + chilling • **Bake:** 35 min.
Makes: 9 servings

- 2 teaspoons canola oil
- 4 ounces thin slices prosciutto, chopped
- 2 large sweet onions, chopped (4 cups)
- 1 carton (8 ounces) egg substitute
- 2½ cups 2% milk
- ¼ teaspoon ground mustard
- ⅛ teaspoon pepper
- 8 cups cubed French bread
- 1½ cups shredded Gruyere or Swiss cheese, divided

1. In a large skillet, heat oil over medium-high heat. Add prosciutto; cook and stir until crisp. Remove from pan with a slotted spoon. Add onions to the same pan; cook and stir until tender.
2. In a large bowl, whisk egg substitute, milk, mustard and pepper. Stir in bread and onions. Reserve 2 tablespoons cooked prosciutto for topping; stir remaining prosciutto into bread mixture.
3. Transfer half of the mixture to a greased 13x9-in. baking dish; sprinkle with half of the cheese. Top with remaining bread mixture. Separately cover and refrigerate the strata and the reserved prosciutto overnight.
4. Preheat oven to 350°. Remove strata from refrigerator while oven heats. Bake, uncovered, 20 minutes. Sprinkle with remaining cheese; top with the reserved prosciutto. Bake 15-20 minutes longer or until a knife inserted in the center comes out clean. Let stand for 5-10 minutes before serving.
Per cup: 267 cal., 11g fat (5g sat. fat), 37mg chol., 609mg sod., 25g carb. (9g sugars, 1g fiber), 17g pro.
Diabetic exchanges: 2 medium-fat meat, 1½ starch, 1 fat.

BERRY DELICIOUS SMOOTHIES F S M FAST FIX

My son and I make this fun, summery smoothie. It's full of wholesome fruit.
—Elizabeth Stewart, Crab Orchard, WV

Start to Finish: 10 min.
Makes: 4 servings

- 1½ cups fat-free strawberry Greek yogurt
- ¾ cup acai mixed berry V8 juice blend
- 1 cup frozen unsweetened strawberries
- 1 cup frozen unsweetened blueberries
- ½ cup frozen unsweetened raspberries
- ½ cup frozen unsweetened blackberries
- ½ cup frozen pitted dark sweet cherries
- ¼ cup wheat bran
- 1 teaspoon ground flaxseed

In a blender, combine all the ingredients; cover and process for 30 seconds or until smooth. Pour into chilled glasses and serve immediately.

Per cup: 167 cal., 1g fat (0 sat. fat), 0 chol., 47mg sod., 33g carb. (26g sugars, 6g fiber), 9g pro.
Diabetic exchanges: 1 starch, 1 fat-free milk.

ALMOND-CHAI GRANOLA S M

This is great to eat with milk or yogurt—or to snack on by the handful.
—Rachel Preus Marshall, MI

Prep: 20 min. • **Bake:** 1 hour 20 min.
Makes: 8 cups

- 2 chai tea bags
- ¼ cup boiling water
- 3 cups quick-cooking oats
- 2 cups almonds, coarsely chopped
- 1 cup sweetened shredded coconut
- ½ cup honey
- ¼ cup olive oil
- ⅓ cup sugar
- 2 teaspoons vanilla extract
- ¾ teaspoon salt
- ¾ teaspoon ground cinnamon
- ¾ teaspoon ground nutmeg
- ¼ teaspoon ground cardamom

1. Preheat oven to 250°. Steep tea bags in boiling water 5 minutes. Meanwhile, combine oats, almonds and coconut. Discard tea bags; stir the remaining ingredients into tea. Pour the tea mixture over the oat mixture; mix well to coat.
2. Spread evenly in a greased 15x10-in. rimmed pan. Bake until golden brown, stirring every 20 minutes, about 1¼ hours. Cool completely without stirring; store in an airtight container.

Per ½ cup: 272 cal., 16g fat (3g sat. fat), 0 chol., 130mg sod., 29g carb. (16g sugars, 4g fiber), 6g pro.
Diabetic exchanges: 3 fat, 2 starch.

ALMOND-CHAI GRANOLA

MINTY PINEAPPLE
FRUIT SALAD

MINTY PINEAPPLE FRUIT SALAD F S M FAST FIX

Fresh mint adds bright flavor to this easy, quick and low-fat pineapple salad. Give it a berry twist by using blueberries and raspberries in place of the grapes, but don't forget the secret dressing ingredient—lemonade!
—Janie Colle, Hutchinson, KS

Start to Finish: 15 min.
Makes: 8 servings

- 4 cups cubed fresh pineapple
- 2 cups sliced fresh strawberries
- 1 cup green grapes
- 3 tablespoons thawed lemonade concentrate
- 2 tablespoons honey
- 1 tablespoon minced fresh mint

Place fruit in a large bowl. In another bowl, mix remaining ingredients; stir gently into fruit. Refrigerate, covered, until serving.

Per ¾ cup: 99 cal., 0 fat (0 sat. fat), 0 chol., 4mg sod., 26g carb. (21g sugars, 2g fiber), 1g pro.
Diabetic exchanges: 1½ fruit, ½ starch.

FLORENCE-INSPIRED SOUFFLE

Light, beautiful and absolutely delicious, this souffle is sure to impress your brunch guests every time you serve it. They will be eager to grab their forks and dig in to this little taste of Italy.
—Jenny Flake, Newport Beach, CA

Prep: 35 min. • **Bake:** 35 min.
Makes: 4 servings

- 6 large egg whites
- ¾ cup onion and garlic salad croutons
- 1 small onion, finely chopped
- ¼ cup finely chopped sweet red pepper
- 2 ounces thinly sliced prosciutto, chopped
- 2 teaspoons olive oil
- 2 cups fresh baby spinach
- 1 garlic clove, minced
- ⅓ cup all-purpose flour
- ½ teaspoon salt
- ¼ teaspoon pepper
- 1¼ cups fat-free milk
- 1 large egg yolk, lightly beaten
- ¼ teaspoon cream of tartar
- ¼ cup shredded Italian cheese blend

1. Place egg whites in a large bowl; let stand at room temperature for 30 minutes.
2. In a food processor, process croutons until ground. Sprinkle evenly onto the bottom and 1 in. up the sides of a greased 2-qt. souffle dish; set aside.
3. In a large saucepan, saute the onion, red pepper and prosciutto in oil for 3-5 minutes or until the vegetables are crisp-tender. Add spinach and garlic; cook just until spinach is wilted. Stir in flour, salt and pepper until blended. Gradually add milk. Bring to a boil; cook and stir for 2 minutes or until thickened.
4. Transfer to a large bowl. Stir a small amount of the hot mixture into egg yolk; return all to the bowl, stirring constantly. Cool slightly.
5. Add cream of tartar to egg whites; beat until stiff peaks form. Fold into vegetable mixture. Transfer to the prepared dish; sprinkle with cheese.
6. Bake at 350° for 35-40 minutes or until top is puffed and center appears set. Serve immediately.

Per serving: 223 cal., 9g fat (3g sat. fat), 73mg chol., 843mg sod., 20g carb. (6g sugars, 2g fiber), 16g pro.
Diabetic exchanges: 2 lean meat, 1½ starch, ½ fat.

FLORENCE-INSPIRED SOUFFLE

HONEY BLUEBERRY COBBLER JAM
F S C M FAST FIX ▸
(PICTURED ON P. 77)

I work at a farmers market, and honey-blueberry jam is my top seller. You've gotta taste it with fresh goat cheese and toasted candied pecans.
—Krystal Wertman, Humble, TX

Start to Finish: 20 min.
Makes: 5 cups

- 5 cups fresh or frozen blueberries, thawed
- 1 cup apple juice
- 1 package (1¾ ounces) pectin for lower sugar recipes
- 1 cup honey
- ½ teaspoon ground nutmeg
- ¼ teaspoon ground cinnamon
- 1 teaspoon vanilla extract

1. Rinse five 1-cup plastic or freezer-safe containers and lids with boiling water. Dry thoroughly.
2. Place blueberries in a large saucepan; mash blueberries. Stir in juice and pectin. Bring to a full rolling boil over high heat, stirring constantly. Stir in honey, nutmeg and cinnamon; return to a full rolling boil. Boil and stir 1 minute. Remove from heat; stir in vanilla.
3. Immediately fill all containers to within ½ in. of tops. Wipe off the top edges of containers; immediately cover with lids. Let stand at room temperature 24 hours.
4. Jam is now ready to use. Refrigerate for up to 2 weeks. Or, freeze for up to 12 months; thaw frozen jam in the refrigerator before serving.
Per 2 tablespoons: 39 cal., 0 fat (0 sat. fat), 0 chol., 13mg sod., 10g carb. (9g sugars, 0 fiber), 0 pro.
Diabetic exchanges: ½ starch.

DUTCH BABY PANCAKE WITH STRAWBERRY-ALMOND COMPOTE

DUTCH BABY PANCAKE WITH STRAWBERRY-ALMOND COMPOTE **M**

Pannekoeken, or Dutch baked pancakes, are a treat in my husband's family. You can also try this recipe with vanilla extract, blueberries and lemon peel.
—Jennifer Beckman, Falls Church, VA

Prep: 15 min. • **Bake:** 20 min.
Makes: 6 servings (3 cups topping)

- 2 tablespoons butter
- 4 large eggs
- ⅔ cup 2% milk
- 2 tablespoons grated orange peel
- ½ teaspoon almond extract
- ⅔ cup all-purpose flour
- 2 tablespoons sugar
- ½ teaspoon kosher salt

TOPPING
- 1 pound fresh strawberries, hulled and quartered
- ½ cup slivered almonds, toasted
- 2 tablespoons orange juice
- 1 tablespoon sugar

1. Preheat oven to 400°. Place butter in a 9-in. pie plate. Place in oven for 4-5 minutes or until butter is melted; carefully swirl to coat evenly.
2. Meanwhile, in a large bowl, whisk eggs, milk, orange peel and extract until blended. Whisk in flour, sugar and salt. Pour into the hot pie plate. Bake for 20-25 minutes or until puffed and the sides are golden brown and crisp.
3. In a small bowl, combine the topping ingredients. Remove pancake from oven; serve immediately with topping.
Note: To toast nuts, bake in a shallow pan in a 350° oven for 5-10 minutes or cook in a skillet over low heat until lightly browned, stirring occasionally.
Per slice with ½ cup topping: 252 cal., 13g fat (4g sat. fat), 153mg chol., 245mg sod., 27g carb. (13g sugars, 3g fiber), 9g pro.
Diabetic exchanges: 1½ fat, 1 starch, 1 medium-fat meat, 1 fruit.

MEDITERRANEAN BROCCOLI & CHEESE OMELET

C M FAST FIX

My Italian mother-in-law taught me to make this omelet years ago. She would make it for breakfast, lunch or dinner and eat it on Italian bread.
—Mary Licata, Pembroke Pines, FL

Start to Finish: 30 min.
Makes: 4 servings

- 2½ cups fresh broccoli florets
- 6 large eggs
- ¼ cup 2% milk
- ½ teaspoon salt
- ¼ teaspoon pepper
- ⅓ cup grated Romano cheese
- ⅓ cup sliced pitted Greek olives
- 1 tablespoon olive oil

Shaved Romano cheese and minced fresh parsley

1. Preheat broiler. In a large saucepan, place steamer basket over 1 in. of water. Place broccoli in basket. Bring water to a boil. Reduce heat to a simmer; steam, covered, 4-6 minutes or until crisp-tender.
2. In a large bowl, whisk eggs, milk, salt and pepper. Stir in cooked broccoli, grated cheese and olives. In a 10-in. ovenproof skillet, heat oil over medium heat; pour in the egg mixture. Cook, uncovered, for 4-6 minutes or until nearly set.
3. Broil 3-4 in. from heat 2-4 minutes or until eggs are completely set. Let stand 5 minutes. Cut into wedges. Sprinkle with shaved cheese and parsley.
Per wedge: 229 cal., 17g fat (5g sat. fat), 290mg chol., 775mg sod., 5g carb. (1g sugars, 1g fiber), 15g pro.

ASPARAGUS FRITTATA

C M FAST FIX

(PICTURED ON P. 76)

You would never guess that egg substitute is used in this fun variation on the classic frittata. I loaded it with fresh asparagus in honor of springtime.
—James Bates, Hermiston, OR

Start to Finish: 25 min.
Makes: 4 servings

- ⅔ pound fresh asparagus, trimmed and cut into 1-inch pieces
- 1½ cups egg substitute
- 5 tablespoons shredded Parmesan cheese, divided
- ¼ teaspoon salt
- ⅛ teaspoon pepper
- 2 teaspoons olive oil
- 1 medium onion, chopped
- 2 tablespoons minced fresh parsley
- ¼ cup shredded reduced-fat cheddar cheese

1. Preheat broiler. In a large saucepan, bring 4 cups water to a boil. Add the asparagus; cook, uncovered, 2-4 minutes or just until crisp-tender. Drain asparagus and immediately drop into ice water. Drain and pat dry.
2. In a small bowl, whisk egg substitute, 3 tablespoons Parmesan cheese, salt and pepper.
3. In a 10-in. ovenproof skillet, heat oil over medium-high heat. Add onion; cook and stir until tender. Stir in asparagus and parsley. Pour in egg mixture. Reduce heat to medium; cook, covered, 8-10 minutes or until eggs are nearly set. Uncover; sprinkle with remaining Parmesan cheese.
4. Broil 5-6 in. from heat 2-3 minutes or until eggs are completely set. Sprinkle with cheddar cheese. Cut into quarters.
Per piece: 134 cal., 6g fat (2g sat. fat), 10mg chol., 480mg sod., 6g carb. (3g sugars, 1g fiber), 15g pro.
Diabetic exchanges: 2 lean meat, 1 vegetable, ½ fat.

MEDITERRANEAN BROCCOLI & CHEESE OMELET

GARDEN FRITTATA C M

I created this dish one day to use up some fresh yellow squash, zucchini and tomato. It's so easy to make because you don't have to make a crust. Give it different twists by trying it with whatever veggies you have on hand.

—Catherine Michel, St. Peters, MO

Prep: 25 min. • **Bake:** 45 min. + standing
Makes: 6 servings

- 1 small yellow summer squash, thinly sliced
- 1 small zucchini, thinly sliced
- 1 small onion, chopped
- 1 cup shredded part-skim mozzarella cheese
- 1 medium tomato, sliced
- ¼ cup crumbled feta cheese
- 4 large eggs
- 1 cup fat-free milk
- 2 tablespoons minced fresh basil
- 1 garlic clove, minced
- ½ teaspoon salt
- ¼ teaspoon pepper
- ¼ cup shredded Parmesan cheese

1. In a microwave-safe bowl, combine the squash, zucchini and onion. Cover and microwave on high for 7-9 minutes or until the vegetables are tender; drain well.

2. Transfer to a 9-in. pie plate coated with cooking spray. Top with the mozzarella, tomato and feta cheese.

3. In a large bowl, whisk the eggs, milk, basil, garlic, salt and pepper; pour over the cheese and tomato layer. Sprinkle with Parmesan cheese.

4. Bake, uncovered, at 375° for 45-50 minutes or until a knife inserted in the center comes out clean. Let stand for 10 minutes before serving.

Per piece: 161 cal., 9g fat (4g sat. fat), 142mg chol., 494mg sod., 7g carb. (5g sugars, 1g fiber), 13g pro.
Diabetic exchanges: 2 medium-fat meat, 1 vegetable.

ORANGE BANANA NUT BREAD S M

I like this recipe because the orange juice gives the banana bread such a distinctive and unusual flavor. The loaf stays tender even after it's been frozen.

—Barbara Roethlisberger, Shepherd, MI

Prep: 15 min. • **Bake:** 50 min. + cooling
Makes: 2 loaves

- 1½ cups sugar
- 3 tablespoons canola oil
- 2 large eggs
- 3 medium ripe bananas, mashed (about 1¼ cups)
- ¾ cup orange juice
- 3 cups all-purpose flour
- 1½ teaspoons baking powder
- 1½ teaspoons baking soda
- ½ teaspoon salt
- 1 cup chopped walnuts

1. Preheat oven to 325°. Combine sugar, oil and eggs; mix well. Stir in bananas and orange juice. Combine the dry ingredients; add to the banana mixture, beating just until moistened. Stir in walnuts. Pour into two greased 8x4-in. loaf pans.

2. Bake for 50-60 minutes or until a toothpick inserted in the center comes out clean. Cool for 10 minutes; remove from pans to a wire rack to cool completely.

Freeze option: Securely wrap and freeze cooled loaves in plastic wrap and foil. To use, thaw at room temperature.

Per slice: 131 cal., 4g fat (0 sat. fat), 13mg chol., 119mg sod., 22g carb. (12g sugars, 1g fiber), 3g pro.

FRUIT-FILLED FRENCH TOAST WRAPS M FAST FIX ▶

(PICTURED ON P. 76)

If you need a lovely dish for breakfast or brunch, these tortilla wraps made like French toast are full of fruity goodness and granola.

—Dawn Jarvis, Breckenridge, MN

Start to Finish: 25 min.
Makes: 2 servings

- ¾ cup (6 ounces) vanilla yogurt
- ⅔ cup sliced ripe banana
- 1 large egg
- ¼ cup 2% milk
- 1 teaspoon ground cinnamon
- ½ teaspoon ground nutmeg
- 2 whole wheat tortillas (8 inches)
- 2 teaspoons butter
- ⅔ cup sliced fresh strawberries
- ⅔ cup fresh blueberries
- ¼ cup granola
  Optional toppings: additional vanilla yogurt, strawberries, blueberries and granola

1. In a small bowl, combine yogurt and banana. In a shallow bowl, whisk egg, milk, cinnamon and nutmeg. Dip both sides of each tortilla in egg mixture. In a skillet, heat butter over medium-high heat. Add tortilla; cook for 1-2 minutes on each side or until golden brown.

2. Spoon yogurt mixture down center of tortillas; top with strawberries, blueberries and granola. Roll up each tortilla and, if desired, top with additional yogurt, berries and granola.

Per wrap: 399 cal., 10g fat (4g sat. fat), 72mg chol., 256mg sod., 68g carb. (29g sugars, 9g fiber), 15g pro.

✱
TEST KITCHEN TIP
When buying strawberries, look for berries that are shiny, firm and very fragrant. A strawberry should be almost completely red, though some whiteness near the leafy cap is acceptable.

ORANGE BANANA NUT BREAD

BLUEBERRY CANTALOUPE SALAD F S M FAST FIX

Add a fresh touch to any meal with these cute cups. The simple citrus dressing really jazzes up the fruit.
—R. Jean Rand, Edina, MN

Start to Finish: 10 min.
Makes: 4 servings

- ¾ cup (6 ounces) orange yogurt
- 1½ teaspoons lemon juice
- ¾ teaspoon poppy seeds
- ½ teaspoon grated orange peel
- 2 cups diced cantaloupe
- 1 cup fresh blueberries

In a small bowl, mix yogurt, lemon juice, poppy seeds and orange peel. To serve, divide cantaloupe and blueberries among four dishes; top with yogurt mixture.

Per ¾ cup with 3 tablespoons dressing: 76 cal., 1g fat (0 sat. fat), 1mg chol., 24mg sod., 17g carb. (15g sugars, 1g fiber), 2g pro.
Diabetic exchanges: 1 fruit.

RASPBERRY-ALMOND
COFFEE CAKE

RASPBERRY-ALMOND COFFEE CAKE M

This fruity coffee cake is an awesome brunch treat. If you can't find raspberries, try blueberries or strawberries instead. I sometimes add a glaze on top.
—Lisa Varner, El Paso, TX

Prep: 20 min. • **Bake:** 30 min. + cooling
Makes: 15 servings

- 2 cups all-purpose flour
- ¾ cup sugar
- ¼ cup packed brown sugar
- 1 teaspoon baking powder
- ½ teaspoon baking soda
- ½ teaspoon salt
- 2 large eggs
- 1 cup buttermilk
- ⅓ cup unsweetened applesauce
- ⅓ cup butter, melted
- ½ teaspoon almond extract
- 2 cups fresh or frozen unsweetened raspberries

TOPPING
- ⅔ cup sliced almonds
- ½ cup packed brown sugar
- 1 teaspoon ground cinnamon

1. Preheat oven to 350°. In a large bowl, whisk the first six ingredients. In another bowl, whisk eggs, buttermilk, applesauce, butter and extract; stir into dry ingredients just until moistened. Gently fold in the raspberries.
2. Transfer batter to a 13x9-in. baking pan coated with cooking spray. In a small bowl, mix topping ingredients; sprinkle over batter. Bake for 30-35 minutes or until a toothpick inserted in center comes out clean. Cool 10 minutes in pan on a wire rack. Serve warm.

Per piece: 229 cal., 7g fat (3g sat. fat), 40mg chol., 207mg sod., 38g carb. (23g sugars, 2g fiber), 4g pro.

SWEET ONION PIE M

Loaded with sweet onions, this creamy pie makes a scrumptious addition to the brunch buffet. By using less butter to cook the onions and substituting lighter ingredients, I cut calories and fat from the tasty dish.
—Barbara Reese, Catawissa, PA

Prep: 35 min. • **Bake:** 30 min.
Makes: 8 servings

2 sweet onions, halved and sliced
1 tablespoon butter
1 frozen deep-dish pie shell
1 cup egg substitute
1 cup fat-free evaporated milk
1 teaspoon salt
¼ teaspoon pepper

1. Preheat oven to 450°. In a large nonstick skillet, cook onions in butter over medium-low heat until very tender, 30 minutes. Line unpricked pastry shell with a double thickness of heavy-duty foil.

2. Bake for 6 minutes. Remove foil; cool on a wire rack. Reduce heat to 425°.
3. Spoon onions into pastry shell. In a small bowl, whisk the egg substitute, milk, salt and pepper; pour over onions. Bake until a knife inserted in the center comes out clean, 30-35 minutes. Let stand for 5-10 minutes before cutting.
Per piece: 169 cal., 7g fat (2g sat. fat), 5mg chol., 487mg sod., 21g carb. (8g sugars, 1g fiber), 7g pro.
Diabetic exchanges: 1 starch, 1 lean meat, 1 fat.

SOFT OATMEAL BREAD F M

My husband loves to make this bread, with its mild oat taste and soft texture. Be sure to try slices toasted up for breakfast, too.
—Nancy Montgomery, Plainwell, MI

Prep: 10 min. • **Bake:** 3 hours
Makes: 1 loaf (2 pounds, 20 slices)

1½ cups water (70° to 80°)
¼ cup canola oil
1 teaspoon lemon juice
¼ cup sugar
2 teaspoons salt
3 cups all-purpose flour
1½ cups quick-cooking oats
2½ teaspoons active dry yeast

1. In bread machine pan, place all ingredients in order suggested by manufacturer. Select the basic bread setting. Choose crust color and loaf size if available.
2. Bake according to bread machine directions (check dough after 5 minutes of mixing; add 1-2 tablespoons of water or flour if needed).
Freeze option: Securely wrap and freeze cooled loaf in foil and place in resealable plastic freezer bag. To use, thaw at room temperature.
Per slice: 127 cal., 3g fat (0 sat. fat), 0 chol., 237mg sod., 21g carb. (3g sugars, 1g fiber), 3g pro.

SWEET ONION PIE

WHOLE WHEAT BUTTERHORNS

WHOLE WHEAT BUTTERHORNS M

I take these rolls to potluck suppers, and I often serve them to guests—I always get many requests for the recipe. They're a favorite when it's just family at home, too. The rolls don't take long to make, and they freeze very well for future use.
—Mary Jane Mullins, Livonia, MO

Prep: 30 min. + rising • **Bake:** 10 min.
Makes: 24 rolls

- 2¾ cups all-purpose flour
- 2 packages (¼ ounce each) active dry yeast
- 1¾ cups water
- ⅓ cup packed brown sugar
- ½ cup butter, divided
- 2 tablespoons honey
- 2 teaspoons salt
- 2 cups whole wheat flour

1. In a large bowl, combine 1½ cups all-purpose flour and yeast.
2. Heat the water, brown sugar, 3 tablespoons butter, honey and salt to 120°-130°; add to flour mixture. Beat on low for 30 seconds with electric mixer; increase speed to high and continue beating 3 minutes. Stir in whole wheat flour and enough of the remaining all-purpose flour to form a soft dough.
3. Turn out onto a lightly floured surface and knead until smooth and elastic, about 6-8 minutes. Place in a greased bowl, turning once to grease the top. Cover with plastic wrap and let rise in a warm place until doubled, about 1½ hours. Punch dough down and divide into thirds. Shape each into a ball, cover and let rest 10 minutes.
4. On a lightly floured surface, roll the balls into three 12-in. circles. Cut each circle into eight wedges. Roll wedges into crescent shapes, starting at the wide end. Place on greased baking sheets. Cover and let rise in a warm place until doubled, about 1 hour. Melt remaining butter and brush some on each crescent.
5. Bake at 400° for 10-15 minutes or until golden brown. Brush again with butter while hot.

Per butterhorn: 137 cal., 4g fat (2g sat. fat), 10mg chol., 237mg sod., 23g carb. (5g sugars, 2g fiber), 3g pro.

SPICED BLUEBERRY QUINOA M

I took up eating quinoa when I found out how much protein it has. This is a really an easy dish to experiment with; my first version of the recipe was made with shredded apples instead of blueberries. It's just as delicious either way!
—Shannon Copley, Upper Arlington, OH

Prep: 10 min. • **Cook:** 30 min.
Makes: 2 servings

- ½ cup quinoa, rinsed and well drained
- 2 cups unsweetened almond milk
- 2 tablespoons honey
- ½ teaspoon ground cinnamon
- ¼ teaspoon salt
- 1 cup fresh or frozen blueberries, thawed
- ¼ teaspoon vanilla extract
- 2 tablespoons chopped almonds, toasted

1. In a small saucepan, cook and stir quinoa over medium heat 5-7 minutes or until lightly toasted. Stir in almond milk, honey, cinnamon and salt; bring to a boil. Reduce heat; simmer, uncovered, 20-25 minutes or until quinoa is tender and liquid is almost absorbed, stirring occasionally.
2. Remove from heat; stir in blueberries and vanilla. Sprinkle with almonds.

Per cup: 352 cal., 10g fat (1g sat. fat), 0 chol., 479mg sod., 59g carb. (25g sugars, 7g fiber), 9g pro.

HEALTH TIP Quinoa is a good source of trace minerals—specifically manganese and copper—that are important in turning carb. into energy.

SPICED BLUEBERRY QUINOA

BUTTERMILK BUCKWHEAT PANCAKES M FAST FIX ▶

This flapjack recipe uses buckwheat flour instead of the wheat-based variety. The light and tender pancakes offer a nutty flavor and hearty texture.
—*Taste of Home* Test Kitchen

Start to Finish: 25 min.
Makes: 4 servings

- 1 cup buckwheat flour
- 2 tablespoons brown sugar
- 1 teaspoon baking powder
- ½ teaspoon baking soda
- ½ teaspoon salt
- ⅛ teaspoon ground cinnamon
- ⅛ teaspoon ground nutmeg
- ⅛ teaspoon ground cloves
- 1 large egg
- 1 cup buttermilk
- 1 tablespoon butter, melted
  Maple syrup, optional
  Additional butter, optional

1. Combine the first eight ingredients. Whisk the egg, buttermilk and butter; stir into dry ingredients just until moistened.
2. Preheat a nonstick griddle coated with cooking spray over medium heat. Pour batter by ¼ cupfuls onto griddle; turn when bubbles on top begin to pop. Cook until second side is golden brown. If desired, serve with maple syrup and additional butter.

Per 2 pancakes: 195 cal., 6g fat (3g sat. fat), 63mg chol., 667mg sod., 31g carb. (11g sugars, 3g fiber), 7g pro.
Diabetic exchanges: 2 starch, 1 fat.

★ ★ ★ ★ ★ **READER REVIEW**

"I really enjoyed these pancakes. Like eating very rich spice cake for breakfast, only better for you. I served them with ham and eggs and maple syrup."

ANNDRIE TASTEOFHOME.COM

EGGS IN PURGATORY
M FAST FIX ▸

Tomatoes and red pepper flakes add the zing in these saucy eggs. Serve them with crusty bread or sauteed polenta rounds.
—Nick Iverson, Denver, CO

Start to Finish: 30 min.
Makes: 4 servings

- 2 tablespoons canola oil
- 1 medium onion, chopped
- ¼ cup tomato paste
- 2 garlic cloves, minced
- 2 teaspoons smoked paprika
- ½ teaspoon sugar
- ½ teaspoon crushed red pepper flakes
- 2 cans (14½ ounces each) fire-roasted diced tomatoes, undrained
- 4 large eggs
- ¼ cup shredded manchego or Monterey Jack cheese
- 2 tablespoons minced fresh parsley
- 1 tube (18 ounces) polenta, sliced and warmed, optional

1. In a large skillet, heat oil over medium-high heat. Add the onion; cook and stir 6-8 minutes or until tender. Stir in tomato paste, garlic, paprika, sugar and pepper flakes; cook 2 minutes longer.
2. Stir in tomatoes; bring to a boil. Reduce heat to maintain a simmer. With the back of a spoon, make four wells in the sauce. Break an egg into each well. Sprinkle with cheese; cook, covered, 8-10 minutes or until egg whites are completely set and yolks begin to thicken but are not hard. Sprinkle with parsley. If desired, serve with polenta.

Per serving: 255 cal., 14g fat (4g sat. fat), 193mg chol., 676mg sod., 20g carb. (9g sugars, 3g fiber), 11g pro.
Diabetic exchanges: 1½ fat, 1 medium-fat meat, 1 starch.
HEALTH TIP Vitamins A and C are an important part of the immune system, so the tomatoes in this dish will help keep you healthy and energized.

EASY HOMEMADE CHUNKY APPLESAUCE **F** **S** **M** FAST FIX ▸

This applesauce is so easy, and my family loves when I make it from scratch. It's good knowing what I'm putting in it!
—Marilee Cardinal, Burlington, NJ

Start to Finish: 30 min.
Makes: 5 cups

- 7 medium apples (about 3 pounds)
- ½ cup sugar
- ½ cup water
- 1 tablespoon lemon juice
- ¼ teaspoon almond or vanilla extract

1. Peel, core and cut each apple into eight wedges. Cut each wedge crosswise in half; place in a large saucepan. Add remaining ingredients.
2. Bring to a boil. Reduce heat; simmer, covered, 15-20 minutes or until desired consistency, stirring occasionally.

Per ¾ cup: 139 cal., 0 fat (0 sat. fat), 0 chol., 0 sod., 36g carb. (33g sugars, 2g fiber), 0 pro.

SPINACH POTATO PIE 🄲

*When we have brunch with relatives,
I often make this crustless quiche with
hash browns and spinach. We add a side
of fruit for a satisfying meal.*
—Deanna Phillips, Ferndale, WA

Prep: 25 min. • **Bake:** 55 min.
Makes: 6 servings

- 5 large eggs, lightly beaten
- 4 cups frozen shredded hash brown potatoes
- 2 cups chopped fresh spinach
- ¾ cup chopped red onion
- ½ cup 2% cottage cheese
- 7 bacon strips, cooked and crumbled
- 3 green onions, chopped
- 4 garlic cloves, minced
- ½ teaspoon salt
- ¼ teaspoon pepper
- ⅛ teaspoon hot pepper sauce
- 3 plum tomatoes, sliced
- ½ cup shredded Parmesan cheese

1. Preheat oven to 350°. In a large bowl, combine the first 11 ingredients. Pour into a greased 9-in. pie plate.
2. Bake 40 minutes. Arrange tomatoes over top; sprinkle with Parmesan cheese. Bake 15-20 minutes longer or until a knife inserted near the edge comes out clean. Let stand 5 minutes before cutting.
Per 1 piece: 204 cal., 10g fat (4g sat. fat), 192mg chol., 624mg sod., 15g carb. (3g sugars, 2g fiber), 15g pro.
Diabetic exchanges: 2 medium-fat meat, 1 starch, ½ fat.

SPINACH POTATO PIE

WAFFLES WITH PEACH-BERRY COMPOTE Ⓜ

*I created my compote recipe one summer
Sunday when I was looking for a more
healthful alternative to butter and maple
syrup to top my waffles. I was amazed at
the results!*
—Brandi Waters, Fayetteville, AR

Prep: 25 min. • **Cook:** 5 min./batch
Makes: 12 waffles (1½ cups compote)

- 1 cup chopped peeled fresh or frozen peaches
- ½ cup orange juice
- 2 tablespoons brown sugar
- ¼ teaspoon ground cinnamon
- 1 cup fresh or frozen blueberries
- ½ cup sliced fresh or frozen strawberries

BATTER
- 1¼ cups all-purpose flour
- ½ cup whole wheat flour
- 2 tablespoons flaxseed
- 1 teaspoon baking powder
- 1 teaspoon baking soda
- ½ teaspoon ground cinnamon
- 1 cup buttermilk
- ¾ cup orange juice
- 1 tablespoon canola oil
- 1 teaspoon vanilla extract

1. In a small saucepan, combine the peaches, orange juice, brown sugar and cinnamon; bring to a boil over medium heat. Add berries; cook and stir for 8-10 minutes or until thickened.
2. In a large bowl, combine the flours, flax, baking powder, baking soda and cinnamon. Combine the buttermilk, orange juice, oil and vanilla; stir into dry ingredients just until moistened.
3. Bake in a preheated waffle iron according to manufacturer's directions until golden brown. Serve with compote.
Per 2 waffles with ¼ cup compote: 251 cal., 4g fat (1g sat. fat), 2mg chol., 324mg sod., 47g carb. (16g sugars, 4g fiber), 7g pro.
Diabetic exchanges: 2½ starch, ½ fruit, ½ fat.

PEACH SMOOTHIE
S **M** **FAST FIX**

Whip up this creamy concoction as a refreshing and nutritious snack. Because you can use frozen fruit, you don't have to wait until peaches are in season to enjoy.
—Martha Polasek, Markham, TX

Start to Finish: 5 min.
Makes: 2 servings

- ½ cup peach or apricot nectar
- ½ cup sliced fresh or frozen peaches
- ¼ cup fat-free vanilla yogurt
- 2 ice cubes

In a blender, combine all ingredients. Cover and process until blended. Pour into chilled glasses; serve immediately.

Per ¾ cup: 68 cal., 0 fat (0 sat. fat), 1mg chol., 4mg sod., 16g carb. (14g sugars, 1g fiber), 2g pro.
Diabetic exchanges: 1 starch.

SPICY HASH BROWN WAFFLES WITH FRIED EGGS

SPICY HASH BROWN WAFFLES WITH FRIED EGGS
M **FAST FIX**

Refrigerated hash brown potatoes help you make quick work of these crunchy waffles. Put out lots of toppings so everyone can design his or her own.
—Nancy Judd, Alpine, UT

Start to Finish: 30 min.
Makes: 4 servings

- 5 large eggs
- ½ teaspoon salt
- ½ teaspoon ground cumin
- ½ teaspoon pepper
- ¼ teaspoon chili powder
- 1¾ cups refrigerated shredded hash brown potatoes
- 1 small onion, finely chopped
- ¼ cup canned chopped green chilies
- 2 tablespoons salsa
- 2 tablespoons canola oil
- ½ cup shredded cheddar-Monterey Jack cheese
  Optional toppings: salsa, guacamole, sour cream and minced fresh cilantro

1. In a large bowl, whisk one egg, salt, cumin, pepper and chili powder. Stir in potatoes, onion, green chilies and salsa. Bake in a preheated waffle iron coated with cooking spray until golden brown and potatoes are tender, 8-12 minutes.
2. In a large skillet, heat oil over medium-high heat. Break remaining eggs, one at a time, into pan. Reduce heat to low. Cook to desired doneness, turning after whites are set if desired. Remove from the heat. Sprinkle with cheese; cover and let stand 3 minutes or until melted.
3. Serve eggs with waffles and toppings of your choice.

Per waffle with 1 fried egg: 273 cal., 17g fat (5g sat. fat), 245mg chol., 570mg sod., 17g carb. (2g sugars, 2g fiber), 12g pro.

BRUNCH BANANA SPLITS

S **M** **FAST FIX**

My whole family loves bananas, fruit and granola for breakfast. I topped all that with yogurt, nuts and honey and called it a split. This is perfect to serve on a busy morning or a special one!
—Nancy Heishman, Las Vegas, NV

Start to Finish: 10 min.
Makes: 4 servings

- 4 small bananas, peeled and halved lengthwise
- 2 cups (16 ounces) fat-free vanilla Greek yogurt
- 2 small peaches, sliced
- 1 cup fresh raspberries
- ½ cup granola without raisins
- 2 tablespoons sliced almonds, toasted
- 2 tablespoons sunflower kernels
- 2 tablespoons honey

Divide bananas among four shallow dishes. Top with remaining ingredients.

Per serving: 340 cal., 6g fat (1g sat. fat), 0 chol., 88mg sod., 61g carb. (38g sugars, 9g fiber), 17g pro.

HEALTH TIP Yogurt's combination of carborhydrates and protein helps give you long-lasting energy. It's also a rich source of phosphorous, which is vital to energy production and storage.

CHEESE TOMATO EGG BAKE **C** **M**

While making eggs, I wanted something different, so I created this egg bake. We loved it! I hope you will, too.
—Jonathan Miller, Naugatuck, CT

Prep: 10 min. • **Bake:** 25 min.
Makes: 2 servings

- ¾ cup egg substitute
- 2 tablespoons reduced-fat ranch salad dressing
- ⅛ teaspoon garlic powder
- 1 plum tomato, seeded and diced
- 1 slice process American cheese

1. Preheat oven to 350°. In a large bowl, whisk the egg substitute, salad dressing and garlic powder. Spray the bottom of a 3-cup round baking dish with cooking spray. Pour half of the egg mixture into the dish; top with tomato and cheese. Pour the remaining egg mixture on top.

2. Bake 22-26 minutes or until completely set and a knife comes out clean.

Per serving: 110 cal., 4g fat (1g sat. fat), 7mg chol., 442mg sod., 6g carb. (3g sugars, 0 fiber), 12g pro.
Diabetic exchanges: 1 lean meat, ½ starch, ½ fat.

BRUNCH BANANA SPLITS

SLOW
COOKER

> *"Enjoy the amazing flavor of homemade cobbler anytime you want. Just let your slow cooker do the work!"*
> —Karen Jarocki, Yuma, AZ

SUNDAY DINNER BRISKET C

You won't believe how tender this brisket comes out of the slow cooker. The sauce has a robust, beefy flavor with a slight tang from the balsamic vinegar, and the rich caramelized onions complete the dish.
—*Taste of Home* Test Kitchen

Prep: 45 min. • **Cook:** 8 hours
Makes: 10 servings

- 3 tablespoons olive oil, divided
- 4 cups sliced onions (about 4 medium)
- 4 garlic cloves, minced
- 1 tablespoon brown sugar
- 1 fresh beef brisket (4 to 5 pounds)
- ⅓ cup all-purpose flour
- 1 teaspoon salt
- 1 teaspoon coarsely ground pepper
- ¼ cup balsamic vinegar
- 1 can (14½ ounces) reduced-sodium beef broth
- 2 tablespoons tomato paste
- 2 teaspoons Italian seasoning
- 1 teaspoon Worcestershire sauce
- ½ teaspoon paprika
- 1 tablespoon cornstarch
- 2 tablespoons cold water

1. In a large skillet, heat 1 tablespoon oil over medium heat. Add onions; cook and stir until softened. Sprinkle with garlic and brown sugar. Reduce heat to medium-low; cook 10 minutes or until onions are golden brown, stirring occasionally. Transfer to an oval 6-qt. slow cooker.

2. If necessary to fit skillet, cut brisket in half. Sprinkle brisket with flour and shake off excess. In skillet, heat remaining oil over medium heat. Brown both sides of brisket; sprinkle with salt and pepper. Place in slow cooker over onions.

3. Add vinegar to skillet; increase heat to medium-high. Cook, stirring to loosen the browned bits from the pan. Stir in the broth, tomato paste, Italian seasoning, Worcestershire sauce and paprika until blended. Pour over brisket. Cook, covered, on low 8-10 hours or until meat is tender.

4. Remove brisket; keep warm. Transfer cooking juices to saucepan; skim fat and bring to a boil. In a small bowl, mix the cornstarch and water until smooth; stir into cooking juices. Return to a boil; cook and stir 1-2 minutes or until thickened.

5. Cut brisket diagonally across the grain into thin slices. Serve with sauce.

Note: This is a fresh beef brisket, not corned beef.

Per 5 ounces cooked beef with ⅓ cup sauce: 319 cal., 12g fat (4g sat. fat), 78mg chol., 381mg sod., 12g carb. (5g sugars, 1g fiber), 39g pro.
Diabetic exchanges: 5 lean meat, 1 starch, 1 fat.

SLOW-COOKED GREEK CHICKEN DINNER

I got this recipe from my sister, and my family just loves it. It's so delicious! The amount of garlic might seem high, but it's actually just right. You get every bit of flavor without garlic overpowering the other ingredients.
—Terri Christensen, Montague, MI

Prep: 25 min. • **Cook:** 5 hours
Makes: 6 servings

- 6 medium Yukon Gold potatoes, quartered
- 1 broiler/fryer chicken (3½ pounds), cut up and skin removed
- 2 large onions, quartered
- 1 whole garlic bulb, separated and peeled
- 3 teaspoons dried oregano
- 1 teaspoon salt
- ¾ teaspoon pepper
- ½ cup plus 1 tablespoon water, divided
- 1 tablespoon olive oil
- 4 teaspoons cornstarch

1. Place potatoes in a 5-qt. slow cooker. Add chicken, onions and garlic; sprinkle with seasonings. Pour ½ cup water over top. Drizzle with oil. Cook, covered, on low until chicken and vegetables are tender, 5-6 hours.
2. In a bowl, mix the cornstarch and remaining water until smooth. Remove chicken and vegetables from slow cooker; keep warm.
3. Strain the cooking juices into a small saucepan; skim fat. Bring juices to a boil. Stir cornstarch mixture; stir into juices. Bring to boil; cook and stir until thickened, 1-2 minutes. Serve with the chicken and vegetables.

Per serving: 404 cal., 9g fat (2g sat. fat), 86mg chol., 482mg sod., 46g carb. (4g sugars, 6g fiber), 34g pro.
Diabetic exchanges: 4 lean meat, 3 starch, ½ fat.

SLOW-COOKED GREEK CHICKEN DINNER

RED BEAN VEGETABLE SOUP F

Cajun seasoning boosts the flavor of my bean soup that's loaded with fresh vegetables. Yum!
—Ronnie Lappe, Brownwood, TX

Prep: 15 min. • **Cook:** 6 hours
Makes: 12 servings (3 quarts)

- 3 large sweet red peppers, chopped
- 3 celery ribs, chopped
- 2 medium onions, chopped
- 4 cans (16 ounces each) kidney beans, rinsed and drained
- 4 cups chicken broth
- 2 bay leaves
- ½ to 1 teaspoon salt
- ½ to 1 teaspoon Cajun seasoning
- ½ teaspoon pepper
- ¼ to ½ teaspoon hot pepper sauce

In a 5-qt. slow cooker, combine peppers, celery, onions and beans. Stir in remaining ingredients. Cover and cook on low for 6 hours or until the vegetables are tender. Discard bay leaves before serving.
Per cup: 158 cal., 0 fat (0 sat. fat), 2mg chol., 701mg sod., 29g carb. (5g sugars, 8g fiber), 11g pro.
Diabetic exchanges: 2 starch, 1 lean meat.

HEARTY HOMEMADE
CHICKEN NOODLE SOUP

CHIPOTLE BEEF CHILI C

I love spicy food, so I think this chili really hits the spot. If you are sensitive to chili peppers, simply start out with just one or two chipotles and increase the amount from there.
—Steven Schend, Grand Rapids, MI

Prep: 15 min. • **Cook:** 6 hours
Makes: 8 servings (about 2½ quarts)

- 2 pounds beef flank steak, cut into 1-inch pieces
- 2 to 4 chipotle peppers in adobo sauce, chopped
- ¼ cup chopped onion
- 1 tablespoon chili powder
- 2 garlic cloves, minced
- 1 teaspoon salt
- ½ teaspoon ground cumin
- 3 cans (15 ounces each) tomato puree
- 1 can (14½ ounces) beef broth
- ¼ cup minced fresh cilantro

In a 4- or 5-qt. slow cooker, combine the first nine ingredients. Cook, covered, on low 6-8 hours or until meat is tender. Stir in cilantro.

Freeze option: Freeze cooled chili in freezer containers. To use, partially thaw in refrigerator overnight. Heat through in a saucepan, stirring occasionally and adding a little broth or water if necessary.
Per 1¼ cups: 230 cal., 9g fat (4g sat. fat), 54mg chol., 668mg sod., 12g carb. (3g sugars, 2g fiber), 25g pro.
Diabetic exchanges: 3 lean meat, 2 vegetable.

HEARTY HOMEMADE
CHICKEN NOODLE SOUP C

This satisfying homemade soup offering a hint of cayenne pepper is brimming with vegetables, chicken and noodles. The recipe came from my father-in-law, but I made some adjustments to give it my own spin.
—Norma Reynolds, Overland Park, KS

Prep: 20 min. • **Cook:** 5½ hours
Makes: 12 servings (3 quarts)

- 12 fresh baby carrots, cut into ½-inch pieces
- 4 celery ribs, cut into ½-inch pieces
- ¾ cup finely chopped onion
- 1 tablespoon minced fresh parsley
- ½ teaspoon pepper
- ¼ teaspoon cayenne pepper
- 1½ teaspoons mustard seed
- 2 garlic cloves, peeled and halved
- 1¼ pounds boneless skinless chicken breast halves
- 1¼ pounds boneless skinless chicken thighs
- 4 cans (14½ ounces each) chicken broth
- 1 package (9 ounces) refrigerated linguine
  Coarsely ground pepper and additional minced fresh parsley, optional

1. In a 5-qt. slow cooker, combine the first six ingredients. Place the mustard seed and garlic on a double thickness of cheesecloth; bring up corners of cloth and tie with kitchen string to form a bag. Place in slow cooker. Add the chicken and broth. Cover and cook on low for 5-6 hours or until meat is tender.
2. Discard spice bag. Remove chicken; cool slightly. Stir linguine into the soup; cover and cook on high for 30 minutes or until tender.
3. Cut the chicken into pieces and return to the soup; heat through. Sprinkle, if desired, with coarsely ground pepper and additional parsley.
Per cup: 199 cal., 6g fat (2g sat. fat), 73mg chol., 663mg sod., 14g carb. (2g sugars, 1g fiber), 22g pro.
Diabetic exchanges: 3 lean meat, 1 starch.

SLOW COOKER CHICKEN TACO SALAD F C

We make good use of this chicken across several meals, including tacos, omelets, sandwiches and enchiladas. My little guys love helping to measure the seasonings.
—Karie Houghton, Lynnwood, WA

Prep: 10 min. • **Cook:** 3 hours
Makes: 6 servings

- 3 teaspoons chili powder
- 1 teaspoon each ground cumin, seasoned salt and pepper
- ½ teaspoon each white pepper, ground chipotle pepper and paprika
- ¼ teaspoon dried oregano
- ¼ teaspoon crushed red pepper flakes
- 1½ pounds boneless skinless chicken breasts
- 1 cup chicken broth
- 9 cups torn romaine
  Optional toppings: sliced avocado, shredded cheddar cheese, chopped tomato, sliced green onions and ranch salad dressing

1. Mix seasonings; rub over the chicken. Place in a 3-qt. slow cooker. Add broth. Cook, covered, on low 3-4 hours or until chicken is tender.
2. Remove chicken; cool slightly. Shred with two forks. Serve over the romaine; top as desired.

Per 1¾ cups: 143 cal., 3g fat (1g sat. fat), 63mg chol., 516mg sod., 4g carb. (1g sugars, 2g fiber), 24g pro.
Diabetic exchanges: 3 lean meat, 1 vegetable.
HEALTH TIP Switch to a baby kale salad blend for more fiber, vitamin C, calcium and iron.

HERBED TURKEY BREASTS C

Tender, moist turkey breast is enhanced with an array of flavorful herbs in this comforting slow-cooked entree.
—Laurie Mace, Los Osos, CA

Prep: 25 min. + marinating
Cook: 3½ hours
Makes: 12 servings

- 1 can (14½ ounces) chicken broth
- ½ cup lemon juice
- ¼ cup packed brown sugar
- ¼ cup fresh sage
- ¼ cup fresh thyme leaves
- ¼ cup lime juice
- ¼ cup cider vinegar
- ¼ cup olive oil
- 1 envelope onion soup mix
- 2 tablespoons Dijon mustard
- 1 tablespoon minced fresh marjoram
- 1½ teaspoons paprika
- 1 teaspoon garlic powder
- 1 teaspoon pepper
- ½ teaspoon salt
- 2 boneless skinless turkey breast halves (2 pounds each)

1. Using a blender, process the first 15 ingredients until blended. Pour marinade into a large resealable plastic bag; add the turkey. Seal the bag and turn to coat; refrigerate for 8 hours or overnight.
2. Transfer turkey and marinade to a 5-qt. slow cooker. Cover and cook on high for 3½ to 4½ hours or until a thermometer reads 165°.

Per 5 ounces cooked turkey: 219 cal., 5g fat (1g sat. fat), 87mg chol., 484mg sod., 5g carb. (3g sugars, 0 fiber), 36g pro.
Diabetic exchanges: 5 lean meat, ½ fat.

SLOW COOKER CHICKEN TACO SALAD

ITALIAN SPAGHETTI SQUASH M

This is a unique and easy way to cook spaghetti squash. Be sure the squash is on the small or medium side so that it fits into the slow cooker after being cut in half.
—Melissa Brooks, Sparta, WI

Prep: 15 min. • **Cook:** 6¼ hours
Makes: 4 servings

- 1 medium spaghetti squash (3 pounds)
- 1 can (14½ ounces) diced tomatoes, undrained
- 1 cup sliced fresh mushrooms
- ½ teaspoon salt
- ½ teaspoon dried oregano
- ¼ teaspoon pepper
- ¾ cup shredded part-skim mozzarella cheese

1. Halve squash lengthwise; discard seeds. Fill with the tomatoes and mushrooms; sprinkle with seasonings. Place in an oval 7-qt. slow cooker, tilting one slightly to fit.
2. Cook, covered, on low until squash is tender, 6-8 hours. Sprinkle with cheese. Cook, covered, on low until the cheese is melted, 10-15 minutes. To serve, cut each half into two portions.

Per ¾ cup: 195 cal., 6g fat (3g sat. fat), 14mg chol., 661mg sod., 31g carb. (4g sugars, 7g fiber), 9g pro.
Diabetic exchanges: 2 starch, 1 medium-fat meat.

CHICKPEA & POTATO CURRY

CHICKPEA & POTATO CURRY M

I make chana masala, the classic Indian dish, in my slow cooker. Browning the onion, ginger and garlic first really makes the sauce amazing.
—Anjana Devasahayam, San Antonio, TX

Prep: 25 min. • **Cook:** 6 hours.
Makes: 6 servings

- 1 tablespoon canola oil
- 1 medium onion, chopped
- 2 garlic cloves, minced
- 2 teaspoons minced fresh gingerroot
- 2 teaspoons ground coriander
- 1 teaspoon garam masala
- 1 teaspoon chili powder
- ½ teaspoon salt
- ½ teaspoon ground cumin
- ¼ teaspoon ground turmeric
- 1 can (15 ounces) crushed tomatoes
- 2 cans (15 ounces each) chickpeas, rinsed and drained
- 1 large baking potato, peeled and cut into ¾-inch cubes
- 2½ cups vegetable stock
- 1 tablespoon lime juice
  Chopped fresh cilantro
  Hot cooked rice
  Sliced red onion, optional
  Lime wedges, optional

1. In a large skillet, heat oil over medium-high heat; saute the onion until tender, 2-4 minutes. Add the garlic, ginger and dry seasonings; cook and stir 1 minute. Stir in the tomatoes; transfer to a 3- or 4-qt. slow cooker.
2. Stir in chickpeas, potato and stock. Cook, covered, on low until potato is tender and flavors are blended, 6-8 hours.
3. Stir in lime juice; sprinkle with cilantro. Serve with rice and, if desired, red onion and lime wedges.

Per 1¼ cups chickpea mixture: 240 cal., 6g fat (0 sat. fat), 0 chol., 767mg sod., 42g carb. (8g sugars, 9g fiber), 8g pro.

CHUNKY CHICKEN CACCIATORE

This recipe is just so versatile! Look in your fridge for anything else you want to throw in, such as red pepper, mushrooms, extra zucchini—you name it. And if you're a vegetarian, go ahead and leave out the chicken.
—Stephanie Loaiza, Layton, UT

Prep: 10 min. • **Cook:** 4 hours
Makes: 6 servings

- 6 boneless skinless chicken thighs (about 1½ pounds)
- 2 medium zucchini, cut into 1-inch slices
- 1 medium green pepper, cut into 1-inch pieces
- 1 large sweet onion, coarsely chopped
- ½ teaspoon dried oregano
- 1 jar (24 ounces) garden-style spaghetti sauce
  Hot cooked spaghetti
  Sliced ripe olives and shredded Parmesan cheese, optional

1. Place chicken and vegetables in a 3-qt. slow cooker; sprinkle with oregano. Pour sauce over top. Cook, covered, on low 4-5 hours or until chicken is tender.
2. Remove chicken; break up slightly with two forks. Return to slow cooker. Serve with spaghetti. If desired, top with olives and cheese.

To make ahead: Place the first six ingredients in a large resealable plastic freezer bag; seal bag and freeze. To use, place filled freezer bag in refrigerator 48 hours or until contents are completely thawed. Cook and serve as directed.
Per serving without spaghetti and optional ingredients: 285 cal., 11g fat (2g sat. fat), 76mg chol., 507mg sod., 21g carb. (14g sugars, 3g fiber), 24g pro.
Diabetic exchanges: 3 lean meat, 1½ starch.

CHUNKY CHICKEN CACCIATORE

EASY GREEN BEANS WITH MUSHROOMS C M

My family actually looks forward to this side dish. I add sliced almonds for crunch and garlic for a little kick.
—Cheryl Wittman, Bergen, NY

Prep: 10 min. • **Cook:** 5 hours
Makes: 10 servings

- 2 pounds fresh green beans, trimmed
- 1 pound sliced fresh mushrooms
- 1 large onion, finely chopped
- 2 tablespoons butter, melted
- 2 tablespoons olive oil
- 3 garlic cloves, minced
- ½ teaspoon salt
- ¼ teaspoon pepper
- ½ cup sliced almonds, toasted

In a 6-qt. slow cooker, combine all of the ingredients except the almonds. Cook, covered, on low until beans are tender, 5-6 hours. Remove with a slotted spoon. Top with almonds.
Note: To toast nuts, bake in a shallow pan in a 350° oven for 5-10 minutes or cook in a skillet over low heat until lightly browned, stirring occasionally.
Per serving: 116 cal., 8g fat (2g sat. fat), 6mg chol., 145mg sod., 11g carb. (4g sugars, 4g fiber), 4g pro.
Diabetic exchanges: 1½ fat, 1 vegetable.

PORK TACOS WITH MANGO SALSA

PORK TACOS WITH MANGO SALSA C

I've made quite a few tacos in my day, but you can't beat a tender filling made in a slow cooker. These are by far the best pork tacos we've had—and we've tried plenty. Make the mango salsa from scratch if you have time! Yum.
—Amber Massey, Argyle, TX

Prep: 25 min. • **Cook:** 6 hours
Makes: 12 servings

- 2 tablespoons lime juice
- 2 tablespoons white vinegar
- 3 tablespoons chili powder
- 2 teaspoons ground cumin
- 1½ teaspoons salt
- ½ teaspoon pepper
- 3 cups cubed fresh pineapple
- 1 small red onion, coarsely chopped
- 2 chipotle peppers in adobo sauce
- 1 bottle (12 ounces) dark Mexican beer
- 3 pounds pork tenderloin, cut into 1-inch cubes
- ¼ cup chopped fresh cilantro
- 1 jar (16 ounces) mango salsa
    Corn tortillas (6 inches), warmed

OPTIONAL TOPPINGS
    Cubed fresh pineapple
    Cubed avocado
    Queso fresco

1. Puree the first nine ingredients in a blender; stir in beer. In a 5- or 6-qt. slow cooker, combine pork and pineapple mixture. Cook, covered, on low until pork is tender, 6-8 hours. Stir to break up pork.
2. Stir cilantro into salsa. Using a slotted spoon, serve pork mixture in tortillas; add salsa and toppings as desired.

Freeze option: Freeze cooled meat mixture and cooking juices in freezer containers. To use, partially thaw in refrigerator overnight. Heat through in a saucepan, stirring occasionally.

Per ⅔ cup pork mixture with 2 tablespoons salsa: 178 cal., 4g fat (1g sat. fat), 64mg chol., 656mg sod., 9g carb. (5g sugars, 2g fiber), 23g pro.
Diabetic exchanges: 3 lean meat, ½ starch.

FALL GARDEN MEDLEY F M

I like to make this recipe in autumn and winter for special occasions because it's colorful, tasty and healthy. It's a hearty side dish that complements many different main courses.
—Krystine Kercher, Lincoln, NE

Prep: 20 min. • **Cook:** 5 hours
Makes: 8 servings

- 4 large carrots, cut into 1½-inch pieces
- 3 fresh beets, peeled and cut into 1½-inch pieces.
- 2 medium sweet potatoes, peeled and cut into 1½-inch pieces
- 2 medium onions, peeled and quartered
- ½ cup water
- 2 teaspoons salt
- ½ teaspoon pepper
- ¼ teaspoon dried thyme
- 1 tablespoon olive oil
    Fresh parsley or dried parsley flakes, optional

1. Place carrots, beets, sweet potatoes, onion and water in a greased 3-qt. slow cooker. Sprinkle with salt, pepper and thyme. Drizzle with olive oil. Cover and cook on low for 5-6 hours or until tender.
2. Stir the vegetables and sprinkle with parsley if desired.

Per ¾ cup: 83 cal., 2g fat (0 sat. fat), 0 chol., 633mg sod., 16g carb. (8g sugars, 3g fiber), 2g pro.
Diabetic exchanges: 1 vegetable, ½ starch.

SLOW-COOKED TURKEY WITH BERRY COMPOTE F C

We love to eat turkey at our house, and this summer entree is a great way to get all that yummy flavor without heating up the house. The berry compote is the ideal addition. For browner turkey, broil for a few minutes before serving.
—Margaret Bracher, Robertsdale, AL

Prep: 35 min. + standing
Cook: 20 min. + releasing
Makes: 12 servings (3¼ cups compote)

- 1 teaspoon salt
- ½ teaspoon garlic powder
- ½ teaspoon dried thyme
- ½ teaspoon pepper
- 2 boneless turkey breast halves (2 pounds each)
- ⅓ cup water

COMPOTE
- 2 medium apples, peeled and finely chopped
- 2 cups fresh raspberries
- 2 cups fresh blueberries
- 1 cup white grape juice
- ¼ teaspoon crushed red pepper flakes
- ¼ teaspoon ground ginger

1. Mix salt, garlic powder, thyme and pepper; rub over turkey breasts. Place in a 5- or 6-qt. slow cooker. Pour water around turkey. Cook, covered, on low 3-4 hours (a thermometer inserted in turkey should read at least 165°).
2. Remove the turkey from slow cooker; tent it with foil. Let it stand for 10 minutes before slicing.
3. Meanwhile, combine the compote ingredients in a large saucepan. Bring to a boil. Reduce heat to medium; cook, uncovered, stirring occasionally, until slightly thickened and apples are tender, 15-20 minutes. Serve the turkey with the berry compote.

Per 5 ounces cooked turkey with ¼ cup compote: 215 cal., 1g fat (0 sat. fat), 94mg chol., 272mg sod., 12g carb. (8g sugars, 2g fiber), 38g pro.
Diabetic exchanges: 5 lean meat, 1 starch.

SLOW-COOKED TURKEY WITH BERRY COMPOTE

SPICED HOT APPLE CIDER F S M

During cool-weather season, my husband and I take this soul-warming cider outside by the fire pit. It tastes as delicious as it smells, and it warms us up instantly.
—Lisa Bynum, Brandon, MS

Prep: 10 min. • **Cook:** 2 hours
Makes: 10 servings (¾ cup each)

- 2 cinnamon sticks (3 inches)
- 1 piece fresh gingerroot (about 1 inch), thinly sliced
- 1 teaspoon whole allspice
- 1 teaspoon whole cloves
- ½ teaspoon cardamom pods, crushed
- 2 quarts apple cider or juice
  Rum, optional

1. Place first five ingredients on a double thickness of cheesecloth. Gather corners of cloth to enclose the spice mixture; tie securely with string.
2. Place the cider and spice bag in a 3-qt. slow cooker. Cook, covered, to allow the flavors to blend, 2-3 hours. Discard spice bag. If desired, stir in rum.

Per ¾ cup without rum: 96 cal., 0 fat (0 sat. fat), 0 chol., 20mg sod., 24g carb. (21g sugars, 0 fiber), 0 pro.

SLOW-COOKED POTATOES WITH SPRING ONIONS S M

I love the simplicity of this recipe, as well as the ease of preparation with my slow cooker. And everyone always likes roasted potatoes, even my pickiest child! If you desire, top the side dish with shredded or crumbled cheese.
—Theresa Gomez, Stuart, FL

Prep: 5 min. • **Cook:** 6 hours
Makes: 12 servings

- 4 pounds small red potatoes
- 8 green onions, chopped (about 1 cup)
- 1 cup chopped sweet onion
- ¼ cup olive oil
- ½ teaspoon salt
- ½ teaspoon pepper

In a 5- or 6-qt. slow cooker, combine all ingredients. Cook, covered, on low 6-8 hours or until potatoes are tender.
Per serving: 157 cal., 5g fat (1g sat. fat), 0 chol., 110mg sod., 26g carb. (2g sugars, 3g fiber), 3g pro.
Diabetic exchanges: 1½ starch, 1 fat.

PULLED CHICKEN SANDWICHES

PULLED CHICKEN SANDWICHES

I was raised as a Southern girl with the love of barbecue built right into my DNA. This slow cooker recipe allows me to enjoy the flavors I grew up eating, while still following a healthy diet.
—Heidi Mulholland, Cumming, GA

Prep: 20 min. • **Cook:** 4 hours
Makes: 6 servings

- 1 medium onion, finely chopped
- 1 can (6 ounces) tomato paste
- ¼ cup reduced-sodium chicken broth
- 2 tablespoons brown sugar
- 1 tablespoon cider vinegar
- 1 tablespoon yellow mustard
- 1 tablespoon Worcestershire sauce
- 2 garlic cloves, minced
- 2 teaspoons chili powder
- ¾ teaspoon salt
- ⅛ teaspoon cayenne pepper
- 1½ pounds boneless skinless chicken breasts
- 6 whole wheat hamburger buns, split

1. In a small bowl, mix the first eleven ingredients. Place chicken in a 3-qt. slow cooker. Pour sauce over top.
2. Cook, covered, on low 4-5 hours or until chicken is tender. Remove chicken; cool slightly. Shred meat with two forks. Return to slow cooker; heat through. Serve in buns.
Freeze option: Freeze cooled chicken mixture in freezer containers. To use, partially thaw in refrigerator overnight. Heat through in a saucepan, stirring occasionally and adding a little broth if necessary.
Per sandwich: 296 cal., 5g fat (1g sat. fat), 63mg chol., 698mg sod., 35g carb. (12g sugars, 5g fiber), 29g pro.
Diabetic exchanges: 3 lean meat, 2 starch.

SLOW-COOKED PEPPER STEAK C

After a long day working in our greenhouse raising bedding plants, I enjoy coming in to this hearty beef dish for supper. It's one of my favorite meals.
—Sue Gronholz, Beaver Dam, WI

Prep: 10 min. • **Cook:** 6½ hours
Makes: 6 servings

- 1½ pounds beef top round steak
- 2 tablespoons canola oil
- 1 cup chopped onion
- ¼ cup reduced-sodium soy sauce
- 1 garlic clove, minced
- 1 teaspoon sugar
- ½ teaspoon salt
- ¼ teaspoon ground ginger
- ¼ teaspoon pepper
- 4 medium tomatoes, cut into wedges or 1 can (14½ ounces) diced tomatoes, undrained
- 1 large green pepper, cut into strips
- 1 tablespoon cornstarch
- ½ cup cold water
  Hot cooked noodles or rice

1. Cut the beef into 3-in.x1-in. strips. In a large skillet, brown the beef in oil. Transfer to a 3-qt. slow cooker. Combine the onion, soy sauce, garlic, sugar, salt, ginger and pepper; pour over beef. Cover and cook on low for 5-6 hours or until the meat is tender. Add tomatoes and green pepper; cook on low 1 hour longer or until the vegetables are tender.
2. Combine cornstarch and cold water until smooth; gradually stir into the slow cooker. Cover and cook on high for 20-30 minutes until thickened. Serve with noodles or rice.
Freeze option: Freeze cooled beef mixture in freezer containers. To use, partially thaw in refrigerator overnight. Heat through in a covered saucepan, gently stirring and adding a little broth or water if necessary.
Per cup without noodles: 232 cal., 8g fat (2g sat. fat), 64mg chol., 639mg sod., 11g carb. (5g sugars, 2g fiber), 28g pro.
Diabetic exchanges: 4 lean meat, 1 vegetable, 1 fat.

SLOW COOKER BERRY COBBLER S M

Enjoy the amazing flavor of homemade cobbler anytime you want. Just let your slow cooker do the work!
—Karen Jarocki, Yuma, AZ

Prep: 15 min. • **Cook:** 1¾ hours
Makes: 8 servings

- 1¼ cups all-purpose flour, divided
- 2 tablespoons plus 1 cup sugar, divided
- 1 teaspoon baking powder
- ¼ teaspoon ground cinnamon
- 1 large egg
- ¼ cup fat-free milk
- 2 tablespoons canola oil
- ⅛ teaspoon salt
- 2 cups fresh or frozen raspberries, thawed
- 2 cups fresh or frozen blueberries, thawed
  Low-fat vanilla frozen yogurt, optional

1. Whisk together the 1 cup flour, 2 tablespoons sugar, baking powder and cinnamon. In another bowl, whisk together egg, milk and oil; add to dry ingredients, stirring just until moistened (batter will be thick). Spread onto the bottom of a 5-qt. slow cooker coated with cooking spray.
2. Mix salt and the remaining flour and sugar; toss with berries. Spoon over the batter. Cook, covered, on high until berry mixture is bubbly, about 1¾ to 2 hours. If desired, serve with frozen yogurt.
Per serving: 260 cal., 5g fat (1g sat. fat), 23mg chol., 110mg sod., 53g carb. (34g sugars, 3g fiber), 4g pro.

SLOW COOKER BERRY COBBLER

**SWEET POTATO
LENTIL STEW**

SWEET POTATO
LENTIL STEW F M

*Years ago, I experienced the spicy flavor
and wonderful aroma of this hearty dish.
Now, it's a staple in my home. You can
serve the stew alone or ladle it over meat
or poultry. It's great either way!*
—Heather Gray, Little Rock, AR

....

Prep: 15 min. • **Cook:** 5 hours
Makes: 6 servings

- 1¼ pounds sweet potatoes
  (about 2 medium), peeled
  and cut into 1-inch pieces
- 1½ cups dried lentils, rinsed
- 3 medium carrots, cut into
  1-inch pieces
- 1 medium onion, chopped
- 4 garlic cloves, minced
- ½ teaspoon ground cumin
- ¼ teaspoon ground ginger
- ¼ teaspoon cayenne pepper
- 1 carton (32 ounces) vegetable broth
- ¼ cup minced fresh cilantro

In a 3-qt. slow cooker, combine the first
nine ingredients. Cook, covered, on low
5-6 hours or until vegetables and lentils are
tender. Stir in cilantro.
Per 1⅓ cups: 290 cal., 1g fat (0 sat. fat),
0 chol., 662mg sod., 58g carb. (16g
sugars, 15g fiber), 15g pro.

TURKEY SAUSAGE
CABBAGE ROLLS

(PICTURED ON P. 97)

*I practically grew up in the kitchen of my
Polish grandmother, watching Babci cook
and listening to her stories. I made her
cabbage roll recipe healthier with whole
grains and turkey, but I kept the same rich
flavors I remember.*
—Fay Moreland, Wichita Falls, TX

....

Prep: 50 min. • **Cook:** 7 hours
Makes: 12 servings

- 12 large plus 6 medium cabbage leaves
- 2 packets (3 ounces each) instant
  multigrain rice mix
- 1 medium onion, finely chopped
- ½ cup finely chopped sweet red pepper
- ¼ cup minced fresh parsley
- 3 teaspoons Italian seasoning
- 1¼ teaspoons salt
- 1 teaspoon garlic powder
- 1 teaspoon pepper
- 1½ pounds lean ground turkey
- 3 Italian turkey sausage links (about
  4 ounces each), casings removed
- 1 bottle (46 ounces) V8 juice

1. In batches, cook cabbage leaves in
boiling water until crisp-tender, about 5
minutes. Drain; cool slightly.

2. In a large bowl, combine rice mix,
onion, red pepper, parsley and seasonings.
Add turkey and sausage; mix lightly but
thoroughly.

3. Line bottom of a 6-qt. slow cooker with
medium cabbage leaves, overlapping the
leaves as needed.

4. Trim thick veins from bottom of large
cabbage leaves, making V-shaped cuts.
Top each with about ½ cup filling. Pull cut
edges together to overlap, then fold over
filling; fold in sides and roll up. Layer in
slow cooker, seam side down. Pour
vegetable juice over top.

5. Cook, covered, on low until cabbage
is tender, 7-9 hours (a thermometer
inserted into the filling should read at
least 165°).
Note: This recipe was tested with
Minute brand Multi-Grain Medley.
**Per cabbage roll with 3 tablespoons
sauce:** 202 cal., 7g fat (2g sat. fat),
49mg chol., 681mg sod., 19g carb.
(5g sugars, 3g fiber), 17g pro.
Diabetic exchanges: 2 lean meat,
1 starch.

ITALIAN TURKEY SANDWICHES

I hope you enjoy these tasty turkey sandwiches as much as our family does. The recipe makes plenty, so it's great for potlucks. Leftovers are just as delicious when reheated the next day.
—Carol Riley, Ossian, IN

Prep: 10 min. • **Cook:** 5 hours
Makes: 12 servings

- 1 bone-in turkey breast (6 pounds), skin removed
- 1 medium onion, chopped
- 1 small green pepper, chopped
- ¼ cup chili sauce
- 3 tablespoons white vinegar
- 2 tablespoons dried oregano or Italian seasoning
- 4 teaspoons beef bouillon granules
- 12 kaiser or hard rolls, split

1. Place turkey breast in a greased 5-qt. slow cooker. Add onion and green pepper.
2. Combine chili sauce, vinegar, oregano and bouillon; pour over the turkey and vegetables. Cover and cook on low for 5-6 hours or until turkey is tender.

3. Shred turkey with two forks and return to the slow cooker; heat through. Spoon ½ cup onto each roll.
Freeze option: Place cooled meat and juice mixture in freezer containers. To use, partially thaw mixture in refrigerator overnight. Microwave, covered, on high in a microwave-safe dish until it is heated through, gently stirring and adding a little water if necessary.
Per sandwich: 374 cal., 4g fat (1g sat. fat), 118mg chol., 724mg sod., 34g carb. (3g sugars, 2g fiber), 49g pro.
Diabetic exchanges: 6 lean meat, 2 starch.

HARVEST BUTTERNUT & PORK STEW

Mix up your dinner routine with this hearty pork entree! Edamame adds an interesting protein-packed touch, and the stew is so comforting with warm bread served on the side.
—Erin Chilcoat, Central Islip, NY

Prep: 20 min. • **Cook:** 8 hours
Makes: 6 servings (2 quarts)

- ⅓ cup plus 1 tablespoon all-purpose flour, divided
- 1 tablespoon paprika
- 1 teaspoon salt
- 1 teaspoon ground coriander
- 1½ pounds boneless pork shoulder butt roast, cut into 1-inch cubes
- 1 tablespoon canola oil
- 2¾ cups cubed peeled butternut squash
- 1 can (14½ ounces) diced tomatoes, undrained
- 1 cup frozen corn, thawed
- 1 medium onion, chopped
- 2 tablespoons cider vinegar
- 1 bay leaf
- 2½ cups reduced-sodium chicken broth
- 1⅔ cups frozen shelled edamame, thawed

1. In a large resealable plastic bag, combine ⅓ cup flour, paprika, salt and coriander. Add pork, a few pieces at a time, and shake to coat.
2. In a large skillet, brown pork in oil in batches; drain. Transfer to a 5-qt. slow cooker. Add the squash, tomatoes, corn, onion, vinegar and bay leaf. In a small bowl, combine broth and remaining flour until smooth; stir into slow cooker.
3. Cover and cook on low for 8-10 hours or until pork and vegetables are tender. Stir in edamame; cover and cook 30 minutes longer. Discard bay leaf.
Per 1⅓ cups: 371 cal., 16g fat (5g sat. fat), 67mg chol., 635mg sod., 30g carb. (7g sugars, 5g fiber), 28g pro.
Diabetic exchanges: 3 medium-fat meat, 1½ starch, 1 vegetable, ½ fat.

ITALIAN TURKEY SANDWICHES

SLOW-COOKED PORK STEW

PUMPKIN SPICE OATMEAL ☰ Ⓜ

There's nothing like a warm cup of oatmeal in the morning, and my spiced version works in a slow cooker. Store leftovers in the fridge.
—Jordan Mason, Brookville, PA

Prep: 10 min. • **Cook:** 5 hours
Makes: 6 servings

- 1 can (15 ounces) solid-pack pumpkin
- 1 cup steel-cut oats
- 3 tablespoons brown sugar
- 1½ teaspoons pumpkin pie spice
- 1 teaspoon ground cinnamon
- ¾ teaspoon salt
- 3 cups water
- 1½ cups 2% milk
  Optional toppings: toasted chopped pecans, ground cinnamon, and additional brown sugar and milk

In large bowl, combine first six ingredients; stir in water and milk. Transfer to a greased 3-qt. slow cooker. Cook, covered, on low 5-6 hours or until oats are tender, stirring once. Serve with toppings as desired.
Per cup: 183 cal., 3g fat (1g sat. fat), 5mg chol., 329mg sod., 34g carb. (13g sugars, 5g fiber), 6g pro.
Diabetic exchanges: 2 starch, ½ fat.

SLOW-COOKED PORK STEW Ⓒ

Try this hearty stew that's easy to put together, but tastes like you've been working real hard in the kitchen all day. It's even better served over polenta, egg noodles or mashed potatoes.
—Nancy Elliott, Houston, TX

Prep: 15 min. • **Cook:** 5 hours
Makes: 8 servings

- 2 pork tenderloins (1 pound each), cut into 2-inch pieces
- 1 teaspoon salt
- ½ teaspoon pepper
- 2 large carrots, cut into ½-inch slices
- 2 celery ribs, coarsely chopped
- 1 medium onion, coarsely chopped
- 3 cups beef broth
- 2 tablespoons tomato paste
- ⅓ cup pitted dried plums, chopped
- 4 garlic cloves, minced
- 2 bay leaves
- 1 fresh rosemary sprig
- 1 fresh thyme sprig
- ⅓ cup Greek olives, optional
  Chopped fresh parsley, optional
  Hot cooked mashed potatoes, optional

1. Sprinkle pork with salt and pepper; transfer to a 4-qt. slow cooker. Add the carrots, celery and onion. In a small bowl, whisk broth and tomato paste; pour over vegetables. Add plums, garlic, bay leaves, rosemary, thyme and, if desired, olives. Cook, covered, on low 5-6 hours or until meat and vegetables are tender.
2. Discard bay leaves, rosemary and thyme. If desired, sprinkle stew with parsley and serve with potatoes.
Per cup without potatoes: 177 cal., 4g fat (1g sat. fat), 64mg chol., 698mg sod., 9g carb. (4g sugars, 1g fiber), 24g pro.
Diabetic exchanges: 3 lean meat, ½ starch.

SWEET POTATO STUFFING

SWEET POTATO STUFFING

Mom likes to make sure there will be enough stuffing to satisfy our large family. For our holiday gatherings, she slow-cooks this tasty sweet potato dressing in addition to the traditional stuffing cooked inside the turkey.
—Kelly Pollock, London, ON

Prep: 15 min. • **Cook:** 4 hours
Makes: 10 servings

- ¼ cup butter, cubed
- ½ cup chopped celery
- ½ cup chopped onion
- ½ cup chicken broth
- ½ teaspoon salt
- ½ teaspoon poultry seasoning
- ½ teaspoon rubbed sage
- ½ teaspoon pepper
- 6 cups dry bread cubes
- 1 large sweet potato, cooked, peeled and cubed
- ¼ cup chopped pecans

1. In a 6-qt. stockpot, heat butter over medium-high heat; saute celery and onion until tender. Stir in broth and seasonings. Stir in remaining ingredients.

2. Transfer to a greased 3-qt. slow cooker. Cook it, covered, on low until it is heated through, about 4 hours.

Per cup: 212 cal., 8g fat (3g sat. fat), 12mg chol., 459mg sod., 33g carb. (6g sugars, 3g fiber), 5g pro.
Diabetic exchanges: 2 starch, 1½ fat.

BEEF & BEANS [F]
(PICTURED ON P. 96)

Served over rice, this deliciously spicy meal-in-one always has family and friends asking for more. It's a favorite from my recipe collection.
—Marie Leamon, Bethesda, MD

Prep: 10 min. • **Cook:** 6½ hours
MAKES: 8 servings

- 1½ pounds boneless round steak
- 1 tablespoon prepared mustard
- 1 tablespoon chili powder
- ½ teaspoon salt
- ¼ teaspoon pepper
- 1 garlic clove, minced
- 2 cans (14½ ounces each) diced tomatoes, undrained
- 1 medium onion, chopped
- 1 teaspoon beef bouillon granules
- 1 can (16 ounces) kidney beans, rinsed and drained
  Hot cooked rice

Cut the steak into thin strips. Combine mustard, chili powder, salt, pepper and garlic in a bowl; add steak and toss to coat. Transfer to a 3-qt. slow cooker; add the tomatoes, onion and bouillon. Cover and cook on low for 6-8 hours. Stir in beans; cook 30 minutes longer. Serve over rice.

Per cup without rice: 185 cal., 3g fat (1g sat. fat), 47mg chol., 584mg sod., 16g carb. (5g sugars, 5g fiber), 24g pro.
Diabetic exchanges: 2 lean meat, 1 starch, 1 vegetable.

MAPLE MUSTARD CHICKEN

My husband loves this chicken dish. It calls for only five ingredients, and we try to have them all on hand for a delicious and cozy dinner anytime.
—Jennifer Seidel, Midland, MI

Prep: 5 min. • **Cook:** 3 hours
Makes: 6 servings

- 6 boneless skinless chicken breast halves (6 ounces each)
- ½ cup maple syrup
- ⅓ cup stone-ground mustard
- 2 tablespoons quick-cooking tapioca
  Hot cooked brown rice

Place chicken in a 3-qt. slow cooker. In a small bowl, combine the syrup, mustard and tapioca; pour over chicken. Cover and cook on low for 3-4 hours or until tender. Serve with rice.

Freeze option: Cool chicken in sauce. Freeze in freezer containers. To use, partially thaw in refrigerator overnight. Heat through slowly in a covered skillet until a thermometer inserted in chicken reads 165°, stirring occasionally and adding a little broth or water if necessary.

Per chicken breast half: 289 cal., 4g fat (1g sat. fat), 94mg chol., 296mg sod., 24g carb. (17g sugars, 2g fiber), 35g pro.

Diabetic exchanges: 5 lean meat, 1½ starch.

ITALIAN SHRIMP & PASTA

ITALIAN SHRIMP & PASTA

This dish will remind you a bit of classic Shrimp Creole, but it has a surprise Italian twist. Slow cooking gives it hands-off ease that's perfect for company.
—Karen Edwards, Sanford, ME

Prep: 20 min. • **Cook:** 7½ hours
Makes: 6 servings

- 1 pound boneless skinless chicken thighs, cut into 2x1-in. strips
- 2 tablespoons canola oil
- 1 can (28 ounces) crushed tomatoes
- 2 celery ribs, chopped
- 1 medium green pepper, cut into 1-inch pieces
- 1 medium onion, coarsely chopped
- 2 garlic cloves, minced
- 1 tablespoon sugar
- ½ teaspoon salt
- ½ teaspoon Italian seasoning
- ⅛ to ¼ teaspoon cayenne pepper
- 1 bay leaf
- 1 cup uncooked orzo or other small pasta
- 1 pound cooked medium shrimp, peeled and deveined

1. In a large skillet, brown chicken in oil; transfer to a 3-qt. slow cooker. Stir in tomatoes, celery, pepper, onion, garlic, sugar and seasonings. Cook, covered, on low 7-8 hours or until the chicken is just tender.

2. Discard bay leaf. Stir in pasta; cook, covered, on high 15 minutes or until pasta is tender. Stir in shrimp; cook, covered, 5 minutes longer or until heated through.

Per 1½ cups: 418 cal., 12g fat (2g sat. fat), 165mg chol., 611mg sod., 40g carb. (10g sugars, 4g fiber), 36g pro.

Diabetic exchanges: 5 lean meat, 2½ starch, 1 fat.

SPICE-BRAISED POT ROAST C

Pour a few ingredients over your pot roast and let the slow cooker do all the work. Herbs and spices give the beef a great savory flavor. I often serve this roast over noodles or with mashed potatoes, using the juices as a gravy.
—Loren Martin, Big Cabin, OK

Prep: 15 min. • **Cook:** 7 hours
Makes: 8 servings

- 1 boneless beef chuck roast (2½ pounds)
- 1 can (14½ ounces) diced tomatoes, undrained
- 1 medium onion, chopped
- ¼ cup white vinegar
- 3 tablespoons tomato puree
- 1 tablespoon poppy seeds
- 1 bay leaf
- 2¼ teaspoons sugar
- 2 teaspoons Dijon mustard
- 2 garlic cloves, minced
- ½ teaspoon salt
- ½ teaspoon ground ginger
- ½ teaspoon dried rosemary, crushed
- ½ teaspoon lemon juice
- ¼ teaspoon ground cumin
- ¼ teaspoon ground turmeric
- ¼ teaspoon crushed red pepper flakes
- ⅛ teaspoon ground cloves
    Hot cooked egg noodles

1. Place roast in a 5-qt. slow cooker. Mix all remaining ingredients except noodles; pour over roast. Cook, covered, on low until meat is tender, 7-9 hours.
2. Discard bay leaf. If desired, skim fat and thicken cooking juices. Serve pot roast with noodles and juices.
Per serving: 276 cal., 14g fat (5g sat. fat), 92mg chol., 305mg sod., 7g carb. (4g sugars, 2g fiber), 29g pro.
Diabetic exchanges: 4 lean meat, ½ starch.

SPICE-BRAISED POT ROAST

STUFFING FROM THE SLOW COOKER M

If you're hosting a big Thanksgiving dinner this year, consider adding this simple slow-cooked stuffing to your menu to ease entertaining. The recipe comes in handy when you run out of oven space at large family gatherings. I use it often.
—Donald Seiler, Macon, MS

Prep: 30 min. • **Cook:** 3 hours
Makes: 10 servings

- 1 cup chopped onion
- 1 cup chopped celery
- ¼ cup butter
- 6 cups cubed day-old white bread
- 6 cups cubed day-old whole wheat bread
- 1 teaspoon salt
- 1 teaspoon poultry seasoning
- 1 teaspoon rubbed sage
- ½ teaspoon pepper
- 1 can (14½ ounces) reduced-sodium chicken broth or vegetable broth
- 2 large eggs, beaten

1. In a small nonstick skillet over medium heat, cook onion and celery in butter until tender.
2. In a large bowl, combine the bread cubes, salt, poultry seasoning, sage and pepper. Stir in onion mixture. Combine broth and eggs; add to bread mixture and toss to coat.
3. Transfer to a 3-qt. slow cooker coated with cooking spray. Cover and cook on low for 3-4 hours or until a thermometer reads 160°.
Per ¾ cup: 178 cal., 7g fat (4g sat. fat), 49mg chol., 635mg sod., 23g carb. (3g sugars, 3g fiber), 6g pro.
Diabetic exchanges: 1½ starch, 1 fat.

THAI CHICKEN
THIGHS

SPLIT PEA SOUP WITH HAM & JALAPENO ⬛

To me, this take on pea soup is total comfort food. I cook it low and slow all day, and it fills the house with a yummy aroma. It's so good with a warm, crispy baguette on the side.
—Chelsea Tichenor, Huntington Beach, CA

Prep: 15 min. • **Cook:** 6 hours
Makes: 6 servings (2¼ quarts)

- 2 smoked ham hocks
- 1 package (16 ounces) dried green split peas
- 4 medium carrots, cut into ½-inch slices
- 1 medium onion, chopped
- 1 jalapeno pepper, seeded and minced
- 3 garlic cloves, minced
- 8 cups water
- 1 teaspoon salt
- 1 teaspoon pepper

In a 4- or 5-qt. slow cooker, combine all ingredients. Cook, covered, on low until meat is tender, 6-8 hours. Remove meat from bones when cool enough to handle; cut ham into small pieces and return to slow cooker.

Note: Wear disposable gloves when cutting hot peppers; the oils can burn skin. Avoid touching your face.

Per 1½ cups: 316 cal., 2g fat (0 sat. fat), 9mg chol., 642mg sod., 55g carb. (9g sugars, 21g fiber), 22g pro.

THAI CHICKEN THIGHS ⬛

Thanks to the slow cooker, a traditional Thai dish that features peanut butter, jalapeno peppers and chili sauce becomes incredibly easy to make. If you want to crank up the spice a bit, then use more jalapeno peppers.
—*Taste of Home* Test Kitchen

Prep: 25 min. • **Cook:** 5 hours
Makes: 8 servings

- 8 bone-in chicken thighs (about 3 pounds), skin removed
- ½ cup salsa
- ¼ cup creamy peanut butter
- 2 tablespoons lemon juice
- 2 tablespoons reduced-sodium soy sauce
- 1 tablespoon chopped seeded jalapeno pepper
- 2 teaspoons Thai chili sauce
- 1 garlic clove, minced
- 1 teaspoon minced fresh gingerroot
- 2 green onions, sliced
- 2 tablespoons sesame seeds, toasted
  Hot cooked basmati rice, optional

1. Place chicken in a 3-qt. slow cooker. In a small bowl, combine the salsa, peanut butter, lemon juice, soy sauce, jalapeno, Thai chili sauce, garlic and ginger; pour over chicken.
2. Cover and cook on low for 5-6 hours or until chicken is tender. Sprinkle with green onions and sesame seeds. Serve with rice if desired.

Note: Wear disposable gloves when cutting hot peppers; the oils can burn skin. Avoid touching your face.

Per chicken thigh with ¼ cup sauce without rice: 261 cal., 15g fat (4g sat. fat), 87mg chol., 350mg sod., 5g carb. (2g sugars, 1g fiber), 27g pro.
Diabetic exchanges: 4 lean meat, 1 fat, ½ starch.

TOMATO BALSAMIC CHICKEN c

I came up with this saucy chicken when I was especially busy and didn't have the time to cook. Since we're new parents, my husband and I both appreciate having a go-to dinner that's easy, homemade and yummy.
—Anne Colvin, Chicago, IL

Prep: 25 min. • **Cook:** 6 hours
Makes: 6 servings

- 2 medium carrots, chopped
- ½ cup thinly sliced shallots
- 2 pounds bone-in chicken thighs, skin removed
- 1 tablespoon all-purpose flour
- ½ cup reduced-sodium chicken broth
- 1 can (14½ ounces) petite diced tomatoes, undrained
- ¼ cup balsamic vinegar
- 1 tablespoon olive oil
- 2 garlic cloves, minced
- 1 bay leaf
- ½ teaspoon Italian seasoning
- ½ teaspoon salt
- ¼ teaspoon pepper
  Hot cooked orzo

1. Place carrots and shallots in a 3- or 4-qt. slow cooker; top with chicken. In a bowl, whisk flour and broth until smooth; stir in tomatoes, vinegar, oil, garlic and seasonings. Pour over chicken. Cook, covered, on low until chicken and carrots are tender, 6-8 hours.
2. Remove chicken; cool slightly. Discard bay leaf and, if desired, skim the fat from carrot mixture.
3. Remove chicken from bones; shred slightly with two forks. Return to slow cooker and heat through. Serve with orzo.
Freeze option: Freeze cooled chicken mixture in freezer containers. To use, partially thaw in refrigerator overnight. Heat through in a saucepan, stirring occasionally.
Per ¾ cup chicken mixture: 235 cal., 11g fat (3g sat. fat), 77mg chol., 433mg sod., 12g carb. (7g sugars, 2g fiber), 23g pro.
Diabetic exchanges: 3 lean meat, 1 vegetable, ½ fat.

SOUTHWESTERN CHICKEN & LIMA BEAN STEW

I always try to have my daughter, son-in-law and grandchildren over when I make this supper. It makes me happy to hear them say, "That was so good!" or watch them quickly filling up their bowls for seconds. It's truly a good-for-you hit.
—Pam Corder, Monroe, LA

Prep: 20 min. • **Cook:** 6 hours
Makes: 6 servings

- 4 bone-in chicken thighs (1½ pounds), skin removed
- 2 cups frozen lima beans
- 2 cups frozen corn
- 1 large green pepper, chopped
- 1 large onion, chopped
- 2 cans (14 ounces each) fire-roasted diced tomatoes, undrained
- ¼ cup tomato paste
- 3 tablespoons Worcestershire sauce
- 3 garlic cloves, minced
- 1½ teaspoons ground cumin
- 1½ teaspoons dried oregano
- ¼ teaspoon salt
- ¼ teaspoon pepper
  Chopped fresh cilantro or parsley

1. Place the first five ingredients in a 5-qt. slow cooker. In a large bowl, combine the tomatoes, tomato paste, Worcestershire sauce, garlic and dry seasonings; pour over the top.
2. Cook, covered, on low 6-8 hours or until chicken is tender. Remove chicken from slow cooker. When cool enough to handle, remove meat from bones; discard the bones. Shred the meat with two forks; return to slow cooker and heat through. If desired, sprinkle with cilantro.
Per 1½ cups: 312 cal., 7g fat (2g sat. fat), 58mg chol., 614mg sod., 39g carb. (9g sugars, 8g fiber), 24g pro.
Diabetic exchanges: 3 lean meat, 2 starch, 1 vegetable.

SOUTHWESTERN CHICKEN & LIMA BEAN STEW

SLOW-COOKED SWISS STEAK ☐

This is one of my favorite dishes to make because I can flour and season the steaks and refrigerate them overnight. The next morning, I just put all the ingredients in the slow cooker, and I have a delicious dinner waiting for us when I arrive home from work.
—Sarah Burks, Wathena, KS

Prep: 10 min. • **Cook:** 6 hours
Makes: 6 servings

- 2 tablespoons all-purpose flour
- ½ teaspoon salt
- ¼ teaspoon pepper
- 1½ pounds beef round steak, cut into six pieces
- 1 medium onion, cut into ¼-inch slices
- 1 celery rib, cut into ½-inch slices
- 2 cans (8 ounces each) tomato sauce

1. In a large resealable plastic bag, combine the flour, salt and pepper. Add the steak; seal bag and shake to coat.
2. Place the onion in a greased 3-qt. slow cooker. Top with the steak, celery and tomato sauce. Cover and cook on low for 6-8 hours or until meat is tender.
Per serving: 171 cal., 4g fat (1g sat. fat), 64mg chol., 409mg sod., 6g carb. (2g sugars, 1g fiber), 27g pro.
Diabetic exchanges: 3 lean meat, 1 vegetable.

SLOW-COOKED
LEMON CHICKEN

SLOW-COOKED LEMON CHICKEN ☐

This is the perfect recipe when you need a taste of spring. A hint of lemon, fresh parsley and few seasonings and you can brighten up everyday chicken.
—Walter Powell, Wilmington, DE

Prep: 20 min. • **Cook:** 5¼ hours
Makes: 6 servings

- 6 bone-in chicken breast halves (12 ounces each), skin removed
- 1 teaspoon dried oregano
- ½ teaspoon seasoned salt
- ¼ teaspoon pepper
- 2 tablespoons butter
- ¼ cup water
- 3 tablespoons lemon juice
- 2 garlic cloves, minced
- 1 teaspoon chicken bouillon granules
- 2 teaspoons minced fresh parsley
  Hot cooked rice

1. Pat chicken dry with paper towels. Combine the oregano, seasoned salt and pepper; rub over chicken. In a skillet over medium heat, brown the chicken in butter; transfer to a 5-qt. slow cooker. Add water, lemon juice, garlic and bouillon to the skillet; bring to a boil, stirring to loosen browned bits. Pour over chicken.
2. Cover and cook on low for 5-6 hours. Baste chicken with cooking juices. Add parsley. Cover and cook 15-30 minutes longer or until meat juices run clear. Serve with rice. (If desired, cooking juices may be thickened before serving.)
Per chicken breast half: 336 cal., 10g fat (4g sat. fat), 164mg chol., 431mg sod., 1g carb. (0 sugars, 0 fiber), 56g pro.

✱

TEST KITCHEN TIP

Browning meats, such as chicken, in a skillet before setting them in a slow cooker adds color and locks in flavor.

SLOW-COOKED VEGETABLES C

I like to simmer an assortment of garden-fresh vegetables for this satisfying side dish. My sister-in-law shared the recipe with me. It's a favorite at potlucks.
—Kathy Westendorf, Westgate, IA

Prep: 10 min. • **Cook:** 7 hours
Makes: 8 servings

- 4 celery ribs, cut into 1-inch pieces
- 4 small carrots, cut into 1-inch pieces
- 2 medium tomatoes, cut into chunks
- 2 medium onions, thinly sliced
- 2 cups cut fresh green beans (1-inch pieces)
- 1 medium green pepper, cut into 1-inch pieces
- ¼ cup butter, melted
- 3 tablespoons quick-cooking tapioca
- 1 tablespoon sugar
- 1 teaspoon salt
- ⅛ teaspoon pepper

1. Place the vegetables in a 3-qt. slow cooker. In a small bowl, combine the butter, tapioca, sugar, salt and pepper; pour over vegetables and stir well.
2. Cover and cook on low for 7-8 hours or until vegetables are tender. Serve with a slotted spoon.
Per cup: 113 cal., 6g fat (4g sat. fat), 15mg chol., 379mg sod., 15g carb. (6g sugars, 3g fiber), 2g pro.
Diabetic exchanges: 1 vegetable, 1 fat, ½ starch.

SLOW-COOKED VEGETABLES

SLOW-COOKED FRUITED OATMEAL WITH NUTS S M

The beauty of this meal is that it slow-cooks overnight and you can nicely feed a crowd in the morning. If the oatmeal is too thick, add a little more milk.
—Trisha Kruse, Eagle, ID

Prep: 15 min. • **Cook:** 6 hours
Makes: 6 servings

- 3 cups water
- 2 cups old-fashioned oats
- 2 cups chopped apples
- 1 cup dried cranberries
- 1 cup fat-free milk
- 2 teaspoons butter, melted
- 1 teaspoon pumpkin pie spice
- 1 teaspoon ground cinnamon
- 6 tablespoons chopped almonds, toasted
- 6 tablespoons chopped pecans, toasted
  Additional fat-free milk

1. In a 3-qt. slow cooker coated with cooking spray, combine the first eight ingredients. Cover and cook on low for 6-8 hours or until liquid is absorbed.
2. Spoon oatmeal into bowls. Sprinkle with almonds and pecans; drizzle with additional milk if desired.
Per cup: 306 cal., 13g fat (2g sat. fat), 4mg chol., 28mg sod., 45g carb. (20g sugars, 6g fiber), 8g pro.
Diabetic exchanges: 3 starch, 2 fat.

SLOW-ROASTED ROOT VEGETABLES

When she was a little girl growing up in Italy, my Aunt Virginia learned to make a dish called Noodles and Nuts. I tried the topping on carrots and parsnips instead of noodles and haven't looked back.
—Terri Collins, Pittsburgh, PA

Prep: 15 min. • **Cook:** 5 hours
Makes: 12 servings

- 2 pounds fresh baby carrots
- 1 medium onion, halved and thinly sliced
- ¼ cup butter, cubed
- 3 garlic cloves, minced
- ¾ teaspoon salt
- ¼ teaspoon pepper
- 1½ pounds medium parsnips
- 2 tablespoons seasoned bread crumbs
- ¾ cup chopped walnuts, toasted
- 3 tablespoons grated Romano cheese, optional

1. In a 5-qt. slow cooker, combine first six ingredients. Cut parsnips crosswise into 2-in. pieces. Cut the thinner pieces in half; cut thicker into quarters. Stir into the carrot mixture.
2. Cook, covered, on low until tender, 5-6 hours. To serve, stir in the bread crumbs; sprinkle with walnuts and, if desired, cheese.
Note: To toast nuts, bake in a shallow pan in a 350° oven for 5-10 minutes or cook in a skillet over low heat until lightly browned, stirring occasionally.
Per ⅔ cup: 158 cal., 9g fat (3g sat. fat), 10mg chol., 263mg sod., 19g carb. (7g sugars, 4g fiber), 3g pro.
Diabetic exchanges: 2 fat, 1 starch.

SLOW-ROASTED ROOT VEGETABLES

SLOW-COOKED CHILI

My hearty chili can simmer for as long as 10 hours on low in the slow cooker. It's so good to come home to its wonderful aroma after a long day away.
—Sue Call, Beech Grove, IN

Prep: 20 min. • **Cook:** 8 hours
Makes: 10 servings (2½ quarts)

- 2 pounds lean ground beef (90% lean)
- 2 cans (16 ounces each) kidney beans, rinsed and drained
- 2 cans (14½ ounces each) diced tomatoes, undrained
- 1 can (8 ounces) tomato sauce
- 2 medium onions, chopped
- 1 green pepper, chopped
- 2 garlic cloves, minced
- 2 tablespoons chili powder
- 1 teaspoon salt
- 1 teaspoon pepper
  Shredded cheddar cheese and thinly sliced green onions, optional

1. In a large skillet, cook beef over medium heat until no longer pink; drain.
2. Transfer to a 5-qt. slow cooker. Add the next nine ingredients. Cover and cook on low for 8-10 hours. If desired, top individual servings with cheese and green onions.
Per cup without cheese: 260 cal., 8g fat (3g sat. fat), 57mg chol., 716mg sod., 23g carb. (6g sugars, 7g fiber), 25g pro.
Diabetic exchanges: 3 lean meat, 1½ starch, 1 vegetable.

PORK & BEEF BARBECUE

It's the combination of beef stew meat and tender pork that keeps friends and family asking about these tangy sandwiches. Add a little lettuce and tomato for a crisp, colorful contrast.
—Corbin Detgen, Buchanan, MI

Prep: 15 min. • **Cook:** 6 hours
Makes: 12 servings

- 1 can (6 ounces) tomato paste
- ½ cup packed brown sugar
- ¼ cup chili powder
- ¼ cup cider vinegar
- 2 teaspoons Worcestershire sauce
- 1 teaspoon salt
- 1½ pounds beef stew meat, cut into ¾-inch cubes
- 1½ pounds pork chop suey meat or pork tenderloin, cut into ¾-inch cubes
- 3 medium green peppers, chopped
- 2 large onions, chopped
- 12 sandwich buns, split
  Lettuce and tomatoes, optional

1. In a 5-qt. slow cooker, combine the first six ingredients. Stir in beef, pork, green peppers and onions. Cover and cook on low for 6-8 hours or until meat is tender.
2. Shred meat with two forks. Serve on buns, with lettuce and tomatoes if desired.
Per sandwich: 444 cal., 12g fat (4g sat. fat), 69mg chol., 684mg sod., 52g carb. (17g sugars, 3g fiber), 32g pro.

SLOW-COOKED MOROCCAN CHICKEN

SLOW-COOKED MOROCCAN CHICKEN

Spices really work their magic on plain chicken in this exciting dish. Dried fruit and couscous add an exotic touch.
—Kathy Morgan, Ridgefield, WA

Prep: 20 min. • **Cook:** 6 hours
Makes: 4 servings

- 4 medium carrots, sliced
- 2 large onions, halved and sliced
- 1 broiler/fryer chicken (3 to 4 pounds), cut up, skin removed
- ½ teaspoon salt
- ½ cup chopped dried apricots
- ½ cup raisins
- 1 can (14½ ounces) reduced-sodium chicken broth
- ¼ cup tomato paste
- 2 tablespoons all-purpose flour
- 2 tablespoons lemon juice
- 2 garlic cloves, minced
- 1½ teaspoons ground ginger
- 1½ teaspoons ground cumin
- 1 teaspoon ground cinnamon
- ¾ teaspoon pepper
  Hot cooked couscous

1. Place carrots and onions in a greased 5-qt. slow cooker. Sprinkle chicken with salt; add to slow cooker. Top with apricots and raisins. In a small bowl, whisk broth, tomato paste, flour, lemon juice, garlic and seasonings until blended; add to the slow cooker.
2. Cook, covered, on low 6-7 hours or until chicken is tender. Serve with couscous.
Per serving without couscous: 435 cal., 9g fat (3g sat. fat), 110mg chol., 755mg sod., 47g carb. (27g sugars, 6g fiber), 42g pro.

BEEF
ENTREES

"When I'm looking for a fast entree, I turn to this beef and broccoli stir-fry. It features a tantalizing sauce made with garlic and ginger."
—Rosa Evans, Odessa, MO

Mexi-Mac Skillet (p. 123) **Sesame Beef Skewers** (p. 127) **Saucy Beef & Cabbage Supper** (p. 133)
Balsamic Steak Salad (p. 125) **Saucy Beef with Broccoli** (p. 126) **Sirloin with Mushroom Sauce** (p. 132)

BEEF ENTREES

TERIYAKI STEAK SKEWERS ©

When these flavorful skewered steaks are sizzling on the grill, the aroma makes everyone around stop what they're doing and come to see what's cooking. The tasty marinade is easy to make, and these little steaks are quick to cook and fun to eat.
—Jeri Dobrowski, Beach, ND

Prep: 15 min. + marinating • **Grill:** 10 min.
Makes: 6 servings

- ½ cup reduced-sodium soy sauce
- ¼ cup cider vinegar
- 2 tablespoons brown sugar
- 2 tablespoons finely chopped onion
- 1 tablespoon canola oil
- 1 garlic clove, minced
- ½ teaspoon ground ginger
- ⅛ teaspoon pepper
- 2 pounds beef top sirloin steak, cut into ½-in.-thick strips

1. In a large bowl, mix the first eight ingredients; toss with beef. Refrigerate, covered, 2-3 hours.
2. Thread beef strips, weaving back and forth, onto six metal or soaked wooden skewers; discard marinade. Grill beef, uncovered, over medium heat until desired doneness, 6-9 minutes, turning occasionally.
Per skewer: 222 cal., 7g fat (2g sat. fat), 61mg chol., 452mg sod., 3g carb. (2g sugars, 0 fiber), 33g pro.
Diabetic exchanges: 4 lean meat.

TACO STUFFED PASTA SHELLS

Here's a kid-friendly dish so flavorful and fun, nobody is likely to guess that it's also lower in fat. It's a great family supper for busy weeknights!
—Anne Thomsen, Westchester, OH

Prep: 25 min. • **Bake:** 25 min.
Makes: 6 servings

- 18 uncooked jumbo pasta shells
- 1½ pounds lean ground beef (90% lean)
- 2 teaspoons chili powder
- 3 ounces fat-free cream cheese, cubed
- 1 bottle (16 ounces) taco sauce, divided
- ¾ cup shredded reduced-fat Mexican cheese blend, divided
- 20 baked tortilla chip scoops, coarsely crushed

1. Preheat oven to 350°. Cook the pasta according to package directions. Drain and rinse in cold water; drain again.
2. Meanwhile, in a large skillet, cook and crumble beef over medium-high heat until no longer pink, 6-8 minutes. Stir in chili powder, cream cheese and ½ cup taco sauce until blended. Stir in ¼ cup shredded cheese.
3. Spoon about 2 tablespoons filling into each shell. Place in an 11x7-in. baking dish coated with cooking spray. Top with the remaining taco sauce.
4. Bake, covered, until heated through, 20-25 minutes. Sprinkle with remaining cheese; bake, uncovered, until the cheese is melted, about 5 minutes. Sprinkle with chips.
Freeze option: Cool unbaked casserole; cover and freeze. To use, partially thaw in refrigerator overnight. Remove from refrigerator 30 minutes before baking. Preheat oven to 350°. Cover casserole with foil; bake as directed, increasing the time as necessary to heat through and for a thermometer inserted in the center to read 165°. Top with cheese and chips as directed.
Per 3 stuffed shells: 384 cal., 13g fat (5g sat. fat), 67mg chol., 665mg sod., 33g carb. (4g sugars, 3g fiber), 33g pro.

SIRLOIN STRIPS OVER RICE

I found this recipe in a movie magazine some 20 years ago. It was the favorite of some male star—but I don't remember who. Its great flavor and the fact that leftovers just get better have made it a family favorite!

—Karen Dunn, Kansas City, MO

Prep: 15 min. • **Cook:** 30 min.
Makes: 6 servings

- 1½ pounds beef top sirloin steak, cut into thin strips
- 1 teaspoon salt
- ¼ teaspoon pepper
- 2 teaspoons olive oil, divided
- 2 medium onions, thinly sliced
- 1 garlic clove, minced
- 1 can (14½ ounces) diced tomatoes, undrained
- ½ cup reduced-sodium beef broth
- ⅓ cup dry red wine or additional reduced-sodium beef broth
- 1 bay leaf
- ½ teaspoon dried basil
- ½ teaspoon dried thyme
- 3 cups hot cooked brown rice

1. Sprinkle the beef strips with salt and pepper. In a large nonstick skillet coated with cooking spray, brown the beef in 1 teaspoon oil. Remove and keep warm.

2. In the same skillet, saute onions in remaining oil until tender. Add garlic; cook for 1 minute longer. Stir in the tomatoes, broth, wine, bay leaf, basil and thyme. Bring to a boil. Reduce heat; simmer, uncovered, for 10 minutes.

3. Return beef to the pan; cook for 2-4 minutes or until tender. Discard bay leaf. Serve with rice.

Per ⅔ cup beef mixture with ½ cup rice: 318 cal., 7g fat (2g sat. fat), 46mg chol., 595mg sod., 33g carb. (4g sugars, 3g fiber), 28g pro.
Diabetic Exchanges: 3 lean meat, 1½ starch, 1 vegetable, ½ fat.

MEXI-MAC SKILLET `FAST FIX`
(PICTURED ON P. 120)

My husband loves this recipe, and I love how simple it is to put together! Because you don't need to precook the macaroni, it's a time-saving dish.

—Maurane Ramsey, Fort Wayne, IN

Start to Finish: 30 min.
Makes: 4 servings

- 1 pound extra-lean ground beef (95% lean)
- 1 large onion, chopped
- 1¼ teaspoons chili powder
- 1 teaspoon dried oregano
- ¼ teaspoon salt
- 1 can (14½ ounces) diced tomatoes, undrained
- 1 can (8 ounces) tomato sauce
- 1 cup fresh or frozen corn
- ½ cup water
- ⅔ cup uncooked elbow macaroni
- ½ cup shredded reduced-fat cheddar cheese

1. In a large nonstick skillet, cook and crumble beef with onion over medium-high heat until no longer pink, 5-7 minutes.

2. Stir in seasonings, tomatoes, tomato sauce, corn and water; bring to a boil. Stir in the macaroni. Reduce the heat; simmer, covered, until macaroni is tender, 15-20 minutes, stirring occasionally. Sprinkle with cheese.

Per 1¼ cups: 318 cal., 10g fat (4g sat. fat), 75mg chol., 755mg sod., 28g carb. (9g sugars, 5g fiber), 32g pro.
Diabetic exchanges: 3 lean meat, 1 starch, 1 vegetable.

SIRLOIN STRIPS OVER RICE

**POTATO-TOPPED
GROUND BEEF SKILLET**

POTATO-TOPPED GROUND BEEF SKILLET

The depth of flavor in this recipe is amazing. I never have leftovers when I take it to potlucks. I love recipes that I can cook and serve in the same skillet. If your butcher has chili grind beef, which is coarsely ground, go for that. It lends an extra-meaty texture.
—Fay Moreland, Wichita Falls, TX

Prep: 25 min. • **Cook:** 45 min.
Makes: 8 servings

- 2 **pounds lean ground beef (90% lean)**
- ½ **teaspoon salt**
- ¼ **teaspoon pepper**
- 1 **tablespoon olive oil**
- 1 **large onion, chopped**
- 4 **medium carrots, sliced**
- 8 **ounces sliced fresh mushrooms**
- 4 **garlic cloves, minced**
- 2 **tablespoons all-purpose flour**
- 2 **teaspoons herbes de Provence**
- 1¼ **cups dry red wine or reduced-sodium beef broth**
- 1 **can (14½ ounces) reduced-sodium beef broth**

TOPPING

- 1¼ **pounds red potatoes (about 4 medium), cut into ¼-inch slices**
- 1 **tablespoon olive oil**
- ¼ **teaspoon salt**
- ⅛ **teaspoon pepper**
- ⅓ **cup shredded Parmesan cheese Minced fresh parsley, optional**

1. In a broiler-safe 12-in. skillet, cook and crumble beef over medium-high heat until no longer pink, 6-8 minutes. Stir in salt and pepper; remove from pan.

2. In same pan, heat oil over medium-high heat; saute onion, carrots, mushrooms and garlic until the onion is tender, 4-6 minutes. Stir in the flour and herbs; cook 1 minute. Stir in wine; bring to a boil. Cook 1 minute, stirring to loosen browned bits from pan. Add beef and broth; return to a boil. Reduce heat; simmer, covered, until flavors are blended, about 30 minutes, stirring occasionally. Remove from heat.

3. Meanwhile, place potatoes in a large saucepan; add water to cover. Bring to a boil. Reduce heat; cook, uncovered, until tender, 10-12 minutes. Drain; cool slightly.

4. Preheat broiler. Arrange potatoes over stew, overlapping slightly; brush lightly with oil. Sprinkle with salt and pepper, then cheese. Broil 5-6 in. from heat until potatoes are lightly browned, 6-8 minutes. Let stand 5 minutes. If desired, sprinkle with parsley.

Per 1¼ cups: 313 cal., 14g fat (5g sat. fat), 74mg chol., 459mg sod., 18g carb. (4g sugars, 3g fiber), 26g pro.
Diabetic exchanges: 3 lean meat, 1 vegetable, ½ starch, ½ fat.

SPINACH DIP BURGERS `FAST FIX`

Every Friday night is burger night at our house. The tomatoes add fresh flavor and the cool spinach dip brings it all together. We often skip the buns and serve these over a bed of grilled cabbage.
—Courtney Stultz, Weir, KS

Start to Finish: 20 min.
Makes: 4 servings

- 1 large egg, lightly beaten
- 2 tablespoons fat-free milk
- ½ cup soft bread crumbs
- 1 teaspoon dried basil
- ½ teaspoon salt
- ¼ teaspoon pepper
- 1 pound lean ground beef (90% lean)
- 4 whole-wheat hamburger buns, split
- ¼ cup spinach dip
- ¼ cup julienned soft sun-dried tomatoes (not packed in oil)
  Lettuce leaves

SPINACH DIP BURGERS

1. Combine the first six ingredients. Add beef; mix lightly but thoroughly. Shape into four ½-in.-thick patties.
2. Place burgers on an oiled grill rack or in a greased 15x1x1-in. pan. Grill, covered, over medium heat or broil 4-5 in. from heat until a thermometer reads 160°, 4-5 minutes per side. Grill buns, cut side down, over medium heat until toasted. Serve burgers on buns; top with spinach dip, tomatoes and lettuce.

Note: To make soft bread crumbs, tear bread into pieces and place in a food processor or blender. Cover and pulse until crumbs form. One slice of bread yields ½-¾ cup crumbs. This recipe was tested with sun-dried tomatoes that do not need to be soaked before use.

Per burger: 389 cal., 17g fat (6g sat. fat), 125mg chol., 737mg sod., 29g carb. (7g sugars, 4g fiber), 29g pro.
Diabetic exchanges: 3 lean meat, 2 starch, 1½ fat.

BALSAMIC STEAK SALAD `C`
(PICTURED ON P. 120)

My husband loves blue cheese and I like a hearty salad that eats like a meal, so I put the two things together in this salad. The sweet-tart dried cranberries pair up deliciously with cheese, creamy avocado and balsamic vinegar. It's irresistible!
—Marla Clark, Albuquerque, NM

Prep: 15 min. + marinating • **Grill:** 15 min.
Makes: 4 servings

- ¼ cup balsamic vinegar
- ¼ cup olive oil
- 2 teaspoons lemon juice
- 1 teaspoon minced fresh thyme or ¼ teaspoon dried thyme
- ¼ teaspoon salt
- ⅛ teaspoon coarsely ground pepper
- 1 beef flat iron steak or top sirloin steak (¾ pound)
- 1 package (9 ounces) ready-to-serve salad greens
- 8 cherry tomatoes, halved
- 4 radishes, sliced
- ½ medium ripe avocado, peeled and thinly sliced
- ¼ cup dried cranberries
  Crumbled blue cheese and additional pepper, optional

1. For dressing, whisk together the first six ingredients. Place steak and ¼ cup dressing in a resealable plastic bag; seal bag and turn to coat. Refrigerate 8 hours or overnight. Reserve remaining dressing; cover and refrigerate until serving.
2. Drain beef, discarding marinade. Grill steak, covered, over medium heat or broil 4 in. from heat until meat reaches desired doneness (for medium-rare, a thermometer should read 135°; medium, 160°), 6-8 minutes per side. Let stand 5 minutes before slicing.
3. To serve, divide salad greens among four plates. Top with steak, tomatoes, radishes and avocado; sprinkle with cranberries and, if desired, cheese and pepper. Serve with reserved dressing.

Per serving: 321 cal., 22g fat (5g sat. fat), 55mg chol., 221mg sod., 15g carb. (9g sugars, 4g fiber), 18g pro.
Diabetic exchanges: 3 fat, 2 lean meat, 2 vegetable.

SAUCY BEEF WITH BROCCOLI `FAST FIX`
(PICTURED ON P. 121)

When I'm looking for a fast entree, I turn to this beef and broccoli stir-fry. It features a tantalizing sauce made with garlic and ginger.
—Rosa Evans, Odessa, MO

Start to Finish: 30 min.
Makes: 2 servings

- 1 tablespoon cornstarch
- ½ cup reduced-sodium beef broth
- ¼ cup sherry or additional beef broth
- 2 tablespoons reduced-sodium soy sauce
- 1 tablespoon brown sugar
- 1 garlic clove, minced
- 1 teaspoon minced fresh gingerroot
- 2 teaspoons canola oil, divided
- ½ pound beef top sirloin steak, cut into ¼-inch-thick strips
- 2 cups fresh small broccoli florets
- 8 green onions, cut into 1-inch pieces

1. Mix first seven ingredients. In a large nonstick skillet, heat 1 teaspoon oil over medium-high heat; stir-fry the beef until browned, 1-3 minutes. Remove from pan.
2. Stir-fry broccoli in the remaining oil until crisp-tender, 3-5 minutes. Add green onions; cook just until tender, 1-2 minutes. Stir cornstarch mixture and add to pan. Bring to a boil; cook and stir until sauce is thickened, 2-3 minutes. Add beef and heat through.

Per 1¼ cups: 313 cal., 11g fat (3g sat. fat), 68mg chol., 816mg sod., 20g carb. (11g sugars, 4g fiber), 29g pro.
Diabetic exchanges: 3 lean meat, 1 starch, 1 vegetable, 1 fat.

★ ★ ★ ★ ★ **READER REVIEW**

"LOVE fresh ginger! The ginger really adds flavor to this dish. It was very simple and great for busy weeknights. We served it over some cauliflower rice for a complete, healthy meal!"

LPHJKITCHEN TASTEOFHOME.COM

ASIAN NOODLE & BEEF SALAD

ASIAN NOODLE & BEEF SALAD `FAST FIX`

My Asian-inspired pasta salad is crunchy, tangy and light. If you have fresh herbs, like basil or cilantro, on hand, add them to the mix. If you like, you can make it ahead, refrigerate it and serve it cold.
—Kelsey Casselbury, Odenton, MD

Start to Finish: 30 min.
Makes: 4 servings

- ¼ cup reduced-sodium soy sauce
- ¼ cup lime juice
- 2 tablespoons sugar
- 2 tablespoons rice vinegar
- 1 tablespoon grated fresh gingerroot
- 1 tablespoon sesame oil
- 1 beef top sirloin steak (1 pound)
- ¼ teaspoon pepper
- 6 ounces thin rice noodles
- 1 cup julienned zucchini
- 2 medium carrots, thinly sliced
- 1 celery rib, sliced

1. For dressing, mix first six ingredients. Sprinkle steak with pepper. Grill, covered, over medium heat until meat reaches desired doneness (for medium-rare, a thermometer should read 135°; medium, 160°), 6-8 minutes per side. Let stand 5 minutes before slicing.
2. Meanwhile, prepare rice noodles according to package directions. Drain; rinse with cold water and drain again. In a large bowl, combine noodles, vegetables and steak; toss with dressing.

Per 1½ cups: 399 cal., 8g fat (2g sat. fat), 46mg chol., 855mg sod., 50g carb. (11g sugars, 2g fiber), 29g pro.

VEGGIE STEAK SALAD
C FAST FIX

This salad just explodes with flavors. It's easy and quick to prepare, tastes delicious, and is a healthy dinner all on one plate.
—Tiffany Martinez, Aliso Viejo, CA

Start to Finish: 30 min.
Makes: 5 servings

- 2 medium ears sweet corn, husked
- 1 beef flank steak (1 pound)
- ¼ teaspoon salt
- ¼ teaspoon pepper
- 2 tablespoons olive oil

DRESSING
- 2 tablespoons olive oil
- 2 tablespoons balsamic vinegar
- 1 teaspoon garlic powder
- 1 teaspoon capers, drained
- 1 teaspoon Dijon mustard

SALAD
- 1 package (5 ounces) spring mix salad greens
- 1 large tomato, chopped
- 4 slices red onion, separated into rings
- ¼ cup minced fresh parsley
- ¼ cup shredded Parmesan cheese

1. In a pot of boiling water, cook corn, uncovered, until tender, 3-5 minutes. Remove; cool slightly. Cut corn from cobs.
2. Sprinkle steak with salt and pepper. In a large skillet, heat 2 tablespoons oil over medium heat. Add the steak; cook until a thermometer reads 145° for medium rare, 6-8 minutes per side. Remove from heat; let stand 5 minutes.
3. In a small bowl, whisk together the dressing ingredients. Thinly slice steak across the grain. Place greens, tomato, onion, parsley, corn and steak in a large bowl; toss with the dressing. Sprinkle with cheese.

Per 2 cups: 301 cal., 19g fat (5g sat. fat), 46mg chol., 301mg sod., 12g carb. (5g sugars, 2g fiber), 21g pro.
Diabetic exchanges: 3 lean meat, 2½ fat, 2 vegetable.

SESAME BEEF SKEWERS FAST FIX
(PICTURED ON P. 120)

A bottle of sesame-ginger dressing makes this amazing dish doable on any weeknight. My pineapple-y salad easily caps off dinner. You can broil the beef, too, but we live in the South, where people grill pretty much all year long.
—Janice Elder, Charlotte, NC

Start to Finish: 30 min.
Makes: 4 servings

- 1 pound beef top sirloin steak, cut into 1-inch cubes
- 6 tablespoons sesame ginger salad dressing, divided
- 1 tablespoon reduced-sodium soy sauce
- 2 cups chopped fresh pineapple
- 2 medium apples, chopped
- 1 tablespoon sweet chili sauce
- 1 tablespoon lime juice
- ¼ teaspoon pepper
- 1 tablespoon sesame seeds, toasted

1. In a bowl, toss beef with 3 tablespoons of dressing and soy sauce; let stand for 10 minutes. Meanwhile, in a large bowl, combine pineapple, apples, chili sauce, lime juice and pepper; toss to combine.
2. Thread beef onto four metal or soaked wooden skewers; discard the remaining marinade. Grill kabobs, covered, over medium heat or broil 4 in. from heat until desired doneness, 7-9 minutes, turning occasionally; brush them generously with the remaining dressing during the last 3 minutes. Sprinkle with sesame seeds. Serve with pineapple mixture.

Per kabob with 1 cup salad: 311 cal., 11g fat (3g sat. fat), 46mg chol., 357mg sod., 28g carb. (21g sugars, 3g fiber), 25g pro.
Diabetic exchanges: 3 lean meat, 1 starch, 1 fruit, ½ fat.

VEGGIE STEAK SALAD

**SPAGHETTI SQUASH
MEATBALL CASSEROLE**

SPAGHETTI SQUASH MEATBALL CASSEROLE

One of our favorite comfort food dinners is spaghetti and meatballs. We really enjoy this healthier version that includes lots of veggies. The same great flavors with nutritious ingredients!
—Courtney Stultz, Weir, KS

Prep: 35 min. • **Bake:** 30 min.
Makes: 6 servings

- 1 medium spaghetti squash (about 4 pounds)
- ½ teaspoon salt, divided
- ½ teaspoon fennel seed
- ¼ teaspoon ground coriander
- ¼ teaspoon dried basil
- ¼ teaspoon dried oregano
- 1 pound lean ground beef (90% lean)
- 2 teaspoons olive oil
- 1 medium onion, chopped
- 1 garlic clove, minced
- 2 cups chopped collard greens
- 1 cup chopped fresh spinach
- 1 cup reduced-fat ricotta cheese
- 2 plum tomatoes, chopped
- 1 cup pasta sauce
- 1 cup shredded part-skim mozzarella cheese

1. Cut squash lengthwise in half; discard seeds. Place halves on a microwave-safe plate, with cut side down. Microwave it, uncovered, on high until tender, 15-20 minutes. Cool slightly.
2. Preheat oven to 350°. Mix ¼ teaspoon salt with remaining seasonings; add to the beef, mixing lightly but thoroughly. Shape into 1½-in. balls. In a large skillet, brown the meatballs over medium heat; remove from pan.
3. In the same pan, heat oil over medium heat; saute onion until tender, about 3-4 minutes. Add the garlic; cook and stir for 1 minute. Stir in collard greens, spinach, ricotta cheese and remaining salt; remove from the heat.
4. Using a fork, separate the strands of spaghetti squash; stir into the greens mixture. Transfer to a greased 13x9-in. baking dish. Top with tomatoes, meatballs, sauce and cheese. Bake, uncovered, until the meatballs are cooked through, about 30-35 minutes.

Per serving: 362 cal., 16g fat (6g sat. fat), 69mg chol., 618mg sod., 32g carb. (7g sugars, 7g fiber), 26g pro.

BEEF BURGUNDY OVER NOODLES

Diabetic exchanges: 3 lean meat, 2 starch, 1 fat.

BEEF BURGUNDY OVER NOODLES

I got this delightful recipe many years ago from my sister-in-law. Whenever I serve it to guests, they always request the recipe. The tender beef, mushrooms and flavorful sauce are delicious over noodles.
—Margaret Welder, Madrid, IA

Prep: 10 min. • **Cook:** 1 hour 20 min.
Makes: 2 servings

- 2 teaspoons butter
- ½ pound beef top sirloin steak, cut into ¼-inch-thick strips
- 2 tablespoons diced onion
- 1½ cups quartered fresh mushrooms
- ¾ cup Burgundy wine or beef broth
- ¼ cup plus 2 tablespoons water, divided
- 3 tablespoons minced fresh parsley, divided
- 1 bay leaf
- 1 whole clove
- ¼ teaspoon salt
- ⅛ teaspoon pepper
- 2 cups uncooked medium egg noodles (about 4 ounces)
- 1 tablespoon all-purpose flour
- ½ teaspoon browning sauce, optional

1. In a Dutch oven or large nonstick skillet, heat butter over medium-high heat; saute beef and onion just until beef is lightly browned, 1-2 minutes. Stir in mushrooms, wine, ¼ cup water, 2 tablespoons parsley and seasonings; bring to a boil. Reduce heat; simmer, covered, until beef is tender, about 1 hour.
2. Meanwhile, cook the egg noodles according to package directions. Drain.
3. In a small bowl, mix flour and remaining water until smooth; stir into the beef mixture. Bring to a boil; cook and stir until thickened, about 2 minutes. Discard bay leaf and clove. If desired, stir in browning sauce. Serve over noodles. Sprinkle with remaining parsley.

Per 1½ cups: 376 cal., 10g fat (5g sat. fat), 88mg chol., 391mg sod., 34g carb. (2g sugars, 2g fiber), 32g pro
Diabetic exchanges: 3 lean meat, 2 starch, 1 vegetable, 1 fat.

ASIAN BEEF & NOODLES

ASIAN BEEF & NOODLES FAST FIX

I created this dish on a whim to feed my hungry teenagers. It has since become a dinnertime staple, and, now, two of my grandchildren make it in their own kitchens.
—Judy Batson, Tampa, FL

Start to Finish: 25 min.
Makes: 4 servings

- 1 beef top sirloin steak (1 pound), cut into ¼-inch-thick strips
- 6 tablespoons reduced-sodium teriyaki sauce, divided
- 8 ounces uncooked whole grain thin spaghetti
- 2 tablespoons canola oil, divided
- 3 cups broccoli coleslaw mix
- 1 medium onion, halved and thinly sliced
  Chopped fresh cilantro, optional

1. Toss beef with 2 tablespoons teriyaki sauce. Cook the spaghetti according to package directions; drain.

2. In a large skillet, heat 1 tablespoon oil over medium-high heat; stir-fry beef until browned, 1-3 minutes. Remove from pan.

3. In same skillet, heat the remaining oil over medium-high heat; stir-fry coleslaw mix and onion until crisp-tender, 3-5 minutes. Add spaghetti and remaining teriyaki sauce; toss and heat through. Stir in beef. If desired, sprinkle with cilantro.

Per 2 cups: 462 cal., 13g fat (2g sat. fat), 46mg chol., 546mg sod., 52g carb. (9g sugars, 8g fiber), 35g pro.

ARTICHOKE STEAK WRAPS FAST FIX

This simple, fast and flavorful dish is one the whole family loves. It's surprisingly easy to make, and you can broil the steak if you don't want to venture outside.
—Greg Fontenot, The Woodlands, TX

Start to Finish: 30 min.
Makes: 6 servings

- 8 ounces frozen artichoke hearts (about 2 cups), thawed and chopped
- 2 medium tomatoes, chopped
- ¼ cup chopped fresh cilantro
- ¾ teaspoon salt, divided
- 1 pound beef flat iron or top sirloin steak (1¼ pounds)
- ¼ teaspoon pepper
- 6 whole wheat tortillas (8 inches), warmed
  Lime wedges

1. Toss artichoke hearts and tomatoes with cilantro and ¼ teaspoon salt.

2. Sprinkle the steak with pepper and the remaining salt. Grill it, covered, over medium heat or broil 4 in. from heat until the meat reaches desired doneness (for medium-rare, a thermometer should read 135°; medium, 150°), about 5-6 minutes per side. Remove from heat; let it stand 5 minutes. Cut into thin slices. Serve steak and salsa in tortillas, folding bottom and sides of tortillas to close.

Per wrap: 301 cal., 11g fat (4g sat. fat), 61mg chol., 506mg sod., 27g carb. (1g sugars, 5g fiber), 24g pro.
Diabetic exchanges: 3 lean meat, 1½ starch.

ROASTED BEEF TENDERLOIN ⓒ

Roast beef marinated overnight in port wine and spices creates a simple but elegant roast I use for special occasions. Here's to a platter of good cheer.
—Schelby Thompson, Camden Wyoming, DE

Prep: 10 min. + marinating
Bake: 40 min. + standing
Makes: 12 servings

- ½ cup port wine or ½ cup beef broth plus 1 tablespoon balsamic vinegar
- ½ cup reduced-sodium soy sauce
- 2 tablespoons olive oil
- 4 to 5 garlic cloves, minced
- 1 teaspoon dried thyme
- 1 teaspoon pepper
- ½ teaspoon hot pepper sauce
- 1 beef tenderloin roast (3 pounds)
- 1 bay leaf

1. For marinade, whisk together the first seven ingredients. Place the roast, bay leaf and ¾ cup marinade into a large resealable plastic bag; seal the bag and turn to coat. Refrigerate 8 hours or overnight. Reserve remaining marinade for basting; cover and refrigerate.

2. Preheat oven to 425°. Place tenderloin on a rack in a roasting pan; discard bay leaf and marinade in bag. Roast until the meat reaches desired doneness (for medium-rare, a thermometer should read 135°; medium, 160°), 40-50 minutes, basting occasionally with the reserved marinade during the last 15 minutes.

3. Remove roast from oven; tent with foil. Let stand 10 minutes before slicing.

Per 3 ounces cooked beef: 193 cal., 8g fat (3g sat. fat), 49mg chol., 257mg sod., 2g carb. (1g sugars, 0 fiber), 25g pro.
Diabetic exchanges: 3 lean meat, ½ fat.

CURRIED BEEF STEW

My mother, who was Japanese, made a dish very similar to this. After a lot of experimenting, I came up with a version that is very close to the one she used to make. This recipe is special to me because it brings back memories of my mother.
—Gloria Gowins, Dalton, OH

Prep: 15 min. • **Cook:** 2 hours
Makes: 4 servings

- ¾ pound beef stew meat (1 to 1½-inch pieces)
- ¼ teaspoon salt
- ⅛ teaspoon pepper
- 2 tablespoons all-purpose flour
- 1 tablespoon canola oil
- 1 large onion, cut into ¾-inch pieces
- 2 tablespoons curry powder
- 2 teaspoons reduced-sodium soy sauce
- 2 bay leaves
- 3 cups beef stock
- 1½ pounds potatoes (about 3 medium), cut into 1-inch cubes
- 2 large carrots, thinly sliced
- 1 tablespoon white vinegar
  Hot cooked brown rice, optional

1. Sprinkle beef with salt and pepper; toss with flour. In a Dutch oven, heat oil over medium heat; cook beef and onion until lightly browned, stirring occasionally. Stir in curry powder, soy sauce, bay leaves and stock; bring to a boil. Reduce heat; simmer, covered, 45 minutes.

2. Stir in potatoes and carrots; return to a boil. Reduce heat; simmer, covered, until meat and vegetables are tender, 1 to 1¼ hours, stirring occasionally. Remove bay leaves; stir in the vinegar. If desired, serve with rice.

Per 1½ cups: 362 cal., 10g fat (3g sat. fat), 53mg chol., 691mg sod., 44g carb. (7g sugars, 7g fiber), 24g pro.
Diabetic exchanges: 3 starch, 3 lean meat, ½ fat.

ROASTED BEEF TENDERLOIN

SUMMER STEAK KABOBS

SUMMER STEAK KABOBS C

These meaty skewers not only satisfy my love of outdoor cooking, they feature a mouthwatering marinade, too. The marinade is terrific with chicken and pork, but I prefer it with beef because it tenderizes remarkably well.
—Christi Ross, Guthrie, TX

Prep: 20 min. + marinating • **Grill:** 10 min.
Makes: 6 servings

- ½ cup canola oil
- ¼ cup soy sauce
- 3 tablespoons honey
- 2 tablespoons white vinegar
- ½ teaspoon ground ginger
- ½ teaspoon garlic powder
- 1½ pounds beef top sirloin steak, cut into 1-inch cubes
- ½ pound whole fresh mushrooms
- 2 medium onions, cut into wedges
- 1 medium sweet red pepper, cut into 1-inch pieces
- 1 medium green pepper, cut into 1-inch pieces
- 1 medium yellow summer squash, cut into ½-inch slices
- Hot cooked rice

1. In a large resealable plastic bag, combine first six ingredients. Add beef; seal bag and turn to coat. Refrigerate 8 hours or overnight.

2. Using 12 metal or soaked wooden skewers, alternately thread the beef and vegetables; discard marinade. Grill kabobs, covered, over medium heat until the beef reaches desired doneness, 10-12 minutes, turning occasionally. Serve with rice.

Per 2 kabobs: 257 cal., 12g fat (2g sat. fat), 46mg chol., 277mg sod., 11g carb. (7g sugars, 2g fiber), 27g pro.
Diabetic exchanges: 3 lean meat, 1½ fat, 1 vegetable.

SIRLOIN WITH MUSHROOM SAUCE C FAST FIX ▶

(PICTURED ON P. 121)

A mouthwatering combination of rich mushroom sauce and peppery steak is a welcome way to finish off a busy day. Whenever visitors drop in around dinnertime, I pull out this recipe and it's ready before we know it.
—Joe Elliott, West Bend, WI

Start to Finish: 30 min.
Makes: 4 servings

- 1 beef top sirloin steak (1 pound and ¾ inch thick)
- 1 teaspoon coarsely ground pepper
- ½ teaspoon salt
- 1 teaspoon butter
- 1½ cups sliced fresh mushrooms
- 1 garlic clove, minced
- ½ cup beef broth
- ½ cup dry red wine or additional beef broth

1. Rub steak with pepper and salt. In a large skillet, heat butter over medium heat; cook the steak until meat reaches desired doneness (for medium-rare, a thermometer should read 135°; medium, 160°), 6-7 minutes per side. Remove from pan; keep warm.

2. Add mushrooms to pan; cook and stir over medium-high heat until lightly browned. Add garlic; cook and stir for 1 minute. Add broth and wine; bring to a boil, stirring to loosen browned bits from pan. Cook until liquid is reduced by half. Slice steak; serve with mushroom sauce.

Per serving: 189 cal., 6g fat (2g sat. fat), 49mg chol., 467mg sod., 2g carb. (1g sugars, 0 fiber), 25g pro.
Diabetic exchanges: 3 lean meat, ½ fat.

ONE-POT MEATY SPAGHETTI `FAST FIX`

I used to help my mom make this when I was growing up, and the recipe stuck. It was a beloved comfort food at college, and is now a weeknight staple for my fiance and me.
—Kristin Michalenko, Seattle, WA

Start to Finish: 30 min.
Makes: 6 servings

- 1 pound extra-lean ground beef (95% lean)
- 2 garlic cloves, minced
- 1 teaspoon sugar
- 1 teaspoon dried basil
- ½ teaspoon dried oregano
- ¼ teaspoon salt
- ¼ teaspoon paprika
- ¼ teaspoon pepper
- 1 can (28 ounces) diced tomatoes, undrained
- 1 can (15 ounces) tomato sauce
- 2 cups water
- ¼ cup chopped fresh parsley
- 8 ounces uncooked whole-wheat spaghetti, broken in half
- ¼ cup grated Parmesan cheese
  Additional chopped parsley

1. In a 6-qt. stockpot, cook and crumble beef with garlic over medium heat until no longer pink, 5-7 minutes. Stir in sugar and seasonings. Add tomatoes, tomato sauce, water and ¼ cup parsley; bring to a boil. Reduce heat; simmer, covered, 5 minutes.
2. Stir in the spaghetti, a little at a time; return to a boil. Reduce heat to medium-low; cook, uncovered, until the spaghetti is al dente, about 8-10 minutes, stirring occasionally. Stir in the cheese. Sprinkle with additional parsley.

Per 1⅓ cups: 292 cal., 6g fat (2g sat. fat), 46mg chol., 737mg sod., 40g carb. (6g sugars, 8g fiber), 24g pro.
Diabetic exchanges: 3 starch, 2 lean meat.

SAUCY BEEF & CABBAGE SUPPER
(PICTURED ON P. 121)

My beef and cabbage supper began as a Reuben sandwich idea without the gluten. We also make it with smoked sausage. It's comforting on cooler days.
—Courtney Stultz, Weir, KS

Prep: 15 min. • **Cook:** 20 min.
Makes: 6 servings

- 1 pound lean ground beef (90% lean)
- 1 medium onion, chopped
- 2 large garlic cloves, minced
- 1 small head cabbage, chopped (about 8 cups)
- 5 medium carrots, peeled and diced
- 3 tablespoons olive oil, divided
- 1 teaspoon salt
- 1 teaspoon pepper
- ½ teaspoon caraway seeds
- ¼ teaspoon ground allspice
- ⅛ teaspoon ground cloves
- ½ cup ketchup
- 2 teaspoons cider vinegar

1. In a 6-qt. stockpot, cook and crumble beef with onion and garlic over medium-high heat until no longer pink, 5-7 minutes. Stir in the cabbage, carrots, 2 tablespoons oil and seasonings; cook and stir until the vegetables are slightly softened, about 7-11 minutes.
2. Stir in ketchup, vinegar and remaining oil. Cook it, uncovered, about 5 minutes, stirring occasionally.

Per 1¼ cups: 260 cal., 13g fat (3g sat. fat), 47mg chol., 671mg sod., 20g carb. (12g sugars, 5g fiber), 17g pro.
Diabetic exchanges: 2 lean meat, 2 vegetable, 1½ fat, ½ starch.

★ ★ ★ ★ ★ **READER REVIEW**

"We throughly enjoyed this recipe and wouldn't change a thing!"
TOTHB TASTEOFHOME.COM

ONE-POT
MEATY SPAGHETTI

FLANK STEAK WITH CILANTRO SALSA VERDE
C **FAST FIX**

Even though steak is always a winner in our house, to make it even more special I add jarred salsa verde and top with freshly chopped tomato and avocado.
—Lily Julow, Lawrenceville, GA

Start to Finish: 25 min.
Makes: 4 servings

- 1 beef flank steak or top sirloin steak, 1 inch thick (about 1¼ pounds)
- ¼ teaspoon salt
- ¼ teaspoon pepper
- 1 cup salsa verde
- ½ cup fresh cilantro leaves
- 1 medium ripe avocado, peeled and diced
- 1 medium tomato, seeded and diced

1. Sprinkle steak with salt and pepper. Grill steak, covered, over medium heat or broil 4 in. from heat until meat reaches desired doneness (for medium-rare, a thermometer should read 135°; medium, 160°), 6-9 minutes per side. Let it stand for 5 minutes.

2. Meanwhile, process salsa and cilantro in a food processor until blended. Slice steak thinly across the grain; serve with salsa mixture, avocado and tomato.

Per serving: 263 cal., 15g fat (4g sat. fat), 54mg chol., 571mg sod., 8g carb. (2g sugars, 4g fiber), 24g pro.
Diabetic exchanges: 3 lean meat, 2 fat.

ROOT STEW

ROOT STEW

While inventing a new form of comfort food, I made a stew of carrots, turnips, parsnips and rutabaga. When I'm in the mood to change things up, I add potatoes or chicken.
—Maria Davis, Flower Mound, TX

Prep: 30 min. • **Bake:** 2 hours
Makes: 8 servings (2½ quarts)

- 2 tablespoons canola oil, divided
- 1½ pounds beef stew meat
- 1½ teaspoons salt
- ½ teaspoon pepper
- 1 medium onion, chopped
- 6 garlic cloves, minced
- 2 bay leaves
- 1 teaspoon dried thyme
- 3 cups reduced-sodium beef broth
- 3 medium carrots
- 2 medium turnips
- 2 medium parsnips
- 1 small rutabaga
- 2 tablespoons cornstarch
- ¼ cup cold water

1. Preheat oven to 325°. In an ovenproof Dutch oven, heat 1 tablespoon oil over medium heat. Brown the beef in batches. Remove from the pan; sprinkle with salt and pepper.

2. In the same pan, heat the remaining oil over medium heat. Add onion; cook and stir until tender, 4-6 minutes. Add garlic; cook and stir 1 minute. Stir in bay leaves, thyme, beef and broth; bring to a boil. Bake, covered, 1 hour.

3. Peel and cut the remaining vegetables into 1-in. pieces; add to Dutch oven. Bake, covered, until beef and vegetables are tender, 1 to 1¼ hours.

4. In a small bowl, mix cornstarch and water until smooth; stir into stew. Bring to a boil; cook and stir until thickened, 1-2 minutes. Discard bay leaves.

Per 1¼ cups: 227 cal., 10g fat (3g sat. fat), 55mg chol., 676mg sod., 16g carb. (6g sugars, 3g fiber), 18g pro.
Diabetic exchanges: 2 lean meat, 1 vegetable, 1 fat, ½ starch.
HEALTH TIP Carrots, turnips and rutabagas are all lower-calorie root vegetables. Adding them to soups and stews is a great way to add volume and nutrients and keep calories in check.

THAI SPINACH BEEF SALAD C FAST FIX

This main-dish salad is as satisfying as it gets. It's crunchy, meaty and a little bit spicy. Best of all, you get a big portion of this dish because it's so good for you.
—Janet Dingler, Cedartown, GA

Start to Finish: 20 min.
Makes: 4 servings

- ¼ cup lime juice
- 2 tablespoons brown sugar
- 2 tablespoons reduced-sodium soy sauce
- 1 teaspoon dried basil
- 1 teaspoon minced fresh mint or ½ teaspoon dried mint
- 1 teaspoon minced fresh gingerroot
- 1 pound beef top sirloin steak, cut into ¼-inch-thick strips
- 1 jalapeno pepper, seeded and chopped
- 1 garlic clove, minced
- 5 ounces fresh baby spinach (about 6 cups)
- 1 large sweet red pepper, julienned
- ½ medium cucumber, julienned

1. For dressing, mix first six ingredients until blended. Place a large nonstick skillet coated with cooking spray over medium-high heat. Add beef and jalapeno; cook and stir until the beef is no longer pink, 1-3 minutes. Add garlic; cook and stir 1 minute. Remove from heat.
2. Place the spinach, red pepper and cucumber in a large bowl. Add beef; toss with dressing. Serve immediately.

Per 2 cups: 207 cal., 5g fat (2g sat. fat), 46mg chol., 383mg sod., 14g carb. (10g sugars, 2g fiber), 27g pro.
Diabetic exchanges: 3 lean meat, 2 vegetable.

TEXAS OVEN-ROASTED BEEF BRISKET C

I was once a brisket novice, but now I cook up a classic dish with the taste of Texas. Thanks to a zesty spice rub, the end result is a fork-tender cut with a crispy crust.
—Audria Ausbern, Tahoka, TX

Prep: 20 min. • **Bake:** 3¼ hours
Makes: 10 servings

- 2 tablespoons chili powder
- 1 tablespoon sugar
- 1 tablespoon onion powder
- 1 tablespoon garlic powder
- 1 tablespoon pepper
- 2 teaspoons ground mustard
- 1 teaspoon salt
- 1 fresh beef brisket (4 pounds), halved
- 1 tablespoon canola oil
- 1½ cups beef broth
- 1 bay leaf

1. Preheat oven to 325°. Mix the first seven ingredients; rub over brisket. In an ovenproof Dutch oven, heat oil over medium heat; brown beef, one piece at a time, on both sides. Return first piece to pan. Add broth and bay leaf; bring to a boil.
2. Bake, covered, until the beef is tender, 3¼ to 3¾ hours. Remove brisket from pan; keep warm. Discard bay leaf; skim fat from the cooking juices. Cut brisket diagonally across the grain into thin slices. Serve it with cooking juices.

Note: This is a fresh beef brisket, not corned beef.
Per 5 ounces cooked beef: 264 cal., 10g fat (3g sat. fat), 77mg chol., 478mg sod., 4g carb. (1g sugars, 1g fiber), 38g pro.
Diabetic exchanges: 5 lean meat.

THAI SPINACH BEEF SALAD

SKILLET BEEF & POTATOES **FAST FIX** ▶

Sirloin strips with red potatoes and fresh rosemary are seriously amazing and ready in a flash. The key here is precooking potatoes in the microwave to speed the process.
—*Taste of Home* Test Kitchen

Start to Finish: 25 min.
Makes: 4 servings

- 1½ pounds red potatoes (about 5 medium), halved and cut into ¼-inch slices
- ⅓ cup water
- ½ teaspoon salt
- 1 pound beef top sirloin steak, cut into thin strips
- ½ cup chopped onion
- 3 tablespoons olive oil, divided
- 2 teaspoons garlic pepper blend
- 1½ teaspoons minced fresh rosemary

1. Place the potatoes, water and salt in a microwave-safe dish; microwave, covered, on high until the potatoes are tender, for 7-9 minutes. Drain.

2. Meanwhile, toss the beef with onion, 2 tablespoons oil and the pepper blend. Place a large skillet over medium-high heat. Add half of the beef mixture; cook and stir until beef is browned, 1-2 minutes. Remove from pan; repeat with remaining beef mixture.

3. In a clean skillet, heat the remaining oil over medium-high heat. Add potatoes; cook until potatoes are lightly browned, 4-5 minutes, turning occasionally. Stir in the beef mixture; heat through. Sprinkle with rosemary.

Per 1½ cups: 320 cal., 16g fat (4g sat. fat), 63mg chol., 487mg sod., 20g carb. (2g sugars, 2g fiber), 23g pro.
Diabetic exchanges: 3 lean meat, 2 fat, 1 starch.

❄

TEST KITCHEN TIP
To keep fresh rosemary all year-round, wrap sprigs in foil and place in a freezer bag. Freeze for up to 3 months. When using, remember that frozen rosemary has a stronger flavor than fresh.

PORTOBELLO BEEF STEW WITH CRANBERRY PILAF

PORTOBELLO BEEF STEW WITH CRANBERRY PILAF

For effortless entertaining, try this hearty stew. You can make it hours ahead, so you have plenty of time to get ready for your party. I serve it with baby greens and blue cheese tossed with balsamic vinaigrette.
—Rebecca Ames, Wylie, TX

Prep: 25 min. • **Cook:** 2 hours
Makes: 4 servings

- 1 pound beef stew meat
- ½ teaspoon salt
- ½ teaspoon coarsely ground pepper
- ¼ cup all-purpose flour
- 3 teaspoons canola oil, divided
- 1 pound sliced baby portobello mushrooms
- 2 garlic cloves, minced
- 1 cup reduced-sodium beef broth
- 1 cup white wine or additional broth
- 1 teaspoon dried thyme
- 1 teaspoon dried rosemary, crushed
- 2 tablespoons cornstarch
- 2 tablespoons water

PILAF

- 1 tablespoon butter
- ⅓ cup chopped celery
- ⅓ cup chopped onion
- 1 cup uncooked long grain rice
- ⅓ cup dried cranberries
- 2 cups reduced-sodium beef broth

1. Sprinkle beef with salt and pepper, then toss with flour to coat lightly; shake off the exxcess. In a Dutch oven, heat 2 teaspoons oil over medium heat; brown the beef. Remove from pan.

2. In the same pan, saute mushrooms in remaining oil over medium-high heat until tender. Add garlic; cook and stir 1 minute. Add broth, wine, thyme and rosemary, stirring to loosen browned bits from pan. Return beef to pan; bring to a boil. Reduce heat; simmer, covered, until beef is tender, 2 to 2½ hours.

3. Mix cornstarch and water until smooth; stir into stew. Bring to a boil; cook and stir until slightly thickened, 1-2 minutes.

4. For pilaf, in a saucepan, heat butter over medium-high heat; saute the celery and onion until tender. Add the rice and cranberries; cook and stir until the rice is lightly browned, 3-4 minutes. Stir in broth; bring to a boil. Reduce the heat; simmer, covered, until the rice is tender, 15-20 minutes. Fluff with a fork. Serve with stew.

Per 1¼ cups stew with ¾ cup rice: 518 cal., 15g fat (5g sat. fat), 82mg chol., 489mg sod., 63g carb. (13g sugars, 3g fiber), 31g pro.

BALSAMIC-SEASONED STEAK S C FAST FIX

This recipe delivers a tender steak without a long marinade. Steak sauce and Balsamic vinegar are a great team, and you can't go wrong with melty Swiss!
—Peggy Woodward, Shullsburg, WI

Start to Finish: 25 min.
Makes: 4 servings

- 1 beef top sirloin steak (¾ inch thick and 1 pound)
- ¼ teaspoon coarsely ground pepper
- 2 tablespoons balsamic vinegar
- 2 teaspoons steak sauce
- 2 ounces sliced reduced-fat Swiss cheese, cut into thin strips

1. Preheat broiler. Place steak on a broiler pan; sprinkle with pepper. Broil 4 in. from heat 7 minutes. Meanwhile, mix vinegar and steak sauce.

2. Turn steak; drizzle with 1 tablespoon vinegar mixture. Broil just until the meat reaches desired doneness (for medium-rare, a thermometer should read 135°; medium, 160°), 4-6 minutes.

3. Remove steak to a cutting board; let it stand 5 minutes. Cut steak into ¼-in. slices; return to broiler pan, arranging slices close together. Drizzle the slices with remaining vinegar mixture; top with cheese. Broil just until cheese is melted, 30-60 seconds.

Per 3 ounces cooked beef with ½ ounce cheese: 188 cal., 8g fat (3g sat. fat), 70mg chol., 116mg sod., 2g carb. (1g sugars, 0 fiber), 26g pro. **Diabetic exchanges:** 3 lean meat, ½ fat.

ARRABBIATA SAUCE WITH ZUCCHINI NOODLES

This popular Italian dish is spicy and full of flavor. We decided to recreate one of our favorite jarred sauces and serve over zucchini pasta for a lighter, healthier meal that's naturally gluten-free.
—Courtney Stultz, Weir, KS

Prep: 10 min. • **Cook:** 35 min.
Makes: 4 servings

- 1 pound lean ground beef (90% lean)
- ½ cup finely chopped onion
- 2 garlic cloves, minced
- 1 can (14½ ounces) petite diced tomatoes, undrained
- ¼ cup dry red wine or beef broth
- 3 tablespoons tomato paste
- 2 teaspoons honey
- 1 teaspoon cider vinegar
- ¾ teaspoon dried basil
- ½ to 1 teaspoon crushed red pepper flakes
- ½ teaspoon salt
- ¼ teaspoon dried oregano
- ¼ teaspoon dried thyme

ZUCCHINI NOODLES

- 2 large zucchini
- 1 tablespoon olive oil
- ¼ teaspoon salt
  Chopped fresh parsley, optional

1. In a large saucepan, cook and crumble beef with onion and garlic over medium-high heat until no longer pink, 5-7 minutes. Stir in the tomatoes, wine, tomato paste, honey, vinegar and seasonings; bring to a boil. Reduce heat; simmer, uncovered, until the flavors are blended, about 25 minutes, stirring occasionally.

2. For noodles, trim ends of zucchini. Using a spiralizer, cut zucchini into thin strands. In a large skillet, heat oil over medium-high heat. Add zucchini; cook until slightly softened, 1-2 minutes, tossing constantly with tongs (do not overcook). Sprinkle with salt. Serve with sauce. If desired, sprinkle with parsley.

Freeze option: Freeze cooled sauce in freezer containers. To use, partially thaw in refrigerator overnight. Heat through in a saucepan, stirring occasionally.

Note: If a spiralizer is not available, use a vegetable peeler to cut zucchini into ribbons. Saute as directed, increasing time as necessary.

Per 1 cup sauce with 1 cup zucchini noodles: 287 cal., 13g fat (4g sat. fat), 71mg chol., 708mg sod., 17g carb. (11g sugars, 4g fiber), 26g pro. **Diabetic exchanges:** 3 lean meat, 2 vegetable, ½ starch.

ARRABIATA SAUCE WITH ZUCCHINI NOODLES

CHICKEN
FAVORITES

"*These are great sandwiches and are a cinch to make. For a spicier taste, eliminate the ketchup and increase the amount of salsa to 1 cup.*"
—Leticia Lewis, Kennewick, WA

Chicken-Stuffed Cubanelle Peppers (p. 140) **Blueberry Chicken Salad** (p. 144) **Chicken & Brussels Sprouts Salad** (p. 141)
Cashew Chicken with Ginger (p. 146) **BBQ Chicken Sandwiches** (p. 143) **Lemon Chicken Pasta** (p. 149)

GARLIC CHICKEN
WITH HERBS

GARLIC CHICKEN WITH HERBS C FAST FIX ►

Pan-roasting garlic cloves turns them into rich, creamy deliciousness. This chicken is fantastic with crusty Italian bread or mashed potatoes on the side.
—Kathy Fleming, Lisle, IL

....

Start to Finish: 30 min.
Makes: 4 servings

- 4 **boneless skinless chicken thighs (about 1 pound)**
- ½ **teaspoon salt**
- ¼ **teaspoon pepper**
- 1 **tablespoon butter**
- 10 **garlic cloves, peeled and halved**
- ¼ **cup white wine or chicken broth**
- 1½ **teaspoons minced fresh rosemary**
- ½ **teaspoon minced fresh sage**
- 1 **cup chicken broth**
  Hot cooked rice of your choice

1. Sprinkle chicken with salt and pepper. In a large skillet, heat butter over medium-high heat; brown chicken on both sides. Remove from pan, reserving drippings.
2. In same skillet, saute garlic in drippings over medium-high heat until light golden brown. Add wine and herbs; bring to a boil, stirring to loosen browned bits from pan. Cook until the mixture is almost evaporated. Add broth and chicken; bring to a boil. Reduce heat; simmer, covered, until a thermometer inserted in chicken reads at least 170°, 10-12 minutes.
3. To serve, spoon pan juices over chicken. Serve with rice.

Per serving: 214 cal., 12g fat (3g sat. fat), 76mg chol., 487mg sod., 3g carb. (0 sugars, 0 fiber), 22g pro.
Diabetic exchanges: 3 lean meat, ½ fat.

CHICKEN-STUFFED CUBANELLE PEPPERS

(PICTURED ON P. 138)

Here's a new take on traditional stuffed peppers. I substituted chicken for the beef and used Cubanelle peppers in place of the usual green peppers.
—Bev Burlingame, Canton, OH

....

Prep: 20 min. • **Bake:** 1 hour
Makes: 6 servings

- 6 **Cubanelle peppers or mild banana peppers**
- 2 **large eggs, lightly beaten**
- 3 **cups shredded cooked chicken breast**
- 1 **cup salsa**
- ¾ **cup soft bread crumbs**
- ½ **cup cooked long grain rice**
- 2 **cups meatless pasta sauce**

1. Preheat oven to 350°. Cut and discard tops from peppers; remove seeds. In a large bowl, mix eggs, chicken, salsa, bread crumbs and rice. Spoon into peppers.
2. Spread pasta sauce onto bottom of a 13x9-in. baking dish coated with cooking spray. Top with peppers. Bake, covered, 60-65 minutes or until peppers are tender and a thermometer inserted in stuffing reads at least 165°.

Note: To make soft bread crumbs, tear bread into pieces and place in a food processor or blender. Cover and pulse until crumbs form. One slice of bread yields ½ to ¾ cup crumbs.

Per stuffed pepper: 230 cal., 4g fat (1g sat. fat), 125mg chol., 661mg sod., 20g carb. (7g sugars, 5g fiber), 26g pro.
Diabetic exchanges: 3 lean meat, 2 vegetable, 1 starch.

PARMESAN CHICKEN WITH LEMON RICE `FAST FIX`

I like the challenge of inventing recipes with ingredients I have on hand. This easy-peasy meal is perfect.
—Colleen Doucette, Truro, NS

Start to Finish: 30 min.
Makes: 4 servings

- 2 cups reduced-sodium chicken broth
- 2 tablespoons lemon juice
- 1 cup uncooked long grain rice
- ½ cup chopped onion
- 1 large egg
- 2 tablespoons fat-free milk
- ¾ cup panko (Japanese) bread crumbs
- ⅔ cup grated Parmesan cheese, divided
- 1 teaspoon dried oregano
- 1 pound boneless skinless chicken breasts
- 2 tablespoons olive oil
- 1 cup frozen peas (about 4 ounces), thawed
- ¼ teaspoon grated lemon zest
  Freshly ground pepper, optional

1. In a saucepan, bring broth and lemon juice to a boil. Stir in rice and onion; return to a boil. Reduce heat; simmer, covered, until liquid is almost absorbed and rice is tender, 15-20 minutes.
2. Meanwhile, in a shallow bowl, whisk together egg and milk. In another bowl, toss bread crumbs with ⅓ cup cheese and oregano. Pound chicken breasts with a meat mallet to ¼-in. thickness. Dip in egg mixture, then in crumb mixture to coat both sides.
3. In a large skillet, heat oil over medium heat. Cook chicken until golden brown and no longer pink, 2-3 minutes per side.
4. When rice is cooked, gently stir in the peas; cook, covered, until heated through, 1-2 minutes. Stir in the lemon zest and remaining cheese. Slice chicken; serve with rice. If desired, sprinkle with pepper.

Per 3 ounces cooked chicken with ¾ cup rice: 500 cal., 14g fat (4g sat. fat), 96mg chol., 623mg sod., 55g carb. (4g sugars, 3g fiber), 36g pro.

CHICKEN & BRUSSELS SPROUTS SALAD `FAST FIX`

(PICTURED ON P. 139)

My mom made the best salads; that's where my love for them started. I've turned her side salads into awesome meals with protein, veggies, nuts and cranberries.
—Lindsay Tanner, Cathedral City, CA

Start to Finish: 30 min.
Makes: 6 servings

- 3 tablespoons olive oil
- 20 fresh Brussels sprouts, trimmed and halved
- 2 shallots, sliced
- ½ teaspoon salt
- ½ cup balsamic vinegar
- 1 skinned rotisserie chicken, shredded
- 3 cups torn romaine
- ⅔ cup chopped roasted sweet red peppers
- ½ cup chopped sun-dried tomatoes (not oil-packed)
- ½ cup balsamic vinaigrette
- ¾ cup pistachios, toasted
- ¾ cup dried cranberries
  Fresh goat cheese, optional

1. In a large skillet, heat oil over medium heat. Add Brussels sprouts and shallots; cook and stir until browned and tender, 10-12 minutes. Sprinkle with salt; drizzle with balsamic vinegar. Cook 2-3 minutes, reducing liquid and stirring to loosen browned bits from pan.
2. Combine the chicken, romaine, red pepper and sun-dried tomatoes. Toss with the Brussels sprouts mixture and balsamic vinaigrette. Top with pistachios and dried cranberries; serve with goat cheese if desired.

Note: To toast nuts, bake in a shallow pan in a 350° oven for 5-10 minutes or cook in a skillet over low heat until lightly browned, stirring occasionally.

Per 1⅓ cups: 500 cal., 25g fat (4g sat. fat), 73mg chol., 657mg sod., 39g carb. (24g sugars, 7g fiber), 30g pro.

PARMESAN CHICKEN WITH LEMON RICE

SKINNY COBB SALAD `FAST FIX`

This skinny version of Cobb salad has all the taste and creaminess with half the fat and calories. If you wish, you can skip the coleslaw mix and do all lettuce, but I like the crunch you get with cabbage.
—Taylor Kiser, Brandon, FL

Start to Finish: 25 min.
Makes: 4 servings

- ¼ cup fat-free plain Greek yogurt
- 2 tablespoons reduced-fat ranch salad dressing
- 1 to 2 teaspoons cold water

SALAD

- 3 cups coleslaw mix
- 3 cups chopped lettuce
- 1 large apple, chopped
- ½ cup crumbled reduced-fat feta or blue cheese
- 1 cup cubed cooked chicken breast
- 2 green onions, chopped
- 4 turkey bacon strips, chopped and cooked
- 1 can (15 ounces) garbanzo beans or chickpeas, rinsed and drained
- 1 small ripe avocado, peeled and cubed

1. Mix yogurt and dressing; thin with water as desired. Toss coleslaw mix with lettuce; divide among four plates.

2. Arrange remaining ingredients in rows over top. Drizzle with yogurt mixture.

HEALTH TIP Combining classic Cobb flavors with healthy ingredients—like Greek yogurt, chopped apple and garbanzo beans—makes this salad a win.

Per serving: 324 cal., 13g fat (3g sat. fat), 48mg chol., 646mg sod., 31g carb. (11g sugars, 9g fiber), 23g pro.
Diabetic exchanges: 2 lean meat, 2 fat, 1½ starch, 1 vegetable.

CHICKEN & GOAT CHEESE SKILLET

CHICKEN & GOAT CHEESE SKILLET `C` `FAST FIX`

My husband was completely bowled over by this on-a-whim skillet meal. I can't wait to make it again very soon!
—Ericka Barber, Eureka, CA

Start to Finish: 20 min.
Makes: 2 servings

- ½ pound boneless skinless chicken breasts, cut into 1-inch pieces
- ¼ teaspoon salt
- ⅛ teaspoon pepper
- 2 teaspoons olive oil
- 1 cup cut fresh asparagus (1-inch pieces)
- 1 garlic clove, minced
- 3 plum tomatoes, chopped
- 3 tablespoons 2% milk
- 2 tablespoons herbed fresh goat cheese, crumbled
  Hot cooked rice or pasta
  Additional goat cheese, optional

1. Toss chicken with salt and pepper. In a large skillet, heat oil over medium-high heat; saute the chicken until it is no longer pink, 4-6 minutes. Remove from the pan; keep warm.

2. Add asparagus to skillet; cook and stir over medium-high heat 1 minute. Add garlic; cook and stir 30 seconds. Stir in tomatoes, milk and 2 tablespoons cheese; cook, covered, over medium heat until cheese begins to melt, 2-3 minutes. Stir in chicken. Serve with rice. If desired, top with additional cheese.

Per 1½ cups chicken mixture: 251 cal., 11g fat (3g sat. fat), 74mg chol., 447mg sod., 8g carb. (5g sugars, 3g fiber), 29g pro.
Diabetic exchanges: 4 lean meat, 2 fat, 1 vegetable.

MANGO & GRILLED CHICKEN SALAD F FAST FIX ▶

We make our home in the hot South, and this awesome fruity chicken salad is a weeknight standout. I buy salad greens and add veggies for color and crunch.
—Sherry Little, Sherwood, AR

Start to Finish: 25 min.
Makes: 4 servings

- 1 pound chicken tenderloins
- ½ teaspoon salt
- ¼ teaspoon pepper

SALAD

- 6 cups torn mixed salad greens
- ¼ cup raspberry or balsamic vinaigrette
- 1 medium mango, peeled and cubed
- 1 cup fresh sugar snap peas, halved lengthwise

1. Toss chicken with salt and pepper. Moisten a paper towel with cooking oil; using long-handled tongs, rub on grill rack to coat lightly. Grill chicken, covered, over medium heat or broil 4 in. from heat 3-4 minutes on each side or until no longer pink. Cut chicken into 1-in. pieces.
2. Divide greens among four plates; drizzle with vinaigrette. Top with chicken, mango and peas; serve immediately.

Per serving: 210 cal., 2g fat (0 sat. fat), 56mg chol., 447mg sod., 22g carb. (16g sugars, 4g fiber), 30g pro.
Diabetic exchanges: 3 lean meat, 2 vegetable, ½ starch, ½ fat.

HEALTH TIP Keep a cold at bay (or at least shorten its duration) with vitamin C-rich mango.

BBQ CHICKEN SANDWICHES
(PICTURED ON P. 139)

These are great sandwiches and are a cinch to make. For a spicier taste, eliminate the ketchup and increase the amount of salsa to 1 cup.
—Leticia Lewis, Kennewick, WA

Prep: 20 min. • **Cook:** 15 min.
Makes: 6 servings

- ½ cup chopped onion
- ½ cup diced celery
- 1 garlic clove, minced
- 1 tablespoon butter
- ½ cup salsa
- ½ cup ketchup
- 2 tablespoons brown sugar
- 2 tablespoons cider vinegar
- 1 tablespoon Worcestershire sauce
- ½ teaspoon chili powder
- ¼ teaspoon salt
- ⅛ teaspoon pepper
- 2 cups shredded cooked chicken
- 6 hamburger buns, split and toasted

1. In a large saucepan, saute the onion, celery and garlic in butter until tender. Stir in the salsa, ketchup, brown sugar, vinegar, Worcestershire sauce, chili powder, salt and pepper.
2. Stir in chicken. Bring to a boil. Reduce heat; cover and simmer for 15 minutes. Serve about ⅓ cup chicken mixture on each bun.

Freeze option: Freeze cooled meat mixture in freezer containers. To use, partially thaw in refrigerator overnight. Heat through in a saucepan, stirring occasionally and adding a little water if necessary. Serve in buns.

Per sandwich: 284 cal., 8g fat (3g sat. fat), 47mg chol., 770mg sod., 35g carb. (12g sugars, 3g fiber), 18g pro.
Diabetic exchanges: 2 starch, 2 lean meat.

MANGO & GRILLED CHICKEN SALAD

BLUEBERRY CHICKEN SALAD
FAST FIX ▸

(PICTURED ON P. 138)

On weekday mornings, I whip up this fresh chicken and blueberry combo to take for lunch. It also works as a nice, light summer supper, and it's a cinch to double for a shower or potluck.
—Kari Kelley, Plains, MT

Start to Finish: 15 min.
Makes: 4 servings

- 2 cups fresh blueberries
- 2 cups cubed cooked chicken breast
- ¾ cup chopped celery
- ½ cup diced sweet red pepper
- ½ cup thinly sliced green onions
- ¾ cup (6 ounces) lemon yogurt
- 3 tablespoons mayonnaise
- ½ teaspoon salt
  Bibb lettuce leaves, optional

1. Set aside a few blueberries for topping salad. In a large bowl, combine chicken, celery, red pepper, green onions and remaining blueberries. In a small bowl, mix yogurt, mayonnaise and salt. Add to chicken mixture; gently toss to coat.
2. Refrigerate until serving. If desired, serve over lettuce. Top with reserved blueberries.

Per cup: 277 cal., 11g fat (2g sat. fat), 60mg chol., 441mg sod., 21g carb. (16g sugars, 3g fiber), 23g pro.
Diabetic exchanges: 3 lean meat, 1 starch, 1 fat, ½ fruit.

CASSOULET FOR TODAY
Traditionally cooked for a number of hours, this version of the rustic French dish offers the same homey taste in less time. It's easy on the wallet, too.
—Virginia Anthony, Jacksonville, FL

Prep: 45 min. • **Bake:** 50 min.
Makes: 6 servings

- 6 boneless skinless chicken thighs (about 1½ pounds)
- ¼ teaspoon salt
- ¼ teaspoon coarsely ground pepper
- 3 teaspoons olive oil, divided
- 1 large onion, chopped
- 1 garlic clove, minced
- ½ cup white wine or chicken broth
- 1 can (14½ ounces) diced tomatoes, drained

CASSOULET FOR TODAY

- 1 bay leaf
- 1 teaspoon minced fresh rosemary or ¼ teaspoon dried rosemary, crushed
- 1 teaspoon minced fresh thyme or ¼ teaspoon dried thyme
- 2 cans (15 ounces each) cannellini beans, rinsed and drained
- ¼ pound smoked turkey kielbasa, chopped
- 3 bacon strips, cooked and crumbled

TOPPING

- ½ cup soft whole wheat bread crumbs
- ¼ cup minced fresh parsley
- 1 garlic clove, minced

1. Preheat oven to 325°. Sprinkle chicken with salt and pepper. In a broiler-safe Dutch oven, heat 2 teaspoons oil over medium heat; brown chicken on both sides. Remove from pan.
2. In same pan, saute onion in remaining oil over medium heat until crisp-tender. Add garlic; cook 1 minute. Add wine; bring to a boil, stirring to loosen browned bits from pan. Add tomatoes, herbs and chicken; return to a boil.
3. Transfer to oven; bake, covered, 30 minutes. Stir in the beans and kielbasa; bake, covered, until the chicken is tender, 20-25 minutes.
4. Remove from oven; preheat broiler. Discard bay leaf; stir in bacon. Toss bread crumbs with parsley and garlic; sprinkle over top. Place in oven so surface of cassoulet is 4-5 in. from heat; broil until crumbs are golden brown, 2-3 minutes.
Note: To make soft bread crumbs, tear bread into pieces and place in a food processor or blender. Cover and pulse until crumbs form. One slice of bread yields ½ to ¾ cup crumbs.
Per serving: 394 cal., 14g fat (4g sat. fat), 91mg chol., 736mg sod., 29g carb. (4g sugars, 8g fiber), 33g pro.
Diabetic exchanges: 4 lean meat, 2 starch, ½ fat.
HEALTH TIP Adding pulses such as cannellini beans to a meat-based main dish bumps up the fiber and protein without adding saturated fat.

GARLIC-GRILLED CHICKEN WITH PESTO ZUCCHINI RIBBONS ⓒ

The first time that I substituted zucchini noodles for regular pasta, it was because I was trying to reduce carbohydrates and calories. Now I make them because we love the flavor and texture they bring to dishes. This dish is just as delicious if you substitute shrimp for the chicken.

—Suzanne Banfield, Basking Ridge, NJ

Prep: 35 min. • **Grill:** 10 min.
Makes: 4 servings

- 2 teaspoons grated lemon zest
- 2 tablespoons lemon juice
- 4 garlic cloves, minced
- ½ teaspoon coarsely ground pepper
- ¼ teaspoon salt
- 4 boneless skinless chicken breast halves (6 ounces each)

ZUCCHINI MIXTURE

- 4 large zucchini (about 2½ pounds)
- ¼ cup chopped oil-packed sun-dried tomatoes
- 1 teaspoon olive oil
- 2 garlic cloves, minced
- ¼ teaspoon salt
- ¼ teaspoon crushed red pepper flakes
- ¼ teaspoon coarsely ground pepper
- ¼ cup prepared pesto
- 4 ounces fresh mozzarella cheese, cut into ½-inch cubes

1. In a large bowl, mix the first five ingredients. Add chicken; turn to coat. Let stand 15 minutes.
2. Meanwhile, for noodles, trim ends of zucchini. Using a cheese slicer or vegetable peeler, cut zucchini lengthwise into long thin slices. Cut zucchini on all sides, as if peeling a carrot, until the seeds become visible. Discard seeded portion or save for another use.
3. Grill chicken, covered, over medium heat or broil 4 in. from heat 4-5 minutes on each side or until a thermometer inserted in chicken reads 165°. Remove from grill; keep warm.
4. In a large nonstick skillet, heat the tomatoes and olive oil over medium-high heat. Add garlic, salt, pepper flakes and pepper; cook and stir 30 seconds. Add zucchini; cook and stir 2-3 minutes or until crisp-tender. Remove from heat. Stir in pesto.
5. Cut chicken into slices. Serve with zucchini noodles. Top with mozzarella.

Per chicken breast half with 1½ cups zucchini noodles: 397 cal., 18g fat (6g sat. fat), 116mg chol., 636mg sod., 14g carb. (7g sugars, 3g fiber), 44g pro.
Diabetic exchanges: 6 lean meat, 1½ fat, 1 vegetable.

ONE-PAN CHICKEN RICE CURRY FAST FIX ▶

I have been loving the subtle spice from curry lately, so I successfully incorporated it into this saucy chicken and rice dish. It's a one-pan meal that has become a go-to dinnertime favorite.

—Mary Lou Timpson, Colorado City, AZ

Start to Finish: 30 min.
Makes: 4 servings

- 2 tablespoons butter, divided
- 1 medium onion, halved and thinly sliced
- 2 tablespoons all-purpose flour
- 3 teaspoons curry powder
- ½ teaspoon salt
- ½ teaspoon pepper
- 1 pound boneless skinless chicken breasts, cut into 1-inch pieces
- 1 can (14½ ounces) reduced-sodium chicken broth
- 1 cup uncooked instant rice
  Chopped fresh cilantro leaves, optional

1. In a large nonstick skillet, heat 1 tablespoon butter over medium-high heat; saute onion until tender and lightly browned, 3-5 minutes. Remove from pan.
2. Mix flour and seasonings; toss with chicken. In same pan, heat remaining butter over medium-high heat. Add chicken; cook just until no longer pink, 4-6 minutes, turning occasionally.
3. Stir in broth and onion; bring to a boil. Stir in rice. Remove from heat; let stand, covered, 5 minutes (mixture will be saucy). If desired, sprinkle with cilantro.

Per cup: 300 cal., 9g fat (4g sat. fat), 78mg chol., 658mg sod., 27g carb. (2g sugars, 2g fiber), 27g pro.
Diabetic exchanges: 3 lean meat, 2 starch, 1½ fat.

GARLIC-GRILLED CHICKEN WITH PESTO ZUCCHINI RIBBONS

ZINGY BAKED CHICKEN NUGGETS FAST FIX

These crispy chicken nuggets have just the right amount of spice. Yogurt makes them extra tender.
—Lee Evans, Queen Creek, AZ

Start to Finish: 30 min.
Makes: 6 servings

- ¼ cup plain yogurt
- 1 tablespoon lemon juice
- 1½ teaspoons seasoned salt
- 1 teaspoon garlic powder
- 1 teaspoon ground coriander
- ½ to ¾ teaspoon cayenne pepper
- 1½ pounds boneless skinless chicken breasts, cut into 1½-inch pieces
- 2 cups whole wheat or regular panko (Japanese) bread crumbs
  Honey mustard, optional

1. Preheat oven to 400°. Mix first six ingredients; stir in chicken to coat.
2. Place bread crumbs in a shallow bowl; add chicken, one piece at a time, and toss to coat. Place 1 in. apart on a greased baking sheet.
3. Bake until lightly browned and chicken is no longer pink, 18-20 minutes. If desired, serve with honey mustard.
Per serving: 222 cal., 4g fat (1g sat. fat), 64mg chol., 481mg sod., 19g carb. (2g sugars, 2g fiber), 26g pro.
Diabetic exchanges: 3 lean meat, 1 starch.

CASHEW CHICKEN WITH GINGER FAST FIX

(PICTURED ON P. 138)

There are lots of recipes for cashew chicken, but my family thinks this one stands alone. We love the flavor from the fresh ginger and the crunch of the cashews. Plus, it's easy to prepare.
—Oma Rollison, El Cajon, CA

Start to Finish: 30 min.
Makes: 6 servings

- 2 tablespoons cornstarch
- 1 tablespoon brown sugar
- 1¼ cups chicken broth
- 2 tablespoons soy sauce
- 3 tablespoons canola oil, divided
- 1½ pounds boneless skinless chicken breasts, cut into 1-inch pieces
- ½ pound sliced fresh mushrooms
- 1 small green pepper, cut into strips
- 1 can (8 ounces) sliced water chestnuts, drained
- 1½ teaspoons grated fresh gingerroot
- 4 green onions, sliced
- ¾ cup salted cashews
  Hot cooked rice

1. Mix first four ingredients until smooth. In a large skillet, heat 2 tablespoons oil over medium-high heat; stir-fry chicken until no longer pink. Remove from pan.
2. In same pan, heat remaining oil over medium-high heat; stir-fry mushrooms, pepper, water chestnuts and ginger until pepper is crisp-tender, 3-5 minutes. Stir broth mixture and add to pan with green onions; bring to a boil. Cook and stir until sauce is thickened, 1-2 minutes.
3. Stir in the chicken and cashews; heat through. Serve with rice.
Per ¾ cup chicken mixture: 349 cal., 19g fat (3g sat. fat), 64mg chol., 650mg sod., 18g carb. (6g sugars, 2g fiber), 28g pro.
Diabetic exchanges: 3 lean meat, 3 fat, 1 starch.

SESAME CHICKEN SLAW SALAD FAST FIX

I tasted many types of Asian chicken salad in California. When I returned to Georgia, I wanted more. Here's a gingery-sweet recipe with crunchy wonton strips.
—Michelle Mulrain, Evans, GA

Start to Finish: 20 min.
Makes: 6 servings

- 4 cups torn romaine
- 1 package (14 ounces) coleslaw mix
- 1 large sweet red pepper, julienned
- 1 small red onion, halved and thinly sliced
- 3 cups shredded rotisserie chicken
- 1 medium ripe avocado, peeled and sliced
- 3 clementines, peeled and segmented, or 1 can (11 ounces) mandarin oranges, drained
- ¾ cup crunchy garlic ginger or plain wonton strips
- ¾ cup reduced-fat Asian toasted sesame salad dressing

Divide all of the ingredients except the salad dressing among six bowls. Serve with dressing.
Note: This recipe was tested with Fresh Gourmet Wonton Strips; look for them in the produce section.
Per 2 cups: Per 2 cups: 309 cal., 13g fat (2g sat. fat), 62mg chol., 414mg sod., 26g carb. (15g sugars, 5g fiber), 25g pro.
Diabetic exchanges: 3 lean meat, 2 vegetable, 2 fat, 1 starch.

DID YOU KNOW?
Avocado is high in monounsaturated fat, a so-called "good fat" that can lower your blood cholesterol along with the risk of stroke and heart disease.

**SESAME CHICKEN
SLAW SALAD**

JERK CHICKEN
WITH TROPICAL COUSCUS

FAST FIX ▶

Caribbean cuisine, we've found, helps brighten up our weeknights thanks to its bold colors and flavors. Done in less than 30 minutes, this chicken dish is one of my go-to easy meals.

—Jeanne Holt, Mendota Heights, MN

Start to Finish: 25 min.
Makes: 4 servings

- 1 can (15.25 ounces) mixed tropical fruit
- 1 pound boneless skinless chicken breasts, cut into 2½-in. strips
- 3 teaspoons Caribbean jerk seasoning
- 1 tablespoon olive oil
- ½ cup chopped sweet red pepper
- 1 tablespoon finely chopped seeded jalapeno pepper
- ⅓ cup thinly sliced green onions (green portion only)
- 1½ cups reduced-sodium chicken broth
- 3 tablespoons chopped fresh cilantro, divided
- 1 tablespoon lime juice
- ¼ teaspoon salt
- 1 cup uncooked whole wheat couscous
  Lime wedges

1. Drain mixed fruit, reserving ¼ cup syrup. Chop fruit.

2. Toss chicken with jerk seasoning. In a large skillet, heat oil over medium-high heat; saute chicken until no longer pink, 4-5 minutes. Remove from pan, reserving the drippings.

3. In same pan, saute peppers and green onions in drippings 2 minutes. Add broth, 1 tablespoon cilantro, lime juice, salt, reserved syrup and chopped fruit; bring to a boil. Stir in couscous; reduce heat to low. Place chicken on top; cook, covered, until liquid is absorbed and chicken is heated through, 3-4 minutes. Sprinkle with the remaining cilantro. Serve with lime wedges.

Per 1½ cups: 411 cal., 7g fat (1g sat. fat), 63mg chol., 628mg sod., 57g carb. (19g sugars, 7g fiber), 31g pro.

DELICIOUS OVEN-BARBECUED CHICKEN

A friend made this juicy chicken when we had our first child. I pared down the recipe to make it healthier. It's now a family favorite, and even the kids ask for it.

—Marge Wagner, Roselle, IL

Prep: 20 min. • **Bake:** 35 min.
Makes: 6 servings

- 6 bone-in chicken breast halves (8 ounces each)
- ⅓ cup chopped onion
- ¾ cup ketchup
- ½ cup water
- ⅓ cup white vinegar
- 3 tablespoons brown sugar
- 1 tablespoon Worcestershire sauce
- 1 teaspoon ground mustard
- ¼ teaspoon salt
- ⅛ teaspoon pepper

1. Preheat oven to 350°. In a nonstick skillet coated with cooking spray, brown chicken breasts over medium heat. Transfer to a 13x9-in. baking dish coated with cooking spray.

2. Recoat skillet with cooking spray. Add onion; cook and stir over medium heat until tender. Stir in remaining ingredients; bring to a boil. Reduce heat; simmer, uncovered, for 15 minutes. Pour over the chicken.

3. Bake, uncovered, until a thermometer inserted in chicken reads 170°, about 35-45 minutes.

Per serving: 324 cal., 10g fat (3g sat. fat), 111mg chol., 602mg sod., 16g carb. (15g sugars, 0 fiber), 39g pro.
Diabetic exchanges: 5 lean meat, 1 starch.

LEMON CHICKEN PASTA

(PICTURED ON P. 139)

This recipe reminds me of the lemony chicken and rice my mom used to make. In my quick update, I saute lightly breaded chicken breasts and serve them over capellini pasta.

—Aileen Rivera, Bronx, NY

Prep: 30 min. • **Cook:** 15 min.
Makes: 6 servings

- 4 boneless skinless chicken breast halves (6 ounces each)
- 1 teaspoon salt, divided
- ¼ teaspoon plus ⅛ teaspoon pepper, divided
- ½ cup all-purpose flour
- 8 ounces uncooked capellini or angel hair pasta
- 3 tablespoons olive oil, divided
- ¼ cup peeled and thinly sliced garlic cloves (about 12 cloves)
- 1 cup white wine or chicken broth
- 2 tablespoons lemon juice
- ½ cup grated Parmigiano-Reggiano cheese
- ⅓ cup plus 3 tablespoons minced fresh parsley, divided
  Lemon wedges, optional

1. Pound chicken breasts with a meat mallet to ¼-in. thickness. Sprinkle with ½ teaspoon salt and ¼ teaspoon pepper. Place flour in a shallow bowl. Dip the chicken in flour to coat both sides; shake off excess.

2. Cook pasta according to package directions for al dente. Meanwhile, in a large skillet, heat 2 tablespoons oil over medium heat. Add chicken; cook for 2-3 minutes on each side or until no longer pink. Remove and keep warm.

3. In same pan, heat remaining oil over medium heat; add garlic. Cook and stir 30-60 seconds or until garlic is lightly browned. Add wine to pan; increase heat to medium-high. Cook, stirring to loosen browned bits from pan, until liquid is reduced by half. Stir in lemon juice.

4. Drain pasta, reserving ½ cup pasta water; place in a large bowl. Add cheese, ⅓ cup parsley, half of the garlic mixture, and remaining salt and pepper; toss to combine, adding enough reserved pasta water to moisten pasta. Serve with chicken. Drizzle with remaining garlic mixture; sprinkle with remaining parsley. If desired, serve with lemon wedges.

Per serving: 403 cal., 12g fat (3g sat. fat), 68mg chol., 577mg sod., 35g carb. (2g sugars, 2g fiber), 31g pro.
Diabetic exchanges: 4 lean meat, 2 starch, 1½ fat.

DELICIOUS OVEN-BARBECUED CHICKEN

THAI RED CURRY CHICKEN & VEGETABLES FAST FIX

The key to this curry chicken is getting complex flavors without a heavy feel. For the veggies, I like colorful pea pods, sweet red peppers and water chestnuts.
—David Dahlman, Chatsworth, CA

Start to Finish: 30 min.
Makes: 4 servings

- 1½ **pounds boneless skinless chicken breasts, cut into 1½-inch pieces**
- 1⅓ **cups light coconut milk**
- 2 **tablespoons red curry paste**
- ½ **teaspoon salt**
- 3 **cups hot cooked brown rice**
- 1 **package (16 ounces) frozen stir-fry vegetable blend**

1. Preheat oven to 425°. Place chicken in a greased 8-in. square baking dish. In a small bowl, mix coconut milk, curry paste and salt; pour over chicken.
2. Bake, covered, 18-22 minutes or until chicken is no longer pink. Meanwhile, cook the vegetables according to the package directions; drain. Serve chicken with rice and vegetables.

Per cup chicken with ¾ cup rice and ¾ cup vegetables: 511 cal., 14g fat (6g sat. fat), 94mg chol., 606mg sod., 51g carb. (6g sugars, 5g fiber), 41g pro.
Diabetic exchanges: 5 lean meat, 3 starch, 1 vegetable, 1 fat.

SESAME CHICKEN VEGGIE WRAPS

SESAME CHICKEN VEGGIE WRAPS FAST FIX

I'm always on the lookout for fast, nutritious recipes that will appeal to my three little kids. They happen to love edamame, so this is a great choice for those on-the-go days.
—Elisabeth Larsen, Pleasant Grove, UT

Start to Finish: 30 min.
Makes: 8 servings

- 1 **cup frozen shelled edamame**

DRESSING

- 2 **tablespoons orange juice**
- 2 **tablespoons olive oil**
- 1 **teaspoon sesame oil**
- ½ **teaspoon ground ginger**
- ¼ **teaspoon salt**
- ⅛ **teaspoon pepper**

WRAPS

- 2 **cups fresh baby spinach**
- 1 **cup thinly sliced cucumber**
- 1 **cup fresh sugar snap peas, chopped**
- ½ **cup shredded carrots**
- ½ **cup thinly sliced sweet red pepper**
- 1 **cup chopped cooked chicken breast**
- 8 **whole wheat tortillas (8 inches), room temperature**

1. Cook edamame according to package directions. Drain; rinse with cold water and drain well. Whisk together all of the dressing ingredients.
2. In a large bowl, combine remaining vegetables, chicken and edamame; toss with dressing. Place about ½ cup mixture on each tortilla. Fold bottom and sides of tortilla over filling and roll up.

Per wrap: 214 cal., 7g fat (1g sat. fat), 13mg chol., 229mg sod., 28g carb. (2g sugars, 5g fiber), 12g pro.
Diabetic exchanges: 2 starch, 1 lean meat, 1 fat.

BUFFALO CHICKEN TENDERS

These chicken tenders get a spicy kick thanks to homemade Buffalo sauce. They taste like they're from a restaurant, but they're so easy to make at home. Blue cheese dipping sauce takes them over the top.

—Dahlia Abrams, Detroit, MI

Start to Finish: 20 min.
Makes: 4 servings

- 1 pound chicken tenderloins
- 2 tablespoons all-purpose flour
- ¼ teaspoon pepper
- 2 tablespoons butter, divided
- ⅓ cup Louisiana-style hot sauce
- 1¼ teaspoons Worcestershire sauce
- 1 teaspoon minced fresh oregano
- ½ teaspoon garlic powder
  Blue cheese salad dressing, optional

1. Toss chicken with flour and pepper. In a large skillet, heat 1 tablespoon butter over medium heat. Add chicken; cook until no longer pink, 4-6 minutes per side. Remove from pan.
2. Mix hot sauce, Worcestershire sauce, oregano and garlic powder. In same skillet, melt the remaining butter; stir in the sauce mixture. Add the chicken; heat it through, turning to coat. If desired, serve with blue cheese dressing.

Per serving: 184 cal., 7g fat (4g sat. fat), 71mg chol., 801mg sod., 5g carb. (1g sugars, 0 fiber), 27g pro.
Diabetic exchanges: 3 lean meat, 1½ fat.

LIME-CILANTRO MARINATED CHICKEN **S** **C**

This marinade is wonderful with chicken, but you can also use it on pork or fish. As an added bonus, it's a low-calorie and low-sodium recipe.

—Roz Walton, Auburn, ME

Prep: 5 min. + marinating • **Grill:** 10 min.
Makes: 6 servings

- ½ cup minced fresh cilantro
- ¼ cup lime juice
- ¼ cup orange juice
- ¼ cup olive oil
- 1 tablespoon chopped shallot
- 1 teaspoon dried minced garlic
- 1 teaspoon pepper
- ⅛ teaspoon salt
- 6 boneless skinless chicken breast halves (5 ounces each)

1. In a blender, combine the first eight ingredients; cover and process until smooth. Place the marinade in a large resealable plastic bag. Add the chicken; seal bag and turn to coat. Refrigerate for at least 2 hours.
2. Drain and discard marinade. Lightly oil the grill rack. Grill chicken, covered, over medium heat or broil 4 in. from the heat for 5-7 minutes on each side or until a thermometer reads 170°.

Per chicken breast half : 175 cal., 6g fat (1g sat. fat), 78mg chol., 80mg sod., 1g carb. (0 sugars, 0 fiber), 29g pro.
Diabetic exchanges: 4 lean meat, ½ fat.

BUFFALO CHICKEN TENDERS

CHICKEN &
SWEET POTATO
POTPIE

CHICKEN & SWEET POTATO POTPIE

Chicken potpie is a top 10 comfort food for me. To save some time, I use rotisserie chicken in the filling and make a crust from phyllo dough.
—Jacyn Siebert, San Francisco, CA

Prep: 40 min. • **Bake:** 10 min.
Makes: 6 servings

- 2 teaspoons olive oil
- ½ pound sliced fresh mushrooms
- 1 small onion, chopped
- 1 large sweet potato, cubed
- 1 cup chopped sweet red pepper
- ½ cup chopped celery
- 2 cups reduced-sodium chicken broth, divided
- ⅓ cup all-purpose flour
- ½ cup 2% milk
- 1 skinned rotisserie chicken, shredded
- 2 tablespoons sherry or reduced-sodium chicken broth
- ¾ teaspoon minced fresh rosemary
- ½ teaspoon salt
- ½ teaspoon dried thyme
- ¼ teaspoon pepper
- 5 sheets phyllo dough (14x9-in. size)
  Butter-flavored cooking spray

1. Preheat oven to 425°. In a large skillet, heat oil over medium-high heat. Add mushrooms and onion; cook and stir until tender, 3-4 minutes. Stir in sweet potato, red pepper and celery; cook 5 minutes longer. Add ¼ cup broth. Reduce heat; cook, covered, over medium-low heat until vegetables are tender, 6-8 minutes.

2. Sprinkle flour over vegetables; cook and stir 1 minute. Gradually add milk and remaining broth. Bring to a boil; cook and stir until thickened, about 1-2 minutes. Stir in chicken, sherry and seasonings. Transfer to an 11x7-in. baking dish coated with cooking spray. Bake, uncovered, until heated through, 10-15 minutes.

3. Meanwhile, stack all five sheets of phyllo dough. Roll up lengthwise; cut crosswise into ½-in.-wide strips. In a bowl, toss strips to separate; spritz with butter-flavored spray. Place on an ungreased baking sheet; spritz again. Bake until golden brown, 4-5 minutes. Arrange phyllo strips over the chicken mixture before serving.

Per cup: 329 cal., 10g fat (2g sat. fat), 75mg chol., 517mg sod., 30g carb. (10g sugars, 3g fiber), 30g pro.
Diabetic exchanges: 4 lean meat, 2 starch, ½ fat.

SPAGHETTI SQUASH LO MEIN
FAST FIX

My colorful lo mein is a lighter version of the classic Chinese dish that everyone at our table loves. Try it with a squirt of Sriracha.
—Loanne Chiu, Fort Worth, TX

Start to Finish: 30 min.
Makes: 4 servings

- 1 small spaghetti squash (about 2 pounds)
- 2 tablespoons sesame oil, divided
- 1 package (12 ounces) fully cooked roasted garlic chicken sausage links or flavor of choice, sliced
- 2½ cups julienned carrots
- 2½ cups shredded red cabbage
- ¼ teaspoon salt
- ⅛ teaspoon pepper
- ¼ cup chopped fresh cilantro
  Reduced-sodium soy sauce and Sriracha Asian hot chili sauce, optional

1. Halve squash lengthwise; discard seeds. Place squash on a microwave-safe plate, cut side down; microwave on high until tender, about 15 minutes. Cool slightly. Separate strands with a fork.

2. In a large skillet, heat 1 teaspoon oil over medium-high heat; saute sausage until browned, 4-6 minutes. Remove from the pan.

3. In same pan, heat 2 teaspoons oil over medium-high heat; saute carrots and cabbage until they are crisp-tender, 4-6 minutes. Stir in the salt and pepper. Add the squash, sausage and remaining oil; toss and heat through. Sprinkle with cilantro. If desired, serve with soy sauce and chili sauce.

Note: This recipe was tested in a 1,100-watt microwave.
Per 1½ cups: 316 cal., 15g fat (3g sat. fat), 70mg chol., 731mg sod., 29g carb. (6g sugars, 7g fiber), 18g pro.
Diabetic exchanges: 2 lean meat, 1½ starch, 1½ fat, 1 vegetable.

SPAGHETTI SQUASH LO MEIN

CONTEST-WINNING CHICKEN WITH MUSHROOM SAUCE
C FAST FIX ▶

This mouthwatering dish is impressive, yet it comes together in no time. I think its flavor rivals that of many full-fat entrees found in fancy restaurants.
—Jennifer Pemberton, Muncie, IN

Start to Finish: 25 min.
Makes: 4 servings

- 2 teaspoons cornstarch
- ½ cup fat-free milk
- 4 boneless skinless chicken breast halves (4 ounces each)
- 1 tablespoon olive oil
- 1 tablespoon butter
- ½ pound sliced fresh mushrooms
- ½ medium onion, thinly sliced
- ¼ cup sherry or chicken broth
- ½ teaspoon salt
- ⅛ teaspoon pepper

1. Mix cornstarch and milk until smooth. Pound the chicken with a meat mallet to ¼-in. thickness.
2. In a large nonstick skillet, heat oil over medium heat; cook chicken until no longer pink, 5-6 minutes per side. Remove from the pan.
3. In same pan, heat butter over medium-high heat; saute mushrooms and onion until tender. Stir in sherry, salt and pepper; bring to a boil. Stir cornstarch mixture and add to pan. Return to a boil; cook and stir until thickened, 1-2 minutes. Return the chicken to the pan; heat through.

Per serving: 225 cal., 9g fat (3g sat. fat), 71mg chol., 541mg sod., 8g carb. (4g sugars, 1g fiber), 26g pro.
Diabetic exchanges: 3 lean meat, 1½ fat, 1 vegetable.

TANDOORI-STYLE CHICKEN WITH CUCUMBER MELON RELISH **C**

We all need a quick meal that's deliciously healthy. Here, I marinate the chicken before I leave for work, and when I get home, I grill the chicken and make the relish. My husband loves the spicy flavor. If more heat is desired, add additional crushed red pepper flakes.
—Naylet LaRochelle, Miami, FL

Prep: 20 min. + marinating • **Grill:** 15 min.
Makes: 4 servings

TANDOORI-STYLE CHICKEN WITH CUCUMBER MELON RELISH

- 1½ cups reduced-fat plain yogurt
- 2 tablespoons lemon juice, divided
- 1½ teaspoons garam masala or curry powder
- ½ teaspoon salt
- ¼ to ½ teaspoon crushed red pepper flakes
- 4 boneless skinless chicken breast halves (6 ounces each)
- 1½ cups chopped cantaloupe
- ½ cup chopped seeded peeled cucumber
- 2 green onions, finely chopped
- 2 tablespoons minced fresh cilantro
- 1 tablespoon minced fresh mint
- ¼ cup toasted sliced almonds, optional

1. In a small bowl, whisk the yogurt, 1 tablespoon lemon juice, garam masala, salt and pepper flakes until blended. Pour 1 cup marinade into a large resealable plastic bag. Add chicken; seal bag and turn to coat. Refrigerate up to 6 hours. Cover and refrigerate remaining marinade.
2. For relish, in a small bowl, mix the cantaloupe, cucumber, green onions, cilantro, mint and remaining lemon juice.
3. Drain chicken, discarding marinade in bag. Moisten a paper towel with cooking oil; using long-handled tongs, rub on the grill rack to coat lightly. Grill the chicken, covered, over medium heat or broil 4 in. from heat 6-8 minutes on each side or until a thermometer reads 165°. Serve with relish and reserved marinade. If desired, sprinkle with almonds.
Note: To toast nuts, bake in a shallow pan in a 350° oven for 5-10 minutes or cook in a skillet over low heat until they are lightly browned, stirring occasionally.
Per serving without almonds: 247 cal., 5g fat (2g sat. fat), 98mg chol., 332mg sod., 10g carb. (9g sugars, 1g fiber), 38g pro.
Diabetic exchanges: 5 lean meat, ½ starch.

CHICKEN & SPANISH CAULIFLOWER "RICE"

I learned about the paleo diet from some friends who now have tons of energy and are super fit. Since then, I've changed my eating habits, too. Everyone from my father to my little nephew loves this recipe for riced cauliflower.
—Megan Schmoldt, Westminster, CO

Start to Finish: 30 min.
Makes: 4 servings

- 1 large head cauliflower
- 1 pound boneless skinless chicken breasts, cut into ½-inch cubes
- ½ teaspoon salt
- ½ teaspoon pepper
- 1 tablespoon canola oil
- 1 medium green pepper, chopped
- 1 small onion, chopped
- 1 garlic clove, minced
- ½ cup tomato juice
- ¼ teaspoon ground cumin
- ¼ cup chopped fresh cilantro
- 1 tablespoon lime juice

1. Core and cut cauliflower into 1-in. pieces. In batches, pulse cauliflower in a food processor until it resembles rice (do not overprocess).
2. Toss chicken with salt and pepper. In a large skillet, heat oil over medium-high heat; saute chicken until lightly browned, about 5 minutes. Add green pepper, onion and garlic; cook and stir 3 minutes.
3. Stir in tomato juice and cumin; bring to a boil. Add cauliflower; cook, covered, over medium heat until the cauliflower is tender, 7-10 minutes, stirring occasionally. Stir in cilantro and lime juice.

Per 1½ cups: 227 cal., 7g fat (1g sat. fat), 63mg chol., 492mg sod., 15g carb. (6g sugars, 5g fiber), 28g pro.
Diabetic exchanges: 3 lean meat, 1 starch, ½ fat.

BACON-GARLIC CHICKEN

Help yourself to my recipe for wonderful Italian stovetop chicken. It can be thrown together in minutes but tastes like you made a big production.
—Yvonne Starlin, Westmoreland, TN

Start to Finish: 30 min.
Makes: 4 servings

- 4 boneless skinless chicken breast halves (5 ounces each)
- ¼ teaspoon salt
- ½ teaspoon pepper
- ¼ cup all-purpose flour
- 3 bacon strips, chopped
- 1 tablespoon butter
- 4 garlic cloves, thinly sliced
- 2 teaspoons minced fresh rosemary or ¾ teaspoon dried rosemary, crushed
- ⅛ teaspoon crushed red pepper flakes
- 1 cup reduced-sodium chicken broth
- 1 tablespoon lemon juice

1. Pound chicken with a meat mallet to ½-in. thickness; sprinkle with the salt and pepper. Lightly coat both sides with flour; shake off excess.
2. In a nonstick skillet, cook the bacon over medium-high heat until crisp, stirring it occasionally. Using a slotted spoon, remove bacon to paper towels; reserve 1 teaspoon drippings.
3. In same pan, heat butter and drippings over medium heat. Add the chicken; cook until no longer pink, 4-6 minutes per side. Remove from pan.
4. Add garlic, rosemary and pepper flakes to pan; cook and stir until garlic begins to color, 1-2 minutes. Stir in broth and lemon juice; bring to a boil, stirring to loosen browned bits from pan. Cook until slightly thickened, 3-4 minutes.
5. Return chicken and bacon to the pan; heat through, turning chicken a few times to coat.

Per chicken breast: 232 cal., 9g fat (4g sat. fat), 88mg chol., 488mg sod., 5g carb. (0 sugars, 0 fiber), 30g pro.
Diabetic exchanges: 4 lean meat, 1 fat.

CHICKEN & SPANISH CAULIFLOWER "RICE"

CHICKEN VEGGIE SKILLET

CHICKEN PARMESAN BURGERS FAST FIX

We have loved chicken Parmesan and thought, "Why not make it a burger?" I like to use fresh mozzarella on these. I've also made the burgers with ground turkey.
—Charlotte Gehle, Brownstown, MI

Start to Finish: 30 min.
Makes: 4 servings

½ cup dry bread crumbs
¼ cup grated Parmesan cheese
3 garlic cloves, minced
1 tablespoon minced fresh basil or 1 teaspoon dried basil
½ teaspoon dried oregano
1 pound lean ground chicken
1 cup meatless spaghetti sauce, divided
2 slices part-skim mozzarella cheese, cut in half
4 slices Italian bread (¾ inch thick)

1. In a large bowl, combine the first five ingredients. Add chicken; mix lightly but thoroughly. Shape into four ½-in.-thick oval patties.
2. Grill burgers, covered, over medium heat or broil 4 in. from heat 4-7 minutes on each side or until a thermometer reads 165°. Top burgers with ½ cup spaghetti sauce and cheese. Cover and grill 30-60 seconds longer or until cheese is melted.
3. Grill bread, uncovered, over medium heat or broil 4 in. from heat 30-60 seconds on each side or until toasted. Top with remaining spaghetti sauce. Serve burgers on toasted bread.
Freeze option: Place patties on a plastic wrap-lined baking sheet; wrap and freeze until firm. Remove from pan and transfer to a resealable plastic freezer bag; return to freezer. To use, grill frozen patties as directed, increasing time as necessary for a thermometer to read 165°.
Per burger: 381 cal., 12g fat (5g sat. fat), 93mg chol., 784mg sod., 32g carb. (5g sugars, 3g fiber), 35g pro.
Diabetic exchanges: 3 lean meat, 2 starch, 1 fat.

CHICKEN VEGGIE SKILLET
C **FAST FIX**

I concocted this chicken and veggie dish to use up some extra mushrooms and asparagus. My husband suggested that I write it down because it's a keeper.
—Rebekah Beyer, Sabetha, KS

Start to Finish: 30 min.
Makes: 6 servings

1½ pounds boneless skinless chicken breasts, cut into ½-inch strips
½ teaspoon salt
¼ teaspoon pepper
6 teaspoons olive oil, divided
½ pound sliced fresh mushrooms
1 small onion, halved and sliced
2 garlic cloves, minced
1 pound fresh asparagus, trimmed and cut into 1-inch pieces
½ cup sherry or chicken stock
2 tablespoons cold butter, cubed

1. Sprinkle chicken with salt and pepper. In a large skillet, heat 1 teaspoon oil over medium-high heat. Add half the chicken; cook and stir 3-4 minutes or until it is no longer pink. Remove from pan. Repeat with 1 teaspoon oil and remaining chicken.
2. In same pan, heat 2 teaspoons oil. Add the mushrooms and onion; cook and stir 2-3 minutes or until tender. Add the garlic; cook 1 minute longer. Add to the chicken.
3. Heat the remaining oil in the pan. Add the asparagus; cook 2-3 minutes or until it is crisp-tender. Add it to chicken and mushrooms.
4. Add sherry to skillet, stirring to loosen browned bits from pan. Bring to a boil; cook 1-2 minutes or until liquid is reduced to 2 tablespoons. Return the chicken and vegetables to pan; heat through. Remove from heat; stir in the butter, 1 tablespoon at a time.
Per cup: 228 cal., 11g fat (4g sat. fat), 73mg chol., 384mg sod., 6g carb. (2g sugars, 1g fiber), 25g pro.
Diabetic exchanges: 3 lean meat, 2 fat, 1 vegetable.

GRILLED CHICKEN CHOPPED SALAD `FAST FIX`

Layered desserts have always grabbed my family's attention, but salads? Not so much. I wondered if I presented a healthy salad in an eye-catching way, whether I could get everyone on board. I'm happy to report that I was correct..
—Christine Hadden, Whitman, MA

Start to Finish: 30 min.
Makes: 4 servings

- 1 pound chicken tenderloins
- 6 tablespoons zesty Italian salad dressing, divided
- 2 medium zucchini, quartered lengthwise
- 1 medium red onion, quartered
- 2 medium ears sweet corn, husks removed
- 1 bunch romaine, chopped
- 1 medium cucumber, chopped
  Additional salad dressing, optional

1. In a bowl, toss the chicken with 4 tablespoons dressing. Brush zucchini and onion with remaining 2 tablespoons of dressing.
2. Place corn, zucchini and onion on a grill rack over medium heat; close lid. Grill corn 10-12 minutes or until tender, turning it occasionally. Grill the zucchini and onion 2-3 minutes on each side or until tender.
3. Drain chicken, discarding marinade. Grill chicken, covered, over medium heat for 3-4 minutes on each side or until no longer pink.
4. Cut corn from cobs; cut the zucchini, onion and chicken into bite-size pieces. In a 3-qt. trifle bowl or other glass bowl, layer romaine, cucumber, grilled vegetables and chicken. If desired, serve with additional salad dressing.
Per 3 cups: 239 cal., 5g fat (0 sat. fat), 56mg chol., 276mg sod., 21g carb. (9g sugars, 5g fiber), 32g pro.
Diabetic exchanges: 3 lean meat, 2 vegetable, ½ starch, ½ fat.

GRILLED CHICKEN CHOPPED SALAD

MAKEOVER SPINACH-STUFFED CHICKEN POCKETS `C` `FAST FIX`

For an easy, upscale chicken dish, you will enjoy these spinach-stuffed chicken breasts. You can also double the recipe without much effort.
—*Taste of Home* Test Kitchen

Start to Finish: 30 min.
Makes: 4 servings

- 3 teaspoons olive oil, divided
- 4 cups fresh baby spinach
- 1 garlic clove, minced
- ½ cup reduced-fat garlic-herb spreadable cheese
- 1 teaspoon Italian seasoning, divided
- ⅓ cup plus ½ cup panko (Japanese) bread crumbs, divided
- 4 boneless skinless chicken breast halves (6 ounces each)
- ¼ teaspoon salt
- ¼ teaspoon pepper
- 1 large egg white
- 1 tablespoon water

1. Preheat oven to 400°. In a large skillet, heat 1 teaspoon oil over medium-high heat. Add the spinach; cook and stir 1-2 minutes or until wilted. Add garlic; cook 1 minute longer. Remove from heat. Stir in spreadable cheese, ¼ teaspoon Italian seasoning and ⅓ cup bread crumbs.
2. Cut a pocket horizontally in the thickest part of each chicken breast. Fill with the spinach mixture; secure with toothpicks.
3. In a shallow bowl, toss remaining bread crumbs with salt, pepper and remaining Italian seasoning. In a separate shallow bowl, whisk egg white and water. Dip both sides of chicken in egg white mixture, then in crumb mixture, patting to help the coating adhere.
4. In a large ovenproof skillet, heat the remaining oil over medium heat. Brown chicken on each side. Place in oven; bake 15-18 minutes or until a thermometer inserted in chicken reads 165°. Discard toothpicks before serving.
Per stuffed chicken breast half: 332 cal., 12g fat (5g sat. fat), 112mg chol., 459mg sod., 11g carb. (1g sugars, 1g fiber), 41g pro.
Diabetic exchanges: 5 lean meat, 1 starch, 1 fat.

MAPLE-THYME CHICKEN THIGHS C FAST FIX

We eat a lot of chicken at our house, and figuring out different ways to serve it gets challenging. My family went nuts for the cozy maple flavors in this recipe, so now I share it at potlucks, too.
—Lorraine Caland, Shuniah, ON

Prep/Total: 15 min.
Makes: 6 servings

- 2 tablespoons stone-ground mustard
- 2 tablespoons maple syrup
- 1 teaspoon minced fresh thyme or ½ teaspoon dried thyme
- ½ teaspoon salt
- ½ teaspoon pepper
- 6 boneless skinless chicken thighs (about 1½ pounds)

1. In a small bowl, mix the first five ingredients. Moisten a paper towel with cooking oil; using long-handled tongs, rub on grill rack to coat lightly.
2. Grill chicken, covered, over medium heat 4-5 minutes on each side or until a thermometer reads 170°. Brush it frequently with mustard mixture during the last 4 minutes of cooking.

Per chicken thigh: 188 cal., 9g fat (2g sat. fat), 76mg chol., 363mg sod., 5g carb. (5g sugars, 0 fiber), 21g pro.
Diabetic exchanges: 3 lean meat.

ONE-POT CHICKEN PESTO PASTA

ONE-POT CHICKEN PESTO PASTA FAST FIX

When my basil goes nuts in the garden, I make pesto and keep it frozen in small containers for the right opportunity, like this saucy one-pot pasta dinner.
—Kimberly Fenwick, Hobart, IN

Start to Finish: 30 min.
Makes: 4 servings

- 1 pound boneless skinless chicken thighs, cut into 1-inch pieces
- 1 teaspoon salt-free seasoning blend
- 2 teaspoons olive oil
- 1 can (14½ ounces) reduced-sodium chicken broth
- 2 tablespoons lemon juice
- 1 cup uncooked gemelli or spiral pasta
- 2 cups fresh broccoli florets
- 1 cup frozen peas
- ⅓ cup prepared pesto

1. Toss chicken with seasoning blend. In a large nonstick skillet, heat oil over medium-high heat. Add chicken and brown evenly; remove from pan.
2. In the same pan, combine broth and lemon juice; bring to a boil, stirring to loosen browned bits from pan. Stir in pasta; return to a boil. Reduce the heat; simmer, covered, 10 minutes.
3. Add the broccoli; cook, covered, for 5 minutes. Return chicken to pan; cook, covered, 2-3 minutes longer or until pasta is tender and the chicken is no longer pink, stirring occasionally. Add the peas; heat through. Stir in pesto.

Per cup: 404 cal., 18g fat (4g sat. fat), 76mg chol., 646mg sod., 29g carb. (4g sugars, 4g fiber), 30g pro.
Diabetic exchanges: 3 lean meat, 2 starch, 2 fat.

BRUSCHETTA CHICKEN

We enjoy serving this tasty chicken to both family and to company. It just might become your new favorite way to use up summer tomatoes and basil.
—Carolin Cattoi-Demkiw, Lethbridge, AB

Prep: 10 min. • **Bake:** 30 min.
Makes: 4 servings

- ½ cup all-purpose flour
- ½ cup egg substitute
- 4 boneless skinless chicken breast halves (4 ounces each)
- ¼ cup grated Parmesan cheese
- ¼ cup dry bread crumbs
- 1 tablespoon butter, melted
- 2 large tomatoes, seeded and chopped
- 3 tablespoons minced fresh basil
- 1 tablespoon olive oil
- 2 garlic cloves, minced
- ½ teaspoon salt
- ¼ teaspoon pepper

1. Preheat oven to 375°. Place flour and egg substitute in separate shallow bowls. Dip chicken in flour, then in egg substitute; place in a greased 13-in.x9-in. baking dish. In a small bowl, mix cheese, bread crumbs and butter; sprinkle over chicken.

2. Loosely cover baking dish with foil. Bake 20 minutes. Uncover; bake 5-10 minutes longer or until a thermometer reads 165°.

3. Meanwhile, in a small bowl, toss the tomatoes with the remaining ingredients. Spoon over chicken; bake 3-5 minutes or until tomato mixture is heated through.

Per serving: 316 cal., 11g fat (4g sat. fat), 75mg chol., 563mg sod., 22g carb. (4g sugars, 2g fiber), 31g pro.
Diabetic exchanges: 3 lean meat, 1½ fat, 1 starch, 1 vegetable.

BRUSCHETTA CHICKEN

ITALIAN CHICKEN TENDERLOINS F C FAST FIX

My friend made this meal for my husband and me after our first child was born. I trimmed it down, and now it's low in fat and carbohydrates. When you shop for chicken tenderloins, keep in mind that some companies label the product chicken tenders.
—Beth Ann Stein, Richmond, IN

Start to Finish: 30 min.
Makes: 6 servings

- ½ cup chopped onion
- 1⅛ teaspoons paprika, divided
- 3 teaspoons olive oil, divided
- 1¼ cups water
- ¼ cup tomato paste
- 1 bay leaf
- ½ teaspoon reduced-sodium chicken bouillon granules
- ½ teaspoon Italian seasoning
- ¼ cup all-purpose flour
- 1½ teaspoons grated Parmesan cheese
- ½ teaspoon salt
- ¼ teaspoon garlic powder
- ¼ teaspoon dried oregano
- 1½ pounds chicken tenderloins

1. In a small saucepan, saute onion and ⅛ teaspoon paprika in 1 teaspoon oil until tender. Stir in the water, tomato paste, bay leaf, bouillon and Italian seasoning. Bring to a boil. Reduce heat; simmer, uncovered, for 10 minutes.

2. Meanwhile, in a large resealable plastic bag, combine the flour, Parmesan cheese, salt, garlic powder, oregano and remaining paprika. Add the chicken; seal the bag and shake to coat.

3. In a large nonstick skillet coated with cooking spray, cook half of the chicken in 1 teaspoon oil for 2-3 minutes on each side or until no longer pink. Remove and keep warm; repeat with remaining chicken and oil. Discard bay leaf. Serve the sauce with chicken.

Per serving: 163 cal., 3g fat (0 sat. fat), 67mg chol., 287mg sod., 8g carb. (3g sugars, 1g fiber), 27g pro.
Diabetic exchanges: 3 lean meat, ½ starch, ½ fat.

CHICKEN WITH CITRUS CHIMICHURRI SAUCE C

Chimichurri is a green sauce from South America that goes with grilled meats. My citrus version brightens up grilled chicken, which gets its juiciness from brining.
—Tyffanie Perez, Springville, UT

Prep: 20 min. + marinating • **Grill:** 10 min.
Makes: 4 servings

- 4 cups water
- ¼ cup kosher salt
- 1 tablespoon honey
- 1 teaspoon grated lemon peel
- 1 teaspoon grated orange peel
- 4 boneless skinless chicken breast halves (6 ounces each)

CHIMICHURRI SAUCE

- ½ cup olive oil
- ¼ cup packed fresh parsley sprigs
- 1 tablespoon minced fresh thyme
- 1 tablespoon lemon juice
- 1 tablespoon orange juice
- 1 garlic clove, peeled
- ¼ teaspoon salt
- ⅛ teaspoon pepper

1. In a large bowl, whisk water, salt, honey and peels until salt is dissolved. Add the chicken, making sure it is submerged. Refrigerate up to 2 hours.
2. Pulse sauce ingredients in a food processor until smooth. Reserve ½ cup sauce for serving.
3. Remove chicken; rinse and pat dry. Brush chicken with remaining sauce. Grill, covered, over medium-high heat or broil 4 in. from heat until a thermometer reads 165°, 4-6 minutes on each side. Serve it with reserved sauce.

Per chicken breast half with 2 tablespoons sauce: 427 cal., 31g fat (5g sat. fat), 94mg chol., 279mg sod., 1g carb. (1g sugars, 0 fiber), 35g pro.

★ ★ ★ ★ ★ **READER REVIEW**

"I trimmed this down, using one chicken breast, but I made the whole batch of chimichurri. I will find other uses for it. So good. Excellent flavor."

BEEMA TASTEOFHOME.COM

CREAMY DIJON CHICKEN

CREAMY DIJON CHICKEN
C FAST FIX

This chicken dish is very fast and economical. It makes a nice sauce that works well over brown rice or wide egg noodles. If you want extra sauce for leftovers, double the recipe.
—Irene Boffo, Fountain Hills, AZ

Start to Finish: 25 min.
Makes: 4 servings

- ½ cup half-and-half cream
- ¼ cup Dijon mustard
- 1 tablespoon brown sugar
- 4 boneless skinless chicken breast halves (6 ounces each)
- ¼ teaspoon salt
- ¼ teaspoon pepper
- 2 teaspoons olive oil
- 2 teaspoons butter
- 1 small onion, halved and very thinly sliced
  Minced fresh parsley

1. Whisk together cream, mustard and brown sugar. Pound chicken breasts with a meat mallet to even thickness; sprinkle with salt and pepper.
2. In a large skillet, heat oil and butter over medium-high heat; brown chicken on both sides. Reduce heat to medium. Add onion and cream mixture; bring to a boil. Reduce heat; simmer, covered, until thermometer inserted in the chicken reads 165°, 10-12 minutes. Sprinkle with parsley.

Per chicken breast half with 3 tablespoons sauce: 295 cal., 11g fat (5g sat. fat), 114mg chol., 621mg sod., 6g carb. (5g sugars, 0 fiber), 36g pro. **Diabetic exchanges:** 5 lean meat, 1 fat, ½ starch.

PEAR CHICKEN SALAD WITH MAPLE VINAIGRETTE `FAST FIX`

Freshen up a classic pear and blue cheese salad with chicken and a drizzle of the maple dressing. Romaine gives the salad a nice crunch.
—Chrysa Duran, Cambridge, MN

Start to Finish: 15 min.
Makes: 2 servings

- 3 cups torn romaine
- 1 cup cubed cooked chicken breast
- 1 medium pear, sliced
- ¼ cup crumbled blue cheese
- ¼ cup dried cranberries
- 2 tablespoons balsamic vinegar
- 2 teaspoons maple syrup
  Dash salt
- 2 tablespoons olive oil

In a large bowl, combine the romaine, chicken, pear, cheese and cranberries. In a small bowl, whisk vinegar, maple syrup and salt. Gradually whisk in the oil until blended. Drizzle over salad; toss to coat.
Per 2½ cups: 420 cal., 21g fat (6g sat. fat), 67mg chol., 365mg sod., 35g carb. (25g sugars, 5g fiber), 25g pro.

THAI CHICKEN PASTA SKILLET `FAST FIX`

This gorgeous Bangkok-style pasta has been a faithful standby for many years and always gets loads of praise. For a potluck, we increase it and do it ahead.
—Susan Ten Pas, Myrtle Creek, OR

Start to Finish: 30 min.
Makes: 6 servings

- 6 ounces uncooked whole wheat spaghetti
- 2 teaspoons canola oil
- 1 package (10 ounces) fresh sugar snap peas, trimmed and cut diagonally into thin strips
- 2 cups julienned carrots (about 8 ounces)
- 2 cups shredded cooked chicken
- 1 cup Thai peanut sauce
- 1 medium cucumber, halved lengthwise, seeded and sliced diagonally
  Chopped fresh cilantro, optional

1. Cook spaghetti according to package directions; drain.
2. Meanwhile, in a large skillet, heat oil over medium-high heat. Add snap peas and carrots; stir-fry 6-8 minutes or until they are crisp-tender. Add the chicken, peanut sauce and spaghetti; heat through, tossing to combine.
3. Transfer to a serving plate. Top with cucumber and, if desired, cilantro.
Per 1⅓ cups: 403 cal., 15g fat (3g sat. fat), 42mg chol., 432mg sod., 43g carb. (15g sugars, 6g fiber), 25g pro.
Diabetic exchanges: 3 lean meat, 2½ starch, 2 fat, 1 vegetable.
HEALTH TIP Fruits are typically associated with the antioxidant vitamin C, but sugar snap peas are an excellent source as well.

THAI CHICKEN PASTA SKILLET

MARRAKESH CHICKEN & COUSCOUS `FAST FIX`

I transformed couscous mix into a one-pot delight that transports you to a faraway land of exotic flavor! My family absolutely loves this recipe.
—Devon Delaney, Westport, CT

Start to Finish: 30 min.
Makes: 6 servings

- 1 tablespoon olive oil
- 1 pound boneless skinless chicken thighs, cut into 1¼-inch pieces
- 1 can (14½ ounces) diced tomatoes, undrained
- 1 jar (7½ ounces) marinated quartered artichoke hearts, drained
- ¼ cup lemon juice
- 2 tablespoons apricot preserves
- ½ teaspoon salt
- ½ teaspoon ground cumin
- ¼ teaspoon crushed red pepper flakes
- ⅛ teaspoon ground cinnamon
- 1 package (5.8 ounces) roasted garlic and olive oil couscous
  Chopped smoked almonds, optional

1. In a 6-qt. stockpot, heat the oil over medium-high heat. Brown chicken on both sides. Stir in tomatoes, artichokes, lemon juice, preserves, salt, spices and seasoning packet from couscous; bring to a boil. Reduce heat; simmer, covered, 10 minutes to allow flavors to develop and for chicken to cook through.
2. Stir in couscous; remove from heat. Let stand, covered, 5 minutes. If desired, sprinkle with almonds.
Per 1⅓ cups: 326 cal., 14g fat (3g sat. fat), 50mg chol., 751mg sod., 30g carb. (8g sugars, 2g fiber), 19g pro.
Diabetic exchanges: 3 lean meat, 2 starch, ½ fat.

SPINACH-FETA CHICKEN PENNE

SPINACH-FETA CHICKEN PENNE `FAST FIX`

I wanted a light sauce for pasta, so I cooked tomatoes with garlic, wine and olive oil. It's a blockbuster combo for seafood, too.
—Lyn Russomanno-Sipos, Blandon, PA

Start to Finish: 30 min.
Makes: 6 servings

- 1 package (12 ounces) whole wheat penne pasta
- 1½ pounds boneless skinless chicken breasts, cut into ¼-in.-thick strips
- 3 tablespoons olive oil, divided
- ¾ teaspoon salt, divided
- ¼ teaspoon pepper
- 3 garlic cloves, minced
- ½ cup reduced-sodium chicken broth
- ½ cup dry white wine or additional broth
- 6 plum tomatoes, chopped
- 2 cups fresh baby spinach
- ¾ cup crumbled feta cheese

1. In a 6-qt. stockpot, cook the pasta according to package directions. Drain; return to pot.
2. Meanwhile, toss chicken with 2 tablespoons oil, ½ teaspoon salt and pepper. In a large skillet, cook and stir chicken, half at a time, over medium-high heat 3-5 minutes or until no longer pink; remove from pan.
3. In same skillet, heat remaining oil over medium heat. Add garlic; cook and stir 1-2 minutes or until tender. Add broth and wine. Bring to a boil, stirring to loosen browned bits from pan; cook 2 minutes. Stir in tomatoes and remaining salt; cook until tomatoes are softened. Stir in the spinach until wilted.
4. Add chicken and tomato mixture to pasta; heat through, tossing to combine. Serve with cheese.
Per 1½ cups: 455 cal., 13g fat (3g sat. fat), 70mg chol., 552mg sod., 46g carb. (3g sugars, 8g fiber), 36g pro.
Diabetic exchanges: 3 lean meat, 2½ starch, 2 fat, 1 vegetable.

CHICKEN SAUSAGE PITA POCKETS `FAST FIX`

Chicken sausage comes in many flavors, so I try different ones when I make pitas with fresh basil and veggies, inspired by the Greek gyro.
—Christina Price, Pittsburgh, PA

Start to Finish: 25 min.
Makes: 4 servings

- 6 teaspoons olive oil, divided
- 1 package (12 ounces) fully cooked roasted garlic chicken sausage links or flavor of your choice, sliced
- 1 cup sliced fresh mushrooms
- 1 small onion, halved and sliced
- 1 medium zucchini, halved lengthwise and sliced
- 1 medium yellow summer squash, halved lengthwise and sliced
- 3 tablespoons chopped fresh basil
- 8 whole wheat pita pocket halves, warmed

Sliced tomato and plain Greek yogurt, optional

1. In a large nonstick skillet, heat 2 teaspoons oil over medium-high heat. Add the sausage; cook and stir 4-6 minutes or until it is lightly browned. Remove from pan.
2. In same skillet, heat 2 teaspoons oil over medium-high heat. Add mushrooms and onion; cook and stir 4-6 minutes or until tender. Remove from pan.
3. Add remaining oil to pan. Add the zucchini and yellow squash; cook and stir 3-5 minutes or until tender. Stir in basil, sausage and mushroom mixture; heat through. Serve in pitas. If desired, add tomato and yogurt.

Per 2 filled pita halves: 376 cal., 16g fat (3g sat. fat), 70mg chol., 736mg sod., 39g carb. (5g sugars, 6g fiber), 22g pro.
Diabetic exchanges: 3 lean meat, 2 starch, 1½ fat, 1 vegetable.

SOUTHWEST CHICKEN DINNER `FAST FIX`

My family orders those gigantic takeout Tex-Mex burritos but can't finish them. I've got a lighter, no-guilt alternative that loses the tortilla.
—Marquisha Turner, Denver, CO

Start to Finish: 30 min.
Makes: 4 servings

- 2 cups water
- 2 tablespoons olive oil, divided
- ½ teaspoon salt
- ¼ teaspoon pepper
- 1 cup uncooked long grain rice
- 1 tablespoon taco seasoning
- 4 boneless skinless chicken breast halves (4 ounces each)
- 1 cup canned black beans or pinto beans, rinsed and drained
- ¼ cup chopped fresh cilantro
- 1 teaspoon grated lime peel
- 2 tablespoons lime juice
  Optional toppings: pico de gallo, shredded Mexican cheese blend and sour cream

1. In a large saucepan, combine water, 1 tablespoon oil, salt and pepper; bring to a boil. Stir in rice. Reduce heat; simmer, covered, 15-17 minutes or until liquid is absorbed and rice is tender.
2. Meanwhile, sprinkle taco seasoning over both sides of chicken. In a large skillet, heat remaining oil over medium heat. Add the chicken; cook 4-5 minutes on each side or until a thermometer reads 165°.
3. In a microwave, heat the beans until warmed. To serve, gently stir cilantro, lime peel and lime juice into rice; divide among four bowls. Cut chicken into slices. Place chicken and beans over rice; serve with toppings as desired.

Per serving: 398 cal., 7g fat (1g sat. fat), 63mg chol., 678mg sod., 52g carb. (1g sugars, 3g fiber), 30g pro.

CHICKEN SAUSAGE PITA POCKETS

TURKEY SPECIALTIES

"My go-to meal after an evening run is this satisfying turkey wrap with jicama, a potato-like root veggie used in Mexican cooking."
—Christie Arp, Blue Ridge, GA

Pizza Spaghetti (p. 171) **Turkey Gyros** (p. 169) **Turkey Salsa Bowls with Tortilla Wedges** (p. 176)
Southwest Turkey Burgers (p. 173) **Spicy Turkey Lettuce Wraps** (p. 172) **Turkey Pepper Kabobs** (p. 177)

TURKEY TENDERLOIN SANDWICHES

We loved these absolutely delicious tenderloins when we visited the Iowa State Fair. We had to wait in line for more that an hour to order them, but with this recipe, we can enjoy them regularly at home.
—Kathy Thompson, Clifton, CO

Prep: 10 min. + marinating • **Grill:** 10 min.
Makes: 4 servings

- 4 turkey breast tenderloins (4 ounces each)
- ¼ cup canola oil
- ¼ cup sherry or chicken broth
- ¼ cup reduced-sodium soy sauce
- 2 tablespoons lemon juice
- 2 tablespoons dried minced onion
- ¼ teaspoon ground ginger
- ⅛ teaspoon pepper
- 4 whole wheat hamburger buns, split
- 1 slice red onion, separated into rings
- 4 slices tomato
- 4 lettuce leaves

1. Flatten tenderloins to ¾-in. thickness. In a large resealable plastic bag, combine the oil, sherry or broth, soy sauce, lemon juice, onion, ginger and pepper; add the turkey. Seal bag and turn to coat; refrigerate for at least 3 hours, turning occasionally.
2. Drain and discard marinade. Grill turkey, uncovered, over medium heat on an oiled rack or broil 4 in. from the heat until juices run clear, about 4 minutes on each side. Serve on buns with onion, tomato and lettuce.

Per sandwich: 279 cal., 7g fat (1g sat. fat), 56mg chol., 423mg sod., 24g carb. (5g sugars, 4g fiber), 31g pro.
Diabetic Exchanges: 4 lean meat, 1½ starch, ½ fat.

DID YOU KNOW?
You can substitute ½ cup of minced fresh onion in the marinade instead of using dried minced onion. For each tablespoon of dried onion called for in a recipe, you can use ¼ cup of minced raw onion.

TURKEY QUESADILLAS WITH CRANBERRY SALSA

TURKEY QUESADILLAS WITH CRANBERRY SALSA FAST FIX ▶

These quesadillas stuffed with turkey and cheese get amped up when you add sweet-tart cranberry salsa. You might want to make extra; the salsa is great with chicken or pork, too!
—Jodi Kristensen, Macomb, MI

Start to Finish: 30 min.
Makes: 4 servings

- ¾ cup fresh or frozen cranberries
- 2 tablespoons sugar
- ¼ cup water
- 1 small pear, chopped
- ¼ cup chopped red onion
- 1 jalapeno pepper, seeded and chopped
- 3 tablespoons chopped celery
- 2 teaspoons grated lemon peel
- 1 tablespoon lemon juice
- ½ teaspoon ground cumin
- 4 flour tortillas (6 inches)
- 2 cups cubed cooked turkey breast
- 1 cup shredded reduced-fat white or yellow cheddar cheese

1. For salsa, in a small saucepan, combine cranberries, sugar and water; bring to a boil. Reduce heat to medium; cook, uncovered, until berries pop, about 10 minutes, stirring occasionally. Remove from heat; cool slightly. Stir in the pear, onion, jalapeno, celery, lemon peel and juice, and cumin.
2. Preheat griddle over medium heat. Top one half of each tortilla with ½ cup turkey; sprinkle with ¼ cup cheese. Fold tortilla to close. Cook on griddle until golden brown and cheese is melted, 1-2 minutes per side. Serve with salsa.
Note: Wear disposable gloves when cutting hot peppers; the oils can burn skin. Avoid touching your face.

Per quesadilla with ⅓ cup salsa: 321 cal., 10g fat (4g sat. fat), 80mg chol., 449mg sod., 27g carb. (12g sugars, 2g fiber), 32g pro.
Diabetic Exchanges: 3 lean meat, 1½ starch, 1 fat, ½ fruit.

SAUSAGE-STUFFED BUTTERNUT SQUASH FAST FIX

Load butternut squash shells with an Italian turkey sausage mixture for a quick and satisfying fall meal. Even better, it's surprisingly low in calories.
—Katia Slinger, West Jordan, UT

Start to Finish: 30 min.
Makes: 4 servings

- 1 medium butternut squash (about 3 pounds)
- 1 pound Italian turkey sausage links, casings removed
- 1 medium onion, finely chopped
- 4 garlic cloves, minced
- ½ cup shredded Italian cheese blend
  Crushed red pepper flakes, optional

1. Preheat broiler. Cut squash lengthwise in half; discard seeds. Place squash in a large microwave-safe dish, cut side down; add ½ in. of water. Microwave, covered, on high until soft, 20-25 minutes. Cool slightly.
2. Meanwhile, in a large nonstick skillet, cook and crumble sausage with onion over medium-high heat until no longer pink, 5-7 minutes. Add garlic; cook and stir 1 minute.
3. Leaving ½-in.-thick shells, scoop pulp from squash and stir into sausage mixture. Place squash shells on a baking sheet; fill with sausage mixture. Sprinkle with the cheese blend.
4. Broil 4-5 in. from heat until cheese is melted, 1-2 minutes. If desired, sprinkle with pepper flakes. To serve, cut each half into two portions.

Per serving: 325 cal., 10g fat (4g sat. fat), 52mg chol., 587mg sod., 44g carb. (10g sugars, 12g fiber), 19g pro.
Diabetic Exchanges: 3 starch, 3 lean meat.

HEALTH TIP Butternut squash is an excellent source of vitamin A in the form of beta-carotene. It's important for normal vision and a healthy immune system, and it helps the heart, lungs and kidneys function properly.

SAUSAGE-STUFFED BUTTERNUT SQUASH

QUINOA-STUFFED ACORN SQUASH

Here's an amazingly flavorful and healthy recipe my family will actually eat. You can omit the sausage if you want to make it a side dish or even lighter.
—Valarree Osters, Lodi, OH

Prep: 15 min. • **Bake:** 45 min.
Makes: 4 servings

- 2 small acorn squash (about 1½ pounds each)
- 1 tablespoon olive oil
- 1 teaspoon Italian seasoning, divided
- ½ teaspoon salt, divided
- ¼ teaspoon garlic powder
- 2 Italian turkey sausage links (about 8 ounces), casings removed
- 1 small onion, finely chopped
- 2 garlic cloves, minced
- ¼ teaspoon pepper
- ¾ cup quinoa, rinsed
- 1½ cups chicken stock
- 1 large egg, lightly beaten
- 1 tablespoon minced fresh parsley
  Shredded Parmesan cheese
  Additional minced fresh parsley

1. Preheat oven to 400°. Cut squash crosswise in half; discard seeds. Cut a thin slice from bottom of each half to allow them to lie flat. Place on a baking sheet, hollow side up; brush tops with oil. Mix ½ teaspoon Italian seasoning, ¼ teaspoon salt and garlic powder; sprinkle over top. Bake until almost tender, 25-30 minutes.
2. Meanwhile, in a large skillet, cook and crumble sausage with onion over medium heat until no longer pink, 4-6 minutes. Add garlic, pepper and the remaining Italian seasoning and salt; cook and stir 1 minute. Stir in quinoa and stock; bring to a boil. Reduce heat; simmer, covered, until liquid is absorbed, 15-20 minutes. Cool slightly. Stir in egg and parsley; spoon into squash.
3. Bake until filling is heated through and squash is tender, 20-25 minutes. Sprinkle with cheese and additional parsley.
Per stuffed squash half: 351 cal., 10g fat (2g sat. fat), 67mg chol., 740mg sod., 53g carb. (7g sugars, 7g fiber), 16g pro.

TURKEY DUMPLING STEW

TURKEY DUMPLING STEW

My mom made this stew when I was young, and it was always a hit. Since it's not too time-consuming, I often make it on weekends for our children, who love the tender dumplings.
—Becky Mohr, Appleton, WI

Prep: 20 min. • **Cook:** 50 min.
Makes: 6 servings

- 4 bacon strips, finely chopped
- 1½ pounds turkey breast tenderloins, cut into 1-inch pieces
- 4 medium carrots, sliced
- 2 small onions, quartered
- 2 celery ribs, sliced
- 1 bay leaf
- ¼ teaspoon dried rosemary, crushed
- 2 cups water, divided
- 1 can (14½ ounces) reduced-sodium chicken broth
- 3 tablespoons all-purpose flour
- ½ teaspoon salt
- ⅛ to ¼ teaspoon pepper
- 1 cup reduced-fat biscuit/baking mix
- ⅓ cup plus 1 tablespoon fat-free milk
  Coarsely ground pepper and chopped fresh parsley, optional

1. In a Dutch oven, cook bacon over medium heat until crisp, stirring occasionally. Remove with a slotted spoon; drain on paper towels. Reserve 2 teaspoons drippings.
2. In drippings, saute turkey over medium-high heat until lightly browned. Add vegetables, herbs, 1¾ cups water and broth; bring to a boil. Reduce heat; simmer, covered, until vegetables are tender, 20-30 minutes.
3. Mix flour and remaining water until smooth; stir into turkey mixture. Bring to a boil; cook and stir until thickened, about 2 minutes. Discard bay leaf. Stir in salt, pepper and bacon.
4. In a small bowl, mix biscuit mix and milk to form a soft dough; drop in six mounds on top of simmering stew. Cover; simmer 15 minutes or until a toothpick inserted in dumplings comes out clean. If desired, sprinkle with pepper and parsley before serving.
Per serving: 284 cal., 6g fat (1g sat. fat), 52mg chol., 822mg sod., 24g carb. (6g sugars, 2g fiber), 34g pro.
Diabetic Exchanges: 4 lean meat, 1 starch, 1 vegetable, ½ fat.

TURKEY MUSHROOM TETRAZZINI

Your family will flip for this rich-tasting turkey and mushroom casserole. The creamy Parmesan-topped tetrazzini is so satisfying that no one will suspect it's lower in fat.
—Irene Banegas, Las Cruces, NM

Prep: 25 min. • **Bake:** 25 min.
Makes: 6 servings

- 8 ounces uncooked spaghetti
- 3 tablespoons cornstarch
- 1 can (14½ ounces) reduced-sodium chicken broth
- ½ teaspoon seasoned salt
  Dash pepper
- 1 tablespoon butter
- ¼ cup finely chopped onion
- 1 garlic clove, minced
- 1 can (12 ounces) fat-free evaporated milk
- 2½ cups cubed cooked turkey breast
- 1 can (4 ounces) mushroom stems and pieces, drained
- 2 tablespoons grated Parmesan cheese
- ¼ teaspoon paprika

1. Preheat oven to 350°. Cook spaghetti according to package directions; drain.
2. Mix cornstarch, broth and seasonings. In a large saucepan, heat butter over medium-high heat; saute onion until tender. Add garlic; cook and stir 1 minute. Stir cornstarch mixture and add to pan. Bring to a boil; cook and stir until thickened, 1-2 minutes. Reduce heat to low. Add milk; cook and stir 2-3 minutes. Stir in turkey, mushrooms and spaghetti.
3. Transfer to an 8-in. square baking dish coated with cooking spray. Bake, covered, 20 minutes. Sprinkle with cheese and paprika; bake, uncovered, until heated through, 5-10 minutes.
Per 1¼ cups: 331 cal., 5g fat (2g sat. fat), 51mg chol., 544mg sod., 41g carb. (10g sugars, 1g fiber), 28g pro.
Diabetic Exchanges: 3 lean meat, 2 starch, 1 vegetable, ½ fat-free milk.

TURKEY GYROS `FAST FIX`
(PICTURED ON P. 164)

Greek seasoning, feta cheese and cucumber sauce give my lightened-up gyros an authentic taste. Instead of feta cheese, we sometimes use cheddar or Monterey Jack.
—Donna Garvin, Glens Falls, NY

Start to Finish: 25 min.
Makes: 4 servings

- 1 medium cucumber, peeled
- ⅔ cup reduced-fat sour cream
- ¼ cup finely chopped onion
- 2 teaspoons dill weed
- 2 teaspoons lemon juice
- 1 teaspoon olive oil
- ½ pound turkey breast tenderloin, cut into ¼-inch-thick strips
- 1½ teaspoons salt-free Greek seasoning
- 1½ cups shredded lettuce
- 8 thin tomato slices
- 4 whole pita breads, warmed
- 2 tablespoons crumbled feta cheese

1. Finely chop a third of the cucumber. For sauce, mix sour cream, onion, dill, lemon juice and chopped cucumber. Thinly slice remaining cucumber.
2. In a nonstick skillet, heat oil over medium-high heat; saute turkey until no longer pink, 4-6 minutes. Stir in Greek seasoning. Serve turkey, lettuce, tomato and sliced cucumber on pitas; top with sauce and cheese.
Per sandwich: 307 cal., 6g fat (2g sat. fat), 28mg chol., 422mg sod., 41g carb. (6g sugars, 3g fiber), 24g pro.
Diabetic Exchanges: 2½ starch, 2 lean meat, 1 vegetable, 1 fat.

✱
TEST KITCHEN TIP
To make your own salt-free Greek seasoning, mix 1½ teaspoons dried oregano; 1 teaspoon each dried mint and dried thyme; ½ teaspoon each dried basil, dried marjoram and dried minced onion; and ¼ teaspoon dried minced garlic. Store in an airtight container in a cool, dry place for up to 6 months. Makes about 2 tablespoons.

TURKEY MUSHROOM TETRAZZINI

MUSHROOM BACON TURKEY BURGERS

MUSHROOM BACON TURKEY BURGERS FAST FIX

If you ask me, a good burger needs to have mushrooms on top, but they tend to slide around and fall out. I decided to put mushrooms right into the patties— problem solved!
—Melissa Obernesser, Utica, NY

Start to Finish: 30 min.
Makes: 4 servings

- 1 cup finely chopped fresh mushrooms (about 4 medium)
- 3 tablespoons soft bread crumbs
- 3 tablespoons barbecue sauce
- ¾ teaspoon onion powder
- ½ teaspoon garlic powder
- ¼ teaspoon pepper
- 1 pound extra-lean ground turkey
- 4 turkey bacon strips, halved
- 4 thin slices cheddar cheese
- 4 whole wheat hamburger buns, split
  Additional barbecue sauce
  Dill pickle slices, optional

1. Combine first six ingredients. Add turkey; mix lightly but thoroughly. Shape into four ½-in.-thick patties.
2. Place burgers on an oiled grill rack over medium heat; grill, covered, until a thermometer reads 165°, 4-5 minutes per side. Grill bacon strips, covered, until crisp, 2-3 minutes per side. Top burgers with cheese and bacon; grill, covered, until cheese is melted, 30 seconds.
3. Serve on buns. Top with additional barbecue sauce and, if desired, pickles.
Note: To make soft bread crumbs, tear bread into pieces and place in a food processor or blender. Cover and pulse until crumbs form. One slice of bread yields ½-¾ cup crumbs.
Per burger: 389 cal., 17g fat (4g sat. fat), 95mg chol., 727mg sod., 30g carb. (9g sugars, 4g fiber), 32g pro.
Diabetic Exchanges: 4 lean meat, 2 starch, 2 fat.

HONEY-BRINED TURKEY BREAST F S C

This recipe will give you a beautifully sweet and spicy, lightly salted turkey roast that also makes great sandwiches, salads and soups. I prefer to use cider or apple juice instead of water for my brine. It makes the turkey so delicious.
—Deirdre Cox, Kansas City, MO

Prep: 50 min. + chilling • **Bake:** 1¾ hours
Makes: 12 servings

- ½ cup kosher salt
- ⅓ cup honey
- 2 tablespoons Dijon mustard
- 1½ teaspoons crushed red pepper flakes
- 2 quarts apple cider or juice, divided
- 1 fresh rosemary sprig
- 2 large oven roasting bags
- 1 bone-in turkey breast (4 to 5 pounds)
- 1 tablespoon olive oil

1. For brine, place first four ingredients and 4 cups cider in a Dutch oven; bring to a boil. Cook and stir until salt is dissolved. Add rosemary; remove from heat. Stir in remaining cider; cool brine to room temperature.
2. Place one roasting bag inside the other. Place turkey breast inside both bags; add brine. Seal bags, pressing out as much air as possible; turn to coat turkey. Place in a baking pan. Refrigerate 6-24 hours, turning occasionally.
3. Preheat oven to 325°. Line bottom of a roasting pan with foil. Drain turkey, discarding brine. Place on a rack in prepared pan; pat dry.
4. Roast turkey 30 minutes. Brush with oil; roast until a thermometer reads 170°, 1¼-1¾ hours. (Cover loosely with foil if turkey browns too quickly.) Remove from oven; tent with foil. Let stand 15 minutes.
Note: It is best not to use prebasted turkey breast for this recipe.
Per 4 ounces cooked turkey (skin removed): 138 cal., 2g fat (0 sat. fat), 78mg chol., 88mg sod., 0 carb. (0 sugars, 0 fiber), 28g pro.
Diabetic Exchanges: 4 lean meat.

TURKEY THYME RISOTTO

This satisfying risotto is a wonderful way to reinvent leftover turkey. I use Romano cheese, garlic and plenty of fresh mushrooms to create it.

—Sunny McDaniel, Cary, NC

Prep: 10 min. • **Cook:** 35 min.
Makes: 4 servings

- 2¾ to 3¼ cups reduced-sodium chicken broth
- 1 tablespoon olive oil
- 2 cups sliced fresh mushrooms
- 1 small onion, chopped
- 1 garlic clove, minced
- 1 cup uncooked arborio rice
- 1 teaspoon minced fresh thyme or ¼ teaspoon dried thyme
- ½ cup white wine or additional broth
- 1½ cups cubed cooked turkey breast
- 2 tablespoons shredded Romano cheese
- ¼ teaspoon salt
- ¼ teaspoon pepper

1. In a small saucepan, bring broth to a simmer; keep hot. In a large nonstick skillet, heat oil over medium-high heat; saute mushrooms, onion and garlic until tender, about 3 minutes. Add rice and thyme; cook and stir 2 minutes.

2. Stir in wine. Reduce heat to maintain a simmer; cook and stir until wine is absorbed. Add hot broth, ½ cup at a time, cooking and stirring until broth has been absorbed after each addition, rice is tender but firm to the bite, and risotto is creamy. (This will take about 20 minutes.)

3. Add the remaining ingredients; cook and stir until heated through. Serve immediately.

Per cup: 337 cal., 6g fat (2g sat. fat), 43mg chol., 651mg sod., 44g carb. (2g sugars, 1g fiber), 24g pro.
Diabetic Exchanges: 3 starch, 2 lean meat, ½ fat.

PIZZA SPAGHETTI
(PICTURED ON P. 164)

The idea for this recipe came to me when I saw someone dip a slice of pizza into a pasta dish. My wife and kids love it and so do my friends!

—Robert Smith, Las Vegas, NV

Prep: 20 min. • **Cook:** 30 min.
Makes: 6 servings

- ½ pound lean ground beef (90% lean)
- ½ pound Italian turkey sausage links, casings removed
- ½ cup chopped sweet onion
- 4 cans (8 ounces each) no-salt-added tomato sauce
- 3 ounces sliced turkey pepperoni
- 1 tablespoon sugar
- 2 teaspoons minced fresh parsley or ½ teaspoon dried parsley flakes
- 2 teaspoons minced fresh basil or ½ teaspoon dried basil
- 9 ounces uncooked whole wheat spaghetti
- 3 tablespoons grated Parmesan cheese

1. In a large nonstick skillet, cook and crumble beef and sausage with onion over medium-high heat until no longer pink, 5-7 minutes. Stir in tomato sauce, pepperoni, sugar and herbs; bring to a boil. Reduce heat; simmer, uncovered, until thickened, 20-25 minutes.

2. Meanwhile, in a 6-qt. stockpot, cook spaghetti according to package directions; drain and return to pot. Toss with sauce. Sprinkle with cheese.

Per 1⅓ cups: 354 cal., 9g fat (3g sat. fat), 57mg chol., 512mg sod., 45g carb. (11g sugars, 7g fiber), 25g pro.
Diabetic Exchanges: 3 starch, 3 lean meat.

✳
TEST KITCHEN TIP
If you don't like whole wheat pasta, try multigrain instead. It looks and tastes like white, but it's better for you.

THYME

ASIAN-STYLE TURKEY PITAS

ASIAN-STYLE TURKEY PITAS
FAST FIX ▶

A neighbor gave me this recipe years ago. It's been my most popular day-after-Turkey-Day dish ever since.
—Beverly Graml, Yorktown, VA

Start to Finish: 25 min.
Makes: 4 servings

½ teaspoon cornstarch
⅓ cup water
2 tablespoons reduced-sodium soy sauce
1 tablespoon honey
1 teaspoon sesame oil
1 tablespoon canola oil
1 medium sweet red pepper, julienned
3 garlic cloves, minced
½ to 1 teaspoon curry powder
¼ teaspoon cayenne pepper
3 cups coarsely shredded cooked turkey
3 green onions, sliced
8 whole wheat pita pocket halves, warmed

1. Mix first five ingredients until smooth. In a large nonstick skillet, heat canola oil over medium-high heat; stir-fry pepper until crisp-tender. Add garlic and spices; cook and stir 1 minute.
2. Stir cornstarch mixture and add to pan. Bring to a boil; cook and stir until slightly thickened, 1-2 minutes. Stir in turkey and green onions; heat through. Serve in pitas.
Per 2 filled pita halves: 394 cal., 10g fat (2g sat. fat), 106mg chol., 692mg sod., 40g carb. (7g sugars, 5g fiber), 37g pro.
Diabetic Exchanges: 4 lean meat, 2½ starch, 1 fat.

SPICY TURKEY LETTUCE WRAPS C FAST FIX ▶

My go-to meal after an evening run is this satisfying turkey wrap with jicama, a potato-like root veggie used in Mexican cooking.
—Christie Arp, Blue Ridge, GA

Start to Finish: 20 min.
Makes: 2 servings

½ pound lean ground turkey
½ cup chopped peeled jicama or celery
¼ cup chopped onion
2 tablespoons reduced-sodium soy sauce
2 teaspoons minced fresh gingerroot
1 garlic clove, minced
⅛ teaspoon cayenne pepper
⅛ teaspoon pepper
¼ cup julienned carrot
6 Bibb lettuce leaves
Hot mustard, optional

1. In a large skillet, cook and crumble turkey with jicama and onion over medium heat until no longer pink, 4-6 minutes. Stir in soy sauce, ginger, garlic and peppers. Add carrot; cook and stir until liquid is absorbed, 1-2 minutes.
2. Serve in lettuce. If desired, serve with mustard.
Per 3 wraps: 212 cal., 9g fat (2g sat. fat), 78mg chol., 655mg sod., 9g carb. (2g sugars, 3g fiber), 24g pro.
Diabetic Exchanges: 3 lean meat, 1 vegetable.

BOW TIES WITH SAUSAGE & ASPARAGUS FAST FIX

We love asparagus, so I look for ways to go green. This veggie pasta comes together fast on hectic nights and makes wonderful leftovers.

—Carol A. Suto, Liverpool, NY

Start to Finish: 30 min.
Makes: 6 servings

- 3 cups uncooked whole wheat bow tie pasta (about 8 ounces)
- 1 pound fresh asparagus, trimmed and cut into 1½-inch pieces
- 1 package (19½ ounces) Italian turkey sausage links, casings removed
- 1 medium onion, chopped
- 3 garlic cloves, minced
- ¼ cup shredded Parmesan cheese
  Additional shredded Parmesan cheese, optional

1. In a 6-qt. stockpot, cook the pasta according to package directions, adding asparagus during the last 2-3 minutes of cooking. Drain, reserving ½ cup pasta water; return pasta and asparagus to pot.
2. Meanwhile, in a large skillet, cook sausage, onion and garlic over medium heat until no longer pink, 6-8 minutes, breaking sausage into large crumbles. Add to stockpot. Stir in ¼ cup cheese and reserved pasta water as desired. Serve with additional cheese if desired.

Per 1⅓ cups: 247 cal., 7g fat (2g sat. fat), 36mg chol., 441mg sod., 28g carb. (2g sugars, 4g fiber), 17g pro.
Diabetic Exchanges: 2 lean meat, 1½ starch, 1 vegetable.

BOW TIES WITH SAUSAGE & ASPARAGUS

SOUTHWEST TURKEY BURGERS FAST FIX
(PICTURED ON P. 164)

I made these turkey burgers with corn, green chilies and taco spice for my parents. They originally weren't sold on an untraditional burger, but absolutely loved them! People gobble up these burgers every time.

—Katie Ring, Menasha, WI

Start to Finish: 30 min.
Makes: 6 servings

- ½ cup seasoned bread crumbs
- ½ cup frozen corn, thawed
- 1 can (4 ounces) chopped green chilies
- 1 tablespoon reduced-sodium taco seasoning
- 1 pound lean ground turkey
- 6 whole wheat hamburger buns, split
- 6 wedges The Laughing Cow queso fresco chipotle cheese, halved
  Lettuce leaves, optional

1. Preheat broiler. Mix first four ingredients. Add the turkey; mix lightly but thoroughly. Shape mixture into six ½-in.-thick patties.
2. In a large nonstick skillet coated with cooking spray, cook burgers in batches over medium heat until a thermometer reads 165°, 4-6 minutes per side. Keep burgers warm.
3. Meanwhile, place buns on a baking sheet, cut side up. Broil 3-4 in. from heat until toasted, about 30 seconds. Spread tops with cheese. Serve burgers in buns with lettuce if desired.

Freeze option: Place uncooked patties on a plastic wrap-lined baking sheet; cover and freeze until firm. Remove from pan and transfer to a large resealable plastic bag; return to freezer. To use, cook frozen patties in a nonstick skillet coated with cooking spray over medium-low heat until a thermometer reads 165°, about 6-8 minutes per side.

Per burger: 316 cal., 10g fat (3g sat. fat), 57mg chol., 812mg sod., 35g carb. (6g sugars, 4g fiber), 22g pro.
Diabetic Exchanges: 3 lean meat, 2 starch, ½ fat.

CHICAGO-STYLE HOT DOGS
FAST FIX

I decided to give a Chicago-style dog a healthy twist for my family. Our kids love it. You can use other fresh toppings to please just about anyone.
—Gregg May, Columbus, OH

Start to Finish: 20 min.
Makes: 4 servings

- 4 turkey hot dogs
- 4 whole wheat tortillas (8 inches), warmed
- 4 thin sandwich pickle slices
- ½ medium cucumber, peeled and thinly sliced
- 2 plum tomatoes, cut into thin wedges
- ½ cup chopped sweet onion
  Optional toppings: prepared mustard, shredded reduced-fat cheddar cheese and sport peppers or other pickled hot peppers

Grill hot dogs according to package directions. Serve in tortillas with pickle, cucumber, tomatoes and onion. Add toppings as desired.
Per serving: 252 cal., 10g fat (2g sat. fat), 35mg chol., 596mg sod., 29g carb. (5g sugars, 3g fiber), 10g pro.
Diabetic Exchanges: 2 starch, 1 medium-fat meat.

ASIAN-STYLE MEAT LOAVES

ASIAN-STYLE MEAT LOAVES
Here's a family-friendly meat loaf with just a hint of Asian flair. Serve it with pea pods or steamed baby bok choy and brown rice.
—Taste of Home Test Kitchen

Prep: 25 min. • **Bake:** 50 min. + standing
Makes: 2 loaves (8 servings each)

- 1⅓ cups panko (Japanese) bread crumbs
- 1 small onion, finely chopped
- 2 large eggs, lightly beaten
- ⅓ cup 2% milk
- ¼ cup hoisin sauce
- 1 tablespoon reduced-sodium soy sauce
- 2 garlic cloves, minced
- 2 teaspoons prepared mustard
- 1¼ teaspoons ground ginger
- 1 teaspoon salt
- 2 pounds extra-lean ground turkey
- 1 pound Italian turkey sausage links, casings removed

TOPPING
- 1 cup ketchup
- ½ cup packed brown sugar
- 2 teaspoons prepared mustard

1. Preheat oven to 350°. In a large bowl, combine first 10 ingredients. Add turkey and sausage; mix lightly but thoroughly. Transfer to two greased 9x5-in. loaf pans. Mix topping ingredients; spread over tops.
2. Bake until a thermometer reads 165°, 50-55 minutes. Let stand 10 minutes before slicing.
Freeze option: Shape meat loaves in plastic wrap-lined loaf pans; cover and freeze until firm. Remove from pans and wrap securely in foil; return to freezer. To use, unwrap and bake meat loaves as directed, increasing time to 1¼-1½ hours, or until a thermometer inserted in center reads 165°.
Per slice: 187 cal., 6g fat (1g sat. fat), 67mg chol., 636mg sod., 17g carb. (12g sugars, trace fiber), 16g pro.
Diabetic Exchanges: 2 lean meat, 1 starch.

✴ TEST KITCHEN TIP
It's smart to double up on your prep and freeze half of the recipe for future meals. Many meatballs, burger patties and taco fillings also freeze well.

TURKEY MARSALA C

This recipe originally called for beef, but I substituted turkey to make it healthier. It's easy to prepare, but the rich sauce makes it seem like you spent all day in the kitchen. I serve this with a baked sweet potato and a green vegetable.
—Deborah Williams, Peoria, AZ

Prep: 10 min. • **Cook:** 30 min.
Makes: 4 servings

- ¼ cup all-purpose flour
- ½ teaspoon salt, divided
- ½ teaspoon pepper, divided
- 1 package (20 ounces) turkey breast tenderloins
- 1 tablespoon olive oil
- 1 tablespoon butter
- ½ pound sliced fresh mushrooms
- ½ cup reduced-sodium chicken broth
- ½ cup Marsala wine
- 1 teaspoon lemon juice

1. Mix the flour, ¼ teaspoon salt and ¼ teaspoon pepper. Cut each tenderloin crosswise in half; pound each piece with a meat mallet to ¾-in. thickness. Toss with the flour mixture; shake off excess.

2. In a large nonstick skillet, heat oil over medium heat. Add turkey; cook until a thermometer reads 165°, 6-8 minutes per side. Remove from pan; keep warm.

3. In same skillet, heat the butter over medium-high heat; saute mushrooms until tender, 3-4 minutes. Stir in broth and wine. Bring to a boil, stirring to loosen browned bits from pan; cook until liquid is reduced by half, 10-12 minutes. Stir in lemon juice and the remaining salt and pepper. Serve with turkey.

Per serving: 295 cal., 8g fat (3g sat. fat), 77mg chol., 482mg sod., 12g carb. (5g sugars, 1g fiber), 36g pro.
Diabetic Exchanges: 4 lean meat, 1½ fat, 1 starch.

TARRAGON-LEMON TURKEY BREAST F S C

If you enjoy the flavors of tarragon and lemon pepper, consider this tasty rub. It's perfect for turkey or even chicken.
—*Taste of Home* Test Kitchen

Prep: 10 min. • **Bake:** 1¾ hours + standing
Makes: 12 servings

- ¼ cup minced fresh tarragon
- 2 tablespoons olive oil
- 1 teaspoon lemon-pepper seasoning
- ½ teaspoon seasoned salt
- 1 bone-in turkey breast (4 pounds)

1. Preheat oven to 325°. Mix first four ingredients. With fingers, carefully loosen skin from turkey breast; rub half of the herb mixture under the skin. Secure skin to underside of turkey breast with toothpicks. Rub outside of turkey with remaining mixture.

2. Place turkey on a rack in a roasting pan. Roast until a thermometer reads 170°, 1¾-2 hours. Remove from oven; tent with foil. Let stand 15 minutes. Remove and discard turkey skin and toothpicks before carving.

Per 4 ounces cooked turkey: 147 cal., 3g fat (1g sat. fat), 78mg chol., 139mg sod., 0 carb. (0 sugars, 0 fiber), 28g pro.
Diabetic Exchanges: 4 lean meat, ½ fat.

TURKEY MARSALA

TURKEY SALSA BOWLS WITH TORTILLA WEDGES

(PICTURED ON P. 165)

Delicious and nutritious, this dish was a favorite of the kids who participated in the junior chef classes I taught at my church. The recipe encouraged creativity and healthy eating as students designed their own salsa bowls using whole grains, vegetables and lean protein.
—Jean Gottfried, Upper Sandusky, OH

Prep: 15 min. • **Cook:** 25 min.
Makes: 8 servings

- 1 pound lean ground turkey
- ½ cup chopped sweet pepper
- ¼ cup thinly sliced celery
- 2 green onions, chopped
- 1 jar (16 ounces) medium salsa
- 1 can (16 ounces) kidney beans, rinsed and drained
- 1 cup uncooked instant brown rice
- 1 cup water
- 4 whole wheat tortillas (8 inches)
- 1 tablespoon canola oil
- 8 cups torn romaine (about 1 head)
  Optional toppings: chopped tomatoes and green onions, sliced ripe olives, cubed avocado, and shredded cheddar cheese

1. Preheat oven to 400°. In a large skillet, cook and crumble turkey with pepper, celery and green onions over medium-high heat until no longer pink, 5-7 minutes. Stir in salsa, beans, rice and water; bring to a boil. Reduce heat; simmer, covered, until liquid is absorbed, about 15 minutes.
2. Brush both sides of tortillas with oil; cut each into eight wedges. Arrange in a single layer on a baking sheet. Bake until lightly browned, 8-10 minutes.
3. To serve, divide lettuce among eight bowls; top with turkey mixture. Serve with tortilla wedges and toppings as desired.
Per serving: 279 cal., 7g fat (1g sat. fat), 39mg chol., 423mg sod., 36g carb. (4g sugars, 6g fiber), 18g pro.
Diabetic Exchanges: 2 starch, 2 lean meat, 1 vegetable.

SOUTHWEST TURKEY LETTUCE WRAPS

SOUTHWEST TURKEY LETTUCE WRAPS C FAST FIX

If you're tired of the same old taco routine, give these a try. I tweaked a friend's recipe to suit our tastes and my family has loved it ever since. It's so tasty and easy to whip up.
—Ally Billhorn, Wilton, IA

Start to Finish: 25 min.
Makes: 6 servings

- 2 pounds extra-lean ground turkey
- 1 small onion, finely chopped
- 2 tablespoons chili powder
- ¾ teaspoon ground cumin
- ½ teaspoon salt
- ½ teaspoon pepper
- 1 can (15 ounces) tomato sauce
- 18 Bibb or iceberg lettuce leaves
- ¾ cup shredded cheddar cheese
  Optional toppings: sour cream, salsa and guacamole

1. In a large skillet, cook and crumble turkey with onion over medium-high heat until no longer pink, 8-10 minutes.
2. Stir in seasonings and tomato sauce; bring to a boil. Reduce heat; simmer, covered, until flavors are blended, about 10 minutes. Serve in lettuce with cheese and toppings as desired.
Freeze option: Freeze cooled meat mixture in freezer containers. To use, partially thaw in refrigerator overnight. Heat through in a saucepan, stirring occasionally and adding a little water if necessary.
Per 3 filled lettuce wraps: 251 cal., 7g fat (3g sat. fat), 75mg chol., 806mg sod., 7g carb. (2g sugars, 2g fiber), 43g pro.
Diabetic Exchanges: 5 lean meat, 1 vegetable.

WINTER VEGETABLE SHEPHERD'S PIE

We eat for comfort during the holidays...but comfort foods aren't always healthy. To make a classic comfort food dish more healthy, I came up with this lovely take on shepherd's pie. It's perfect for putting out on your holiday buffet table.
—Ann Sheehy, Lawrence, MA

Prep: 55 min. • **Bake:** 30 min. + standing
Makes: 8 servings

- 3 cups cubed peeled butternut squash (1-inch pieces)
- 1 large potato, peeled and cut into 1-inch cubes (about 2 cups)
- 2 medium carrots, thinly sliced
- 2 cups vegetable broth
- ½ teaspoon plus ¾ teaspoon salt, divided
- ¾ teaspoon pepper, divided
- 2 pounds ground turkey
- 1 large onion, chopped
- 1 tablespoon olive oil
- ¾ pound sliced fresh mushrooms
- 3 garlic cloves, minced
- ½ cup white wine
- 1 teaspoon dried thyme
- ¼ cup all-purpose flour
- 2 cups frozen peas (about 8 ounces)

1. Preheat oven to 350°. Place first four ingredients in a large saucepan; bring to a boil. Reduce heat; simmer, covered, until vegetables are tender, 10-15 minutes. Drain vegetables, reserving broth. Mash vegetables until smooth, stirring in ½ teaspoon salt and ¼ teaspoon pepper.
2. In two batches, cook turkey and onion in a Dutch oven over medium-high heat until turkey is no longer pink, 5-7 minutes, breaking meat into crumbles. Remove from pan.
3. In same pan, heat oil over medium-high heat; saute mushrooms until tender, about 7-9 minutes. Add garlic; cook and stir 1 minute. Add wine, thyme and the remaining salt and pepper; bring to a boil, stirring to remove browned bits from pan. Cook until liquid is evaporated. Stir in flour until blended; gradually stir in reserved broth. Bring to a boil; cook and stir until thickened. Stir in peas and turkey mixture; heat through.
4. Transfer to a greased 2½-quart baking dish. Spread with mashed vegetables. Bake, uncovered, until filling is bubbly, 30-35 minutes. Let stand 10 minutes before serving.
Per serving: 314 cal., 11g fat (2g sat. fat), 75mg chol., 654mg sod., 29g carb. (6g sugars, 5g fiber), 28g pro.
Diabetic Exchanges: 3 lean meat, 2 starch.

TURKEY PEPPER KABOBS

(PICTURED ON P. 165)

This is a summertime favorite at our house. While the turkey is a nice change of pace and tastes great with the sweet basting sauce and pineapple, the recipe also works well with cubed chicken.
—Traci Goodman, Paducah, KY

Prep: 15 min. + marinating • **Grill:** 10 min.
Makes: 4 servings

- 1 can (8 ounces) unsweetened pineapple chunks
- ¼ cup packed brown sugar
- 2 tablespoons canola oil
- 2 tablespoons Worcestershire sauce
- 1 garlic clove, minced
- 1 teaspoon prepared mustard
- 1 pound turkey breast tenderloins, cut into 1-inch cubes
- 1 large sweet onion, cut into ¾-inch pieces
- 1 each large green and sweet red peppers, cut into 1-inch pieces

1. Drain pineapple, reserving ¼ cup juice. For the marinade, mix brown sugar, oil, Worcestershire sauce, garlic, mustard and reserved juice.
2. In another bowl, toss turkey with ⅓ cup marinade; refrigerate, covered, 2-3 hours. Cover and refrigerate remaining marinade.
3. On metal or soaked wooden skewers, alternately thread turkey, vegetables and pineapple; discard remaining marinade in bowl. Grill kabobs, covered, on an oiled grill rack over medium heat until meat is no longer pink, 8-10 minutes, turning occasionally. Baste frequently with reserved marinade during last 3 minutes.
Per 2 kabobs: 298 cal., 6g fat (0 sat. fat), 45mg chol., 146mg sod., 34g carb. (28g sugars, 3g fiber), 30g pro.
Diabetic Exchanges: 4 lean meat, 2 vegetable, 1 starch, 1 fat.

★ ★ ★ ★ ★ **READER REVIEW**

"I used chicken instead of turkey, but I followed the rest of the recipe exactly and it was delicious. A nice hint of sweetness."

WOMER TASTEOFHOME.COM

WINTER VEGETABLE SHEPHERD'S PIE

PORK, HAM & MORE

"This breaded tenderloin rekindles memories of a sandwich shop in my Ohio hometown. Even though I've moved away, I'm happy to say my family can still enjoy the sandwiches thanks to this recipe."
—Erin Fitch, Sherrills Ford, NC

Mexican Pork & Pinto Beans (p. 189) **Pork with Sweet Potatoes** (p. 195) **Chili-Spiced Pork Chops** (p. 182)
Light Linguine Carbonara (p. 194) **Crispy Pork Tenderloin Sandwiches** (p. 192) **Rosemary Pork Medallions with Peas** (p. 191)

LIME-GLAZED PORK CHOPS **S** FAST FIX▶

A wonderfully sweet-sour citrus glaze makes these grilled chops tangy and tasty. They are perfect for weeknight dinners and weekend barbecues alike.
—Jacqueline Correa, Landing, NJ

Start to Finish: 25 min.
Makes: 4 servings

- ⅓ cup orange marmalade
- 1 jalapeno pepper, seeded and finely chopped
- 2 tablespoons lime juice
- 1 teaspoon grated fresh gingerroot
- 4 bone-in pork loin chops (8 ounces each)
- 4 teaspoons minced fresh cilantro Lime wedges

1. For glaze, in a small saucepan, combine marmalade, jalapeno, lime juice and ginger; cook and stir over medium heat 4-6 minutes or until marmalade is melted.
2. Moisten a paper towel with cooking oil; using long-handled tongs, rub on grill rack to coat lightly.
3. Grill chops, covered, over medium heat or broil 4 in. from heat 6-8 minutes on each side or until a thermometer reads 145°, brushing with glaze during the last 5 minutes. Let stand 5 minutes. Sprinkle with cilantro; serve with lime wedges.
Note: Wear disposable gloves when cutting hot peppers; the oils can burn skin. Avoid touching your face.
Per pork chop: 303 cal., 10g fat (4g sat. fat), 98mg chol., 87mg sod., 19g carb. (16g sugars, 0 fiber), 35g pro.
Diabetic exchanges: 4 lean meat, 1 starch.

CARAMELIZED PORK SLICES

CARAMELIZED PORK SLICES **C** FAST FIX▶

This easy treatment for pork caught my eye when I saw the word caramelized. I like to serve this over noodles or rice, or with mashed potatoes.
—Elisa Lochridge, Beaverton, OR

Start to Finish: 25 min.
Makes: 4 servings

- 1 pork tenderloin (1 pound)
- 2 teaspoons canola oil, divided
- 2 garlic cloves, minced
- 2 tablespoons brown sugar
- 1 tablespoon orange juice
- 1 tablespoon molasses
- ½ teaspoon salt
- ¼ teaspoon pepper

1. Cut tenderloin into eight slices; pound each with a meat mallet to ½-in. thickness. In a nonstick skillet, heat 1 teaspoon oil over medium-high heat; brown pork on both sides. Remove from pan.
2. In same skillet, heat remaining oil over medium-high heat; saute garlic 1 minute. Stir in remaining ingredients. Add pork, turning to coat; cook, uncovered, until a thermometer reads 145°, 3-4 minutes. Let stand 5 minutes before serving.
Per 2 pork slices: 198 cal., 6g fat (2g sat. fat), 64mg chol., 344mg sod., 12g carb. (11g sugars, 0 fiber), 23g pro.
Diabetic exchanges: 3 lean meat, ½ starch.

THYME & BASIL ROAST PORK C

Dad's favorite roast pork was rubbed with cinnamon, thyme, basil and lemon. He loved thick slices and wanted only a salad to finish off the meal.
—Lorraine Caland, Shuniah, ON

Prep: 30 min. • **Bake:** 1 hour + standing
Makes: 8 servings

- 1 tablespoon all-purpose flour
- 2 teaspoons dried basil
- 2 teaspoons dried thyme
- 2 teaspoons ground cinnamon
- 1½ teaspoons salt
- ½ teaspoon pepper
- 1 boneless pork loin roast (3 to 4 pounds)
- 2 tablespoons canola oil
- 1 medium apple, cut into wedges
- 1 medium onion, cut into wedges
- 1 medium lemon, cut into wedges
- 1 fresh rosemary sprig

1. Preheat oven to 325°. In a small bowl, mix flour, basil, thyme, cinnamon, salt and pepper; rub over pork.

2. In a large skillet, heat oil over medium-high heat. Brown roast on all sides. Place roast in a shallow roasting pan, fat side up. Arrange apple and onion around the roast. Squeeze lemon juice from one wedge over pork; add lemon wedges to pan. Place the rosemary over pork.

3. Roast for 1 to 1½ hours or until a thermometer reads 145°. Remove the roast, onion and apple to a serving platter; tent with foil. Let it stand for 15 minutes before slicing.

Per 4 ounces cooked pork: 266 cal., 11g fat (3g sat. fat), 85mg chol., 493mg sod., 6g carb. (3g sugars, 1g fiber), 33g pro.
Diabetic exchanges: 4 lean meat, 1 fat, ½ starch.

THYME & BASIL ROAST PORK

GLAZED PORK CHOPS
C FAST FIX ▶

When I was a new mom, I needed good, healthy meals that were fast to fix. These juicy chops were just what I wanted. Since this is a one-pan dish, cleanup's quick, too.
—Kristin Tanis, Hatfield, PA

Start to Finish: 30 min.
Makes: 4 servings

- 4 bone-in pork loin chops (¾ inch thick and 7 ounces each)
- ⅓ cup plus 1 tablespoon cider vinegar, divided
- 3 tablespoons soy sauce
- 3 garlic cloves, minced
- 1½ teaspoons cornstarch

1. In a large nonstick skillet, brown pork chops over medium heat, about 2 minutes per side. Mix ⅓ cup vinegar, soy sauce and garlic; pour over the chops. Bring to a boil. Reduce the heat; simmer, covered, until a thermometer inserted in pork reads 145°, 7-9 minutes.

2. Mix cornstarch and remaining vinegar until smooth; stir into pan. Bring to a boil; cook and stir until sauce is thickened, about 1 minute.

Per pork chop with 2 tablespoons sauce: 224 cal., 8g fat (3g sat. fat), 86mg chol., 754mg sod., 2g carb. (0 sugars, 0 fiber), 32g pro.
Diabetic exchanges: 4 lean meat.

✳

TEST KITCHEN TIP
Cornstarch needs just a minute or two of boiling to thicken a sauce, gravy or dessert filling. If it cooks too long, the cornstarch will begin to lose its thickening power. Carefully follow the recipe for the best results.

ITALIAN
HERB-CRUSTED
PORK LOIN

ITALIAN HERB-CRUSTED PORK LOIN ⓒ

I like to change things up during the holidays by roasting pork loin with my favorite herbs and veggies. This dish is a showpiece that really dazzles my family.
—Kim Palmer, Kingston, GA

Prep: 15 min. + chilling
Bake: 50 min. + standing
Makes: 8 servings

- 3 tablespoons olive oil
- 5 garlic cloves, minced
- 1 teaspoon salt
- 1 teaspoon each dried basil, thyme and rosemary, crushed
- ½ teaspoon Italian seasoning
- ½ teaspoon pepper
- 1 boneless pork loin roast (3 to 4 pounds)
- 8 medium carrots, halved lengthwise
- 2 medium onions, quartered

1. In a small bowl, mix oil, garlic and seasonings; rub over roast. Arrange carrots and onions on the bottom of a 13x9-in. baking pan. Place the roast over vegetables, fat side up. Refrigerate, covered, 1 hour.
2. Preheat oven to 475°. Roast the pork for 20 minutes.
3. Reduce oven setting to 425°. Roast for another 30-40 minutes or until a thermometer reads 145° and vegetables are tender. Remove the roast from the oven; tent it with foil. Let stand 20 minutes before slicing.

Per serving: 295 cal., 13g fat (4g sat. fat), 85mg chol., 388mg sod., 9g carb. (4g sugars, 2g fiber), 34g pro.
Diabetic exchanges: 5 lean meat, 1 vegetable, 1 fat.

CHILI-SPICED PORK CHOPS
ⓒ **FAST FIX ▸**
(PICTURED ON P. 179)

I like my food spicy, and my husband likes his mild. This pleasantly spiced dish makes us both happy—and our son enjoys it, too. It's easy to make, and I always have all the ingredients on hand.
—Andrea Keith, Kentwood, MI

Start to Finish: 30 min.
Makes: 6 servings

- ¾ cup seasoned bread crumbs
- 3 tablespoons chili powder
- ½ teaspoon seasoned salt
- 1 large egg
- ¼ cup fat-free milk
- 6 bone-in pork rib chops (7 ounces each, ¾ inch thick)

1. Preheat oven to 350°. In a shallow bowl, combine the bread crumbs, chili powder and seasoned salt. In another shallow bowl, combine the egg and milk. Dip chops in egg mixture, then coat with crumb mixture.
2. Transfer to a 15x10x1-in. baking pan coated with cooking spray. Bake 20-25 minutes or until the meat reaches the desired doneness (for medium-rare, a thermometer should read 145°; medium, 160°). Let the meat stand 5 minutes before serving.

Per pork chop: 261 cal., 10g fat (4g sat. fat), 95mg chol., 506mg sod., 12g carb. (2g sugars, 2g fiber), 29g pro.
Diabetic exchanges: 4 lean meat, 1 starch.

APPLE-BALSAMIC PORK CHOPS & RICE `FAST FIX`

Thanks to tangy balsamic vinegar and sweet apples, this one-pot dish lets you have a little something special anytime.
—Greg Hageli, Elmhurst, IL

Start to Finish: 30 min.
Makes: 4 servings

- 4 boneless pork loin chops (6 ounces each)
- ½ teaspoon salt, divided
- ½ teaspoon pepper, divided
- 1 tablespoon canola oil
- 2 medium Gala apples, cut into ½-inch pieces
- 2 cups sliced fresh mushrooms
- 1 medium onion, chopped
- 1½ cups instant brown rice
- 1 cup reduced-sodium chicken broth
- 2 tablespoons balsamic vinegar
- ¼ teaspoon dried thyme

1. Sprinkle pork chops with ¼ teaspoon salt and ¼ teaspoon pepper. In a large skillet, heat oil over medium heat. Brown pork chops on both sides; remove from the pan.

2. Add apples, mushrooms and onion to the skillet; cook and stir 4-5 minutes or until tender. Stir in rice, broth, vinegar, thyme, and remaining salt and pepper. Bring to a boil. Reduce the heat; cook, covered, 5 minutes.

3. Place the pork chops over the top; cook, covered, 4-6 minutes or until a thermometer inserted in pork reads 145°. Let meat stand 5 minutes before serving.

Per pork chop with 1 cup rice: 454 cal., 15g fat (4g sat. fat), 82mg chol., 498mg sod., 42g carb. (11g sugars, 4g fiber), 38g pro.

Diabetic exchanges: 5 lean meat, 2 starch, 1 fat, ½ fruit.

HAM & MANDARIN SALAD `FAST FIX`

I created this salad at the request of all the men in our house. They asked for something tangy, sweet, spicy and manly.
—Patricia Swart, Galloway, NJ

Start to Finish: 25 min.
Makes: 4 servings

- ⅓ cup fat-free mayonnaise
- 2 tablespoons fat-free milk
- 1 tablespoon cider vinegar
- 1 garlic clove, minced
- ¼ teaspoon pepper
- 8 slices deli ham (about 6 ounces), cut into strips
- 1 can (11 ounces) mandarin oranges, drained
- 2 celery ribs, thinly sliced
- ⅓ cup chopped walnuts, toasted
- 2 green onions, chopped
- 6 cups torn romaine

In a large bowl, mix first five ingredients. Stir in ham, mandarin oranges, celery, walnuts and green onions. Serve it over romaine, tossing before serving if desired.

Note: To toast nuts, bake in a shallow pan in a 350° oven for 5-10 minutes or cook in a skillet over low heat until lightly browned, stirring occasionally.

Per 2¼ cups: 172 cal., 8g fat (1g sat. fat), 21mg chol., 586mg sod., 17g carb. (11g sugars, 4g fiber), 11g pro.

Diabetic exchanges: 2 lean meat, 1 vegetable, 1 fat, ½ starch.

APPLE-BALSAMIC PORK CHOPS & RICE

HERBED LEMON PORK CHOPS

C FAST FIX

You'll receive plenty of compliments on these tender and juicy pork chops. Mixed herbs and a final squeeze of lemon pack on the flavor in just 20 minutes!
—Billi Jo Sylvester, New Smyrna Beach, FL

Start to Finish: 20 min.
Makes: 2 servings

- 1 teaspoon salt-free garlic seasoning blend
- ½ teaspoon dried basil
- ½ teaspoon dried oregano
- ½ teaspoon dried parsley flakes
- ¼ teaspoon salt
- ¼ teaspoon garlic powder
- ¼ teaspoon dried rosemary, crushed
- 2 bone-in pork loin chops (6 ounces each)
- 1 teaspoon olive oil
- 1 tablespoon lemon juice

1. Mix seasonings; rub over both sides of chops. In a large nonstick skillet, heat oil over medium-high heat. Add pork; cook until a thermometer reads 145°, about 5-8 minutes per side.
2. Remove from the heat; drizzle with lemon juice. Let stand, covered, 5 minutes before serving.

Per pork chop: 200 cal., 10g fat (3g sat. fat), 74mg chol., 350mg sod., 1g carb. (0 sugars, 0 fiber), 26g pro.
Diabetic exchanges: 4 lean meat, ½ fat.

BREADED MUSTARD & SAGE PORK CUTLETS

BREADED MUSTARD & SAGE PORK CUTLETS FAST FIX

After attending my child's back-to-school program and receiving a complimentary package of instant potatoes, I had to make something with them. I created these pork cutlets and they were fantastic.
—Carrie Farias, Oak Ridge, NJ

Start to Finish: 25 min.
Makes: 4 servings

- 1 large egg
- 2 tablespoons fat-free milk
- 2 tablespoons Dijon mustard
- ¾ cup panko (Japanese) bread crumbs
- ¾ cup mashed potato flakes
- 2 teaspoons ground mustard
- 2 teaspoons minced fresh sage
- ⅓ cup all-purpose flour
- 8 thin boneless pork loin chops (2 ounces each)
- ½ teaspoon salt
- 4 teaspoons canola oil, divided

1. In a shallow bowl, whisk egg, milk and Dijon mustard. In another shallow bowl, mix bread crumbs, potato flakes, ground mustard and sage. Place flour in another shallow bowl. Sprinkle pork with salt.
2. Dip pork in flour to coat both sides; shake off excess. Dip in egg mixture, then in bread crumb mixture, patting to help coating adhere.
3. In a large skillet, heat 2 teaspoons oil over medium heat. Add pork in batches; cook 2-3 minutes on each side or until a thermometer reads at least 145°, adding additional oil as needed.

Per 2 pork cutlets: 328 cal., 13g fat (3g sat. fat), 101mg chol., 567mg sod., 23g carb. (1g sugars, 1g fiber), 27g pro.
Diabetic exchanges: 3 lean meat, 1½ starch, 1 fat.

DIXIE LAMB CHOPS

DIXIE LAMB CHOPS **FAST FIX**

These saucy chops may seem fancy, but mine work for both special occasions and busy evenings, too. We love them with spinach salad and crusty bread.
—Barbara Burge, Los Gatos, CA

Start to Finish: 20 min
Makes: 4 servings

- 4 lamb loin chops (5 to 6 ounces each)
- ½ teaspoon salt
- ¼ teaspoon pepper
- 1 tablespoon olive oil
- ¼ cup molasses
- 2 tablespoons steak sauce
- 1 tablespoon cider vinegar

1. Sprinkle chops with salt and pepper. In a large skillet, heat the oil over medium heat; cook chops, covered, until bottoms are browned, 5-7 minutes.
2. Mix molasses, steak sauce and vinegar. Turn chops; pour molasses mixture over top. Cook, covered, over medium-low heat until lamb reaches desired doneness (for medium-rare, a thermometer should read 145°; medium, 160°), 5-7 minutes.

Per lamb chop with 1 tablespoon glaze: 225 cal., 9g fat (3g sat. fat), 57mg chol., 493mg sod., 17g carb. (16g sugars, 0 fiber), 18g pro.
Diabetic exchanges: 3 lean meat, 1 starch, ½ fat.

BARBECUE PORK SALAD

C FAST FIX

All it requires is 2 teaspoons of barbecue seasoning to put a tasty, unexpected twist on this simple main-dish salad.
—*Taste of Home* Test Kitchen

Start to Finish: 30 min.
Makes: 4 servings

- 1 pork tenderloin (1 pound), cut into 1-inch cubes
- 1 teaspoon barbecue seasoning
- ⅛ teaspoon salt
- 2 teaspoons olive oil
- 1 bunch romaine, torn
- 1 cup cherry tomatoes, quartered
- ¾ cup canned black beans

VINAIGRETTE
- ½ cup cider vinegar
- ¼ cup olive oil
- 2 green onions, sliced
- 1 teaspoon barbecue seasoning
- ⅛ teaspoon salt
- ⅛ teaspoon pepper

1. Toss pork with barbecue seasoning and salt. In a large skillet, saute pork in oil until no longer pink; set aside.
2. In a large bowl, combine the romaine, tomatoes, black beans and pork. In a small bowl, combine vinaigrette ingredients; drizzle over salad and toss to coat.

Per 2 cups: 339 cal., 20g fat (3g sat. fat), 63mg chol., 757mg sod., 12g carb. (2g sugars, 4g fiber), 27g pro.

SAVORY BEER
PORK CHOPS

SAVORY BEER PORK CHOPS

C **FAST FIX** ▶

These tender chops in savory sauce are perfect for a hectic weeknight because they're so easy to prep. They use only five ingredients! Try them with hot buttery noodles.
—Jana Christian, Farson, WY

....

Start to Finish: 20 min.
Makes: 4 servings

    4   boneless pork loin chops
        (4 ounces each)
    ½   teaspoon salt
    ½   teaspoon pepper
    1   tablespoon canola oil
    3   tablespoons ketchup
    2   tablespoons brown sugar
    ¾   cup beer or nonalcoholic beer

1. Sprinkle pork chops with salt and pepper. In a large skillet, heat oil over

medium heat; brown chops on both sides.
2. Mix ketchup, brown sugar and beer; pour over chops. Bring to a boil. Reduce the heat; simmer it, uncovered, until a thermometer inserted in the pork reads 145°, 4-6 minutes. Let stand 5 minutes before serving.
Per pork chop: 239 cal., 10g fat (3g sat. fat), 55mg chol., 472mg sod., 11g carb. (11g sugars, 0 fiber), 22g pro.
Diabetic exchanges: 3 lean meat, 1 fat, ½ starch.

BACON & SPINACH PIZZA
FAST FIX ▶

Our go-to pizza is a snap to make using packaged pizza crust and ready-to-serve bacon. The kids don't even mind the spinach on top!
—Annette Riva, Naperville, IL

....

Start to Finish: 20 min.
Makes: 6 servings

    1   prebaked 12-inch pizza crust
    ⅓   cup pizza sauce
    1   cup shaved Parmesan cheese
    2   cups fresh baby spinach, thinly sliced
    8   ready-to-serve fully cooked bacon
        strips, cut into 1-inch pieces

Preheat oven to 450°. Place crust on an ungreased baking sheet. Spread with sauce; top with ½ cup cheese, spinach and bacon. Sprinkle with remaining cheese. Bake until cheese is melted, 8-10 minutes.
Per slice: 269 cal., 10g fat (4g sat. fat), 10mg chol., 726mg sod., 31g carb. (2g sugars, 2g fiber), 15g pro.
Diabetic exchanges: 2 starch, 2 medium-fat meat.

CREOLE PORK TENDERLOIN
WITH VEGETABLES

CREOLE PORK TENDERLOIN WITH VEGETABLES C

Fresh summer vegetables are paired with lean pork and tasty Greek olives for a healthy and quick dinner, great for family and friends.

—Judy Armstrong, Prairieville, LA

Prep: 30 min. • **Bake:** 20 min.
Makes: 8 servings

3½ teaspoons reduced-sodium Creole seasoning, divided
2 pork tenderloins (1 pound each)
2 tablespoons canola oil
2 medium fennel bulbs, trimmed and cut into 1-inch wedges
1 medium eggplant, cut into 1-inch cubes
2 medium yellow summer squash, halved and cut into ½-inch slices
1 large sweet red pepper, cut into 1-inch pieces
2 shallots, thinly sliced
½ cup pitted Greek olives, coarsely chopped
3 garlic cloves, minced
½ cup vegetable broth
4 teaspoons minced fresh thyme or 1¼ teaspoons dried thyme

1. Preheat the oven to 350°. Sprinkle 3 teaspoons of Creole seasoning over tenderloins. In a 6-qt. stockpot, heat the oil over medium-high heat. Brown the tenderloins on all sides. Transfer to a roasting pan.
2. Add fennel, eggplant, squash, pepper and shallots to stockpot; cook and stir over medium heat 3-4 minutes or until lightly browned. Add olives and garlic; cook and stir 1 minute longer. Stir in the broth, thyme and remaining Creole seasoning; bring to a boil. Reduce heat; simmer, covered, 6-8 minutes or until fennel is crisp-tender. Spoon vegetables and liquid around pork.
3. Bake, uncovered, 20-25 minutes or until the vegetables are tender and a thermometer inserted in pork reads 145°. Let stand 5 minutes before serving. Cut pork into slices; serve with vegetables.

Per 3 ounces cooked pork with 1 cup vegetables: 247 cal., 10g fat (2g sat. fat), 64mg chol., 575mg sod., 15g carb. (7g sugars, 5g fiber), 25g pro.
Diabetic exchanges: 3 lean meat, 2 vegetable, 1 fat.

PORK CHOPS WITH TOMATO CURRY

This flavorful dish is great on cold winter nights. I love the sweetness of the apples, the heat of the curry, and the bite of crunchy almonds.
—Mary Marlowe Leverette, Columbia, SC

Prep: 15 min. • **Cook:** 25 min.
Makes: 6 servings

- 4 teaspoons butter, divided
- 6 boneless pork loin chops (6 ounces each)
- 1 small onion, finely chopped
- 3 medium apples, thinly sliced (about 5 cups)
- 1 can (28 ounces) whole tomatoes, undrained
- 4 teaspoons sugar
- 2 teaspoons curry powder
- ½ teaspoon salt
- ½ teaspoon chili powder
- 4 cups hot cooked brown rice
- 2 tablespoons toasted slivered almonds, optional

1. In a 6-qt. stockpot, heat 2 teaspoons butter over medium-high heat. Brown pork chops in batches. Remove from pan.
2. In same pan, heat remaining butter over medium heat. Add onion; cook and stir 2-3 minutes or until tender. Stir in apples, tomatoes, sugar, curry powder, salt and chili powder. Bring to a boil, stirring to break up tomatoes.
3. Return chops to pan. Reduce the heat; simmer, uncovered, 5 minutes. Turn the chops; cook 3-5 minutes longer or until a thermometer inserted in pork reads 145°. Let stand 5 minutes before serving. Serve with rice and, if desired, sprinkle with toasted almonds.
Note: To toast nuts, bake in a shallow pan in a 350° oven for 5-10 minutes or cook them in a skillet over low heat until lightly browned, stirring occasionally.
Per pork chop with ¾ cup tomato mixture and ⅔ cup rice: 478 cal., 14g fat (5g sat. fat), 89mg chol., 475mg sod., 50g carb. (15g sugars, 7g fiber), 38g pro.
Diabetic exchanges: 5 lean meat, 2 starch, 2 vegetable, ½ fruit, ½ fat.

MEXICAN PORK & PINTO BEANS
(PICTURED ON P. 178)

We've lived in Arizona for decades, so Mexican-style cooking has become the same as Arizona-style cooking for us. Nothing tastes better than chili-spiced pork with tortillas.
—Anne Fatout, Phoenix, AZ

Prep: 30 min. • **Cook:** 4 hours
Makes: 16 servings (4 quarts)

- 1 bone-in pork loin roast (3 pounds), trimmed
- 1 package (16 ounces) dried pinto beans, soaked overnight
- 4 to 5 cloves garlic, minced
- 2 tablespoons chili powder
- 1 to 1½ teaspoons ground cumin
- 1 teaspoon dried oregano
- 2 cans (4 ounces each) chopped green chilies
  Pepper to taste
- 5 medium carrots, sliced
- 4 celery ribs, sliced
- 1 can (14½ ounces) diced tomatoes, undrained
- 3 small zucchini, sliced
  Flour tortillas, warmed

1. In a stockpot, combine the first eight ingredients; cover with water. Bring to a boil. Reduce heat; simmer, covered, 3 to 4 hours or until meat and beans are tender.
2. Remove pork; cool slightly. Stir carrots, celery and tomatoes into bean mixture; return to a boil. Reduce heat; simmer, covered, until vegetables are crisp-tender. Add zucchini; cook 8-10 minutes longer or until crisp-tender.
3. Meanwhile, remove pork from bone; discard bone. Cut pork into bite-size pieces; return to pot and heat through. Serve with tortillas.
Freeze option: Freeze cooled pork mixture in freezer containers. To use, partially thaw in refrigerator overnight. Microwave, covered, on high in a microwave-safe dish until heated through, gently stirring and adding a little broth or water if necessary.
Per cup: 211 cal., 5g fat (2g sat. fat), 34mg chol., 181mg sod., 23g carb. (3g sugars, 6g fiber), 19g pro.
Diabetic exchanges: 2 lean meat, 1½ starch, 1 vegetable.

PORK CHOPS WITH TOMATO CURRY

SKILLET PORK CHOPS WITH APPLES & ONION FAST FIX

Simple recipes that land on the table fast are a lifesaver. I serve these pork chops with cooked veggies and, when there's time, corn bread stuffing.
—Tracey Karst, Ponderay, ID

Start to Finish: 20 min.
Makes: 4 servings

- 4 boneless pork loin chops (6 ounces each)
- 3 medium apples, cut into wedges
- 1 large onion, cut into thin wedges
- ¼ cup water
- ⅓ cup balsamic vinaigrette
- ½ teaspoon salt
- ¼ teaspoon pepper

1. Place a large nonstick skillet over medium heat; brown pork chops on both sides, about 4 minutes. Remove from pan.
2. In same skillet, combine apples, onion and water. Place pork chops over apple mixture; drizzle chops with vinaigrette. Sprinkle with salt and pepper. Reduce heat; simmer, covered, 3-5 minutes or until a thermometer inserted in chops reads 145°.

Per pork chop with ¾ cup apple mixture: 360 cal., 15g fat (4g sat. fat), 82mg chol., 545mg sod., 22g carb. (15g sugars, 3g fiber), 33g pro.
Diabetic exchanges: 5 lean meat, 1 fruit, 1 fat.

MEDITERRANEAN PORK & ORZO

MEDITERRANEAN PORK & ORZO FAST FIX

On a really busy day, this meal-in-a-bowl is one of my top picks. It's quick to put together, leaving me a lot more time to relax at the table.
—Mary Relyea, Canastota, NY

Start to Finish: 30 min.
Makes: 6 servings

- 1½ pounds pork tenderloin
- 1 teaspoon coarsely ground pepper
- 2 tablespoons olive oil
- 3 quarts water
- 1¼ cups uncooked orzo pasta
- ¼ teaspoon salt
- 1 package (6 ounces) fresh baby spinach
- 1 cup grape tomatoes, halved
- ¾ cup crumbled feta cheese

1. Rub pork with pepper; cut into 1-in. cubes. In a large nonstick skillet, heat oil over medium heat. Add pork; cook and stir 8-10 minutes or until no longer pink.
2. Meanwhile, in a Dutch oven, bring water to a boil. Stir in orzo and salt; cook, uncovered, 8 minutes. Stir in spinach; cook 45-60 seconds longer or until orzo is tender and spinach is wilted. Drain.
3. Add tomatoes to pork; heat through. Stir in orzo mixture and cheese.

Per ⅓ cups: 372 cal., 11g fat (4g sat. fat), 71mg chol., 306mg sod., 34g carb. (2g sugars, 3g fiber), 31g pro.
Diabetic exchanges: 3 lean meat, 2 starch, 1 vegetable, 1 fat.

MANDARIN PORK STIR-FRY
FAST FIX

When my husband and I were dating, he told me he liked Asian food. I got a wok and discovered the joy of preparing quick dishes like this pork stir-fry.
—Laurie Martignon, Niagara, WI

Start to Finish: 25 min.
Makes: 4 servings

- 2 cups uncooked instant rice
- 1 tablespoon cornstarch
- ½ teaspoon garlic powder
- ½ teaspoon ground ginger
- ½ cup orange juice
- ¼ cup water
- 2 tablespoons soy sauce
- 1 pork tenderloin (1 pound), cut into 2-inch strips
- 2 tablespoons canola oil
- 1 package (14 ounces) frozen sugar snap peas
- 1 can (11 ounces) mandarin oranges, drained

1. Cook rice according to package directions. Meanwhile, in a small bowl, combine the cornstarch, garlic powder and ginger. Stir in orange juice until smooth. Stir in the water and soy sauce; set aside.

2. In a large wok or skillet, stir-fry pork in oil until the juices run clear; remove to a platter and keep warm. In the same skillet, stir-fry peas until tender. Return pork to skillet. Stir orange juice mixture; add to skillet. Cook and stir for 2 minutes or until thickened. Gently stir in oranges. Serve with rice.

Per serving: 473 cal., 11g fat (2g sat. fat), 63mg chol., 514mg sod., 61g carb. (14g sugars, 5g fiber), 30g pro.

ROSEMARY PORK MEDALLIONS WITH PEAS
C **FAST FIX**

(PICTURED ON P. 179)

It's nice to have a quick meal to fix after coming home from work. These pork cutlets are simple to prepare and don't use a lot of ingredients, so they're great for beginner cooks.
—Laura McAllister, Morganton, NC

Start to Finish: 25 min.
Makes: 4 servings

- 1 pound pork tenderloin, cut into ½-inch slices
- ½ teaspoon salt
- ¼ teaspoon pepper
- ¼ cup all-purpose flour
- 1 tablespoon olive oil
- 2 teaspoons butter
- 1 cup reduced-sodium chicken broth
- 1 garlic clove, minced
- 1 teaspoon dried rosemary, crushed
- 2 cups frozen peas

1. Sprinkle pork with salt and pepper. Toss with flour to coat lightly; shake off the excess.

2. In a large skillet, heat oil and butter over medium heat. Add pork; cook 1-2 minutes on each side or until tender. Remove from pan; keep warm.

3. In same pan, add the broth, garlic and rosemary; bring to a boil, stirring to loosen browned bits from pan. Cook 2-3 minutes or until liquid is reduced by a third. Stir in peas; cook 2-3 minutes longer or until heated through. Serve with pork.

Per 3 ounces cooked pork with ⅓ cup peas: 260 cal., 10g fat (3g sat. fat), 69mg chol., 571mg sod., 15g carb. (4g sugars, 3g fiber), 28g pro.
Diabetic exchanges: 3 lean meat, 1 starch, ½ fat.

MANDARIN PORK STIR-FRY

CRISPY PORK TENDERLOIN SANDWICHES FAST FIX

(PICTURED ON P. 179)

This breaded tenderloin rekindles memories of a sandwich shop in my Ohio hometown. Even though I've moved away, I'm happy to say my family can still enjoy the sandwiches thanks to this recipe.

—Erin Fitch, Sherrills Ford, NC

Start to Finish: 25 min.
Makes: 4 servings

- 2 tablespoons all-purpose flour
- ½ teaspoon salt
- ¼ teaspoon pepper
- 1 large egg, lightly beaten
- ½ cup seasoned bread crumbs
- 3 tablespoons panko (Japanese) bread crumbs
- ½ pound pork tenderloin
- 2 tablespoons canola oil
- 4 hamburger buns or kaiser rolls, split
  Optional toppings: lettuce leaves, tomato and pickle slices, and mayonnaise

1. In a shallow bowl, mix flour, salt and pepper. Place egg and the combined bread crumbs in two separate shallow bowls.
2. Cut the tenderloin crosswise into four slices; pound each slice with a meat mallet to ¼-in. thickness. Dip in the flour mixture to coat both sides; shake off the excess. Dip in egg, then in crumb mixture, patting to help adhere.
3. In a large skillet, heat oil over medium heat. Cook pork 2-3 minutes on each side or until golden brown. Remove from pan; drain on paper towels. Serve in buns, with toppings as desired.

Per sandwich: 289 cal., 11g fat (2g sat. fat), 43mg chol., 506mg sod., 29g carb. (3g sugars, 1g fiber), 17g pro.
Diabetic exchanges: 2 starch, 2 lean meat, 1½ fat.
HEALTH TIP Keep the carbs to about 10 grams per serving by skipping the bun and serving the pork on grilled portobello mushrooms or eggplant slices.

BLACKBERRY-SAUCED PORK CHOPS

BLACKBERRY-SAUCED PORK CHOPS FAST FIX

My family loved these chops from the first time I fixed them. They're as tasty in a skillet as they are grilled, so you can eat them all year long. The sauce is also fantastic with chicken.

—Priscilla Gilbert, Indian Harbour Beach, FL

Start to Finish: 30 min.
Makes: 4 servings

- ½ cup seedless blackberry spreadable fruit
- 1 tablespoon lemon juice
- 1 tablespoon reduced-sodium soy sauce
  Dash ground cinnamon
- 4 boneless pork loin chops (5 ounces each)
- 2 teaspoons steak seasoning
- 2 teaspoons olive oil
- 1 cup fresh blackberries

1. In a small saucepan, combine the spreadable fruit, lemon juice, soy sauce and cinnamon. Cook and stir over low heat until spreadable fruit is melted. Remove from heat.
2. Sprinkle the pork chops with steak seasoning. In a large nonstick skillet coated with cooking spray, heat oil over medium heat. Add pork chops; cook 5-7 minutes on each side or until a thermometer reads 145°. Let stand 5 minutes. Serve with sauce and blackberries.

Per pork chop with 2 tablespoons sauce and ¼ cup berries: 311 cal., 10g fat (3g sat. fat), 68mg chol., 531mg sod., 25g carb. (19g sugars, 2g fiber), 28g pro.
Diabetic exchanges: 4 lean meat, 1½ starch, ½ fat.

HERBED PORK ROAST WITH GRAVY C

An easy rub made with pantry ingredients packs on surprising flavor. This irresistible pork roast is my husband's favorite dish.
—Jean Harris, Central Point, OR

Prep: 10 min. • **Bake:** 2 hours
Makes: 8 servings

- ¼ cup packed brown sugar
- 1 tablespoon dried thyme
- 1 teaspoon each garlic salt, pepper, rubbed sage and dried rosemary, crushed
- 1 boneless pork loin roast (3 to 4 pounds)
- ¼ cup all-purpose flour

1. Combine brown sugar and seasonings; rub over roast. Place roast, fat side up, on a rack in a roasting pan. Bake, uncovered, at 325° for 2 hours or until a thermometer reads 160°.

2. Remove roast from pan. Pour the pan drippings into a large measuring cup; add water to measure 2 cups. Place flour in a small saucepan; stir in pan drippings until blended. Bring to a boil over medium heat. Cook and stir gravy for 2 minutes or until thickened. Serve gravy with roast.

Freeze option: Place the sliced roast in freezer containers; top with gravy. Cool and freeze. To use, partially thaw meat in the refrigerator overnight. Microwave, covered, on high in a microwave-safe dish until heated through, gently stirring and adding a little water if necessary.

Per 5 ounces cooked pork: 254 cal., 8g fat (3g sat. fat), 85mg chol., 172mg sod., 10g carb. (7g sugars, 0 fiber), 33g pro.
Diabetic exchanges: 5 lean meat, ½ starch.

HERBED PORK ROAST WITH GRAVY

PORK MEDALLIONS WITH SAUTEED APPLES C FAST FIX ▶

Pork and apples are such a good match, and this down-home supper is proof. I really like the fact that the lean cut of meat is tender and juicy, but healthy, too.
—Clara Coulson Minney
Washington Court House, OH

Start to Finish: 30 min.
Makes: 4 servings

- 2 teaspoons cornstarch
- ⅔ cup reduced-sodium chicken broth
- ¼ cup apple juice
- 1 tablespoon butter
- 2 medium apples, thinly sliced
- 2 green onions, sliced
- 1 garlic clove, minced
- ¾ teaspoon dried thyme
- ½ teaspoon paprika
- ¼ teaspoon salt
- ¼ teaspoon pepper
- 1 pound pork tenderloin, cut into 1-inch slices

1. Preheat broiler. In a small bowl, mix cornstarch, broth and apple juice. In a nonstick skillet, heat butter over medium-high heat. Add apples, green onions and garlic; cook and stir 2-3 minutes or until apples are crisp-tender. Stir cornstarch mixture and add to pan. Bring to a boil; cook and stir for 1-2 minutes or until thickened. Keep warm.

2. Mix thyme, paprika, salt and pepper. Pound pork slices with a meat mallet to ½-in. thickness; sprinkle both sides with seasonings.

3. Place pork on a broiler pan. Broil 3 in. from heat 3-4 minutes on each side or until a thermometer reads 145°. Let the pork stand 5 minutes before serving. Serve with apples.

Per 3 ounces cooked pork with ½ cup apples: 251 cal., 10g fat (4g sat. fat), 85mg chol., 335mg sod., 15g carb. (10g sugars, 3g fiber), 25g pro.
Diabetic exchanges: 3 lean meat, 1 fruit, ½ fat.

SOUTHERN PORK & RICE

SOUTHERN PORK & RICE
FAST FIX

At our house, we're big on healthy eating. These ultra tender pork chops with colorful rice and black-eyed peas are a meal fancy enough for a dinner party.
—Annie Holmes, Murfreesboro, TN

Start to Finish: 25 min.
Makes: 4 servings

- 4   boneless pork loin chops (6 ounces each)
- 1   teaspoon seafood seasoning, divided
- 1   tablespoon olive oil
- 1   medium sweet red pepper, chopped
- 1   medium onion, chopped
- 2   teaspoons Worcestershire sauce
- 1   can (15½ ounces) black-eyed peas, rinsed and drained
- 1   can (14½ ounces) diced tomatoes with mild green chilies
- 1   cup uncooked instant rice
- 1   cup reduced-sodium chicken broth

1. Sprinkle pork with ¾ teaspoon seafood seasoning. In a large skillet, heat oil over medium heat; brown chops on both sides. Remove from pan.

2. Add the pepper and onion to the skillet; cook and stir until tender, 4-5 minutes. Stir in the remaining seafood seasoning, Worcestershire sauce, peas, tomatoes, rice and broth. Bring to a boil. Place chops over top. Reduce heat; simmer, covered, until a thermometer inserted in pork reads 145°, 2-3 minutes. Let it stand, covered, 5 minutes before serving.

Per pork chop with 1¼ cups rice mixture: 484 cal., 13g fat (4g sat. fat), 82mg chol., 764mg sod., 45g carb. (7g sugars, 6g fiber), 42g pro.
Diabetic exchanges: 5 lean meat, 3 starch, ½ fat.

HEALTH TIP You can make this meal gluten-free by using gluten-free broth and Worcestershire sauce.

LIGHT LINGUINE CARBONARA
FAST FIX

(PICTURED ON P. 178)

When we have to rush off at night, I make this speedy pasta with veggies and bacon. Serve with breadsticks or garlic toast, and dinner's done.
—Mary Jo Miller, Mansfield, OH

Start to Finish: 25 min.
Makes: 4 servings

- 8   ounces uncooked linguine
- ½   cup frozen peas
- 1   large egg
- 1   cup fat-free evaporated milk
- ¼   cup finely chopped sweet red pepper
- ⅛   teaspoon crushed red pepper flakes
- ⅛   teaspoon pepper
- ½   cup grated Parmesan cheese, divided
- 2   bacon strips, cooked and crumbled

1. In a 6-qt. stockpot, cook the linguine according to package directions, adding peas during the last 2 minutes of cooking. Meanwhile, in a small saucepan, whisk the egg, milk, red pepper, pepper flakes and pepper until blended; cook and stir over medium-low heat until mixture is just thick enough to coat spoon and a thermometer reads at least 160°. Stir in ¼ cup cheese and bacon; remove from heat.

2. Drain the linguine; return to pot. Add the sauce and toss to coat. Serve it with remaining cheese.

Per cup: 349 cal., 7g fat (3g sat. fat), 62mg chol., 366mg sod., 53g carb. (10g sugars, 3g fiber), 19g pro.

GRILLED PORK TENDERLOINS C

We do a lot of grilling during the summer months, and this recipe is one my family asks for again and again.
—Betsy Carrington, Lawrenceburg, TN

Prep: 10 min. + marinating • **Grill:** 20 min.
Makes: 8 servings

⅓ cup honey
⅓ cup reduced-sodium soy sauce
⅓ cup teriyaki sauce
3 tablespoons brown sugar
1 tablespoon minced fresh gingerroot
3 garlic cloves, minced
4 teaspoons ketchup
½ teaspoon onion powder
½ teaspoon ground cinnamon
¼ teaspoon cayenne pepper
2 pork tenderloins (about 1 pound each)
Hot cooked rice

1. In a large bowl, combine the first 10 ingredients. Pour half of the marinade into a large resealable plastic bag; add tenderloins. Seal bag and turn to coat; refrigerate 8 hours or overnight, turning occasionally. Cover and refrigerate the remaining marinade.

2. Drain and discard the marinade from the meat. Grill it, covered, over indirect medium-hot heat for 20-35 minutes or until a thermometer reads 145°, turning occasionally and basting with reserved marinade. Let stand 5 minutes before slicing. Serve with rice.

Freeze option: Freeze uncooked pork in bag with marinade. Transfer reserved marinade to a freezer container; freeze. To use, completely thaw tenderloins and marinade in refrigerator. Grill as directed.

Per 3 ounces cooked pork: 196 cal., 4g fat (1g sat. fat), 64mg chol., 671mg sod., 15g carb. (14g sugars, 0 fiber), 24g pro.
Diabetic exchanges: 3 lean meat, 1 starch.

PORK WITH SWEET POTATOES
(PICTURED ON P. 178)

With sweet potatoes, dried cranberries and apple slices, this pork dish is especially popular during fall and winter. Your family will love not only the taste, but also the colorful medley of ingredients.
—Mary Relyea, Canastota, NY

Prep: 20 min. • **Cook:** 20 min.
Makes: 4 servings

½ cup all-purpose flour
½ teaspoon salt
¼ teaspoon pepper
1 pork tenderloin (about 1 pound)
1 tablespoon canola oil
2 medium sweet potatoes (about 1 pound), peeled and cubed
½ cup dried cranberries
1 can (14½ ounces) reduced-sodium chicken broth
1 tablespoon Dijon mustard
1 medium apple, sliced
4 green onions, chopped

1. In a shallow bowl, mix flour, salt and pepper. Cut the tenderloin into 12 slices; pound each with a meat mallet to ¼-in. thickness. Dip the pork in flour mixture to coat both sides; shake off excess.

2. In a large nonstick skillet coated with cooking spray, heat oil over medium-high heat; brown pork in batches. Remove from pan.

3. Add sweet potatoes, cranberries and broth to same pan. Bring to a boil. Reduce heat; simmer, covered, 4-6 minutes or until potatoes are almost tender. Stir in the mustard.

4. Return pork to pan; add apple and green onions. Return to a boil. Reduce heat; simmer, covered, 4-6 minutes or until pork and sweet potatoes are tender.

Per 3 slices pork with 1 cup potato mixture: 315 cal., 8g fat (2g sat. fat), 63mg chol., 513mg sod., 36g carb. (20g sugars, 4g fiber), 26g pro.
Diabetic exchanges: 3 lean meat, 2½ starch, ½ fat.

GRILLED PORK TENDERLOINS

FISH &
SEAFOOD

"*I'm always up for new ways to cook salmon. In this dish, a sweet sauce gives the fish and green beans some down-home barbecue tang. Even our kids love it.*"
—Aliesha Caldwell, Robersonville, NC

Lemon-Basil Grilled Shrimp & Couscous (p. 202) **Greek Fish Bake** (p. 201) **Sea Scallops & Fettuccine** (p. 203)
Summer Garden Fish Tacos (p. 207) **Sweet & Tangy Salmon with Green Beans** (p. 199) **Sesame Cilantro Shrimp** (p. 214)

BLACKENED TILAPIA
WITH ZUCCHINI NOODLES

BLACKENED TILAPIA
WITH ZUCCHINI NOODLES

C **FAST FIX**

*I love quick and bright meals like this
one-skillet wonder. Homemade pico de
gallo is easy to make the night before.*
—Tammy Brownlow, Dallas, TX

Start to Finish: 30 min.
Makes: 4 servings

 2 large zucchini (about 1½ pounds)
 1½ teaspoons ground cumin
 ¾ teaspoon salt, divided
 ½ teaspoon smoked paprika
 ½ teaspoon pepper

 ¼ tsp garlic powder
 4 tilapia fillets (6 ounces each)
 2 teaspoons olive oil
 2 garlic cloves, minced
 1 cup pico de gallo

1. Trim ends of zucchini. Using a spiralizer,
cut zucchini into thin strands.
2. Mix cumin, ½ teaspoon salt, smoked
paprika, pepper and garlic powder;
sprinkle generously onto both sides of
tilapia. In a large nonstick skillet, heat oil
over medium-high heat. In batches, cook
tilapia until fish just begins to flake easily
with a fork, 2-3 minutes per side. Remove
from pan; keep warm.

3. In same pan, cook zucchini with garlic
over medium-high heat until it is slightly
softened, 1-2 minutes, tossing constantly
with tongs (do not overcook). Sprinkle
with remaining salt. Serve with tilapia and
pico de gallo.
Note: If a spiralizer is not available,
zucchini may also be cut into ribbons
using a vegetable peeler. Saute it as
directed, increasing time as necessary.
Per serving: 203 cal., 4g fat (1g sat. fat),
83mg chol., 522mg sod., 8g carb. (5g
sugars, 2g fiber), 34g pro.
Diabetic exchanges: 5 lean meat,
1 vegetable, ½ fat.

SOUTHERN SEAFOOD GUMBO

A local restaurant serves a terrific gumbo, and I duplicated it pretty closely with this recipe. I did lighten it up a bit, but no one in my family seems to mind.
—Susan Wright, Champaign, IL

Prep: 25 min. • **Cook:** 35 min.
Makes: 12 servings

- 1 medium onion, chopped
- 2 celery ribs with leaves, chopped
- 1 medium green pepper, chopped
- 1 tablespoon olive oil
- 3 garlic cloves, minced
- 1 bottle (46 ounces) spicy hot V8 juice
- 1 can (14½ ounces) diced tomatoes, undrained
- ¼ teaspoon cayenne pepper
- 1 package (16 ounces) frozen sliced okra, thawed
- 1 pound catfish fillets, cut into ¾-inch cubes
- ¾ pound uncooked medium shrimp, peeled and deveined
- 3 cups cooked long grain rice

1. In a Dutch oven, saute the onion, celery and green pepper in oil until tender. Add garlic; cook 1 minute longer. Stir in the V8 juice, tomatoes and cayenne; bring to a boil. Reduce heat; cover and simmer for 10 minutes.
2. Stir in okra and catfish; cook 8 minutes longer. Add the shrimp; cook 7 minutes longer or until the shrimp turn pink. Place the rice in 12 individual serving bowls; top with gumbo.
Per serving: 180 cal., 5g fat (1g sat. fat), 60mg chol., 512mg sod., 22g carb. (7g sugars, 3g fiber), 14g pro.
Diabetic exchanges: 2 lean meat, 2 vegetable, 1 starch.

SWEET & TANGY SALMON WITH GREEN BEANS

(PICTURED ON P. 197)

I'm always up for new ways to cook salmon. In this dish, a sweet sauce gives the fish and green beans some down-home barbecue tang. Even our kids love it.
—Aliesha Caldwell, Robersonville, NC

Prep: 20 min. • **Bake:** 15 min.
Makes: 4 servings

- 4 salmon fillets (6 ounces each)
- 1 tablespoon butter
- 2 tablespoons brown sugar
- 2 tablespoons reduced-sodium soy sauce
- 2 tablespoons Dijon mustard
- 1 tablespoon olive oil
- ½ teaspoon pepper
- ⅛ teaspoon salt
- 1 pound fresh green beans, trimmed

1. Preheat oven to 425°. Place the fillets on a 15x10x1-in. baking pan coated with cooking spray. In a small skillet, melt the butter; stir in the brown sugar, soy sauce, mustard, oil, pepper and salt. Brush half of the mixture over salmon.
2. Place the green beans in a large bowl; drizzle with the remaining brown sugar mixture and toss to coat. Arrange green beans around fillets. Roast 14-16 minutes or until fish just begins to flake easily with a fork and green beans are crisp-tender.
Per fillet with ¾ cup green beans: 394 cal., 22g fat (5g sat. fat), 93mg chol., 661mg sod., 17g carb. (10g sugars, 4g fiber), 31g pro.
Diabetic exchanges: 5 lean meat, 1½ fat, 1 vegetable, ½ starch.

SOUTHERN SEAFOOD GUMBO

PEPPER & SALSA COD
F **C** **FAST FIX** ▶

After tasting a similar dish at the grocery store, my husband figured out how to make this awesome cod topped with salsa and peppers.
—Robyn Gallagher, Yorktown, VA

Start to Finish: 30 min.
Makes: 2 servings

- 2   cod or haddock fillets (6 ounces each)
- 1   teaspoon olive oil
- ¼   teaspoon salt
      Dash pepper
- ⅓   cup orange juice
- ¼   cup salsa
- ⅓   cup julienned green pepper
- ⅓   cup julienned sweet red pepper
      Hot cooked rice

1. Preheat oven to 350°. Brush both sides of the fillets with oil; place them in a greased 11x7-in. baking dish. Sprinkle with salt and pepper. Pour orange juice over fish; top with salsa and peppers.
2. Bake, covered, 17-20 minutes or until fish just begins to flake easily with a fork. Serve with rice.

Per serving without rice: 183 cal., 3g fat (1g sat. fat), 65mg chol., 512mg sod., 9g carb. (6g sugars, 1g fiber), 27g pro.
Diabetic exchanges: 4 lean meat, 1 vegetable, ½ fat.

SHRIMP & CORN STIR-FRY

SHRIMP & CORN STIR-FRY
FAST FIX ▶

I make this seafood stir-fry at summer's end when my garden offers plenty of tomatoes, yellow squash, garlic and corn. For a quick supper, my family loves it over rice.
—Lindsay Honn, Huntingdon, PA

Start to Finish: 20 min.
Makes: 4 servings

- 2   tablespoons olive oil
- 2   small yellow summer squash, sliced
- 1   small onion, chopped
- 1   pound uncooked shrimp (26-30 per pound), peeled and deveined
- 1½ cups fresh or frozen corn, thawed
- 1   cup chopped tomatoes
- 4   garlic cloves, minced
- ½   teaspoon salt
- ¼   teaspoon pepper
- ¼   teaspoon crushed red pepper flakes, optional
- ¼   cup chopped fresh basil
      Hot cooked brown rice

1. In a large skillet, heat oil over medium-high heat. Add squash and onion; stir-fry until squash is crisp-tender, 2-3 minutes.
2. Add next six ingredients and, if desired, pepper flakes; stir-fry until shrimp turn pink, 3-4 minutes longer. Top with basil. Serve with rice.

Per serving: 239 cal., 9g fat (1g sat. fat), 138mg chol., 443mg sod., 19g carb. (8g sugars, 3g fiber), 22g pro.
Diabetic exchanges: 3 lean meat, 1½ fat, 1 starch, 1 vegetable.

STIR-FRIED SCALLOPS & ASPARAGUS FAST FIX

Served over some quick-cooking ramen noodles, this stir-fry is perfect for busy families on hurried weeknights. It comes together in about half an hour.
—Barbara Schindler, Napoleon, OH

Start to Finish: 25 min.
Makes: 4 servings

- 1 package (3 ounces) chicken ramen noodles
- 1 pound fresh asparagus, trimmed and cut into 1-inch pieces
- 1 medium sweet red pepper, julienned
- 1 tablespoon olive oil
- 3 green onions, thinly sliced
- 1 garlic clove, minced
- 1 pound sea scallops, halved horizontally
- 1 tablespoon lime juice
- 2 tablespoons reduced-sodium soy sauce
- 1 teaspoon sesame oil
- 1 teaspoon hot pepper sauce

1. Discard seasoning package from ramen noodles or save for another use. Cook the ramen noodles according to the package directions; keep warm.

2. Meanwhile, in a nonstick skillet or wok, stir-fry the asparagus and red pepper in oil for 2 minutes or until the vegetables are crisp-tender. Add green onions and garlic, stir-fry 1 minute longer. Stir in the scallops. Stir-fry for 3 minutes or until scallops are firm and opaque.

3. Combine the lime juice, soy sauce, sesame oil and hot pepper sauce; stir into skillet. Serve with ramen noodles.

Per cup: 269 cal., 9g fat (3g sat. fat), 37mg chol., 578mg sod., 22g carb. (2g sugars, 2g fiber), 24g pro.
Diabetic exchanges: 3 lean meat, 1 starch, 1 vegetable, 1 fat.

GREEK FISH BAKE C FAST FIX
(PICTURED ON P. 196)

As a military spouse living overseas, I was given the chance to try many styles of cooking. Here is a Mediterranean-inspired recipe that we still love today.
—Stacey Boyd, Springfield, VA

Start to Finish: 30 min.
Makes: 4 servings

- 4 cod fillets (6 ounces each)
- 2 tablespoons olive oil
- ¼ teaspoon salt
- ⅛ teaspoon pepper
- 1 small green pepper, cut into thin strips
- ½ small red onion, thinly sliced
- ¼ cup pitted Greek olives, sliced
- 1 can (8 ounces) tomato sauce
- ¼ cup crumbled feta cheese

1. Preheat oven to 400°. Place cod in a greased 13x9-in. baking dish. Brush with oil; sprinkle with salt and pepper. Top with green pepper, onion and olives.

2. Pour tomato sauce over top; sprinkle with cheese. Bake until fish just begins to flake easily with a fork, 15-20 minutes.

Per fillet with toppings: 246 cal., 12g fat (2g sat. fat), 68mg chol., 706mg sod., 6g carb. (2g sugars, 2g fiber), 29g pro.
Diabetic exchanges: 4 lean meat, 1½ fat, 1 vegetable.

DID YOU KNOW?

Salty, crumbly Greek feta cheese is traditionally made with sheep's or goat's milk, but most American brands are made with cow's milk instead.

STIR-FRIED SCALLOPS & ASPARAGUS

LEMON-BASIL GRILLED SHRIMP & COUSCOUS

FAST FIX ▶

(PICTURED ON P. 196)

The basil and lemon flavors in this grilled shrimp dish are a perfect complement to each other. There is lemon and basil in the marinade as well as the garnish on the finished dish. Make sure to use fresh basil and fresh lemon juice and zest. They really make a big difference.
—Trisha Kruse, Eagle, ID

Start to Finish: 30 min.
Makes: 6 servings

- 1½ cups uncooked pearl (Israeli) couscous
- ⅓ cup lemon juice
- ¼ cup olive oil
- 2 tablespoons Dijon mustard
- 3 garlic cloves, minced
- ½ teaspoon salt
- ¼ teaspoon pepper
- ½ cup minced fresh basil, divided
- 2 pounds uncooked large shrimp, peeled and deveined
- 2 teaspoons grated lemon peel

1. Cook couscous according to package directions; remove from heat. Meanwhile, in a large bowl, whisk lemon juice, oil, mustard, garlic, salt and pepper until blended; stir in ¼ cup basil. Stir ¼ cup dressing into cooked couscous; reserve remaining dressing.
2. Thread shrimp onto metal or soaked wooden skewers. Moisten a paper towel with cooking oil; using long-handled tongs, rub on grill rack to coat lightly. Grill the shrimp, covered, over medium-high heat 2-3 minutes on each side or until shrimp turn pink.
3. Remove shrimp from skewers; toss with reserved dressing. Serve with couscous. Sprinkle with lemon peel and remaining basil.

Per 8 shrimp with ½ cup couscous: 363 cal., 12g fat (2g sat. fat), 184mg chol., 497mg sod., 34g carb. (0 sugars, 0 fiber), 29g pro.
Diabetic exchanges: 3 lean meat, 2 starch, 2 fat.

EASY CRAB CAKES

EASY CRAB CAKES **C** **FAST FIX** ▶

Ready-to-go crabmeat makes these delicate patties ideal for dinner when you are pressed for time. You can also form the crab mixture into four thick patties instead of eight cakes.
—Charlene Spelock, Apollo, PA

Start to Finish: 25 min.
Makes: 4 servings

- 1 cup seasoned bread crumbs, divided
- 2 green onions, finely chopped
- ¼ cup finely chopped sweet red pepper
- 1 large egg, lightly beaten
- ¼ cup reduced-fat mayonnaise
- 1 tablespoon lemon juice
- ½ teaspoon garlic powder
- ⅛ teaspoon cayenne pepper
- 2 cans (6 ounces each) crabmeat, drained, flaked and cartilage removed
- 1 tablespoon butter

1. In a large bowl, combine ⅓ cup bread crumbs, green onions, red pepper, egg, mayonnaise, lemon juice, garlic powder and cayenne; fold in crab.
2. Place remaining bread crumbs in a shallow bowl. Divide mixture into eight portions; shape into 2-in. balls. Gently coat with bread crumbs and shape into ½-in.-thick patties.
3. In a large nonstick skillet, heat butter over medium-high heat. Add crab cakes; cook 3-4 minutes on each side or until golden brown.

Per 2 crab cakes: 239 cal., 11g fat (3g sat. fat), 141mg chol., 657mg sod., 13g carb. (2g sugars, 1g fiber), 21g pro.
Diabetic exchanges: 3 lean meat, 2 fat, 1 starch.

FISH & CHIPS

Dine like you're in a traditional British pub. These moist fish fillets from the oven have a fuss-free coating that's healthier but just as crunchy and golden as the deep-fried kind. Simply seasoned and baked, the crispy fries are perfect on the side.
—Janice Mitchell, Aurora, CO

Prep: 10 min. • **Bake:** 35 min.
Makes: 4 servings

- 1 pound potatoes (about 2 medium)
- 2 tablespoons olive oil
- ¼ teaspoon pepper

FISH
- ⅓ cup all-purpose flour
- ¼ teaspoon pepper
- 1 large egg
- 2 tablespoons water
- ⅔ cup crushed cornflakes
- 1 tablespoon grated Parmesan cheese
- ⅛ teaspoon cayenne pepper
- 1 pound haddock or cod fillets
  Tartar sauce, optional

1. Preheat oven to 425°. Peel and cut potatoes lengthwise into ½-in.-thick slices; cut slices into ½-in.-thick sticks.
2. In a large bowl, toss potatoes with oil and pepper. Transfer to a 15x10x1-in. baking pan coated with cooking spray. Bake, uncovered, 25-30 minutes or until golden brown and crisp, stirring once.
3. Meanwhile, in a shallow bowl, mix the flour and pepper. In another shallow bowl, whisk egg with water. In a third bowl, toss cornflakes with cheese and cayenne. Dip the fish in flour mixture to coat both sides; shake off excess. Dip in egg mixture, then in the cornflake mixture, patting to help the coating adhere.
4. Place on a baking sheet coated with cooking spray. Bake 10-12 minutes or until fish just begins to flake easily with a fork. Serve with potatoes and, if desired, the tartar sauce.
Per serving: 376 cal., 9g fat (2g sat. fat), 120mg chol., 228mg sod., 44g carb. (3g sugars, 2g fiber), 28g pro.
Diabetic exchanges: 3 starch, 3 lean meat, 1½ fat.

SEA SCALLOPS & FETTUCCINE
FAST FIX
(PICTURED ON P. 197)

When we decided to lose weight, my husband and I tried this recipe and loved it so much we had it every Tuesday. It's so easy, he would fix it on nights I was running late.
—Donna Thompson, Laramie, WY

Start to Finish: 30 min.
Makes: 2 servings

- 4 ounces uncooked fettuccine
- 1 tablespoon olive oil
- ½ medium sweet red pepper, julienned
- 1 garlic clove, minced
- ½ teaspoon grated lemon peel
- ¼ teaspoon crushed red pepper flakes
- ½ cup reduced-sodium chicken broth
- ¼ cup white wine or additional broth
- 1 tablespoon lemon juice
- 6 sea scallops (about ¾ pound)
- 2 teaspoons grated Parmesan cheese

1. Cook fettuccine according to package directions; drain.
2. Meanwhile, in a large skillet, heat oil over medium-high heat. Add red pepper, garlic, lemon peel and pepper flakes; cook and stir 2 minutes. Stir in broth, wine and lemon juice. Bring to a boil. Reduce heat; simmer, uncovered, 5-6 minutes or until liquid is reduced by half.
3. Cut each scallop horizontally in half; add to skillet. Cook, covered, 4-5 minutes or until the scallops are firm and opaque, stirring occasionally. Serve with fettuccine. Sprinkle with cheese.
Per serving: 421 cal., 10g fat (2g sat. fat), 42mg chol., 861mg sod., 49g carb. (4g sugars, 3g fiber), 30g pro.

DID YOU KNOW?
Farmed scallops are becoming more common. Because scallops are filter-feeders that live on plankton, they don't require much feed. Their low environmental impact makes farmed scallops a green choice.

FISH & CHIPS

PAN-SEARED COD

PAN-SEARED COD C FAST FIX

Cod has a soft, buttery appeal that goes great with cilantro, onions and crunchy pine nuts. This is the easiest, tastiest cod preparation I've found.
—Lucy Lu Wang, Seattle, WA

Start to Finish: 25 min.
Makes: 2 servings

- 2 cod fillets (6 ounces each)
- ½ teaspoon salt
- ¼ teaspoon pepper
- 3 tablespoons olive oil, divided
- ½ large sweet onion, thinly sliced
- ½ cup dry white wine
- ¼ cup coarsely chopped fresh cilantro
- 1 tablespoon pine nuts or sliced almonds

1. Pat the cod dry with paper towels then sprinkle with salt and pepper. In a large nonstick skillet, heat 2 tablespoons oil over medium-high heat. Brown fillets lightly on both sides; remove from pan.

2. In same skillet, heat remaining oil over medium heat. Add onion; cook and stir 4-5 minutes or until softened. Stir in wine; cook 3-4 minutes longer or until the onion is lightly browned, stirring occasionally. Return cod to pan. Reduce heat to low; cook, covered, 2-3 minutes or until fish just begins to flake easily with a fork.

3. Remove cod from pan. Stir cilantro and pine nuts into onion; serve with fish.
Per fillet with ¼ cup onion mixture:
378 cal., 24g fat (3g sat. fat), 65mg chol., 691mg sod., 8g carb. (5g sugars, 1g fiber), 28g pro.

✳ TEST KITCHEN TIP
Here's a great way to keep parsley, cilantro and basil fresh for up to a month. Trim stems with kitchen scissors and place the herb bunch in a short tumbler containing an inch or two of water. Remove any loose leaves so only the stems (and no greenery) touch the water. Loosely tie a produce bag around the tumbler to trap humidity around the leaves and pop the tumbler in the fridge. Each time you use the herbs, change the water. Turn the produce bag inside before placing it on the herbs so any excess moisture that has built up inside the bag can evaporate.

SEAFOOD PASTA DELIGHT

SEAFOOD PASTA DELIGHT
FAST FIX

I once made this dish while visiting friends. These days, whenever I eat it, the meal feels like a festive occasion.
—Debbie Campbell, Dartmouth, NS

Start to Finish: 30 min.
Makes: 6 servings

- ½ cup chicken broth
- ½ cup dry white wine or additional chicken broth
- ¼ cup reduced-sodium soy sauce
- 2 tablespoons cornstarch
- 1 teaspoon sugar
- ½ teaspoon salt
  Dash pepper
- 12 ounces uncooked vermicelli
- 4 teaspoons olive oil, divided
- ½ pound sea scallops
- ½ pound uncooked medium shrimp, peeled and deveined
- 1 medium sweet red pepper, julienned
- 1 medium sweet yellow pepper, julienned
- 1 cup fresh or frozen sugar snap peas
- 2 to 3 garlic cloves, minced
- 1 teaspoon minced fresh gingerroot
- 2 teaspoons sesame oil

1. In a small bowl, mix the first seven ingredients until smooth. Cook vermicelli according to package directions.

2. Meanwhile, in a large nonstick skillet, heat 2 teaspoons olive oil over medium-high heat. Add scallops and shrimp; stir-fry 3-4 minutes or until scallops are firm and opaque and shrimp turn pink. Remove from pan.

3. Stir-fry peppers, snap peas, garlic and ginger in remaining olive oil 3-5 minutes or just until vegetables are crisp-tender. Stir cornstarch mixture and add to pan. Bring to a boil; cook and stir 1-2 minutes or until sauce is thickened.

4. Return seafood to pan; heat through. Stir in sesame oil. Drain vermicelli; add to pan and toss to combine.
Per serving: 372 cal., 6g fat (1g sat. fat), 59mg chol., 794mg sod., 53g carb. (6g sugars, 3g fiber), 22g pro.

DE-LIGHTFUL
TUNA CASSEROLE

SEARED SALMON WITH STRAWBERRY BASIL RELISH

C FAST FIX ▶

Here, try a sweet new approach to salmon by topping it off with a relish of strawberries, basil, honey and pepper.

—Stacy Mullens, Gresham, OR

Start to Finish: 20 min.
Makes: 6 servings

- 6 salmon fillets (4 ounces each)
- 1 tablespoon butter, melted
- ¼ teaspoon salt
- ⅛ teaspoon freshly ground pepper

RELISH
- 1¼ cups finely chopped fresh strawberries
- 1 tablespoon minced fresh basil
- 1 tablespoon honey
  Dash freshly ground pepper

1. Brush the fillets with melted butter; sprinkle with salt and pepper. Heat a large skillet over medium-high heat. Add fillets, skin side up, in batches if necessary; cook 2-3 minutes on each side or until fish just begins to flake easily with a fork.
2. In a small bowl, toss strawberries with basil, honey and pepper. Serve salmon with relish.

Per salmon fillet with 3 tablespoons relish: 215 cal., 12g fat (3g sat. fat), 62mg chol., 169mg sod., 6g carb. (5g sugars, 1g fiber), 19g pro.
Diabetic exchanges: 3 lean meat, ½ starch, ½ fat.

DE-LIGHTFUL TUNA CASSEROLE

This mild homemade tuna casserole will truly satisfy your family's craving for comfort food without all the fat!
—Colleen Willey, Hamburg, NY

Prep: 15 min. • **Bake:** 25 min.
Makes: 5 servings

- 1 package (7 ounces) elbow macaroni
- 1 can (10¾ ounces) reduced-fat reduced-sodium condensed cream of mushroom soup, undiluted
- 1 cup sliced fresh mushrooms
- 1 cup shredded reduced-fat cheddar cheese
- 1 cup fat-free milk
- 1 can (5 ounces) light water-packed tuna, drained and flaked
- 2 tablespoons diced pimientos
- 3 teaspoons dried minced onion
- 1 teaspoon ground mustard
- ¼ teaspoon salt
- ⅓ cup crushed cornflakes

1. Cook macaroni according to package directions. Meanwhile, in a large bowl, combine the soup, mushrooms, cheese, milk, tuna, pimientos, onion, mustard and salt. Drain macaroni; add to tuna mixture and mix well.
2. Transfer to a 2-qt. baking dish that is coated with cooking spray. Sprinkle with cornflakes. Bake, uncovered, at 350° for 25-30 minutes or until bubbly.
Freeze option: Cool unbaked casserole before topping with cornflakes; cover and freeze. To use, partially thaw casserole in the refrigerator overnight. Remove from refrigerator 30 minutes before baking. Preheat oven to 350°. Top casserole with cornflakes and bake as directed; increase time as necessary for a thermometer inserted in center to read 165°.
Per 1¼ cups: 329 cal., 8g fat (4g sat. fat), 32mg chol., 684mg sod., 43g carb. (7g sugars, 2g fiber), 23g pro.
Diabetic exchanges: 3 starch, 2 lean meat.

SHRIMP PANZANELLA SALAD
FAST FIX ▶

These days I'm cooking for two. After working in the garden, I can dash indoors and have this shrimp and bread salad on the table pronto.
—Kallee Krong-Mccreery, Escondido, CA

Start to Finish: 20 min.
Makes: 2 servings

- 1 cup cubed French bread (¾ inch)
- 1 teaspoon olive oil
- ⅛ teaspoon garlic salt
- 1 teaspoon butter
- ½ pound uncooked shrimp (31-40 per pound), peeled and deveined
- 1 garlic clove, minced
- 3 cups fresh baby spinach
- ½ medium ripe avocado, peeled and cubed
- 1 medium tomato, chopped
- 2 tablespoons Italian salad dressing
- 1 tablespoon grated Parmesan cheese

1. In a large nonstick skillet, toss bread cubes with oil and garlic salt. Cook over medium heat 3-4 minutes or until bread is toasted, stirring frequently. Remove from the pan.

2. In the same skillet, heat the butter over medium heat. Add shrimp and garlic; cook and stir 2-3 minutes or until shrimp turn pink. Remove from heat.

3. In a large bowl, combine the spinach, avocado, tomato, toasted bread and shrimp; drizzle this with dressing and toss gently to coat. Sprinkle with cheese; serve immediately.

Per serving: 306 cal., 16g fat (3g sat. fat), 145mg chol., 567mg sod., 19g carb. (4g sugars, 5g fiber), 23g pro.
Diabetic exchanges: 3 lean meat, 2 vegetable, 1 fat, ½ starch.

HEALTH TIP Whole-wheat French bread is becoming more popular, but can still be hard to find. Substitute cubed bread from a crusty whole-wheat dinner roll to increase fiber in this salad.

SHRIMP PANZANELLA SALAD

SUMMER GARDEN FISH TACOS
(PICTURED ON P. 196)

I like to serve fish tacos with quinoa and black beans for a complete and satisfying meal. If you've got them, add summer toppings like bright peppers, green onions or purple carrots.
—Camille Parker, Chicago, IL

Prep: 20 min. • **Grill:** 20 min.
Makes: 4 servings

- 1 medium ear sweet corn, husk removed
- 1 poblano pepper, halved and seeds removed
- 4 tilapia fillets (4 ounces each)
- ⅛ teaspoon salt
- 1 yellow summer squash, halved lengthwise
- 1 medium heirloom tomato, chopped
- ⅓ cup chopped red onion
- 3 tablespoons coarsely chopped fresh cilantro
- 1 teaspoon grated lime peel
- 3 tablespoons lime juice
- 8 taco shells, warmed
- ½ medium ripe avocado, peeled and sliced

1. Moisten a paper towel with cooking oil; using long-handled tongs, rub on grill rack to coat lightly. Grill the corn and pepper, covered, over medium heat 10-12 minutes or until tender, turning them occasionally. Cool slightly.

2. Meanwhile, sprinkle fish with salt. Grill fish and squash, covered, over medium heat 7-9 minutes or until fish just begins to flake easily with a fork and squash is tender, turning once.

3. Cut corn from cob and place in a bowl. Chop pepper and squash; add to corn. Stir in tomato, onion, cilantro, lime peel and lime juice. Serve fish in taco shells; top with corn mixture and avocado slices.
Note: Wear disposable gloves when cutting hot peppers; the oils can burn skin. Avoid touching your face.

Per 2 tacos: 278 cal., 10g fat (2g sat. fat), 55mg chol., 214mg sod., 26g carb. (5g sugars, 5g fiber), 25g pro.
Diabetic exchanges: 3 lean meat, 1½ starch, 1 vegetable, ½ fat.

CRISPY ALMOND TILAPIA

C **FAST FIX** ▶

Since changing over to a healthier style of cooking, I've come up with new coatings for baked fish. I use almonds, panko bread crumbs and a smidge of hot sauce to add crunchy texture with nice heat.
—Amanda Flinner, Beaver, PA

Start to Finish: 30 min.
Makes: 4 servings

- 1 large egg
- ¼ cup Louisiana-style hot sauce
- ¾ cup slivered almonds, chopped and toasted
- ⅓ cup panko (Japanese) bread crumbs
- 1 teaspoon grated lemon peel
- 1 teaspoon seafood seasoning
- ¼ teaspoon garlic powder
- 4 tilapia fillets (4 ounces each)
- ½ teaspoon salt
- ¼ teaspoon pepper

1. Preheat oven to 400°. Whisk together egg and hot sauce in a shallow bowl. In a separate shallow bowl, toss the almonds, bread crumbs, lemon peel and spices.

2. Halve fillets lengthwise; sprinkle with salt and pepper. Dip in egg mixture, then in almond mixture, patting to adhere; place on a greased or parchment-lined baking sheet. Bake until lightly browned and fish just begins to flake easily with a fork, about 12-15 minutes.

Note: To toast nuts, bake in a shallow pan in a 350° oven for 5-10 minutes or cook in a skillet over low heat until lightly browned, stirring occasionally.

Per 2 fillet pieces: 251 cal., 13g fat (2g sat. fat), 102mg chol., 537mg sod., 9g carb. (1g sugars, 3g fiber), 28g pro.
Diabetic exchanges: 4 lean meat, 2 fat.

SALMON & FETA WILTED SPINACH SALAD

SALMON & FETA WILTED SPINACH SALAD **FAST FIX** ▶

My friend mentioned a Turkish salmon and couscous dish that sounded fantastic, so I started experimenting. I prefer this salad warm, but it's also tasty served cold.
—Jeni Pittard, Statham, GA

Start to Finish: 30 min.
Makes: 2 servings

- 1 salmon fillet (8 ounces)
- 2 teaspoons lemon juice
- ½ teaspoon Greek seasoning
- ½ cup quinoa, rinsed
- 1 cup reduced-sodium chicken broth
- 1 teaspoon olive oil
- 4 cups coarsely chopped fresh spinach
- 1 cup grape tomatoes, halved
- ¼ cup crumbled feta cheese
- 2 tablespoons chopped fresh parsley
- 1 tablespoon minced fresh oregano
- ⅛ teaspoon pepper
  Lemon wedges

1. Preheat oven to 375°. Place salmon on foil-lined baking sheet, skin side down. Sprinkle with the lemon juice and Greek seasoning. Bake until fish just begins to flake easily with a fork, 15-18 minutes.

2. Meanwhile, in small saucepan, combine the quinoa, broth and oil; bring to a boil. Reduce heat; simmer, covered, until the liquid is absorbed and quinoa is tender, 12-15 minutes.

3. To serve, break salmon into 1-in. pieces using a fork. Place the spinach, tomatoes, quinoa and salmon in a large bowl. Add the cheese, herbs and pepper; toss gently to combine. Serve with lemon wedges.

Per 2 cups: 427 cal., 18g fat (4g sat. fat), 64mg chol., 773mg sod., 34g carb. (3g sugars, 6g fiber), 32g pro.
Diabetic exchanges: 3 lean meat, 2 vegetable, 1½ starch, 1 fat.

GARLIC SHRIMP & RICE SALAD

FAST FIX

For this easy-to-make main dish salad, you can prepare the rice mixture and chop the vegetables ahead of time. Cook the shrimp at the last minute, then assemble it all together for a light yet satisfying meal.
—Diane Nemitz, Ludington, MI

Start to Finish: 30 min.
Makes: 4 servings

- 1 pound uncooked shrimp (31-40 per pound), peeled and deveined
- 2 tablespoons olive oil
- 2 garlic cloves, minced
- 1 teaspoon dried oregano
- 1 package (8.8 ounces) ready-to-serve brown rice
- ¼ cup mayonnaise
- ¼ cup sour cream
- 2 tablespoons minced fresh basil or 1 teaspoon dried basil
- 2 tablespoons lemon juice
- 1 celery rib, chopped
- ¼ cup minced fresh parsley
- 2 tablespoons chopped green pepper
- 4 cups fresh baby arugula or baby spinach

1. Toss the shrimp with oil, garlic and oregano; let stand 15 minutes. Meanwhile, cook rice according to package directions. Transfer rice to a large bowl; cool slightly. For dressing, mix mayonnaise, sour cream, basil and lemon juice.

2. In a large skillet, saute shrimp mixture over medium-high heat until shrimp turns pink, 2-3 minutes. Add to rice; stir in the celery, parsley and pepper. Add arugula and toss lightly; serve with dressing.

Per serving: 397 cal., 23g fat (5g sat. fat), 142mg chol., 232mg sod., 21g carb. (1g sugars, 2g fiber), 22g pro.

PARMESAN BAKED COD

C FAST FIX

This is a goof-proof way to keep cod moist and flavorful. My mom shared this recipe with me years ago.
—Mary Jo Hoppe, Pewaukee, WI

Start to Finish: 25 min.
Makes: 4 servings

- 4 cod fillets (4 ounces each)
- ⅔ cup mayonnaise
- 4 green onions, chopped
- ¼ cup grated Parmesan cheese
- 1 teaspoon Worcestershire sauce

1. Preheat oven to 400°. Place the cod in an 8-in. square baking dish coated with cooking spray. Mix remaining ingredients; spread over fillets.

2. Bake, uncovered, until fish just begins to flake easily with a fork, 15-20 minutes.

Per fillet: 247 cal., 15g fat (2g sat. fat), 57mg chol., 500mg sod., 7g carb. (2g sugars, 0 fiber), 20g pro.
Diabetic exchanges: 3 lean meat, 3 fat.

GARLIC SHRIMP & RICE SALAD

OVEN-FRIED FISH NUGGETS
F **C** **FAST FIX** ▶

My husband and I love fried fish, but we're both trying to cut back on dietary fat. I made up this recipe and it's a hit with us both. He says he likes it as much as deep-fried fish, and that's saying a lot!
—LaDonna Reed, Ponca City, OK

Start to Finish: 25 min.
Makes: 4 servings

- ⅓ cup seasoned bread crumbs
- ⅓ cup crushed cornflakes
- 3 tablespoons grated Parmesan cheese
- ½ teaspoon salt
- ¼ teaspoon pepper
- 1½ pounds cod fillets, cut into 1-inch cubes
  Butter-flavored cooking spray

1. In a shallow bowl, combine the bread crumbs, cornflakes, Parmesan cheese, salt and pepper. Coat fish with butter-flavored spray, then roll in crumb mixture.

2. Place on a baking sheet coated with cooking spray. Bake at 375° for 15-20 minutes or until the fish flakes easily with a fork.

Freeze option: Cover and freeze the unbaked fish nuggets on waxed paper-lined baking sheet until firm. Transfer to a resealable plastic freezer bag; return to freezer. To use, preheat oven to 375°. Bake the nuggets on a rack on a greased baking sheet 15-20 minutes or until fish flakes easily with a fork.

Per 9 pieces: 171 cal., 2g fat (1g sat. fat), 66mg chol., 415mg sod., 7g carb. (1g sugars, 0 fiber), 29g pro.
Diabetic exchanges: 5 lean meat, ½ starch.

MAPLE TERIYAKI SALMON FILLETS

MAPLE TERIYAKI SALMON FILLETS

Maple syrup and apple juice provide the mildly sweet marinade for this salmon. Whether broiled or grilled, the fillets glaze nicely when basted.
—Kathy Schrecengost, Oswego, NY

Prep: 10 min. + marinating • **Grill:** 10 min.
Makes: 4 servings

- ⅓ cup apple juice
- ⅓ cup maple syrup
- 3 tablespoons reduced-sodium soy sauce
- 2 tablespoons finely chopped onion
- 2 garlic cloves, minced
- 4 salmon fillets (6 ounces each)

1. In a small bowl, whisk the first five ingredients until blended. Remove ½ cup for basting; cover and refrigerate. Pour remaining marinade into a large resealable plastic bag. Add salmon; seal bag and turn to coat. Refrigerate 1-3 hours.

2. Drain salmon, discarding marinade in bag. Moisten a paper towel with cooking oil; using long-handled tongs, rub on grill rack to coat lightly. Place salmon on grill rack, skin side down. Grill, covered, over medium heat or broil 4 in. from heat for 10-12 minutes or until fish flakes easily with a fork, basting frequently during the last 4 minutes.

Per fillet: 349 cal., 16g fat (3g sat. fat), 85mg chol., 512mg sod., 20g carb. (17g sugars, 0 fiber), 30g pro.
Diabetic exchanges: 5 lean meat, 1 starch.

CHRISTMAS EVE CONFETTI PASTA `FAST FIX`

Our Christmas Eve tradition is to make linguine with red and green peppers and shrimp. We serve it with a snappy salad and garlic bread.
—Ellen Fiore, Montvale, NJ

Start to Finish: 25 min.
Makes: 8 servings

- 1 package (16 ounces) linguine
- 1 cup chopped sweet red pepper
- 1 cup chopped green pepper
- ⅓ cup chopped onion
- 3 garlic cloves, peeled and thinly sliced
- ¼ teaspoon salt
- ¼ teaspoon dried oregano
- ⅛ teaspoon crushed red pepper flakes
- ⅛ teaspoon pepper
- ¼ cup olive oil
- 2 pounds peeled and deveined cooked shrimp (61-70 per pound)
- ½ cup shredded Parmesan cheese

1. Cook the linguine according to the package directions. Meanwhile, using a Dutch oven, saute the peppers, onion, garlic and seasonings in oil until the vegetables are tender.
2. Add shrimp; cook and stir 2-3 minutes longer or until heated through. Drain the linguine and toss with shrimp mixture. Sprinkle with cheese.

Per 1⅓ cups: 418 cal., 11g fat (2g sat. fat), 176mg chol., 331mg sod., 46g carb. (3g sugars, 3g fiber), 33g pro.
Diabetic exchanges: 3 starch, 3 lean meat, 1½ fat.

ZUCCHINI-WRAPPED SCALLOPS `C`

This dish gets a little heat from red pepper flakes and Caribbean jerk seasoning. These kabobs are special enough for a summer dinner party.
—Julie Gwinn, Hershey, PA

Prep: 20 min. + marinating • **Grill:** 10 min.
Makes: 4 servings

- 2 tablespoons orange juice
- 1 tablespoon olive oil
- 1 teaspoon Caribbean jerk seasoning
- 1 teaspoon grated orange peel
- ⅛ teaspoon crushed red pepper flakes
- 1½ pounds sea scallops (about 16)
- 2 medium zucchini

1. In a small bowl, combine the orange juice, oil, seasoning, orange peel and red pepper flakes; set aside 1 tablespoon for basting. Pour the remaining marinade into a large resealable plastic bag; add the scallops. Seal bag and turn to coat; refrigerate for 30 minutes.
2. Using a vegetable peeler or metal cheese slicer, cut zucchini into very thin lengthwise strips. Drain and discard the marinade. Wrap a zucchini strip around each scallop. Secure by threading where the zucchini ends overlap onto metal or soaked wooden skewers.
3. Using long-handled tongs, moisten a paper towel with cooking oil and lightly coat the grill rack. Grill seafood, covered, over medium heat or broil 4 in. from the heat for 3-4 minutes on each side or until scallops are opaque, brushing once with reserved marinade.

Per serving: 194 cal., 5g fat (1g sat. fat), 56mg chol., 346mg sod., 7g carb. (2g sugars, 1g fiber), 29g pro.
Diabetic exchanges: 4 lean meat, ½ starch, ½ fat.

CHRISTMAS EVE CONFETTI PASTA

**BARBECUED SHRIMP &
PEACH KABOBS**

*We enjoy fish frequently, and this b
version has a tempting mild orange
It comes out of the oven flaky and r*
—Jacquelyn Dixon, La Porte City, IA

Start to Finish: 25 min.
Makes: 4 servings

- 4 cod fillets (4 ounces each)
- 2 tablespoons butter
- ½ cup chopped onion
- 1 garlic clove, minced
- 1 teaspoon grated orange peel
- ⅓ cup orange juice
- 1 tablespoon lemon juice
- ⅛ teaspoon pepper
- 1 tablespoon minced fresh pars

1. Preheat oven to 375°. Place fille
an 11x7-in. baking dish that is coate
cooking spray.
2. In a skillet, heat butter over med
high heat; saute the onion and garli
tender. Spoon over fish. Mix orange
and citrus juices; drizzle over fish.
3. Bake, uncovered, until fish just b
to flake easily with a fork, 15-20 mi
Sprinkle with pepper and parsley.
Per 3 ounces cooked fish: 153 c
fat (4g sat. fat), 58mg chol., 108m
5g carb. (3g sugars, 0 fiber), 18g p
Diabetic exchanges: 3 lean meat.

★ ★ ★ ★ ★ **READER REVIEW**

"Excellent, easy to ma
The flavors were light
and tasty. This recipe
made my short list. I w
definitely make it aga
TIGERLILY61 TASTEOFHOME.COM

BARBECUED SHRIMP & PEACH KABOBS F

*Shrimp grilled with peaches and green
onions really sets off fireworks! The spicy
seasonings even helped me win a ribbon
at a county fair.*
—Jen Smallwood, Portsmouth, VA

Prep: 25 min. • **Grill:** 10 min.
Makes: 4 servings

- 1 tablespoon packed brown sugar
- 1 teaspoon paprika
- ½ to 1 teaspoon ground ancho
  chili pepper
- ½ teaspoon ground cumin
- ¼ teaspoon salt
- ¼ teaspoon freshly ground pepper
- ⅛ to ¼ teaspoon cayenne pepper
- 1 pound uncooked shrimp (16-20
  per pound), peeled and deveined
- 3 medium peaches, each cut into
  8 wedges

- 8 green onions (light green and white
  portion only), cut into 2-inch pieces
  Olive oil-flavored cooking spray
  Lime wedges

1. Mix brown sugar and seasonings. Place
shrimp, peaches and green onions in large
bowl; sprinkle with brown sugar mixture
and toss to coat. On four or eight metal
or soaked wooden skewers, alternately
thread shrimp, peaches and green onions.
2. Lightly spritz both sides of kabobs with
cooking spray. Grill, covered, over medium
heat or broil 4 in. from heat 3-4 minutes
on each side or until the shrimp turn pink.
Squeeze lime wedges over kabobs.
Per kabob: 170 cal., 2g fat (0 sat. fat),
138mg chol., 289mg sod., 18g carb.
(13g sugars, 3g fiber), 20g pro.
Diabetic exchanges: 3 lean meat, 1 fruit.

CITRUS COD

SESAME CILANTRO SHRIMP

C **FAST FIX**

(PICTURED ON P. 197)

On days when I don't feel like spending much time in the kitchen, I reach for shrimp. I can have a hot meal in the table in 10 minutes.
—Tami Penunuri, League City, TX

Start to Finish: 10 min.
Makes: 4 servings

- 1 tablespoon plus ½ cup reduced-fat Asian toasted sesame salad dressing, divided
- 1 pound uncooked shrimp (31-40 per pound), peeled and deveined
  Lime wedges
- ¼ cup chopped fresh cilantro
- 3 cups cooked brown rice, optional

1. Using a large nonstick skillet, heat 1 tablespoon dressing over medium heat. Add the shrimp; cook and stir 1 minute.
2. Stir in the remaining dressing; cook, uncovered, 1-2 minutes longer or until shrimp turn pink. To serve, squeeze lime juice over top; sprinkle with cilantro. If desired, serve with rice.

Per ½ cup shrimp mixture without rice: 153 cal., 4g fat (0 sat. fat), 138mg chol., 461mg sod., 9g carb. (7g sugars, 0 fiber), 20g pro.
Diabetic exchanges: 3 lean meat, ½ starch, ½ fat.

★ ★ ★ ★ ★ **READER REVIEW**

"I forgot the cilantro, so mine was just the dressing and shrimp over white rice. It was still tasty and I couldn't ask for a faster meal!"

VEGGIEMAMA TASTEOFHOME.COM

TOMATO WALNUT TILAPIA

TOMATO WALNUT TILAPIA

C **FAST FIX**

Tomato, bread crumbs and crunchy walnuts dress up tilapia fillets in this delightful main dish. I often serve the fish with cooked green beans and julienned carrots.
—Phyl Broich-Wessling, Garner, IA

Start to Finish: 20 min.
Makes: 4 servings

- 4 tilapia fillets (4 ounces each)
- ¼ teaspoon salt
- ¼ teaspoon pepper
- 1 tablespoon butter
- 1 medium tomato, thinly sliced

TOPPING

- ½ cup soft bread crumbs
- ¼ cup chopped walnuts
- 2 tablespoons lemon juice
- 1½ teaspoons butter, melted

1. Sprinkle the fillets with salt and pepper. In a large skillet coated with cooking spray, cook the fillets in butter over medium-high heat for 2-3 minutes on each side or until lightly browned.
2. Transfer fish to a broiler pan or baking sheet; top with the tomato. Combine the topping ingredients; spoon over the tops.
3. Broil 3-4 in. from heat for 2-3 minutes or until topping is lightly browned and fish flakes easily with a fork.

Per fillet: 205 cal., 10g fat (3g sat. fat), 67mg chol., 265mg sod., 7g carb. (2g sugars, 1g fiber), 24g pro.
Diabetic exchanges: 3 lean meat, 2 fat, ½ starch.

PISTACHIO SALMON

This simple salmon gets its crunch from a coating of crushed pistachios, panko bread crumbs and Parmesan cheese. Add some steamed veggies and rice and it's dinnertime!
—Anthony Oraczewski, Port St. Lucie, FL

Start to Finish: 25 min
Makes: 4 servings

⅓ cup pistachios, finely chopped
¼ cup panko (Japanese) bread crumbs
¼ cup grated Parmesan cheese
1 salmon fillet (1 pound)
½ teaspoon salt
¼ teaspoon pepper

1. Preheat oven to 400°. In a shallow bowl, toss pistachios with bread crumbs and cheese.
2. Place salmon on a greased foil-lined 15x10x1-in. pan, skin side down; sprinkle with salt and pepper. Top with pistachio mixture, pressing to make it adhere. Bake, uncovered, until fish just begins to flake easily with a fork, 15-20 minutes.
3. **Per 3 ounces cooked fish:** 269 cal., 17g fat (3g sat. fat), 61mg chol., 497mg sod., 6g carb. (1g sugars, 1g fiber), 23g pro. **Diabetic exchanges:** 3 lean meat, 1 fat, ½ starch.

HEALTH TIP Save leftover pistachios for snacking! One serving (about 50 nuts) has 6 grams protein, 3 grams fiber and more than 10 percent of the daily value of B6, thiamin, copper and phosphorous.

GRILLED HERB TILAPIA

Trust me: This super tilapia with ginger and lemon takes dinner over the top with minimal prep. Grilling the fish in foil is about as easy as it gets.
—Trisha Kruse, Eagle, ID

Start to Finish: 30 min.
Makes: 4 servings

1 cup fresh cilantro leaves
1 cup fresh parsley leaves
2 tablespoons olive oil
2 teaspoons grated lemon peel
2 tablespoons lemon juice
1 tablespoon coarsely chopped fresh gingerroot
¾ teaspoon sea salt or kosher salt, divided
2 cups grape tomatoes, halved lengthwise
1½ cups fresh or frozen corn (about 8 ounces), thawed
4 tilapia fillets (6 ounces each)

1. Place the first six ingredients in a food processor; add ½ teaspoon salt. Pulse until mixture is finely chopped.
2. In a bowl, combine tomatoes and corn; stir in 1 tablespoon herb mixture and the remaining salt.
3. Place each fillet on a piece of heavy-duty foil (about 12-in. square). Top with herb mixture; spoon tomato mixture alongside fish. Fold foil around fish and vegetables, sealing tightly.
4. Grill, covered, over medium-high heat 6-8 minutes or until fish just begins to flake easily with a fork. Open foil carefully to allow steam to escape.
Per serving: 270 cal., 9g fat (2g sat. fat), 83mg chol., 443mg sod., 15g carb. (6g sugars, 3g fiber), 35g pro.
Diabetic exchanges: 5 lean meat, 1½ fat, 1 vegetable, ½ starch.

PISTACHIO SALMON

MEATLESS MAINS

"We're always up for good ways to use our bumper crop of zucchini. Here's one of our favorites. I serve meatless meals two or three times a week—we can make sure we eat our veggies and save a little on groceries while we're at it."
—Heather Savage, Wood River Junction, RI

White Beans & Bow Ties (p. 218) Black Bean & Sweet Potato Tostadas (p. 223) Spinach-Basil Lasagna (p. 219)
Grilled Tomato Pizzas (p. 224) White Beans & Veggies with Couscous (p. 227) Lentil Burritos (p. 231)

**BLACK BEAN &
SWEET POTATO
RICE BOWLS**

BLACK BEAN &
SWEET POTATO RICE BOWLS

M FAST FIX

*With three hungry boys
in my house, dinners
need to be quick and
filling, and it helps to
sneak in some veggies,
too. This one is a favorite because it's
hearty and simple to customize with
different ingredients.*

—Kim Van Dunk, Caldwell, NJ

Start to Finish: 30 min.
Makes: 4 servings

- ¾ cup uncooked long grain rice
- ¼ teaspoon garlic salt
- 1½ cups water
- 3 tablespoons olive oil, divided
- 1 large sweet potato, peeled and diced
- 1 medium red onion, finely chopped
- 4 cups chopped fresh kale (tough stems removed)
- 1 can (15 ounces) black beans, rinsed and drained
- 2 tablespoons sweet chili sauce
  Lime wedges, optional
  Additional sweet chili sauce, optional

1. Place rice, garlic salt and water in a large saucepan; bring to a boil. Reduce heat; simmer, covered, until water is absorbed and the rice is tender,
15-20 minutes. Remove from heat; let stand for 5 minutes.
2. Meanwhile, in a large skillet, heat 2 tablespoons oil over medium-high heat; saute sweet potato 8 minutes. Add the onion; cook and stir until potato is tender, 4-6 minutes. Add the kale; cook and stir until tender, 3-5 minutes. Stir in beans; heat through.
3. Gently stir 2 tablespoons chili sauce and remaining oil into rice; add to potato mixture. If desired, serve with lime wedges and additional chili sauce.

Per 2 cups: 435 cal., 11g fat (2g sat. fat), 0 chol., 405mg sod., 74g carb. (15g sugars, 8g fiber), 10g pro.

HEALTH TIP Sweet potato + kale + black beans = nearly ⅓ of the daily value for fiber!

WHITE BEANS & BOW TIES

M FAST FIX

(PICTURED ON P. 216)

When we have fresh veggies, we toss them with pasta shapes like penne or bow ties. What a tasty way to enjoy a meatless meal!

—Angela Buchanan, Longmont, CO

Start to Finish: 25 min.
Makes: 4 servings

- 2½ cups uncooked whole wheat bow tie pasta (about 6 ounces)

- 1 tablespoon olive oil
- 1 medium zucchini, sliced
- 2 garlic cloves, minced
- 2 large tomatoes, chopped (about 2½ cups)
- 1 can (15 ounces) cannellini beans, rinsed and drained
- 1 can (2¼ ounces) sliced ripe olives, drained
- ¾ teaspoon freshly ground pepper
- ½ cup crumbled feta cheese

1. Cook pasta according to package directions. Drain, reserving ½ cup pasta water.
2. Meanwhile, in a large skillet, heat oil over medium-high heat; saute zucchini until crisp-tender, 2-4 minutes. Add garlic; cook and stir 30 seconds. Stir in tomatoes, beans, olives and pepper; bring to a boil. Reduce heat; simmer, uncovered, until tomatoes are softened, 3-5 minutes, stirring occasionally.
3. Stir in pasta and enough pasta water to moisten as desired. Stir in cheese.

Per 1½ cups: 348 cal., 9g fat (2g sat. fat), 8mg chol., 394mg sod., 52g carb. (4g sugars, 11g fiber), 15g pro.

HEALTH TIP Boost protein in meatless pasta dishes by using whole wheat noodles, adding white beans or stirring in a little cheese—or all three!

ZUCCHINI CRUST PIZZA ▣

My mother-in-law shared the recipe for this unique pizza with me. It's just right for brunch, lunch or a light supper. Loosen the nutritious zucchini crust from the pan with a metal spatula.

—Ruth Denomme, Englehart, ON

Prep: 20 min. • **Bake:** 25 min.
Makes: 6 slices

- 2 cups shredded zucchini (1 to 1½ medium), squeezed dry
- ½ cup egg substitute or 2 large eggs, lightly beaten
- ¼ cup all-purpose flour
- ¼ teaspoon salt
- 2 cups shredded part-skim mozzarella cheese, divided
- ½ cup grated Parmesan cheese, divided
- 2 small tomatoes, halved, seeded and sliced
- ½ cup chopped onion
- ½ cup julienned green pepper
- 1 teaspoon dried oregano
- ½ teaspoon dried basil

1. Preheat oven to 450°. In a large bowl, combine first four ingredients; stir in ½ cup mozzarella cheese and ¼ cup Parmesan cheese. Transfer to a 12-in. pizza pan coated generously with cooking spray; spread to an 11-in. circle.
2. Bake until golden brown, about 13-16 minutes. Reduce oven setting to 400°. Sprinkle with remaining mozzarella cheese; top with tomatoes, onion, pepper, herbs and remaining Parmesan cheese. Bake until edges are golden brown and cheese is melted, 10-15 minutes.

Per slice: 188 cal., 10g fat (5g sat. fat), 30mg chol., 514mg sod., 12g carb. (4g sugars, 1g fiber), 14g pro.
Diabetic exchanges: 2 vegetable, 2 lean meat, ½ fat.

SPINACH-BASIL LASAGNA ▣
(PICTURED ON P. 217)

In the kitchen, my husband and I like to use classic ingredients in new ways. I came up with this lasagna one day and haven't made another type since. We love it!

—Charlotte Gehle, Brownstown, MI

Prep: 20 min. • **Bake:** 45 min.
Makes: 9 servings

- 1 large egg, lightly beaten
- 2 cups reduced-fat ricotta cheese
- 4 ounces crumbled feta cheese
- ¼ cup grated Parmesan cheese
- ¼ cup chopped fresh basil
- 2 garlic cloves, minced
- ¼ teaspoon pepper
- 1 jar (24 ounces) pasta sauce
- 9 no-cook lasagna noodles
- 3 cups fresh baby spinach
- 2 cups shredded part-skim mozzarella cheese

1. Preheat oven to 350°. Mix the first seven ingredients.
2. Spread ½ cup pasta sauce into a greased 13x9-in. baking dish. Layer with three lasagna noodles, ¾ cup ricotta mixture, 1 cup spinach, ½ cup mozzarella cheese and ⅔ cup sauce. Repeat layers twice. Sprinkle with the remaining mozzarella cheese.
3. Bake, covered, 35 minutes. Uncover; bake until heated through and cheese is melted, 10-15 minutes. Let stand for 5 minutes before serving.

Freeze option: Cover and freeze unbaked lasagna. To use, partially thaw in refrigerator overnight. Remove from refrigerator 30 minutes before baking. Preheat oven to 350°. Bake lasagna as directed, increasing time as necessary to heat through and for a thermometer inserted in center to read 165°.

Per piece: 292 cal., 12g fat (6g sat. fat), 59mg chol., 677mg sod., 27g carb. (10g sugars, 3g fiber), 18g pro.
Diabetic exchanges: 2 starch, 2 medium-fat meat.

ZUCCHINI CRUST PIZZA

NO-COOK FRESH TOMATO SAUCE S C M

Try this sauce at times when you have a box of pasta or a store-bought pizza shell and need a surefire topping. Dinner is served.
—Julianne Schnuck, Milwaukee, WI

Prep: 15 min. + standing
Makes: about 3½ cups

1½ pounds assorted fresh tomatoes, coarsely chopped (about 4½ cups)
⅓ cup minced fresh basil
1 tablespoon olive oil
2 garlic cloves, coarsely chopped
Salt and pepper to taste
Hot cooked angel hair pasta or spaghetti
Grated Parmesan cheese

1. Place tomatoes in a large bowl; stir in basil, oil and garlic. Season with salt and pepper to taste. Let stand at room temperature until juices are released from tomatoes, 30-60 minutes, stirring occasionally.
2. Serve with hot pasta. Sprinkle with Parmesan cheese.

Per ¾ cup sauce: 64 cal., 4g fat (1g sat. fat), 0 chol., 9mg sod., 7g carb. (5g sugars, 2g fiber), 2g pro.
Diabetic exchanges: 1 vegetable, 1 fat.

VEGGIE TACOS

VEGGIE TACOS M FAST FIX

These vegetarian tacos are stuffed with a blend of sauteed cabbage, peppers and black beans that is so filling you won't miss the meat. Top with avocado, cheese or a dollop of sour cream.
—*Taste of Home* Test Kitchen

Start to Finish: 30 min.
Makes: 4 servings

2 tablespoons canola oil
3 cups shredded cabbage
1 medium sweet red pepper, julienned
1 medium onion, halved and sliced
2 teaspoons sugar
1 can (15 ounces) black beans, rinsed and drained
1 cup salsa
1 can (4 ounces) chopped green chilies
1 teaspoon minced garlic
1 teaspoon chili powder
¼ teaspoon ground cumin
8 taco shells, warmed
½ cup shredded cheddar cheese
1 medium ripe avocado, peeled and sliced

1. In a large skillet, heat oil over medium-high heat; saute cabbage, pepper and onion until crisp-tender, about 5 minutes. Sprinkle with sugar.
2. Stir in beans, salsa, chilies, garlic, chili powder and cumin; bring to a boil. Reduce heat; simmer, covered, until flavors are blended, about 5 minutes.
3. Serve in taco shells. Top with cheese and avocado.

Per 2 tacos: 430 cal., 22g fat (5g sat. fat), 14mg chol., 770mg sod., 47g carb. (8g sugars, 10g fiber), 12g pro.

VEGGIE NICOISE SALAD M

More and more people in my workplace are becoming vegetarians. When we cook or eat together, the focus is on fresh produce. This salad combines some of our favorite ingredients in one dish— and with the hard-cooked eggs and kidney beans, it delivers enough protein to satisfy those who are skeptical of vegetarian fare.
—Elizabeth Kelley, Chicago, IL

Prep: 40 min. • **Cook:** 25 min.
Makes: 8 servings

- ⅓ cup olive oil
- ¼ cup lemon juice
- 2 teaspoons minced fresh oregano
- 2 teaspoons minced fresh thyme
- 1 teaspoon Dijon mustard
- 1 garlic clove, minced
- ¼ teaspoon coarsely ground pepper
- ⅛ teaspoon salt

- 1 can (16 ounces) kidney beans, rinsed and drained
- 1 small red onion, halved and thinly sliced
- 1 pound small red potatoes (about 9), halved
- 1 pound fresh asparagus, trimmed
- ½ pound fresh green beans, trimmed
- 12 cups torn romaine (about 2 small bunches)
- 6 hard-boiled large eggs, quartered
- 1 jar (6½ ounces) marinated quartered artichoke hearts, drained
- ½ cup Nicoise or kalamata olives

1. For vinaigrette, whisk together first eight ingredients. In another bowl, toss kidney beans and onion with 1 cup vinaigrette. Set aside bean mixture and remaining vinaigrette.

2. Place potatoes in a saucepan and cover with water. Bring to a boil. Reduce heat; simmer, covered, until tender, 10-15 minutes. Drain. While warm, toss with 1 tablespoon vinaigrette; set aside.

3. In a pot of boiling water, cook asparagus just until crisp-tender, 2-4 minutes. Remove with tongs and immediately drop in ice water. Drain and pat dry. In the same pot of boiling water, cook green beans until crisp-tender, 3-4 minutes. Remove beans; place in ice water. Drain and pat dry.

4. To serve, toss the asparagus with 1 tablespoon vinaigrette; toss green beans with 2 teaspoons vinaigrette. Toss romaine with remaining vinaigrette; place on a platter. Arrange vegetables, kidney bean mixture, eggs, artichoke hearts and olives over top.

Per serving: 329 cal., 19g fat (4g sat. fat), 140mg chol., 422mg sod., 28g carb. (6g sugars, 7g fiber), 12g pro.
Diabetic exchanges: 3 fat, 2 medium-fat meat, 2 vegetable, 1½ starch.

SPINACH PIZZA QUESADILLAS
M FAST FIX ▶

This simple five-ingredient dinner is special to me because my daughter and I created it together. You can make variations with other veggies you might have at home. It's a smart way to get kids to eat their veggies.
—Tanna Mancini, Gulfport, FL

Start to Finish: 20 min.
Makes: 6 servings

- 6 whole wheat tortillas (8 inches)
- 3 cups shredded part-skim mozzarella cheese
- 3 cups chopped fresh spinach
- 1 can (8 ounces) pizza sauce

1. Preheat oven to 400°. On one half of each tortilla, layer ½ cup cheese, ½ cup spinach and about 2 tablespoons sauce. Fold other half over filling. Place on baking sheets coated with cooking spray.

2. Bake until the cheese is melted, about 10-12 minutes.

Per quesadilla: 301 cal., 13g fat (7g sat. fat), 36mg chol., 650mg sod., 29g carb. (3g sugars, 4g fiber), 19g pro.
Diabetic exchanges: 2 starch, 2 medium-fat meat.

VEGGIE NICOISE SALAD

**CHICKPEA & CHIPOTLE
TOSTADAS**

CHICKPEA & CHIPOTLE TOSTADAS M

My young twins love colorful meals they can eat with their hands. In this meatless dish, they eat the chickpeas first and save the tostada for the end.
—Amber Massey, Argyle, TX

Prep: 20 min. • **Cook:** 25 min.
Makes: 6 servings

¾ cup fat-free sour cream
½ cup salsa verde
1 medium sweet red pepper, chopped
1 medium onion, chopped
2 garlic cloves, minced
1 cup vegetable broth
2 cans (15 ounces each) chickpeas, rinsed and drained

2 chipotle peppers in adobo sauce, minced
1 teaspoon ground cumin
½ teaspoon salt
½ cup minced fresh cilantro
2 tablespoons lime juice
12 corn tortillas (6 inches)
 Cooking spray
½ medium head iceberg lettuce, shredded
3 plum tomatoes, chopped
1 medium ripe avocado, peeled and cubed
 Shredded reduced-fat cheddar cheese

1. Preheat broiler. For sauce, mix sour cream and salsa.
2. In a large skillet coated with cooking spray, cook and stir red pepper and onion over medium heat until tender, about 6-8 minutes. Add garlic; cook and stir 1 minute. Stir in broth, chickpeas, chipotles, cumin and salt; bring to a boil. Reduce heat; simmer, covered, 5 minutes.
3. Coarsely mash mixture with a potato masher; stir in cilantro and lime juice. If desired, cook over low heat to thicken, stirring frequently.
4. In batches, spritz both sides of tortillas with cooking spray and place on a baking sheet; broil 4-5 in. from heat until crisp and lightly browned, about 1 minute per side. To serve, top tortillas with chickpea mixture, lettuce, tomatoes, avocado and sauce. Sprinkle with cheese.

Per 2 tostadas: 347 cal., 9g fat (1g sat. fat), 5mg chol., 752mg sod., 59g carb. (11g sugars, 12g fiber), 12g pro.

ROASTED CURRIED CHICKPEAS & CAULIFLOWER

M

When there's not much time to cook, try roasting potatoes and cauliflower with chickpeas for a warm-you-up dinner. Add tofu to the sheet pan if you like.
—Pam Correll, Brockport, PA

Prep: 15 min. • **Bake:** 30 min.
Makes: 4 servings

- 2 pounds potatoes (about 4 medium), peeled and cut into ½-inch cubes
- 1 small head cauliflower, broken into florets (about 3 cups)
- 1 can (15 ounces) chickpeas, rinsed and drained
- 3 tablespoons olive oil
- 2 teaspoons curry powder
- ¾ teaspoon salt
- ¼ teaspoon pepper
- 3 tablespoons minced fresh cilantro or parsley

1. Preheat oven to 400°. Place first seven ingredients in a large bowl; toss to coat. Transfer to a 15x10x1-in. baking pan coated with cooking spray.
2. Roast until the vegetables are tender, 30-35 minutes, stirring occasionally. Sprinkle with cilantro.

Per 1½ cups: 339 cal., 13g fat (2g sat. fat), 0 chol., 605mg sod., 51g carb. (6g sugars, 8g fiber), 8g pro.
Diabetic exchanges: 3 starch, 2 fat, 1 vegetable, 1 lean meat.

ROASTED CURRIED CHICKPEAS & CAULIFLOWER

BLACK BEAN & SWEET POTATO TOSTADAS

M FAST FIX

(PICTURED ON P. 216)

These spicy veggie-packed tostadas won over my meat-loving husband. To make them even faster, shop for baked tostada shells.
—Lauren Delaney-Wallace, Glen Carbon, IL

Start to Finish: 30 min.
Makes: 4 servings

- 1 medium sweet potato, peeled and cut into ½-in. cubes
- ¼ cup fat-free mayonnaise
- 2 teaspoons lime juice
- 1 to 3 teaspoons minced chipotle pepper in adobo sauce
- 2 teaspoons olive oil
- 1 small onion, chopped
- 2 garlic cloves, minced
- 1½ teaspoons ground cumin
- ½ teaspoon onion powder
- ½ teaspoon pepper
- ¼ teaspoon cayenne pepper
- ¼ teaspoon salt
- 1 can (15 ounces) black beans, rinsed and drained
- 8 corn tortillas (6 inches)
  Cooking spray
- 1 cup shredded Monterey Jack cheese
  Shredded lettuce, optional

1. Preheat broiler. Place sweet potato in a microwave-safe bowl; microwave, covered, on high until tender, 2-3 minutes. For sauce, mix mayonnaise, lime juice and chipotle pepper.
2. In a large saucepan, heat oil over medium heat; saute onion until tender, 3-4 minutes. Add garlic and seasonings; cook and stir 1 minute. Stir in beans; heat through. Stir in sweet potato; keep warm.
3. In two batches, spritz both sides of tortillas with cooking spray and place on a baking sheet; broil 4-5 in. from heat until crisp and lightly browned, about 1 minute per side. Sprinkle immediately with cheese. To serve, top tortillas with sauce, bean mixture and, if desired, lettuce.

Per 2 tostadas: 407 cal., 15g fat (6g sat. fat), 27mg chol., 676mg sod., 54g carb. (8g sugars, 10g fiber), 16g pro.

GRILLED TOMATO PIZZAS M
(PICTURED ON P. 216)

My husband and I make grilled pizza with a tangy balsamic glaze, and it tastes as if we used a wood-burning oven.

—Michele Tungett, Rochester, IL

Prep: 30 min. + rising • **Grill:** 5 min./batch
Makes: 6 servings

- 1 package (¼ ounce) active dry yeast
- 1 cup warm water (110° to 115°)
- 6 tablespoons olive oil, divided
- 1 tablespoon honey
- ¼ teaspoon salt
- 2 to 3 cups all-purpose flour
  Cooking spray
- 6 cups cherry tomatoes, halved
- 1 cup fresh basil, torn
- ½ cup balsamic glaze
  Shaved Parmesan cheese, optional

1. Dissolve yeast in warm water. Combine 2 tablespoons oil, honey, salt, yeast mixture and 1½ cups flour; beat on medium speed until smooth. Stir in enough remaining flour to form a soft dough (dough will be sticky).
2. Turn dough onto a floured surface; knead until smooth and elastic, about 6-8 minutes. Place in a greased bowl, turning once to grease the top. Cover; let rise in a warm place until doubled, about 1 hour.
3. Punch down dough; divide into six portions. On a lightly floured surface, roll each portion into an 8x6-in. rectangle. Place each on a greased piece of foil. Spritz with cooking spray; cover with plastic wrap and let rest 10 minutes.
4. In batches, carefully invert crusts onto greased grill rack; peel off foil. Grill, covered, over medium heat until bottom is golden brown, 2-3 minutes. Turn; grill until bottom begins to brown, 1-2 minutes.
5. Remove from grill. Brush tops with remaining oil; top with tomatoes. Grill, covered, until bottom is golden brown and tomatoes are heated through, 1-2 minutes. To serve, add basil, drizzle with glaze and, if desired, top with cheese.
Per pizza: 363 cal., 15g fat (2g sat. fat), 0 chol., 115mg sod., 53g carb. (15g sugars, 3g fiber), 6g pro.

LEMONY GARBANZO SALAD

LEMONY GARBANZO SALAD
M **FAST FIX**

Everybody goes for this super fresh salad with the cumin-coriander dressing, especially on warm days.

—Sonya Labbe, West Hollywood, CA

Start to Finish: 15 min.
Makes: 4 servings

- ¼ cup olive oil
- 3 tablespoons lemon juice
- ¾ teaspoon ground cumin
- ¼ teaspoon salt
- ¼ teaspoon ground coriander
- ¼ teaspoon pepper
- 2 cans (15 ounces each) garbanzo beans or chickpeas, rinsed and drained
- 3 green onions, chopped
- ½ cup plain yogurt
- 1 tablespoon minced fresh parsley
- 1 tablespoon orange marmalade
- 4 cups spring mix salad greens

1. In a large bowl, whisk together the first six ingredients; stir in beans and green onions. In another bowl, mix yogurt, parsley and marmalade.
2. To serve, divide greens among four plates; top with bean mixture. Serve with yogurt sauce.
Per serving: 363 cal., 19g fat (3g sat. fat), 4mg chol., 478mg sod., 41g carb. (10g sugars, 10g fiber), 11g pro.
HEALTH TIP The garbanzo beans are responsible for most of the 10 grams fiber in this salad. They also add folate, vitamin B6, manganese, phosphorous and iron.

CHEESY RIGATONI BAKE M

This is a family favorite. One of our four children always asks for it as a birthday dinner entree.
—Nancy Urbine, Lancaster, OH

Prep: 20 min. • **Bake:** 30 min.
Makes: 2 casseroles (6 servings each)

- 1 package (16 ounces) rigatoni or large tube pasta
- 2 tablespoons butter
- ¼ cup all-purpose flour
- ½ teaspoon salt
- 2 cups whole milk
- ¼ cup water
- 4 large eggs, lightly beaten
- 2 cans (8 ounces each) tomato sauce
- 2 cups shredded part-skim mozzarella cheese
- ¼ cup grated Parmesan cheese

1. Preheat oven to 375°. In a 6-qt. stockpot, cook pasta according to the package directions. Drain; return to the pot. Cool slightly.

2. Meanwhile, in a small saucepan, melt butter over low heat. Stir in flour and salt until smooth; gradually whisk in milk and water. Bring to a boil, stirring constantly; cook and stir until thickened, 1-2 minutes. Remove from heat.

3. Add eggs to pasta, tossing to coat. Divide mixture between two greased 8-in. square baking dishes. Layer each dish with one can tomato sauce, 1 cup mozzarella cheese and half of the white sauce. Sprinkle with Parmesan cheese. Bake, uncovered, until a thermometer reads 160°, 30-35 minutes.

Freeze option: Cover and freeze unbaked casseroles. To use, partially thaw in refrigerator overnight. Remove from refrigerator 30 minutes before baking. Preheat oven to 375°. Cover casserole with foil; bake 40 minutes. Uncover; bake until a thermometer inserted in center reads 165°, 7-10 minutes.

Per 1⅓ cups: 282 cal., 10g fat (5g sat. fat), 85mg chol., 486mg sod., 35g carb. (4g sugars, 2g fiber), 14g pro.
Diabetic exchanges: 2 starch, 1 medium-fat meat, ½ fat.

BLACK-EYED PEAS & PASTA
M FAST FIX

Tradition has it that if you eat black-eyed peas on New Year's Day, you'll enjoy prosperity all year through—but I serve this tasty combination of pasta, peas and tangy tomatoes anytime.
—Marie Malsch, Bridgman, MI

Start to Finish: 30 min.
Makes: 6 servings

- 1 tablespoon olive oil
- 1 cup chopped green pepper
- ½ cup chopped onion
- 1 jalapeno pepper, seeded and chopped
- 3 garlic cloves, minced
- 1 can (28 ounces) crushed tomatoes
- 8 ounces uncooked bow tie pasta (about 3 cups)
- 1 can (15½ ounces) black-eyed peas, rinsed and drained
- 1 to 3 tablespoons minced fresh cilantro
- 1 teaspoon cider vinegar
- 1 teaspoon sugar
- 1 teaspoon salt
- ⅛ teaspoon pepper

1. In a large skillet, heat oil over medium-high heat; saute green pepper, onion, jalapeno and garlic until onion is tender. Add tomatoes; bring to a boil. Simmer, uncovered, 10 minutes.

2. Meanwhile, in a 6-qt. stockpot, cook pasta according to package directions.

3. Add remaining ingredients to tomato mixture; return to a boil. Reduce heat; simmer, uncovered, 10 minutes. Drain pasta; return to pot. Stir in black-eyed pea mixture.

Note: Wear disposable gloves when cutting hot peppers; the oils can burn skin. Avoid touching your face.

Per cup: 266 cal., 4g fat (1g sat. fat), 0 chol., 731mg sod., 50g carb. (10g sugars, 6g fiber), 11g pro.

CHEESY RIGATONI BAKE

SOUTHWEST
VEGETARIAN BAKE

SOUTHWEST
VEGETARIAN BAKE M

*This veggie-packed casserole hits the spot
on chilly nights. But it's equally good any
time I have a taste for Mexican food with
all the fixings, too.*
—Trish Gale, Monticello, IL

Prep: 40 min. • **Bake:** 35 min. + standing
Makes: 8 servings

¾ cup uncooked brown rice
1½ cups water
1 can (15 ounces) black beans, rinsed
    and drained
1 can (11 ounces) Mexicorn, drained
1 can (10 ounces) diced tomatoes and
    green chilies
1 cup shredded reduced-fat cheddar
    cheese

1 cup salsa
1 cup (8 ounces) reduced-fat sour
    cream
¼ teaspoon pepper
½ cup chopped red onion
1 can (2¼ ounces) sliced ripe olives,
    drained
1 cup shredded reduced-fat Mexican
    cheese blend

1. In a small saucepan, bring rice and
water to a boil. Reduce heat; simmer,
covered, until the rice is tender, about
35-40 minutes.
2. Preheat oven to 350°. Place beans,
corn, tomatoes, cheddar cheese and rice
in a large bowl; stir in salsa, sour cream
and pepper. Transfer to a shallow 2½-qt.
baking dish coated with cooking spray.
Sprinkle with onion and olives.

3. Bake, uncovered, 30 minutes. Sprinkle
with Mexican cheese; bake, uncovered,
until heated through and cheese is melted,
5-10 minutes. Let stand for 10 minutes
before serving.
Per cup: 285 cal., 10g fat (5g sat. fat),
21mg chol., 759mg sod., 36g carb.
(6g sugars, 4g fiber), 15g pro.
Diabetic exchanges: 2 starch,
2 vegetable, 1 lean meat, 1 fat.

DID YOU KNOW?
Reduced-fat cheeses have about half the
fat and saturated fat of regular cheeses.
They work well in recipes where the
cheese is melted into a casserole or
baked pasta dish, or blended into a meat
loaf mixture where it can melt and blend
with other flavors.

SPAGHETTI WITH FRESH TOMATO SAUCE M

When my mom made spaghetti sauce, the house would smell so good that I'd open the windows to torture the neighbors. It tastes even more wonderful the next day, when the flavors have really melded.
—Vera Schulze, Holbrook, NY

Prep: 15 min. • **Cook:** 30 min.
Makes: 4 servings

- 2 tablespoons olive oil
- 1 large onion, finely chopped
- 2 pounds plum tomatoes, chopped (about 5 cups)
- 1 teaspoon salt
- ¼ teaspoon pepper
- 8 ounces uncooked spaghetti
- ¼ cup thinly sliced fresh basil
- 1 teaspoon sugar, optional
- Grated Romano cheese and additional basil

1. In a 6-qt. stockpot, heat oil over medium heat; saute onion until tender, 4-6 minutes. Stir in tomatoes, salt and pepper; bring to a boil. Reduce heat; simmer, uncovered, until thickened, 20-25 minutes. Meanwhile, cook spaghetti according to package directions; drain.
2. Stir ¼ cup basil and, if desired, sugar into sauce. Serve over spaghetti. Top with cheese and additional basil.
Freeze option: Freeze cooled sauce in freezer containers. To use, partially thaw in refrigerator overnight. Heat through in a saucepan, stirring occasionally.
Per cup spaghetti with ¾ cup sauce: 327 cal., 8g fat (1g sat. fat), 0 chol., 607mg sod., 55g carb. (9g sugars, 5g fiber), 10g pro.

SPAGHETTI WITH FRESH TOMATO SAUCE

WHITE BEANS & VEGGIES WITH COUSCOUS M FAST FIX
(PICTURED ON P. 217)

We're always up for good ways to use our bumper crop of zucchini. Here's one of our favorites. I serve meatless meals two or three times a week—we can make sure we eat our veggies and save a little on groceries while we're at it.
—Heather Savage, Wood River Junction, RI

Start to Finish: 25 min.
Makes: 4 servings

- 1 tablespoon olive oil
- 1 medium zucchini, quartered lengthwise and thinly sliced
- 1 medium onion, finely chopped
- 4 garlic cloves, minced
- 1 can (15 ounces) white kidney or cannellini beans, rinsed and drained
- 1 can (14½ ounces) diced tomatoes, undrained
- ½ teaspoon dried basil
- ¼ teaspoon dried rosemary, crushed
- ¼ teaspoon pepper
- ⅛ teaspoon salt

COUSCOUS

- 1½ cups water
- 1 tablespoon butter
- ¼ teaspoon salt
- 1 cup uncooked couscous

1. In a large skillet, heat oil over medium-high heat; saute zucchini and onion until tender, 3-4 minutes. Add garlic; cook and stir 1 minute.
2. Stir in beans, tomatoes and seasonings; bring to a boil. Reduce heat; simmer, uncovered, until slightly thickened and zucchini is tender, 3-4 minutes, stirring occasionally.
3. Meanwhile, in a small saucepan, combine water, butter and salt; bring to a boil. Stir in couscous. Remove from heat; let stand, covered, until water is absorbed, about 5 minutes. Fluff with a fork. Serve bean mixture with couscous.
Freeze option: Freeze cooled bean mixture in freezer containers. To use, partially thaw in refrigerator overnight. Heat through in a saucepan, stirring occasionally.
Per cup bean mixture with ¾ cup couscous: 350 cal., 8g fat (2g sat. fat), 8mg chol., 521mg sod., 60g carb. (7g sugars, 9g fiber), 13g pro.

MUSHROOM CAPRESE PIZZA

MUSHROOM CAPRESE PIZZA M

When my tomatoes ripen all at once, I use them up in simple recipes like this one. Cheesy baguette pizzas, served with a salad, are ideal for lunch—and they make standout appetizers, too.
—Lorraine Caland, Shuniah, ON

Prep: 25 min. • **Bake:** 10 min.
Makes: 6 servings

- 2 teaspoons olive oil
- 8 ounces sliced fresh mushrooms
- 2 medium onions, halved and sliced
- 2 garlic cloves, minced
- ½ teaspoon Italian seasoning
- ¼ teaspoon salt
    Dash pepper
- 1 French bread baguette
    (10½ ounces), halved lengthwise
- 1½ cups shredded part-skim mozzarella cheese
- ¾ cup thinly sliced fresh basil leaves, divided
- 3 medium tomatoes, sliced

1. Preheat oven to 400°. In a large skillet, heat oil over medium-high heat; saute mushrooms and onions until tender. Add garlic and seasonings; cook and stir 1 minute.
2. Place baguette halves on a baking sheet, cut side up; sprinkle with half of the cheese and ½ cup basil. Top with the mushroom mixture, tomatoes and remaining cheese.
3. Bake until the cheese is melted, about 10-15 minutes. Sprinkle with remaining basil. Cut each half into three portions.

Per piece: 260 cal., 7g fat (4g sat. fat), 18mg chol., 614mg sod., 36g carb. (5g sugars, 3g fiber), 13g pro.
Diabetic exchanges: 2 starch, 1 vegetable, 1 medium-fat meat.

✳

TEST KITCHEN TIP
If you don't have Italian seasoning, you can mix up your own with equal amounts of basil, thyme, rosemary and oregano. You can also add parsley flakes, marjoram, sage, savory or garlic powder.

VEGETARIAN PAD THAI

VEGETARIAN PAD THAI
M FAST FIX

This is a simple pad Thai loaded with crisp vegetables and zesty flavor. It's quick, simple, and fresh-tasting.
—Colleen Doucette, Truro, NS

Start to Finish: 30 min.
Makes: 4 servings

- 6 ounces uncooked thick rice noodles
- 2 tablespoons packed brown sugar
- 3 tablespoons reduced-sodium soy sauce
- 4 teaspoons rice vinegar
- 2 teaspoons lime juice
- 2 teaspoons olive oil
- 3 medium carrots, shredded
- 1 medium sweet red pepper, cut into thin strips
- 4 green onions, chopped
- 3 garlic cloves, minced
- 4 large eggs, lightly beaten
- 2 cups bean sprouts
- ⅓ cup chopped fresh cilantro
    Chopped peanuts, optional
    Lime wedges

1. Prepare noodles according to package directions. Drain; rinse well and drain again. In a small bowl, mix together brown sugar, soy sauce, vinegar and lime juice.
2. In a large nonstick skillet, heat oil over medium-high heat; stir-fry carrots and pepper until crisp-tender, 3-4 minutes. Add green onions and garlic; cook and stir 2 minutes. Remove from pan.
3. Reduce heat to medium. Pour eggs into the same pan; cook and stir until no liquid egg remains. Stir in carrot mixture, noodles and sauce mixture; heat through. Add bean sprouts; toss to combine. Top with cilantro and, if desired, peanuts. Serve with lime wedges.

Per 1¼ cups: 339 cal., 8g fat (2g sat. fat), 186mg chol., 701mg sod., 55g carb. (15g sugars, 4g fiber), 12g pro.

LENTIL BOWLS F M FAST FIX

An Ethiopian recipe inspired this feel-good dinner that's tangy, creamy and packed with hearty comfort.
—Rachael Cushing, Portland, OR

Start to Finish: 30 min.
Makes: 6 servings

- 1 tablespoon olive oil
- 2 medium onions, chopped
- 4 garlic cloves, minced
- 2 cups dried brown lentils, rinsed
- 1 teaspoon salt
- ½ teaspoon ground ginger
- ½ teaspoon paprika
- ¼ teaspoon pepper
- 3 cups water
- ¼ cup lemon juice
- 3 tablespoons tomato paste
- ¾ cup fat-free plain Greek yogurt
  Chopped tomatoes and minced fresh cilantro, optional

1. In a large saucepan, heat oil over medium-high heat; saute onions for 2 minutes. Add garlic; cook 1 minute. Stir in lentils, seasonings and water; bring to a boil. Reduce heat; simmer, covered, until lentils are tender, 25-30 minutes.
2. Stir in lemon juice and tomato paste; heat through. Serve with yogurt and, if desired, tomatoes and cilantro.

Per ¾ cup: 294 cal., 3g fat (0 sat. fat), 0 chol., 419mg sod., 49g carb. (5g sugars, 8g fiber), 21g pro.
Diabetic exchanges: 3 starch, 2 lean meat, ½ fat.

HEALTH TIP Cup for cup, lentils have twice as much protein and iron as quinoa.

SAUCY VEGGIE SPIRALS

SAUCY VEGGIE SPIRALS
M FAST FIX

This is my daughter Tonya's favorite meal. Sometimes we make it with rigatoni and call it Riga-Tonya. Either way, it's a quick, wonderful way to prepare some yummy vegetables for your kids.
—Sandra Eckert, Pottstown, PA

Start to Finish: 20 min.
Makes: 6 servings

- 8 ounces uncooked gluten-free spiral pasta
- 1 tablespoon olive oil
- 1 large onion, coarsely chopped
- 1 large sweet red or green pepper, coarsely chopped
- 1 medium zucchini, halved lengthwise and sliced
- 1 package (16 ounces) firm tofu, drained and cut into ½-inch cubes
- 2 cups gluten-free meatless pasta sauce

1. Cook pasta according to package directions; drain.
2. Meanwhile, in a large skillet, heat oil over medium heat; saute the onion, pepper and zucchini until crisp-tender, 6-8 minutes. Stir in tofu and pasta sauce; heat through. Stir in pasta.

Note: Read all ingredient labels for possible gluten content prior to use. Ingredient formulas can change, and production facilities vary among brands. If you're concerned that your brand may contain gluten, contact the company.

Per 1¼ cups tofu mixture with ⅔ cup pasta: 267 cal., 7g fat (1g sat. fat), 0 chol., 380mg sod., 43g carb. (8g sugars, 4g fiber), 11g pro.
Diabetic exchanges: 2½ starch, 1 vegetable, 1 lean meat, ½ fat.

WARM SQUASH & QUINOA SALAD M FAST FIX

Whenever I see butternut squash at the supermarket, I buy one. It's amazing tossed with earthy quinoa, Italian spices and crunchy pine nuts. And don't get me started on the browned butter! Yum.
—Carly Taylor, Libertyville, IL

Start to Finish: 30 min.
Makes: 6 servings

- 2 cups quinoa, rinsed
- 3 teaspoons ground cumin
- 3 cups water
- 2 tablespoons butter
- 3½ cups cubed peeled butternut squash (about ½ medium)
- 1 teaspoon sea salt
- ¾ teaspoon Italian seasoning
- ¼ teaspoon coarsely ground pepper
- ½ cup crumbled feta cheese
  Toasted pine nuts, optional

1. In a large saucepan, combine quinoa, cumin and water; bring to a boil. Reduce heat; simmer, covered, until liquid is absorbed, 10-13 minutes. Remove from heat; keep warm.

2. Meanwhile, in a large skillet, heat the butter over medium-low heat until golden brown, 3-5 minutes, stirring constantly. Immediately stir in the cubed squash and seasonings; cook, covered, until tender, 10-12 minutes, stirring occasionally. Add to quinoa, stirring gently to combine. Top with cheese and, if desired, pine nuts.

Per cup: 314 cal., 9g fat (4g sat. fat), 15mg chol., 449mg sod., 49g carb. (2g sugars, 7g fiber), 11g pro.

LENTIL BURRITOS M FAST FIX
(PICTURED ON P. 217)

I'm constantly trying to incorporate healthy but tasty meals into our menu. Both kids and adults love these burritos that combine lentils and zucchini.
—Pam Masters, Wickenburg, AZ

Start to Finish: 30 min.
Makes: 8 burritos

- 2 cups water
- 1 cup dried brown lentils
- 2 tablespoons dried minced onion
- ½ teaspoon dried minced garlic
- ½ teaspoon ground cumin
- ⅛ teaspoon hot pepper sauce
- 1 small zucchini, chopped
- 1 cup taco sauce
- 1 cup shredded part-skim mozzarella cheese
- 8 flour tortillas (8 inches), warmed

1. Place first six ingredients in a large saucepan; bring to a boil. Reduce heat; simmer, covered, until lentils are tender, 15-20 minutes. Drain if necessary.

2. Stir zucchini, taco sauce and cheese into lentils. To serve, place about ½ cup lentil mixture on each tortilla and roll up.

Per burrito: 313 cal., 7g fat (3g sat. fat), 9mg chol., 452mg sod., 47g carb. (4g sugars, 5g fiber), 14g pro.

Diabetic exchanges: 3 starch, 2 lean meat, 1 fat.

WARM SQUASH & QUINOA SALAD

TREAT
YOURSELF

"These cool, creamy pops are a deliciously different way to use up the bounty from your rhubarb patch. They really hit the spot on a warm summer day."
—Donna Linihan, Moncton, NB

Marinated Oranges (p. 238) **Old-Fashioned Rice Pudding** (p. 253) **Ribbon Pudding Pie** (p. 247)
Triple-Berry Cobbler (p. 244) **Strawberry-Rhubarb Ice Pops** (p. 237) **Chocolate-Dipped Phyllo Sticks** (p. 239)

CHOCOLATY S'MORES BARS

CHOCOLATY S'MORES BARS

One night, my husband had some friends over to play poker and he asked for these s'mores bars. They polished off the pan and asked for more! I shared the recipe, and now his friends can make them at home, too.

—Rebecca Shipp, Beebe, AR

Prep: 15 min. + cooling
Makes: 1½ dozen

- ¼ cup butter, cubed
- 1 package (10 ounces) large marshmallows
- 1 package (12 ounces) Golden Grahams cereal
- ⅓ cup milk chocolate chips, melted

1. In a large saucepan, melt butter over low heat. Add marshmallows; cook and stir until blended. Remove from heat. Stir in cereal until coated.
2. Press into a greased 13x9-in. pan using a buttered spatula. Drizzle with melted chocolate. Cool completely before cutting. Store in an airtight container.

Per bar: 159 cal., 4g fat (2g sat. fat), 7mg chol., 197mg sod., 30g carb. (17g sugars, 1g fiber), 1g pro.

YUMMY ZUCCHINI CHOCOLATE CAKE M

As a confirmed chocoholic, I'd rank this as my all-time favorite treat. I found the original recipe more than 20 years ago, but have lightened it up quite a bit. Everyone asks for the recipe, and no one suspects that it's lighter than most chocolate cakes.

—Carleta Foltz, Sunrise Beach, MO

Prep: 20 min. • **Bake:** 30 min.
Makes: 18 servings

- 1¾ cups sugar
- ½ cup canola oil
- 2 large eggs
- ⅔ cup unsweetened applesauce
- 1 teaspoon vanilla extract
- 2½ cups all-purpose flour
- ½ cup baking cocoa
- 1 teaspoon baking soda
- ½ teaspoon salt
- ½ cup buttermilk
- 2 cups shredded zucchini
- 1 cup (6 ounces) miniature semisweet chocolate chips
- ½ cup chopped pecans, toasted

1. Preheat oven to 350°. Coat a 13x9-in. baking pan with cooking spray.
2. Beat sugar and oil on medium speed 1 minute. Add the eggs, applesauce and vanilla; beat 1 minute. In another bowl, whisk together flour, cocoa, baking soda and salt; add to sugar mixture alternately with buttermilk, beating just until blended. Stir in zucchini.

Transfer to the prepared pan. Bake for 20 minutes. Sprinkle with chocolate chips and pecans. Bake until toothpick inserted in center comes out clean, 10-15 minutes. Cool in pan on a wire rack.

Note: To toast nuts, bake in a shallow pan in a 350° oven for 5-10 minutes or cook in a skillet over low heat until they are lightly browned, stirring occasionally.

Per piece: 285 cal., 12g fat (3g sat. fat), 21mg chol., 159mg sod., 43g carb. (27g sugars, 2g fiber), 4g pro.

NO-BAKE APPLE PIE

We always have an abundance of apples in the fall, so I like to make this easy pie. My husband has diabetes, and this recipe fits into his diet...but everyone enjoys it.
—Shirley Vredenburg, Ossineke, MI

Prep: 20 min. + chilling
Makes: 8 servings

- 1 package (0.3 ounce) sugar-free lemon gelatin
- ½ teaspoon ground cinnamon
- ¼ teaspoon ground nutmeg
- 1¾ cups water, divided
- 5 medium tart apples, peeled and sliced
- 1 package (0.8 ounce) sugar-free cook-and-serve vanilla pudding mix
- ½ cup chopped nuts
- 1 reduced-fat graham cracker crust (6 ounces)
  Whipped topping, optional

1. In a large saucepan, mix the gelatin, cinnamon, nutmeg and 1½ cups water. Add apples; bring to a boil. Reduce heat; simmer, covered, until apples are tender, about 5 minutes.

2. In a bowl, mix the pudding mix and remaining water; stir into apple mixture. Cook until thickened, about 1 minute, stirring occasionally. Remove from heat; stir in nuts. Transfer to crust.

3. Refrigerate for at least 2 hours before serving. If desired, serve the apple pie with whipped topping.

Per piece: 202 cal., 8g fat (1g sat. fat), 0 chol., 152mg sod., 30g carb. (17g sugars, 2g fiber), 3g pro.
Diabetic exchanges: 1½ fat, 1 starch, 1 fruit.

DID YOU KNOW?

Cinnamon comes in two basic types: Ceylon and cassia. Ceylon cinnamon's delicate, complex flavor is ideal for ice creams, sauces, and quick fillings like this one. The spicy, bolder cassia cinnamon (often labeled simply as cinnamon) is preferred for baking.

CRANBERRY PEAR CRISP ⑤ Ⓜ

A dollop of fat-free frozen yogurt tames the tartness of juicy cranberries in this treasured recipe. I don't recall just where I found it, but it's been a family favorite for at least 20 years.
—Ruth Fox, Elmhurst, IL

Prep: 20 min. • **Bake:** 30 min.
Makes: 8 servings

- 1 package (12 ounces) fresh or frozen cranberries, thawed
- 2 large pears, peeled and sliced
  Sugar substitute equivalent to ½ cup sugar
- ¼ cup sugar
- 6 teaspoons all-purpose flour, divided
- ¾ teaspoon ground cinnamon
- ⅓ cup old-fashioned oats
- 2 tablespoons brown sugar
- 2 tablespoons butter, softened
- ¼ cup chopped walnuts
  Low-fat vanilla frozen yogurt, optional

1. Preheat the oven to 375°. Place the cranberries and pears in a large bowl. Mix sugar substitute, sugar, 1 teaspoon flour and cinnamon; toss with fruit. Transfer to an 8-in. square baking dish coated with cooking spray.

2. In a small bowl, mix oats, brown sugar, butter and remaining flour until crumbly; stir in walnuts. Sprinkle over fruit.

3. Bake, uncovered, until the topping is golden brown and pears are tender, about 30-35 minutes. Serve warm. If desired, top with frozen yogurt.

Note: This recipe was tested with Splenda no-calorie sweetener.

Per serving: 165 cal., 6g fat (2g sat. fat), 8mg chol., 25mg sod., 29g carb. (17g sugars, 4g fiber), 2g pro.
Diabetic exchanges: 1 starch, 1 fruit, 1 fat.

NO-BAKE APPLE PIE

OLD-FASHIONED HONEY BAKED APPLES F S M

My baked apple recipe may be very old-fashioned, but it's tried and true. It's definitely a comfort food.
—Rachel Hamilton, Greenville, PA

Prep: 10 min. • **Bake:** 35 min.
Makes: 2 servings

- 2 medium tart apples
- ¼ cup dried cranberries
- ⅔ cup water
- ¼ cup packed brown sugar
- 1 tablespoon honey
  Vanilla ice cream or sweetened whipped cream, optional

1. Preheat oven to 350°. Core apples, leaving bottoms intact; peel top third of each. Place in a greased 8x4-in. glass loaf pan; fill with cranberries.
2. In a small saucepan, combine the water, brown sugar and honey; cook and stir over medium heat until sugar is dissolved. Pour over apples.
3. Bake, uncovered, until the apples are tender, 35-40 minutes, basting occasionally with juices. If desired, serve with ice cream.

Per baked apple: 253 cal., 0 fat (0 sat. fat), 0 chol., 13mg sod., 67g carb. (59g sugars, 4g fiber), 0 pro.

COCONUT CREAM CAKE

COCONUT CREAM CAKE M

Have the urge to splurge? Try this moist and mouthwatering cake. No one who's ever eaten a piece can believe it's from a lower-fat recipe.
—Deborah Protzman, Bloomington, IL

Prep: 20 min. + chilling
Bake: 20 min. + cooling
Makes: 15 servings

- 1 package white cake mix (regular size)
- 3 large egg whites
- 1¼ cups water
- ⅓ cup sweetened shredded coconut
- 1 can (14 ounces) fat-free sweetened condensed milk
- 1 teaspoon coconut extract

TOPPING
- 1½ cups reduced-fat whipped topping
- ⅓ cup sweetened shredded coconut, toasted

1. Preheat oven to 350°. Coat a 13x9-in. pan with cooking spray.
2. Beat cake mix, egg whites, water and coconut on low speed 30 seconds. Beat on medium for 2 minutes. Transfer to the prepared pan. Bake until a toothpick inserted in center comes out clean, 20-25 minutes. Cool on a wire rack 10 minutes.
3. Mix milk and extract. Using a large meat fork, poke holes in cake. Gently spread half of the milk mixture over cake; let stand for 3 minutes. Spread with the remaining milk mixture; cool 1 hour.
4. Spread with whipped topping; sprinkle with the toasted coconut. Refrigerate, covered, until cold, about 4 hours.

Note: To toast coconut, bake in a shallow pan in a 350° oven for 5-10 minutes or cook in a skillet over low heat until golden brown, stirring occasionally.

Per piece: 231 cal., 4g fat (3g sat. fat), 3mg chol., 266mg sod., 44g carb. (32g sugars, 1g fiber), 4g pro.

CHOCOLATE MACAROON CUPCAKES F S M

A delightful coconut and ricotta cheese filling is hidden inside these cupcakes.
—Dolores Skrout, Summerhill, PA

Prep: 20 min. • **Bake:** 30 min. + cooling
Makes: 1½ dozen

- 2 large egg whites
- 1 large egg
- ⅓ cup unsweetened applesauce
- 1 teaspoon vanilla extract
- 1¼ cups all-purpose flour
- 1 cup sugar
- ⅓ cup baking cocoa
- ½ teaspoon baking soda
- ¾ cup buttermilk

FILLING

- 1 cup reduced-fat ricotta cheese
- ¼ cup sugar
- 1 large egg white
- ⅓ cup sweetened shredded coconut
- ½ teaspoon coconut or almond extract
  Confectioners' sugar

1. Preheat oven to 350°. Coat 18 muffin cups with cooking spray.
2. Beat first four ingredients until well blended. In another bowl, whisk together the flour, sugar, cocoa and baking soda; gradually beat into egg mixture alternately with buttermilk.
3. For filling, beat ricotta cheese, sugar and egg white until blended. Stir in the coconut and extract.
4. Fill the prepared cups with half of the batter. Drop filling by tablespoonfuls into the center of each cupcake; cover with remaining batter.
5. Bake until a toothpick inserted in the cupcake portion comes out clean, about 28-33 minutes. Cool 10 minutes before removing from pans to wire racks; cool completely. Dust the cupcakes with confectioners' sugar.

Per cupcake: 126 cal., 2g fat (1g sat. fat), 14mg chol., 85mg sod., 24g carb. (16g sugars, 1g fiber), 4g pro.
Diabetic exchanges: 1½ starch.

STRAWBERRY-RHUBARB ICE POPS F S M

(PICTURED ON P. 233)

These cool, creamy pops are a deliciously different way to use up the bounty from your rhubarb patch. They really hit the spot on a warm summer day.
—Donna Linihan, Moncton, NB

Prep: 10 min. + freezing
Cook: 15 min. + cooling
Makes: 8 pops

- 3 cups chopped fresh or frozen rhubarb (½ inch)
- ¼ cup sugar
- 3 tablespoons water
- 1 cup (8 ounces) strawberry yogurt
- ½ cup unsweetened applesauce
- ¼ cup finely chopped fresh strawberries
- 2 drops red food coloring, optional
- 8 freezer pop molds or 8 paper cups (3 ounces each) and wooden pop sticks

1. Place rhubarb, sugar and water in a large saucepan; bring to a boil. Reduce heat; simmer, uncovered, until thick and blended, 10-15 minutes. Remove ¾ cup mixture to a bowl; cool completely. (Save remaining rhubarb for another use).
2. Add the yogurt, applesauce and strawberries to bowl; stir until blended. If desired, tint with food coloring. Fill each mold or cup with about ¼ cup rhubarb mixture. Top molds with holders; top cups with foil and insert sticks through foil. Freeze until firm.
Note: If using frozen rhubarb, measure rhubarb while still frozen, then thaw completely. Drain in a colander, but do not press liquid out.
Per pop: 72 cal., 0 fat (0 sat. fat), 2mg chol., 18mg sod., 16g carb. (14g sugars, 1g fiber), 2g pro.
Diabetic exchanges: 1 fruit.

CHOCOLATE MACAROON CUPCAKES

**LIME & SPICE
PEACH COBBLER**

LIME & SPICE PEACH COBBLER M

This was my grandmother's favorite recipe to make when the peaches were in great abundance. Now I bake it often for my family and friends.
—Mary Ann Dell, Phoenixville, PA

Prep: 25 min. • **Bake:** 35 min.
Makes: 8 servings

- 3 **tablespoons sugar**
- 3 **tablespoons brown sugar**
- 2 **tablespoons minced crystallized ginger**
- 4 **teaspoons cornstarch**
- 2 **teaspoons ground cinnamon**
- ½ **teaspoon grated lime peel**
- 8 **medium peaches, peeled and sliced (about 5 cups)**
- 1 **tablespoon lime juice**

TOPPINGS

- 3 **tablespoons butter, softened**
- ¼ **cup packed brown sugar**
- 2 **tablespoons sugar**
- 1 **cup cake flour**
- ½ **teaspoon baking powder**
- ¼ **teaspoon salt**
- 2 **tablespoons cold water**
- ¼ **cup chopped pecans**
- 1 **large egg yolk**
- 2 **tablespoons buttermilk**

1. Preheat oven to 375°. Mix the first six ingredients; toss with peaches and lime juice. Transfer to an 8-in. square baking dish coated with cooking spray.
2. For topping, beat the butter and sugars until blended. Whisk together flour, baking powder and salt; beat into butter mixture. Beat in water just until crumbly. Stir in the pecans; crumble over filling.
3. Whisk together the egg yolk and buttermilk; brush carefully over crumb mixture. Bake until the topping is golden brown and filling is bubbly, 35-40 minutes. Serve warm.

Per serving: 287 cal., 8g fat (3g sat. fat), 35mg chol., 152mg sod., 53g carb. (33g sugars, 3g fiber), 4g pro

MARINATED ORANGES F S M
(PICTURED ON P. 232)

I marinated oranges for a cake topping. Then I discovered they make a puckery good dessert all by themselves, topped with vanilla yogurt.
—Carol Poindexter, Norridge, IL

Prep: 15 min. + marinating
Makes: 4 servings

- 1 **tablespoon grated orange peel**
- 1 **cup orange juice**
- 1 **teaspoon grated lemon peel**
- 1 **tablespoon lemon juice**
- 1 **tablespoon sugar**
- 1 **teaspoon vanilla extract**
- 4 **medium oranges, peeled and thinly sliced (about 3 cups)**
  Lime peel strips and vanilla yogurt, optional

1. Mix first six ingredients, stirring until sugar is dissolved. Place oranges in a glass bowl; add juice mixture.
2. Refrigerate, covered, until flavors are blended, 2-3 hours. If desired, top with lime peel and serve with yogurt.

Per ¾ cup: 86 cal., 0 fat (0 sat. fat), 0 chol., 7mg sod., 20g carb. (16g sugars, 0 fiber), 1g pro.
Diabetic exchanges: 1½ fruit.

★ ★ ★ ★ ★ **READER REVIEW**
"This is a nice refreshing dessert, but it's also great for breakfast."

LINDAS_WI TASTEOFHOME.COM

MAKEOVER FRUIT PIZZA

CHOCOLATE-DIPPED PHYLLO STICKS F S C M
(PICTURED ON P. 233)

Looking for something light and special to bake up for the holidays? Try these crunchy treats. They're great with coffee or alongside sorbet and sherbet.
—Peggy Woodward, Shullsburg, WI

Prep: 30 min. • **Bake:** 5 min.
Makes: 20 sticks

  4 sheets phyllo dough (14x9-inch size)
  2 tablespoons butter, melted
  1 tablespoon sugar
  ¼ teaspoon ground cinnamon
     Cooking spray
  2 ounces semisweet chocolate, finely chopped
  ½ teaspoon shortening
  ½ ounce white baking chocolate, melted

1. Preheat oven to 425°. Place one sheet of phyllo dough on a work surface; brush with butter. Cover with a second sheet of phyllo; brush with butter. (Keep remaining phyllo dough covered with plastic wrap and a damp towel to stop it from drying out.) Cut phyllo lengthwise in half; cut each half crosswise into five rectangles (4½x2¾ in.). Tightly roll up rectangles jelly-roll style, starting with a long side.
2. Mix the sugar and cinnamon. Lightly coat sticks with cooking spray; sprinkle with 1½ teaspoons sugar mixture. Place on an ungreased baking sheet. Bake until lightly browned, 3-5 minutes. Remove to a wire rack to cool. Repeat with the remaining ingredients.
3. In a microwave, melt the semisweet chocolate and shortening; stir until it is smooth. Dip one end of each phyllo stick in chocolate; allow extra to drip off. Place on waxed paper; let stand until set. Drizzle with white chocolate.
Per phyllo stick: 42 cal., 3g fat (2g sat. fat), 3mg chol., 19mg sod., 3g carb. (2g sugars, 0 fiber), 0 pro.

MAKEOVER FRUIT PIZZA S M

Refreshing fruit pizzas are now growing in popularity from coast to coast. That's why we skimmed the calories and fat from a traditional version and created this delightful treat. It has nearly half of the calories, fat and cholesterol of the dessert pizzas you'd find at a gourmet bakery.
—*Taste of Home* Test Kitchen

Prep: 25 min. + chilling
Bake: 10 min. + cooling
Makes: 16 servings

  1 cup all-purpose flour
  ¼ cup confectioners' sugar
  ½ cup cold butter, cubed
GLAZE
  5 teaspoons cornstarch
  1¼ cups unsweetened pineapple juice
  1 teaspoon lemon juice
TOPPINGS
  1 package (8 ounces) reduced-fat cream cheese
  ⅓ cup sugar
  1 teaspoon vanilla extract
  2 cups halved fresh strawberries
  1 cup fresh blueberries
  1 can (11 ounces) mandarin oranges, drained

1. Preheat oven to 350°. In a large bowl, mix flour and confectioners' sugar; cut in butter until crumbly. Press onto an ungreased 12-in. pizza pan. Bake until very lightly browned, 10-12 minutes. Cool completely on a wire rack.
2. In a small saucepan, mix the glaze ingredients until smooth; bring to a boil. Cook and stir until thickened, about 2 minutes. Cool slightly.
3. In a bowl, beat cream cheese, sugar and vanilla until smooth. Spread over crust. Top with berries and mandarin oranges. Drizzle with glaze. Refrigerate until cold.
Per slice: 170 cal., 9 fat (6g sat. fat), 25mg chol., 120mg sod., 20g carb. (13g sugars, 1g fiber), 3g pro.
Diabetic exchanges: 1½ fat, 1 starch, ½ fruit.

SWEET POTATO CRISP

SOUR CREAM BAVARIAN ⒻⓈ

Are you perhaps sweet on someone who is counting calories? Show them you care with this light and refreshing dessert. It's sinfully creamy and so pretty with the tart raspberry sauce. No one would ever guess that it's fat-free!
—Judi Janczewski, Berwyn, IL

Prep: 10 min. + chilling • **Cook:** 5 min.
Makes: 8 servings (1¼ cups sauce)

- 1 envelope unflavored gelatin
- ¾ cup cold water
- ⅔ cup sugar
- 1 cup (8 ounces) fat-free sour cream
- 1 teaspoon vanilla extract
- 2 cups fat-free whipped topping

SAUCE
- 1 package (10 ounces) frozen sweetened raspberries or sliced strawberries, thawed
- 1 tablespoon cornstarch
- 1 tablespoon sugar

1. In a small saucepan, sprinkle gelatin over cold water; let stand 1 minute. Add sugar; heat and stir over low heat until gelatin and sugar are completely dissolved. Transfer to a bowl; whisk in sour cream and vanilla. Refrigerate 10 minutes.
2. Fold in whipped topping. Pour into a 4-cup mold coated with cooking spray. Refrigerate, covered, 4 hours or until firm.
3. For sauce, drain berries, reserving syrup. Add enough water to the syrup to measure ¾ cup. In a small saucepan, mix cornstarch, sugar and syrup mixture until smooth. Bring to a boil; cook and stir until thickened, about 2 minutes. Cool slightly. Stir in the drained berries; refrigerate until serving.
4. To serve, unmold the dessert onto a serving plate. Serve with sauce.
Per piece: 176 cal., 0 fat (0 sat. fat), 1mg chol., 37mg sod., 33g carb. (30g sugars, 2g fiber), 3g pro.

SWEET POTATO CRISP Ⓜ

My not-too-sweet potato crisp features a wonderful buttery crumb topping. I found it a welcome change from candied sweet potatoes.
—Kathy Hamsher, Moon Township, PA

Prep: 40 min. • **Bake:** 35 min.
Makes: 12 servings

- 4 medium sweet potatoes (about 2½ pounds), peeled and cut into 1-inch cubes
- 1 package (8 ounces) fat-free cream cheese
- ¼ teaspoon ground cinnamon
- 2 medium apples, quartered
- 1 cup fresh or frozen cranberries
- ½ cup all-purpose flour
- ½ cup quick-cooking oats
- ½ cup packed brown sugar
- 3 tablespoons cold butter
- ¼ cup chopped pecans

1. Preheat oven to 350°. Place the sweet potatoes in a large saucepan; add water to cover. Bring to a boil. Reduce heat; cook, uncovered, until tender, 10-15 minutes. Drain well.
2. In a large bowl, beat the potatoes, cream cheese and cinnamon until smooth. Spread into an 11x7-in. baking dish coated with cooking spray. In a food processor, pulse the apples and cranberries until chopped; spread over potato mixture.
3. In a small bowl, mix the flour, oats and brown sugar; cut in butter until crumbly. Stir in the pecans; sprinkle over top. Bake, uncovered, until topping is golden brown and apples are tender, 35-40 minutes.
Per serving: 206 cal., 5g fat (2g sat. fat), 10mg chol., 165mg sod., 36g carb. (19g sugars, 3g fiber), 5g pro.
Diabetic exchanges: 2 starch, 1 fat.

SOUR CREAM BAVARIAN

COOKOUT CARAMEL S'MORES F S FAST FIX

These classic treats make a great finish to an informal meal. And toasting the marshmallows extends our after-dinner time together, giving us something fun to do as a family.
—Martha Haseman, Hinckley, IL

Start to Finish: 10 min.
Makes: 4 servings

- 4 whole graham crackers, halved
- 8 large marshmallows, toasted
- 2 teaspoons hot caramel ice cream topping, warmed if necessary
- 2 teaspoons chocolate syrup

Top four graham cracker halves with toasted marshmallows. Drizzle with caramel topping and chocolate syrup; top with remaining crackers.

Per s'more: 127 cal., 2g fat (0 sat. fat), 0 chol., 119mg sod., 28g carb. (16g sugars, 1g fiber), 1g pro.

★ ★ ★ ★ ★ **READER REVIEW**

"This is a new twist on the classic s'mores. Very nice!"

TOM1234 TASTEOFHOME.COM

FLUFFY KEY LIME PIE

FLUFFY KEY LIME PIE F

For a taste of paradise, try this light and creamy confection. It's low in fat, sugar and fuss. Dessert doesn't get any better than that!
—Frances VanFossan, Warren, MI

Prep: 20 min. + chilling
Makes: 8 servings

- ¼ cup boiling water
- 1 package (0.3 ounce) sugar-free lime gelatin
- 2 cartons (6 ounces each) Key lime yogurt
- 1 carton (8 ounces) frozen fat-free whipped topping, thawed
- 1 reduced-fat graham cracker crust (6 ounces)

1. In a large bowl, add boiling water to the gelatin; stir 2 minutes to completely dissolve. Whisk in yogurt. Fold in whipped topping. Pour into crust.

2. Refrigerate, covered, until set, about 2 hours.

Per piece: 194 cal., 3g fat (1g sat. fat), 2mg chol., 159mg sod., 33g carb. (18g sugars, 0 fiber), 3g pro.

Diabetic exchanges: 2 starch, ½ fat.

ICE CREAM CONE TREATS
FAST FIX

I came up with this recipe as a way for my grandkids to enjoy Rice Krispies Treats without getting sticky hands. You can also pack the cereal mixture into paper cups and insert a freezer pop stick to create cute pops.

—Mabel Nolan, Vancouver, WA

Start to Finish: 20 min.
Makes: 12 servings

12 ice cream sugar cones
   Melted semisweet chocolate,
      optional
   Colored sprinkles
 4 cups miniature marshmallows
 3 tablespoons butter
 6 cups Rice Krispies

1. If desired, dip the ice cream cones in melted chocolate to coat edges; stand in juice glasses or coffee mugs.
2. Place sprinkles in a shallow bowl. In a microwave or in a large saucepan over low heat, melt marshmallows and butter; stir until smooth. Remove from heat; stir in cereal.
3. Working quickly, use buttered hands to shape mixture into 12 balls; pack firmly into cones. Dip tops in sprinkles.
Per serving: 174 cal., 4g fat (2g sat. fat), 8mg chol., 142mg sod., 34g carb. (14g sugars, 0 fiber), 2g pro.

ANGEL FOOD CAKE ROLL **F M**

There's always some room for dessert, especially when it's this eye-catching cake roll. We like strawberry yogurt for our filling, but different flavors work well, too. The treat is a summertime staple.

—Joan Colbert, Sigourney, IA

Prep: 30 min. + freeezing
Bake: 15 min. + cooling
Makes: 12 servings

 1 package (16 ounces) angel food
   cake mix
   Confectioners' sugar
 1 cup (8 ounces) strawberry yogurt
 1 package (3.4 ounces) instant
   vanilla pudding mix
 3 drops red food coloring, optional
 2 cups whipped topping

1. Preheat the oven to 350°. Line an ungreased 15x10x1-in. pan with parchment paper.
2. Prepare cake batter according to package directions. Transfer to prepared pan. Bake until top springs back when lightly touched, 15-20 minutes. Cool 5 minutes. Invert onto a tea towel dusted with confectioners' sugar. Gently peel off paper. Roll up cake in the towel jelly-roll style, starting with a short side. Cool completely on a wire rack.
3. Whisk together yogurt, pudding mix and, if desired, food coloring. Fold in whipped topping.
4. Unroll cake; spread yogurt mixture over cake to within ½ in. of edges. Roll up again, without towel. Cover tightly and freeze. Remove from freezer 30 minutes before slicing.
Per slice: 243 cal., 3g fat (3g sat. fat), 1mg chol., 427mg sod., 50g carb. (37g sugars, 0 fiber), 4g pro.

ICE CREAM CONE TREATS

TRIPLE-BERRY COBBLER M

(PICTURED ON P. 232)

I combined several recipes to come up with this winner, and it's really versatile. Sometimes I use other fruits depending on what is available or on hand.
—Edna Woodard, Fredericksburg, TX

Prep: 20 min. • **Bake:** 25 min.
Makes: 6 servings

- ½ cup sugar
- 3 tablespoons cornstarch
- ¼ teaspoon ground cinnamon
- 1 cup water
- 1 cup fresh or frozen cranberries, thawed
- 1 cup fresh blueberries
- 1 cup fresh blackberries

TOPPING

- ¼ cup sugar
- 2 tablespoons butter, softened
- ¼ teaspoon vanilla extract
- ⅓ cup fat-free milk
- ⅔ cup all-purpose flour
- ¾ teaspoon baking powder
- ¼ teaspoon salt

1. Preheat the oven to 375°. In a small heavy saucepan, mix sugar, cornstarch, cinnamon and water until smooth; bring to a boil. Cook and stir until thickened, about 2 minutes. Remove from heat; stir in berries. Transfer to an 8-in. square baking dish coated with cooking spray.

2. For topping, beat the sugar and butter until crumbly. Beat in the vanilla and milk. Whisk together flour, baking powder and salt; add to butter mixture, stirring just until moistened. Drop by tablespoonfuls over the fruit.

3. Bake until the filling is bubbly and a toothpick inserted in topping comes out clean, 25-30 minutes. Serve warm.

Per serving: 234 cal., 4g fat (2g sat. fat), 10mg chol., 196mg sod., 48g carb. (30g sugars, 3g fiber), 3g pro.

CARAMEL APPLE-PEAR CRISP

CARAMEL APPLE-PEAR CRISP S M

This crisp is packed with a combination of healthy pears and apples, and just the right amount of walnuts in the topping.
—Amanda Pettit, Logan, OH

Prep: 20 min. • **Bake:** 40 min.
Makes: 6 servings

- 2 tablespoons sugar
- ¼ teaspoon ground allspice
- 3 medium pears, peeled and sliced (about 3 cups)
- 2 medium tart apples, peeled and sliced (about 2 cups)
- ⅓ cup sugar-free caramel topping

OAT TOPPING

- ¼ cup quick-cooking oats
- ¼ cup packed brown sugar
- 2 tablespoons all-purpose flour
- 3 tablespoons cold reduced-fat butter
- ¼ cup chopped walnuts
  Reduced-fat vanilla ice cream, optional

1. Preheat oven to 375°. Mix sugar and allspice; toss with fruit. Place in an 8-in. square baking pan coated with cooking spray. Drizzle with caramel topping.

2. Mix oats, brown sugar and flour. Cut in butter until crumbly; stir in the walnuts. Sprinkle over filling.

3. Bake until top is golden brown and the fruit is tender, 40-45 minutes. Serve warm. If desired, top with ice cream.

Note: This recipe was tested with Land O'Lakes light stick butter.

Per serving: 241 cal., 7g fat (2g sat. fat), 8mg chol., 80mg sod., 48g carb. (26g sugars, 4g fiber), 2g pro.

MAKEOVER CREAM CHEESE STREUSEL BARS Ⓜ

Even with a chocolaty crust, crispy topping and soft cream cheese filling, these delectable bars are still guilt-free!
—Janet Coops, Duarte, CA

....

Prep: 20 min. • **Bake:** 30 min. + cooling
Makes: 16 servings

- 1 cup all-purpose flour
- ¾ cup confectioners' sugar
- ¼ cup baking cocoa
- ⅛ teaspoon salt
- ⅛ teaspoon baking soda
- ½ cup cold butter, cubed

FILLING
- 1 package (8 ounces) reduced-fat cream cheese
- 1 can (14 ounces) fat-free sweetened condensed milk
- 1 large egg, lightly beaten
- 2 teaspoons vanilla extract

1. Preheat oven to 350°. In a large bowl, whisk together first five ingredients; cut in butter until fine crumbs form (mixture will be powdery). Reserve ½ cup mixture for topping. Lightly press remaining mixture into an 8-in. square baking pan coated with cooking spray. Bake just until set, 8-10 minutes.

2. Beat the cream cheese until smooth. Gradually beat in milk. Add egg and vanilla; beat just until blended. Pour over crust. Bake 15 minutes.

3. Sprinkle the reserved topping over the filling. Bake until filling is set, 5-10 minutes. Cool completely on a wire rack. Store in the refrigerator.

Per piece: 216 cal., 9g fat (6g sat. fat), 40mg chol., 164mg sod., 28g carb. (21g sugars, 0 fiber), 5g pro.
Diabetic exchanges: 2 starch, 2 fat.

FROSTY LEMONADE PIE Ⓜ

This creamy pie gets its citrus flavor from lemonade mix and crushed lemon sandwich cookies. It's a wonderful dessert to store in the freezer for nights when you need a low-sugar treat in a hurry.
—Emma Overby, East Prairie, MS

....

Prep: 15 min. + freezing
Makes: 8 servings

- 1 package (8 ounces) fat-free cream cheese
- 1 tub sugar-free lemonade soft drink mix
- 1 cup cold fat-free milk
- 1 package (1 ounce) sugar-free instant vanilla pudding mix
- 1 carton (8 ounces) frozen fat-free whipped topping, thawed
- 10 sugar-free lemon sandwich cookies, crushed
- 1 reduced-fat graham cracker crust (6 ounces)
  Lemon slices and fresh mint leaves, optional

1. Beat cream cheese and drink mix until smooth. In another bowl, whisk milk and pudding mix 1½ minutes (mixture will be very thick). Beat into the cream cheese mixture. Beat in a third of the whipped topping. Fold in the remaining whipped topping.

2. Reserve 3 tablespoons cookie crumbs; fold remaining crumbs into cream cheese mixture. Spoon into the crust, spreading evenly. Sprinkle with reserved crumbs.

3. Freeze, covered, until firm, 4-5 hours. Remove from the freezer 15-30 minutes before serving. If desired, top with lemon slices and mint.

Note: This recipe was tested using Crystal Light lemonade soft drink mix. One container (2.1 ounces) contains four tubs.

Per piece: 257 cal., 6g fat (2g sat. fat), 4mg chol., 404mg sod., 35g carb. (13g sugars, 0 fiber), 7g pro.
Diabetic exchanges: 2 starch, 1 fat.

MAKEOVER CREAM CHEESE
STREUSEL BARS

STRAWBERRY SORBET
SENSATION

STRAWBERRY SORBET SENSATION F M

On hot days in Colorado, we chill out with slices of this berries-and-cream dessert. The layered effect is so much fun. Use any flavor of sorbet you like.
—Kendra Doss, Colorado Springs, CO

....

Prep: 20 min. + freezing
Makes: 8 servings

- 2 cups strawberry sorbet, softened if necessary
- 1 cup cold fat-free milk
- 1 package (1 ounce) sugar-free instant vanilla pudding mix
- 1 carton (8 ounces) frozen reduced-fat whipped topping, thawed
  Sliced fresh strawberries

1. Line an 8x4-in. loaf pan with plastic wrap. Spread sorbet onto bottom of pan; place in freezer 15 minutes.

2. In a bowl, whisk milk and pudding mix 2 minutes. Let stand until soft-set, about 2 minutes. Fold in the whipped topping; spread over the sorbet. Freeze, covered, 4 hours or overnight.

3. Remove from freezer 10-15 minutes before serving. Invert the dessert onto a serving plate; remove the plastic wrap. Cut into slices. Serve with strawberries.
Per slice: 153 cal., 3g fat (3g sat. fat), 1mg chol., 163mg sod., 27g carb. (18g sugars, 2g fiber), 1g pro.
Diabetic exchanges: 2 starch, ½ fat.

CHOCOLATE PUDDING SANDWICHES F S C

These frozen cookie sandwiches are a favorite dessert and after-school snack for my kids...and even my diabetic husband enjoys one now and then.
—Jan Thomas, Richmond, VA

....

Prep: 20 min. + freezing
Makes: about 3½ dozen

- 1½ cups cold fat-free milk
- 1 package (1.4 ounces) sugar-free instant chocolate pudding mix
- 1 carton (8 ounces) frozen reduced-fat whipped topping, thawed
- 1 cup miniature marshmallows
- 2 packages (9 ounces each) chocolate wafers

1. For filling, whisk milk and pudding mix 2 minutes; let stand 2 minutes. Fold in whipped topping, then marshmallows.
2. For each sandwich, spread about 2 tablespoons of filling onto bottom of a wafer; top with another wafer. Stack sandwiches in covered containers.
3. Freeze until firm, about 3 hours. Remove from the freezer 5 minutes before serving.
Per sandwich cookie: 75 cal., 2g fat (1g sat. fat), 0 chol., 107mg sod., 12g carb. (6g sugars, 1g fiber), 1g pro.
Diabetic exchanges: 1 starch, ½ fat.

FROZEN BERRY & YOGURT SWIRLS F S C M

These are a great treat to have on a warm summer day! They're a favorite at our summer block party.
—Colleen Ludovice, Wauwatosa, WI

Prep: 15 min. + freezing
Makes: 10 pops

- 10 plastic or paper cups (3 ounces each)
- 2¾ cups fat-free honey Greek yogurt
- 1 cup mixed fresh berries
- ¼ cup water
- 2 tablespoons sugar
- 10 wooden pop sticks

1. Fill each cup with about ¼ cup yogurt. Place berries, water and sugar in a food processor; pulse until berries are finely chopped. Spoon 1½ tablespoons berry mixture into each cup. Stir gently with a pop stick to swirl.
2. Top cups with foil; insert pop sticks through foil. Freeze until firm.

Per pop: 60 cal., 0 fat (0 sat. fat), 0 chol., 28mg sod., 9g carb. (8g sugars, 1g fiber), 6g pro.
Diabetic exchanges: 1 starch.
Frozen Clementine & Yogurt Swirls: Substitute 1 cup seeded clementine segments (about 5 medium) and ¼ cup orange juice for berries, water and sugar; proceed as directed.

RIBBON PUDDING PIE F M
(PICTURED ON P. 233)

Cool, smooth and creamy, this pretty pie is a slice of heaven for anyone who likes an easy yet impressive dessert. The lovely pudding layers feature a yummy combination of vanilla, chocolate and butterscotch.
—Doris Morgan, Verona, MS

Prep: 20 min. + chilling
Makes: 8 servings

- 4 cups cold fat-free milk, divided
- 1 package (1 ounces) sugar-free instant vanilla pudding mix
- 1 reduced-fat graham cracker crust 6 ounces)
- 1 package (1 ounces) sugar-free instant butterscotch pudding mix
- 1 package (1.4 ounces) sugar-free instant chocolate pudding mix
  Whipped topping and finely chopped pecans, optional

1. Whisk 1⅓ cups milk and the vanilla pudding mix 2 minutes. Spread into crust.
2. In another bowl, whisk 1⅓ cups milk and butterscotch pudding mix 2 minutes. Carefully spoon it over the vanilla layer, spreading evenly.
3. In a third bowl, whisk the remaining 1⅓ cups milk and chocolate pudding mix 2 minutes. Carefully spread over the top. Refrigerate until set, at least 30 minutes. If desired, serve with whipped topping and chopped pecans.

Per piece: 184 cal., 3g fat (1g sat. fat), 2mg chol., 427mg sod., 32g carb. (13g sugars, 1g fiber), 6g pro.
Diabetic exchanges: 2 starch, 1 fat.

FROZEN BERRY & YOGURT SWIRLS

CHEWY CHOCOLATE PEANUT BUTTER COOKIES
S C M

This soft and chewy low-carb cookie recipe, developed by our Test Kitchen, calls for canola oil instead of butter to reduce the saturated fat. It's hard to eat just one!
—*Taste of Home* Test Kitchen

Prep: 20 min. • **Bake:** 10 min./batch
Makes: about 4 dozen

- 1 cup chunky peanut butter
- ¼ cup canola oil
- ¾ cup packed brown sugar
- ½ cup sugar
- 1 tablespoon vanilla extract
- 2 large eggs
- 1 cup all-purpose flour
- ⅓ cup baking cocoa
- 1 teaspoon baking soda
- ½ teaspoon salt
- ½ cup miniature chocolate chips

1. Preheat oven to 350°. Beat the first four ingredients until blended. Beat in vanilla and eggs, one at a time. Whisk together flour, cocoa, baking soda and salt; gradually beat into peanut butter mixture (dough will be sticky). Stir in the chocolate chips.
2. Drop dough by rounded teaspoonfuls 2 in. apart onto ungreased baking sheets. Flatten slightly with a glass.
3. Bake cookies until the tops are cracked and cookies are set, 8-10 minutes. Cool 2 minutes before removing to wire racks to cool.
Per cookie: 86 cal., 5g fat (1g sat. fat), 8mg chol., 81mg sod., 10g carb. (7g sugars, 1g fiber), 2g pro.

NO-BAKE CEREAL COOKIE BARS

NO-BAKE CEREAL COOKIE BARS S

We pull out all the goodies, like raisins and coconut, to make these chewy bars. For added color, sprinkle on the M&M's once the bars are in the pan. Then press them in.
—Connie Craig, Lakewood, WA

Prep: 10 min. • **Cook:** 15 min. + cooling
Makes: 3 dozen

- 4½ cups Rice Krispies
- 3¼ cups quick-cooking oats
- ½ cup cornflakes
- ½ cup sweetened shredded coconut
- ½ cup butter, cubed
- 1 package (16 ounces) miniature marshmallows
- ¼ cup honey
- ½ cup M&M's minis
- ¼ cup raisins

1. Grease a 15x10x1-in. pan. In a large bowl, combine first four ingredients.
2. In a large saucepan, melt butter over low heat. Add marshmallows; stir until completely melted. Stir in honey until blended. Pour over cereal mixture; stir until evenly coated. Cool 5 minutes.
3. Stir in M&M's and raisins; press into prepared pan using a greased spatula. Let stand 30 minutes before cutting. Store between layers of waxed paper in an airtight container.
Per bar: 137 cal., 4g fat (3g sat. fat), 8mg chol., 58mg sod., 24g carb. (13g sugars, 1g fiber), 2g pro.
Diabetic exchanges: 1½ starch, ½ fat.
HEALTH TIP The M&M's only add 15 calories , so go ahead and add a little fun.

GLAZED CHOCOLATE ANGEL FOOD CAKE F S M

Light as air and loaded with the sort of chocolate flavor everyone craves, this delightful cake offers all of the taste and none of the guilt. It's an all-time favorite of mine.

—Mary Relyea, Canastota, NY

....

Prep: 20 min. • **Bake:** 40 min. + cooling
Makes: 12 servings

- 1½ cups egg whites (about 10 large)
- 1 cup cake flour
- 2 cups sugar, divided
- ½ cup baking cocoa
- 1 teaspoon cream of tartar
- 1 teaspoon vanilla extract
- ¼ teaspoon salt
GLAZE
- ½ cup semisweet chocolate chips
- 3 tablespoons half-and-half cream

1. Place egg whites in a large bowl; let stand at room temperature 30 minutes.

2. Preheat oven to 350°. Sift flour, 1 cup sugar and cocoa together twice.

3. Add cream of tartar, vanilla and salt to egg whites; beat on medium speed until soft peaks form. Gradually add remaining sugar, 2 tablespoons at a time, beating on high after each addition until sugar is dissolved. Continue beating until stiff glossy peaks form. Gradually fold in flour mixture, about ½ cup at a time.

4. Gently transfer to an ungreased 10-in. tube pan. Cut through batter with a knife to remove air pockets. Bake on lowest oven rack 40-50 minutes or until top springs back when lightly touched and cracks feel dry. Immediately invert pan; cool completely in pan, about 1 hour.

5. Run a knife around sides and center tube of pan. Remove cake to a serving plate. For glaze, in a microwave, melt chocolate chips with cream; stir until smooth. Drizzle over cake.

Per slice: 235 cal., 3g fat (2g sat. fat), 2mg chol., 102mg sod., 49g carb. (37g sugars, 1g fiber), 5g pro.

FRUIT & ALMOND BITES S C M

Featuring big handfuls of dried apricots, cherries, almonds and pistachios, these are some seriously tasty and satisfying no-bake treats. You can take them anywhere.

—Donna Stelmach, Morristown, NJ

....

Prep: 40 min. + chilling
Makes: about 4 dozen

- 3¾ cups sliced almonds, divided
- ¼ teaspoon almond extract
- ¼ cup honey
- 2 cups finely chopped dried apricots
- 1 cup finely chopped dried cherries or cranberries
- 1 cup finely chopped pistachios, toasted

1. Place 1¼ cups almonds in a food processor; pulse until finely chopped. Remove almonds to a shallow bowl; reserve for coating.

2. Add remaining 2½ cups almonds to food processor; pulse until finely chopped. Add extract. While processing, gradually add honey. Remove to a large bowl; stir in apricots and cherries. Divide mixture into six portions; shape each into a ½-in.-thick roll. Wrap in plastic; refrigerate 1 hour or until firm.

3. Unwrap and cut the rolls into 1½-in. pieces. Roll half of the pieces in reserved almonds, pressing gently to make the nuts adhere. Roll remaining half in pistachios. If desired, wrap them individually in waxed paper, twisting the ends to close. Store in airtight containers, layered between waxed paper if unwrapped.

Note: To toast nuts, bake in a shallow pan in a 350° oven for 5-10 minutes or cook them in a skillet over low heat until lightly browned, stirring occasionally.

Per piece: 86 cal., 5g fat (0 sat. fat), 0 chol., 15mg sod., 10g carb. (7g sugars, 2g fiber), 2g pro.
Diabetic exchanges: 1 fat, ½ starch.
HEALTH TIP Per ounce, almonds contain more fiber and protein than any other tree nut.

GLAZED CHOCOLATE ANGEL FOOD CAKE

PEAR TART

PEAR TART S M

This pretty pastry looks like it came from a fancy bakery. My sister-in-law brought this fruity dessert to dinner one night, and we all went back for seconds. It is truly scrumptious.
—Kathryn Rogers, Suisun City, CA

Prep: 15 min. • **Bake:** 25 min. + chilling
Makes: 12 servings

3 tablespoons butter, softened
½ cup sugar
¾ teaspoon ground cinnamon
¾ cup all-purpose flour
⅓ cup finely chopped walnuts

FILLING

1 package (8 ounces) reduced-fat cream cheese
¼ cup plus 1 tablespoon sugar, divided
1 large egg
1 teaspoon vanilla extract
1 can (15 ounces) sliced pears in light syrup, drained well and thinly sliced
¼ teaspoon ground cinnamon

1. Preheat oven to 425°. Beat the butter, sugar and cinnamon until crumbly. Beat in flour and walnuts. Press onto the bottom and up the sides of a 9-in. fluted tart pan with a removable bottom coated with cooking spray.
2. For filling, beat the cream cheese and ¼ cup sugar until smooth. Beat in egg and vanilla. Spread into crust. Arrange pears over top. Mix cinnamon and remaining sugar; sprinkle over pears.
3. Bake for 10 minutes. Reduce the oven setting to 350°; bake until the filling is set, 15-20 minutes. Cool 1 hour on a wire rack. Refrigerate at least 2 hours before serving.
Per piece: 199 cal., 9g fat (5g sat. fat), 36mg chol., 112mg sod., 25g carb. (18g sugars, 1g fiber), 4g pro.
Diabetic exchanges: 2 fat, 1½ starch.

DID YOU KNOW?
Most vanilla comes from Madagascar and Reunion Island—formerly known as Bourbon Island—off the southeast coast of Africa. Bourbon vanilla is celebrated for its strong, clear vanilla flavor and creamy finish.

PLUM GOOD CRISP

PLUM GOOD CRISP S M

This is a great crisp that goes well with any meal, but you can also serve it as a breakfast treat or snack. When it's served warm, it can't be beat!
—Peter Halferty, Corpus Christi, TX

Prep: 20 min. • **Bake:** 30 min. + standing
Makes: 8 servings

4 cups sliced fresh plums (about 1½ pounds)
3 medium nectarines, sliced
1½ cups fresh blueberries
3 tablespoons brown sugar
2 tablespoons cornstarch
¼ teaspoon ground ginger
⅛ teaspoon ground nutmeg
¼ cup maple syrup
2 tablespoons lemon juice

TOPPING

½ cup old-fashioned oats
½ cup all-purpose flour
¼ cup packed brown sugar
¼ teaspoon salt
4 teaspoons unsweetened apple juice
4 teaspoons canola oil
1½ teaspoons butter, melted

1. Preheat oven to 400°. Place fruit in a large bowl. Mix brown sugar, cornstarch, spices, syrup and lemon juice; toss with fruit. Transfer to an 11x7-in. baking dish coated with cooking spray.
2. For topping, mix oats, flour, brown sugar and salt; stir in remaining ingredients until crumbly. Sprinkle over fruit.
3. Bake, uncovered, until filling is bubbly and topping is golden brown, about 30 minutes. Let stand for 15 minutes before serving.
Per ¾ cup: 233 cal., 4g fat (1g sat. fat), 2mg chol., 85mg sod., 49g carb. (33g sugars, 3g fiber), 3g pro.

CHOCOLATE-TOPPED STRAWBERRY CHEESECAKE

Perfect for entertaining, this light and airy cheesecake draws its unique flavor from the chocolate crust. It always garners some compliments while adding a touch of elegance to your table.
—Kathy Berger, Dry Ridge, KY

Prep: 35 min. + chilling
Bake: 10 min. + cooling
Makes: 12 servings

1¼ cups chocolate graham cracker
    crumbs (about 9 whole crackers)
¼ cup butter, melted
2 envelopes unflavored gelatin
½ cup cold water
16 ounces fresh or frozen unsweetened
    strawberries, thawed

2 packages (8 ounces each) fat-free
    cream cheese, cubed
1 cup fat-free cottage cheese
    Sugar substitute equivalent
      to ¾ cup sugar
1 carton (8 ounces) frozen reduced-
    fat whipped topping, thawed, divided
½ cup chocolate ice cream topping
1 cup quartered fresh strawberries

1. Preheat oven to 350°. Mix cracker crumbs and butter; press onto bottom and 1 in. up sides of a 9-in. springform pan coated with cooking spray. Place on a baking sheet. Bake until set, about 10 minutes. Cool completely on a wire rack.
2. In a small saucepan, sprinkle gelatin over cold water; let stand 1 minute. Heat over low heat, stirring until the gelatin is completely dissolved; remove from heat.

3. Hull strawberries if necessary; puree in a food processor. Remove to a bowl. Add cream cheese, cottage cheese and sugar substitute to food processor; process until smooth. While processing, gradually add gelatin mixture. Add pureed strawberries; process until blended. Transfer to a large bowl; fold in 2 cups of whipped topping. Pour into the crust. Refrigerate, covered, until set, 2-3 hours.
4. Loosen sides of cheesecake with a knife; remove rim. To serve, top with chocolate topping, remaining whipped topping and quartered strawberries.
Note: This recipe was tested with Splenda no-calorie sweetener.
Per slice: 244 cal., 8g fat (5g sat. fat), 16mg chol., 463mg sod., 29g carb. (17g sugars, 2g fiber), 10g pro.
Diabetic exchanges: 2 starch, 1½ fat.

BANANA CHOCOLATE CAKE M

This light-as-air chocolate cake from our Test Kitchen has lots of banana flavor. It's scrumptious as is, but you can also dress it up with nuts.
—*Taste of Home* Test Kitchen

....

Prep: 15 min. • **Bake:** 25 min. + cooling
Makes: 12 servings

- ⅓ cup butter, softened
  Sugar substitute equivalent
    to ¾ cup sugar
- ⅓ cup packed brown sugar
- 2 teaspoons vanilla extract
- 2 large eggs
- ½ cup water
- 1⅓ cups all-purpose flour
- ½ cup nonfat dry milk powder
- 3 tablespoons baking cocoa
- 1 teaspoon baking powder
- ½ teaspoon baking soda
- ½ teaspoon salt
- 1 cup mashed ripe bananas
    (about 2 medium bananas)
  Confectioners' sugar

1. Preheat oven to 375°. Coat a 9-in. square baking pan with cooking spray.
2. Cream the butter, sugar substitute and brown sugar until light and fluffy. Add the vanilla and eggs, one at a time, beating well after each addition. Stir in water. Whisk together flour, milk powder, cocoa, baking powder, baking soda and salt; add to the creamed mixture just until combined. Stir in the bananas.
3. Transfer to prepared pan. Bake until a toothpick inserted in center comes out clean and cake begins to pull from sides of pan, 23-28 minutes. Cool it completely in the pan on a wire rack. Dust it with confectioners' sugar.
Note: This recipe was tested with Splenda no-calorie sweetener.
Per piece: 169 cal., 6g fat (4g sat. fat), 45mg chol., 261mg sod., 25g carb. (10g sugars, 1g fiber), 4g pro.
Diabetic exchanges: 1½ starch, 1 fat.

OLD-FASHIONED RICE PUDDING F M
(PICTURED ON P. 232)

This dessert is a wonderful way to end any meal. As a girl, I always waited eagerly for the first heavenly bite. Today, my husband likes to top his with a scoop of ice cream.
—Sandra Melnychenko, Grandview, MB

....

Prep: 10 min. • **Bake:** 1 hour
Makes: 6 servings

- 3½ cups 2% milk
- ½ cup uncooked long grain rice
- ⅓ cup sugar
- ½ teaspoon salt
- ½ cup raisins
- 1 teaspoon vanilla extract
  Ground cinnamon, optional

1. Preheat oven to 325°. Place first four ingredients in a large saucepan; bring to a boil over medium heat, stirring constantly. Transfer to a greased 1½-qt. baking dish.
2. Bake, covered, 45 minutes, stirring every 15 minutes. Stir in raisins and vanilla; bake, covered, until rice is tender, about 15 minutes. If desired, sprinkle pudding with cinnamon. Serve warm or refrigerate and serve cold.
Per ¾ cup: 214 cal., 3g fat (2g sat. fat), 11mg chol., 266mg sod., 41g carb. (25g sugars, 1g fiber), 6g pro.

★ ★ ★ ★ ★ **READER REVIEW**

"This is so so good! Been making it for years. Cut back on the sugar and use golden raisins, top with Cool Whip or vanilla ice cream. The whole family just loves this rice pudding."

KATHY2838 TASTEOFHOME.COM

BANANA CHOCOLATE CAKE

Index

INDEX